SOCIAL WORK IN HEALTH CARE

A GUIDE TO PROFESSIONAL PRACTICE

SOCIAL WORK IN HEALTH CARE

A GUIDE TO PROFESSIONAL PRACTICE

WRITTEN AND EDITED BY

NEIL F. BRACHT

THE HAWORTH PRESS

NEW YORK

The Haworth Press, 149 Fifth Avenue, New York, New York 10010

Library of Congress Cataloging in Publication Data:

Bracht, Neil F
   Social work in health care.

   Includes bibliographies and index.
   1. Medical social work—United States—Addresses, essays, lectures.   I. Title. [DNLM: 1.
Social work. 2. Delivery of health care. 3. Health services.
W322 B796s]
HV687.5.U5B7   362.1'0973   78-7881
ISBN 0-917724-04-6
ISBN 0-917724-05-4 pbk.

Printed in the United States of America

*No medical discovery made during the recent decades can compare in practical impor-
tance with the introduction of social and economic decency in the life of the average man.
The greatest advances in health for the people were probably the indirect results of better
housing and working conditions, the general availability of soap, of linen for undercloth-
ing, of glass for windows, and a humanitarian concern for higher living standards....
The health field is no longer the monopoly of the medical professions; it requires the
services of all sorts of other skills. Collaboration will become increasingly urgent as the
community demands steps be taken not only to treat its diseases, but also to protect its
health.*

—*René Dubos,* Man Adapting

CONTENTS

Contents

PART VII
SOCIAL WORK IN PRIMARY HEALTH CARE
AND PREVENTION PROGRAMS

PART VIII
INTERPROFESSIONAL CONSULTATION AND TEACHING

PART IX
ORGANIZING AND PLANNING
COMMUNITY HEALTH SERVICES

PART X
STRATEGIES FOR RESEARCH

CONTRIBUTORS

BARBARA BERKMAN, D.S.W., Adjunct Assistant Professor of Community Medicine (Social Work), Mount Sinai School of Medicine, City University of New York

DONA LANSING BRACHT, B.S.W., M.S.W., Candidate, School of Social Work, University of Washington, Seattle

SIDNEY HIRSCH, M.S.W. Chief, Social Work Service, Veterans Administration Hospital, New York, New York

PETER HOOKEY, M.S.W., Ph.D., Assistant Professor, School of Social Work, University of Illinois at Urbana-Champaign

ROSALIE A. KANE, D.S.W., Consultant, The Rand Corporation, Santa Monica, California

RONA LEVY, M.S.W., Ph.D., M.P.H., Assistant Professor, School of Social Work, University of Washington, Seattle

LU PEARMEN, ACSW, Consultant, L. M. Pearman and Associates, Minneapolis

HELEN REHR, D.S.W., Director, Department of Social Work Services, and Edith J. Baerwald Professor of Community Medicine (Social Work), Mount Sinai School of Medicine, City University of New York

ELAINE SCHROEDER, M.S.W., Ph.C., School of Social Work, University of Washington, Seattle

JEAN SEARLES, M.S.W., Mental Retardation Consultant, Minneapolis

LAWRENCE C. SHULMAN, M.S.W., ACSW, Divisional Director, Department of Social Work Services, Long Island Jewish-Hillside Medical Center, New Hyde Park, New York

PATRICIA VOLLAND, ACSW, LCSW, Director, Department of Social Work, The Johns Hopkins Hospital, Baltimore

CINDY COOK WILLIAMS, R.N., ACSW, Social Worker, Veterans Administration Hospital, Seattle, Washington

REG ARTHUR WILLIAMS, R.N., M.N., Assistant Professor, School of Nursing, University of Washington, Seattle

MILTON WITTMAN, D.S.W., Chief, Social Work Education Branch, Division of Manpower and Training Programs, National Institute of Mental Health, Alcohol, Drug Abuse, and Mental Health Administration, PHS, U.S. Department of Health, Education, and Welfare, Rockville, Maryland

MARGO WYCKOFF, M.S.W., Clinical Instructor, Pain Clinic, Department of Anesthesiology, University of Washington, Seattle

PREFACE

Beginning with a handful of early social workers employed in a hospital dispensary in Boston at the turn of the century, thousands of professional social workers in health settings have over the years made significant but infrequently recognized contributions to the health and mental health of individuals, families, and communities. Often these contributions came through timid collaboration with physicians in order to have the opportunity to "suggest" consideration of the social components of illness and rehabilitation. Sometimes social work's contributions were better made by leaving the walls of established institutions and organizing neighborhood groups and health clinics, advocating reform of deleterious social and economic conditions related to poor health, or collaborating in new models of health care delivery. After seventy-five years of struggling professional growth, social work is now involved in nearly every facet of American health services; and it is expanding. Social work is "coming of age" in the health care field.

It seems to the author that there is a need for an up-to-date reference book to serve as a guide to professional social work practice in the health field—a book that would incorporate the past, summarize current activities, and provide some direction to future practice trends and opportunities. With national health insurance and other health care reforms looming on the horizon, the contributions of social work must be made more visible. Social-work leadership in combination with other provider and consumer groups can offer ways of solving our society's complex health care problems. This book draws together the numerous works of past and present practitioners and educators whose joint efforts have made social work an essential ingredient of modern, comprehensive health care.

It has been sixteen years since Harriet Bartlett published *Social Work Practice in the Health Field* (NASW). Many, many changes have occurred during this period. *Health in the Community* (Free Press), written by Katz and Felton in 1965, was an excellent contribution with a focus on community-wide health services and programs. *Medicine and Social Work* (Prodist, 1974) confined its collection of papers, edited by Helen Rehr, to the study of interprofessional education. Two recent specialized contributions dealing with social work in health care are Georgia Travis' book *Chronic Illness in Children: Its Impact on Child and Family* (Stanford University Press, 1976) and *Long Term Care of Older People* (Human Sciences Press, 1977), written by Elaine Brody. Goldberg and Neill's 1972 study of *Social Work in General Practice* (George Allen and Unwin Ltd., London) is an important contribution but is related primarily to the British health system. Faculty of the Public Health Social Work programs at both Berkeley and Pittsburgh have made enormous contributions to the field as editors of at least ten specialized monographs on social work in the health field. These resources are identified in appropriate chapters of this book. The National Association of Social Work has published several documents related to social work in health care, as has the Society for Hospital Social Work Directors. In short, there have been many excellent published contributions on social work practice in health, but no single text, other than Bartlett's in 1961, is available as a comprehensive guide to the field. It has been my intent to provide such a text; one that would be viewed as complementary to the fine specialized publications just mentioned.

In this task I have been assisted by many individuals throughout the past sixteen years of my own clinical, administrative, and academic experience in health and social work. To those who encouraged my advanced training in public health, I shall be ever grateful. In this regard I would especially like to thank Darwin Palmiere and other faculty previously or currently associated with the Michigan School of Public Health. Grace White and Leone Renn, formerly of the University of Kentucky, helped immensely in the professional task of integrating social-work and public health concepts in practice. From several colleagues in medicine, Lester Evans, Kurt Deuschle, Andrew Hunt, and Jesse Tapp, I learned much about the social aspects of health care.

To numerous social-work faculty colleagues and students at graduate schools where I have taught, I acknowledge your attempts, if not always your success, in helping me see other viewpoints or expand my horizons. I have also profited from continuing close associations with social-work practitioners in health settings.

Among those who have reviewed draft portions of my book or discussed particular concepts, I should like to thank Sylvia Clarke, Bruce Mobberly, John Suttinger, Eleanor Klein, and Cindy Williams. To those who contributed chapters to the book or gave permission to quote from their materials, I am most appreciative. I wish to thank Sandy Brown, who assisted with the typing, and Marvel Shangle, who has for several years helped considerably to keep my bibliographical references and file materials up to date.

A very special note of thanks to my parents and children, all of whom assisted in this effort. From Dona, my colleague and spouse, I received invaluable editorial assistance and, in addition, a lot of inspiration along the way.

NEIL F. BRACHT

INTRODUCTION AND USE OF BOOK

This book is concerned with the scope and contribution of professional social work in health settings. It documents social work's accumulated expertise, knowledge, and research evaluations in patient care during the past seventy-five years. It analyzes individual and community health needs and the social and behavioral aspects of illness, and discusses essential practice components and skills required of social workers in health care. The early chapters provide a broad framework and set of premises within which to view the profession's role(s) and functions in health care systems. A number of cited empirical studies suggest a firm base and rationale for the importance of social work's involvement in health care. The reader is encouraged to make independent evaluations by familiarizing himself/herself with the extensive reference notes and suggested additional readings at the conclusion of each chapter.

The book can escort the relatively new worker or student through the range of social work activities in health care settings, including clinical practice, community organization and planning, and administration and consultation practice. The experienced worker may find, among other things, the reference notes and additional readings useful in his/her case consultations, in the interpretation of new program needs, or in conducting and promoting research efforts. Other health professionals such as hospital administrators, nurses, and physicians, as well as consumer groups, will find in the book a source of information and documentation regarding the rationale, practice, contribution, and outcomes of social work.

Primarily, the book is intended as an overall reference guide for social workers in the health field, not as a prescriptive manual or casebook for all of the specialized aspects of day-to-day social work practice in health settings. It does, however, make available to the self-directed learner an up-to-date reference list on the far-ranging scope and practice techniques of social workers in health care. Throughout the chapters that follow, the reader will find a comprehensive listing of social work and related literature in health (principally American, but some British and Canadian) spanning three-quarters of a century, including the author's review and selection from among some 1500 "social work in health" references obtained from *MEDLARS* Bibliographic Search Service (1966–1977). In Chapter 9 references to social treatment interventions with some sixty different illness states or socio-health conditions are highlighted in order to facilitate further library study by the practitioner.

In Part I the current scope of social work practice in nearly all facets of health care is described, including the historical development of social work from the early 1900s through 1975. Social work contributions to health care are placed in the conceptual framework of comprehensive health care. Five basic premises are asserted as a foundation and rationale for social work practice and intervention in health care delivery.

In Part II a discussion of health care delivery issues and trends in the United States and their implications for social work practice is provided. The author's interest, or perhaps bias, is reflected in Chapter 4 when HMOs are suggested as a model for the organization and financing of comprehensive health and mental health care. Part III deals with some of the basic tools and knowledge useful to social workers in entering health care practice. Chapter 5 provides a model for orienting new social workers and students to health settings, using a hospital as an illustration. Relevant topic areas frequently covered in health orientation programs are related to pertinent pages and sections of this book for the convenience of the trainer. (See page 71.) Because the team approach is so important in health settings, Chapter 6 reviews the relationship of small-group theory to the interprofessional team.

Changing health and illness patterns are having a dramatic effect on the health care delivery system. In Part IV life style, poverty, and other socioeconomic factors associated with these changes are discussed, including approaches to assessing the psychosocial effects of specific illnesses or community health problems. In Part V a reference source to treatment interventions with selected illnesses is provided, including a case illustration involving social work treatment of a growing problem area, namely, patients experiencing the chronic pain syndrome. Social work services in nursing homes is dealt with in Part VI. Social work practice in hospitals has been, both historically and currently, the largest arena for social work employment in the health care field. Owing to a heightened controversy over the quality and cost of hospital care, I have chosen to highlight the major changing directions and new opportunities in hospitals rather than to provide a detailed account of the rich and varied experiences of hospital social workers. While hospital social work will remain an important practice dimension, equal attention must be given to new focuses on primary health care, prevention, and community outreach and planning. In this connection, Part VII deals with the application of prevention knowledge to health and mental health practice and provides information on the contribution and cost-benefit of social work practice in primary care and ambulatory health settings (Chapter 14). Two special areas of expertise, interprofessional consultation and teaching, developed by social workers during the past thirty years in health programs are described in Part VIII.

The organizing and planning of community health services is outlined in Part IX, with special emphasis on public health social work and the development of health care services for women. In Part X, strategies for social work research in health are outlined. Steps in applied hospital social work research are identified, as well as new developments in patient compliance techniques an how these can be used by social workers (Chapter 19). Issues in administration and accountability related to social work services are dealt with in Part XI. Most of this content focuses on the hospital setting, since administrative practices have developed on a larger scale and the issues of financial accountability are more acute. The concluding part of the book deals with educating social workers for quality health care practice. Guidelines for developing a health care concentration in schools of social work are suggested (Chapter 22).

Two helpful appendixes are included for the social work practitioner. These are (A) a list of common abbreviations and symbols used in clinical medicine and (B) selected federal health acts (1935–1975) related to the practice and development of social work in health care.

Part I

THE SCOPE OF SOCIAL WORK AND ITS CONTRIBUTION TO HEALTH CARE

1/THE SCOPE AND HISTORICAL DEVELOPMENT OF SOCIAL WORK, 1900–1975

NEIL F. BRACHT

After seventy-five years of developing and providing social services for clients in health care systems, social workers in the mid-1970s are prominent in nearly every facet of health care delivery. Today it is far easier to point to areas where social workers are than areas where they are not. Social workers are active as health care providers, planners, consultants, and administrators in hundreds of health care programs. Approximately 70 percent of all social workers in health care hold a master's or higher degree. In the pages that follow, the scope and historical development of social workers in health and mental health services is examined in detail. First, a brief overview highlighting the range of professional social work services in health care is provided.

Professional employment of social workers in health ranges from outreach specialists in neighborhood health clinics to program developers in the dean's office of medical schools; from regional health planners to recognized psychosocial experts in pain treatment, home dialysis care, mental health rehabilitation, and hospital discharge management. Social workers are teachers of medical students, consultants to doctors and health institutions, and collaborators on interdisciplinary primary health care teams. Social workers conduct research on access to and utilization of health services and on psychosocial aspects of illness; they link patients and their families to necessary community support services and increasingly staff hospital emergency rooms as advocates for victims of child abuse, rape, robbery, and accompanying social dislocations. Social workers train volunteers and paraprofessionals as staff assistants in social and health programs. They initiate new services, such as counseling to prevent possible trauma resulting from the relocation of elderly patients to community institutions. Social work's historical concern for and commitment to the problems of the poor, the badly housed and nourished, and the chronically disabled are continued in the development and staffing of alternative health clinics, special services to the developmentally disabled, adult day care programs, consultation services for consumer and self-help citizen groups, and patient grievance offices directed by social work ombudsmen.

3

Social workers serve as policy analysts at the state and federal levels, staff health planning agencies, and organize community groups for health action. They provide services to the armed forces and the Veterans Administration, as well as to special governmental programs to assist Indians, migrants, blacks (sickle cell anemia centers), and other groups. Increasingly the attention of social work is being directed toward illness prevention, health education, and health maintenance. In Figure 1.1 the range of health programs employing social workers is illustrated. Nearly seventy different components of the health care or broader human services delivery system are found to have social work involvement.

A CURRENT PROFILE OF SOCIAL WORK DEPLOYMENT IN THE HEALTH FIELD

Social work employment in the health field is now estimated at nearly 40,000 and is expanding.[1] Between 1960 and 1970 the number of social workers employed in health care nearly doubled.[2] In 1974 the number of social workers employed in group medical practices increased by 50 percent.[3] Finney, in a recent (1975) study of the academic backgrounds of professional staff in health planning agencies (196 of 218 federally funded agencies), found that among staff-level planners social work represented the largest employed group and ranked third largest among directors and deputy directors of those planning agencies.[4] According to the American Hospital Association, nearly half (3,179) of the nation's 7,174 hospitals have social service departments or provide social services.[5] (In 1955 only 967 of all general hospitals had social service departments.) A 1971 Medicare report on participating providers lists 9,101 qualified social workers and 7,475 other social workers employed in the 6,935 participating hospitals. In the same report 2,759 social workers (1,026 qualified and 1,733 other social workers) are listed as employed among the 4,829 extended-care facilities, and 316 social workers are on the staffs of the country's 2,410 home health agencies.[6] Twenty-one percent of all home health agencies offer social services.

The Veterans Administration alone employs some 3,600 social workers nationally. By 1966 social work employment in local and state health departments had reached 1,000.[7] The social work section of the American Public Health Association now lists 355 members. The Society for Hospital Social Work Directors of the American Hospital Association now has approximately 1,800 members. At the federal level some 339 social workers are employed throughout the various programs of the Department of Health, Education and Welfare. In 1972 the Department of Defense listed 441 social workers serving throughout the various armed services. (Not all of these social workers are in the health area, however.)

In the mental health field social work is by far the largest of the traditional professions providing services. Some 17,687 (42 percent) of the staff of all

Preventive–Educational

Public health departments:
  Maternal and child health projects
  Children and youth health projects
  Health screening programs
  Family planning
Self-help/recovery groups (e.g., mastectomy patients)
Pregnancy prevention
Geriatric transfer counseling
Alcohol–drug abuse services
Sex education/counseling
Patient ombudsman offices
Child abuse and rape prevention
Crisis clinics and health referral

Hospital–Institutional Care

Community general hospitals
Teaching hospitals
Military hospitals
Government hospitals:
  U.S. Public Health Service
  Veterans Administration
  Indian health
  Tuberculosis and chronic disease
  State mental hospitals
  State mental-retardation facilities
Typical hospital sites staffed by social workers:
  Emergency room
  Medical–surgical areas
  Pediatrics and maternity care
  Rehabilitation–burn units
  Mental health/psychiatric
  Intake and discharge planning
  Intensive-care units
  Neurology–orthopedics
Nursing care facilities
Day hospitals and aftercare programs
Domiciliary–personal care
Long-term care facilities
Hospital-based home health care

Primary Care Programs

Solo and group medical practices
Health maintenance organization
Neighborhood health centers
Free clinics (women's, etc.)
Family medicine programs
Specialty outpatient clinics:
  Genetic counseling
  Developmental disabilities
  Sickle cell anemia
  Seizure clinics
  Crippled children
  Pain clinics
Community mental health centers
Family health team projects
Community home health agencies

Community Health Planning

National voluntary and United Way health agencies
Health systems agencies (planners)
Mental health–retardation boards
State developmental disability programs
State–local offices on aging
Health and disaster relief programs
Rural health planning (Appalachia)
Vocational rehabilitation offices
Human resource agencies
Health information–referral
HEW—federal, regional
  Medicaid–Medicare
  PSRO
  Migrant health
  Human development
  National Institute of Mental Health
  Health Resources Administration

Health Professions Education

Medical schools
Schools of public health
Nursing schools
Pharmacy schools
Allied health schools
Dentistry schools

FIG. 1.1. Health agencies and programs that employ professional social workers.

mental health facilities are social workers. (In contrast to psychiatrists, 30.7 percent; psychologists, 22.4 percent; and psychiatric nurses, 4.9 percent.) In federally funded community mental health centers social work again is the largest profession, comprising 44.8 percent (3,044) of the staff of these centers.[8]

Social workers with regular faculty appointments in American medical schools now number 595. A survey of medical school deans (1976) indicates a desire to increase the number of such appointments.[9] Social workers also hold faculty appointments in schools of nursing, dentistry, public health, and allied health care programs and have been educational collaborators in schools of pharmacy. Expanded utilization of the social worker is occurring in highly specialized medical areas such as regional burn centers and pain clinics, in sickle cell diagnostic centers, in hospital intensive-care and coronary care units, in genetic counseling (15 percent of these programs employed social workers in 1975),[10] and in other preventive-health programs. Social work services are now required under the Health Maintenance Organization Act of 1973 and the end-stage renal disease amendments to Medicare (1972). A 1975 national survey of primary health care centers, including fee-for-service, prepaid group practices and family medicine programs, identified 161 programs with social workers.[11] Sixty percent of the 96 programs responding to the questionnaire indicated that two or more social workers were employed by the program.

Membership in the National Association of Social Workers is now 70,000 (1977), and since 1969 one-third of the members have consistently designated their employment as in the health and mental health field. The Association has sponsored at the national level a Quality Assurance Council and newsletter (PSRO). This council is monitoring the extensive efforts under way nationally by social workers in health and mental health settings to develop audit procedures, utilization and peer review mechanisms, cost-benefit studies, and improved information systems. Social work's response to quality assurance, including pilot demonstration programs, is an excellent example of proactive effort as opposed to postreactive aspects to changes in health care systems. In addition, a national register of clinical social work practitioners was established in 1976.

SOCIAL WORKERS AS QUALIFIED HEALTH CARE PROVIDERS AND VENDORSHIP STATUS

Recognition of social workers as "qualified health care providers" by third-party payors continues to grow.[12] Social services reimbursement is already established under major federal insurance plans such as Medicare, hospital, home health, and extended-care benefits and the Civilian Health and Medical Program of the Uniformed Services (CHAMPUS). Underwriters for the Federal Employees Health Benefits Association (FEHBA) such as Prudential, Aetna, Mutual of Omaha, and Blue Cross/Blue Shield recognize social workers as third-party vendors. Other vendor insurance companies include Banker's Life of Des Moines, the Union Labor Life Insurance Company, and New England Mutual. In 1977 the NASW backed Senate Bill No. 532 to provide for greater utilization of social work under both Medicare and Medicaid programs.

Each year more social workers are legally regulated through state licensure, certification, and registration mechanisms. These efforts help protect consumers and, at the same time, provide them with greater freedom of choice in obtaining professional health and mental health services from social workers. Current data suggest that such services are less costly when provided by social workers.[13]

EDUCATION FOR SOCIAL WORK PRACTICE

In the academic realm, the prospects for specialized training of social workers entering the health care field are beginning to brighten. Some twelve schools have well-developed health care concentrations, and many others are considering curriculum changes in this area.[14] Perretz has found that significant numbers of social work students are placed in health settings and particularly in new health delivery programs such as neighborhood health centers, HMOs, and interdisciplinary team projects.[15] Finney has found that one in four social work students placed in health planning agencies for practicum experience were hired on a full-time basis following completion of their master's degrees. He has also found a significant increase in the number of social work doctoral students who are concentrating in in the health policy planning area.[16] In a 1974 study conducted by the NIMH in conjunction with the Council on Social Work Education, 16,590 full-time students in schools of social work were identified according to practicum experience and field of interest. Nearly 6,000 students were placed in health and mental health field practicum sites according to the following categories:[17]

Students	Sites
1,881	community mental health centers
1,708	psychiatric services
1,107	medical and public health settings
754	medical and psychiatric settings
458	alcoholism and drug abuse programs

Social work faculty have many kinds of affiliations and interests in the health care field. Faculty members are represented on the committees and task forces of comprehensive health planning agencies and serve as consultants to health agencies.[18] Joint health courses and research interrelationships between schools of social work and other university health professional schools and centers are becoming more prominent.[19] Several schools of social work have joint MSW-MPH degree options at both the master's and doctoral levels. Each year approximately thirty students in social work gain advanced degrees in public health. An increasing number of social work faculty are also trained in public health and teach in graduate health care concentrations. For additional discussion of preparing social work students for practice in health care, see Chapt. 22.

RESEARCH AND SCHOLARLY DEVELOPMENTS

A research base on the effectiveness and cost-benefit of social work services is developing.[20, 21, 22, 23] The development of two new specialty journals (*Social Work in Health Care*, 1975, and *Health and Social Work*, 1976) adds greater visibility to social work's practice and research contributions to health care. A recent book by Travis, *Chronic Illness in Children*,[24] is a major scholarly addition to the field, as is *Long Term Care: A Handbook for Researchers, Planners and Providers*,[25] which contains the writings of several social workers.

Empirically based studies of social work practice in health care are summarized later. Their numbers are growing. A MEDLARS search conducted by the author on "social work–health" produced 1510 references between 1966 and 1977. It is of some historical interest to note that Gordon, in reviewing contributions of medical social workers in 14 social work and health journals, found only 100 items between 1950 and 1955. He said, "We realized the tendency of social workers to think in terms of what should be rather than what is. Perhaps this characteristic results from the desire of a young and under-developed profession to move its practice ahead. But goals, principles and directives actually rest on knowledge from scientific theory and social work experience. This knowledge must be pulled up from the depths where it is now hidden and laid out in the open for all to examine."[26]

PERSONNEL FORECASTS

Social service employment forecasts in the health field are promising. The fact that social work is involved in nearly every facet of health care suggests both its adaptability and its relevance to health care programs. In a recent comprehensive review of studies on social work in the job market, Hardcastle and Katz suggest, "A third area that social workers and social work education should be concerned with is the expanding health care arena. This includes not only traditional jobs of medical social work but also jobs in health care systems planning and management."[27]

Most trends suggest a future demand for personal health care counseling, health education, and increased consumer participation. Social workers have developed specialized skills in these areas of intervention. Although the potential opportunities for social workers in the expanding health field are considerable, the predominance of one-to-one clinical practice has created a noticeable gap in the supply of social work professionals trained for management, coordinating, and planning functions. Perhaps the recent amendments to the 1976 Health Profession Educational Assistance Act (which allows health training funds for schools of social work) will help correct the deficiency in social workers qualified to assume management and planning roles.

Schools of social work continue to attract many more qualified applicants than can be accepted. In 1974 the Gallup poll confirmed the increased appeal for social work as a career choice among college students. Overall, 6 percent of college students—9 percent of college women and 4 percent of college men —say they plan to go into the helping profession of social work when they complete their education. With social work enrollments remaining high in graduate schools, the "pool" of students who would be potentially interested in the challenging and well-paid positions available in health care settings seem to be sufficient to meet future employment needs.

THE HISTORICAL DEVELOPMENT OF SOCIAL WORK IN HEALTH CARE

The relationship between social work and health care in the United States has beginnings that extend to the late 1800s. Developments in social medicine and later in public health were in large part due "to social work being 'medicine's' first professional ally from the social field."[28] Rosen, the noted historian and public health physician, says:

To a large extent the history of social medicine is also the history of social policy (welfare). . . . The roots of social medicine are to be found in organized social work. It was here that medicine and social science found a common ground for action in the prevention of tuberculosis, securing better housing and work conditions.[29]

One example of social work's early leadership in public health campaigns was the work of Edward Devine. Under his direction the committee on the prevention of TB was established in 1902. The committee "utilized the services of capable phsycians and lay persons in working out a program of research into the social and medical aspects of tuberculosis, education of the public, encouragement of sanitaria for the care of patients and relief of indigent consumptives."[30] The Charity Organization Societies were actively involved in programs to combat infant mortality, rickets, and scurvy. In New York City the Association for Improving the Conditions of the Poor collaborated with the New York City Health Department in establishing in 1917 a center for maternal and child care in one of the city's settlement houses.

Social workers were essential to the success of many public health programs that had to work through citizen groups and settlements in order to be effective.[31] As early as 1893, Jane Addams had established a medical dispensary at Chicago's Hull House. Later social workers contributed substantially to the mental hygiene movement and the development of child guidance clinics.

Today's social worker has much to learn from the early successes and vicissitudes encountered by pioneering social workers. In this section we briefly review some of the historical highlights in the development of social work in health care. Nacman's historical analysis (see suggested additional readings) will also be helpful to the reader.

In Chart 1.1 important dates in the development of social work in health care are highlighted. Social work's development can be viewed in three distinct historical frameworks. In the *early period,* between 1890 and 1935, social work took the lead in efforts to prevent the serious infectious diseases that decimated large populations, and in developing health resources for the poor and indigent. During this period social work was also introduced into health care settings and became institutionalized.

The development of free dispensaries for the poor was not without controversy. In 1912 the New York County Medical Society hired, surprisingly, Anne Moore, a social worker, to conduct the study of possible "dispensary abuse."[32] Moore's findings indicated that 90 percent of those investigated were "worthy" of free treatment. Fears of pauperization during that time were related partly to the dream of social Darwinism and partly to organized medicine's historical ambivalence toward the concept of health care as a basic right. In this early interaction between social work and medicine we glimpse some of the differing social goals and values among the two professions. More recently, the Seebohm Report in Britain sees

the more fundamental sources of the difference between medicine and social work in the contrasting developments of the two professions. The social worker's emphasis is on patients gaining understanding of their situation and on the acquisition of personal insight and empathy on the part of the social workers. Medicine on the other hand is concerned with refining its objectivity and technology. . . . These two approaches are as different as they are obviously complimentary.[33]

ORIGINS OF HOSPITAL SOCIAL WORK

The eighteenth and early nineteenth centuries saw the growth of hospitals in both Great Britain and America. "With increasing complexity of medical care and increased acceptance of hospital services there developed a need for adjunct services in addition to the usual medical and nursing care. These have ushered in social work, nutrition, etc."[34] It was Dr. Richard Cabot who first introduced social work into the hospital dispensary at Massachusetts General Hospital in 1905. Cabot saw social work as the major linkage between medical and environmental resources. In his book, *Social Service and the Art of Healing,* he said:

Unless the doctor has already acquired the "social point of view" to the extent of seeing that his treatment of dispensary patients is slovenly, without some knowledge of their homes, their finances, their thoughts and worries—he will think that the social worker is trying to teach him how to do his work whenever she does what he didn't and couldn't do before. Naturally he will resent this indignantly.[35]

CHART 1.1

Some Important Dates in the Development of Social Work in Health Care.

1893	Jane Addams organizes medical dispensary at Hull House Settlement.
1902	Johns Hopkins medical students do field training at Charity Organization Society of Baltimore. New York COS establishes committee on prevention of TB, utilizing services of physicians.
1905	Dr. Richard Cabot employs first social worker in Outpatient Department at Massachusetts General Hospital.
1908	Clifford Beers and other professionals, including social workers, organize the first Society for Mental Hygiene in New Haven, Connecticut.
1909	First woman almoner appointed at St. Thomas Hospital, England.
1912	National Social Welfare Conference hosts first public discussion on national health insurance.
1917	Cincinnati social unit experiment initiated (neighborhood health center).
1918	Social work department established at the University of Chicago clinics. American Association of Hospital Social Workers formed.
1921	American Hospital Association conducts first survey of social workers.
1922	clinics. (Dr. Adolf Meyer was proud to point out that his wife was the first person to do this work.)
1923	Social work department established at Washington University in St. Louis.
1926	Harry Hopkins discusses the close relationship between social work and public health at the Cleveland National Conference.
1926	Social service established in Veterans Bureau (later Veterans Administration).
1927	Beginning of public health social work practice in Los Angeles Health Department (TB program).
1927	Committee on the Cost of Medical Care documents health needs of the elderly in the United States, recommends prepaid programs.
1936	Title V of the Social Security Act creates the Crippled Children's Division, which allows for the development of the medical-social consultants in the Children's Bureau's regional offices.
1942	"Social Insurance and Allied Services" (Beveridge Plan) report issued in England, leads to development of National Health Service (1948).
1946	National Foundation for Infantile Paralysis makes available training grants to social work students.
1947	National Institute of Mental Health (HEW) awards training stipends for social workers.
1949	First almoners used in medical group practices in England.
1954	Montiefiore–Family Health Maintenance Demonstration Project in progress.
1955	Joint Commission on Mental Illness and Health established by Congress.
1956	NASW develops a definition statement on medical social work.
1958	Cornell Welfare Project on coordinated care for the poor established.
1962	Princeton Seminar on Public Health Concepts in Social Work Education (proceedings published by the CSWE).
1962	American Public Health Association publishes "Educational Qualifications of Social Workers in Public Health Programs."
1962–1963	Community Mental Health–Mental Retardation Centers Act, Maternal and Child Health Act, and Migrant Health Act passed by Congress.

(continued)

11

CHART 1.1 (Continued)

1965–	Medicaid and Medicare (provision for social work consultations in nursing
1966	homes) created along with OEO Health Centers, regional medical programs, Comprehensive Health Planning Act, Appalachian Regional Act. The Civil Rights Act had a major impact on hospitals and health facilities.
1970	Joint Committee on Accreditation of Hospitals requires that "social services must be available to patients and families."
1971	American Hospital Association publishes manual on "Essentials of Social Work Programs in Hospitals."
1973	Health Maintenance Organization Act requires social services.

Cabot was joined by a number of other medical social reformers (see *The Medical Profession and Social Reform*). For example, Alice Hamilton, a graduate of the Johns Hopkins School of Medicine, joined Jane Addams at Hull House in 1897 and founded one of the first child welfare and outpatient pediatric clinics in the nation. While Cabot saw a clear role for social work, he acknowledged that social workers and, to some extent, even nurses were encountered with suspicion and hostility in hospitals. When Margaret Brogden initiated social services at the Johns Hopkins Hospital in 1907, social workers were barred from the medical wards by physicians. Social workers, much like patients, can feel ill at ease and not "at home" in hospitals. Even today there is ambivalence among social workers about assuming leadership roles in hospitals.[36] As in the case of the early dispensary abuse "flap," once social work moved into institutional settings some of its values and professional ideology came into sharper contrast with those of the dominant medical establishment. Social work's complementary and supportive relationships with the broader public health movement of the late 1800s had already started to change.

Following the development of medical-social consultants resulting from the passage of the Social Security amendments in 1935, social work moved into its *middle period* of development. This came at a time when medicine was in the throes of specialization and the resulting fragmentation of medical care practice. During the 1940s and 1950s, issues of coordination of care surfaced as a major concern of health care delivery. During these years social workers became more recognized as health care professionals participating in health teams and comprehensive health care projects. Considerable expansion of social workers in mental health agencies occurred during this period. Social work skills in consultation and teaching in health agencies and medical schools were important practices. It was also a time when various specialty groups of social workers combined to form the National Association of Social Work. The *Medical Social Work Journal* was published during this period.

In Chart 1.2 some of the early important writings, publications, and addresses related to social work are shown. In 1939 Bartlett wrote on social work teaching in medical schools, followed in 1948 by the publication *Widening*

Horizons in Medical Education. Silver described the development of family health teams including social workers.[37] The Cornell-Welfare Medical Care Project, which began in 1958, was a demonstration effort to combat fragmentation in health care to the poor.[38]

As a result of the specialization focus in medicine, social work too had become more specialized. Serious fractures between medical and psychiatric social work were well established by the 1940s. Freudian thought, which provided a facade of "scientific respectability," had a profound influence on social work education and practice. Internal conflict superseded external factors as a cause of personal and social breakdown. Institutionally based program orientations slowed community outreach and social-action efforts. The expanding mental health movement following World War II further widened the split between medical and psychiatric social work.

Out of the experiences of the middle period of development, social work gained respected skills in clinical treatment, teaching, and consultation. Research and evaluative studies of social work intervention were left wanting. In retrospect the distinctions between medical and psychiatric social work were better suited to the needs and orientations of medical care than to the client, who was in need of a unitary approach to his/her physical and mental health and environmental problems-in-living situation. While distinctions still remain, the future of social work in health care will require social workers skilled in a wide range of interventions related to the individual's physical, mental health, and social-environmental ills. The contribution that social work makes to health care is in its holistic approach to problems of both body and mind. It is hoped that in the future social work will not be "addicted" to one methodology such as Freudianism or behaviorism or seduced into fragmenting its rich repertoire of professional competencies so as to gain status within a medical system. Social work's uniqueness comes from its persistent focus on the physical, sociopsychological, and environmental health needs of clients.

During the *current period,* the 1960s and 1970s, social work in the health care field has expanded rapidly. When the mushrooming problems of civil rights, poverty, and social disorder surfaced in the 1960s, it was painfully apparent that social work's focus on institutional and remedial interventions was deficient. New alternatives to health care delivery, such as OEO neighborhood health centers, expanded programs for the prevention of maternal and infant health problems, community mental health centers, special outreach services to the rural poor, and new day care, home care, and self-care programs were needed. In all of these programs social work has made substantial contributions. Regardless of the criticisms of the "war on poverty," important new findings and successes have emerged in ways to provide comprehensive care to high-risk populations. Social and medical care, it was learned, can be provided in a satisfactory way to low-income groups.[39]

Consultation services for nursing homes and support by the Joint Commission on Accreditation of Hospitals for social service departments have

CHART 1.2

Early Writings, Publications, and Addresses Related to the Development of
Social Work in Health Care.

1907	Jane Addams addresses the American Hospital Association on "Layman's View of Hospital Work Among the Poor."
1910	Edward Devine discusses ill health in his book *Misery and Its Causes* (pp. 53–112).
1915	Dr. Richard Cabot, *Social Service and the Art of Healing*, New York: Moffat, Yard and Company.
1918	Michael Davis describes the work of hospital social service in his book *Dispensaries* (Macmillan).
1919	*Hospital Social Service Journal* initiated (published until 1933).
1921	Dr. Adolf Meyer delivers speech on "Historical Sketch and Outlook for Psychiatric Social Work."
1928	Dr. Cabot addresses the International Conference of Social Workers in Paris on the subject of "Social Services in Health Settings."
1930	Ida Cannon, *Social Work in Hospitals* (Russell Sage Foundation).
1931	J. H. Means writes on "The Social Component of Medicine" in *Hospital Social Service* 27, no. 74 (1931):93.
1940	Harriett Bartlett, *Some Aspects of Social Casework in a Medical Setting* (George Banta Publishing Co.).
1945	*Medical Social Work Journal* published.
1948	*Widening Horizons in Medical Education: A Study of the Teaching of Social and Environmental Factors in Medicine* published by the New York Commonwealth Fund (jointly sponsored by the American Association of Medical Social Workers).
1952	Ida Cannon, *Social Frontier of Medicine* (Harvard Press).
1956	William Gordon, "The Challenge of Research to Today's Medical Social Worker," *Social Work*, January 1956, pp. 81–87.
1956	National Association of Social Work, *A Pilot Study of Medical Social Workers' Interdisciplinary Conferences*. New York.
1956	Publication of *Expanding Horizons in Medical-Social Work* by Eleanor Cockerill, University of Chicago (Harper Press).
1957	Harriet Bartlett, *Fifty Years of Social Work in the Medical Setting* (NASW). New York.
1957	Doris Siegel describes the function of "Social Work in a Medical Setting" in *Social Work*, April 1957, pp. 70–77, and Grace White publishes "A View From Reservoir Hill" *Social Work* vol 2, no. 1, 1957, pp. 68–74.
1958	Elizabeth Rice, faculty member of the Harvard School of Public Health, authors chapter on medical social work in *Readings in Medical Care* (University of North Carolina Press).
1959	Medical-Social Work Section of the NASW develops monograph on "The Medical Social Worker as Mental Health Worker." New York.
1961	The NASW publishes first monograph on "Participation of Social Workers in Medical Education." New York.
1961	Harriet Bartlett, "Social Work Practice in the Health Field" (NASW). New York.
1961	Milton Wittman, "Preventive Social Work—A Goal for Practice in Education," *Journal of Social Work*, vol 6, no. 1, Jan., pp. 19–28.

(continued)

CHART 1.2 (Continued)

1962	Stanley King, ed., *Perceptions of Illness and Medical Practice*, includes chapter on medical social work (Russell Sage Foundation).
1962	*Proceedings of Seminar on Public Health Concepts in Social Work Education*, Princeton University (CSWE). New York.
1962	Elizabeth Rice publishes "Concepts of Prevention as Applied to the Practice of Social Work." *American Journal of Public Health* vol. 52, no. 2, Feb. 1962, pp. 266–274.
1962	American Public Health Association publishes "Educational Qualifications of Social Workers in Public Health Programs." *American Journal of Public Health*, vol 52, no. 2, Feb., pp. 317–324.

been major factors influencing social work development in recent years. Social work's involvement in Medicaid and Medicare programs has also been visible.[40] Innovative practice in emergency rooms, intensive-care units, and patient advocacy programs are also developing. Social work has increasingly participated in new educational programs in medical schools such as community medicine, family medicine, and the teaching programs of schools of nursing, pharmacy, and public health. Community organization and planning for health care have become more frequently associated with social work competence and skill. Unfortunately, during this period schools of social work have not been preparing practitioners to deal with the many new roles for social workers in health care.

Current trends toward health maintenance (HMOs), home care, self-care, better nutrition, and other environmental health measures are once again uniting themes for the involvement of social work with its historical partners in medicine, public health, nursing, and allied health professions. Social work's contribution to the foundations of health care in this country are significant. The profession has helped earn for each American the right to medical care. Now we must join in the efforts to provide *health* care on an equitable basis. Health services are but one force to better the human condition. However, in the years to come innovations in health promotion, delivery, and care will be an ever more important factor in improving the general welfare of this and, it is hoped, other countries.[41]

NOTES

1. *Health Resources Statistics,* Health Resources Administration Publication no. 75–1509 (Washington, D.C.: Government Printing office, 1974), chap. 33.
2. Neil Bracht, "Health Care: The Largest Human Service System," *Social Work* 19, no. 5 (September 1974):532–42.
3. Peter Hookey, "Social Work in Primary and Ambulatory Health Care: Access, Utilization, Attitudinal and Economic Aspects of an Emergent Field of Practice," St. Louis, Mo.,

Washington University doctoral dissertation, May 1976. University Microfilms, International no. 762–23–076, Ann Arbor, Michigan.

4. Robert Finney, Rita Pessin, and Larry Matheis, "Prospects for Social Workers in Health Planning," *Health and Social Work* 1, no. 3 (August 1976):7–26.

5. Bracht, op. cit.

6. *Medicare,* 1971, sec. 3, "Participating Providers," U.S. Department of Health, Education and Welfare, Office of Research and Statistics, Social Security Administration Publication no. SSA 76–11706 (Washington, D.C., January 1976).

7. Bracht, op. cit.

8. National Institute of Mental Health, *Staffing of Mental Health Facilities, United States,* (Washington, D.C., 1972), Table 1.6 on p. 35.

9. Richard Grinnell, et al., "The Status of Graduate-Level Social Workers Teaching in Medical Schools," *Social Work in Health Care* 1, no. 3 (Spring 1976):317–23.

10. Sylvia Schild, "Social Work with Genetic Problems," *Health and Social Work* 2, no. 1 (February 1977):58–77.

11. Hookey, op. cit.

12. Chauncey Alexander, "Pilot Project May Help Third-Party Vendorship Status," *NASW News,* February 1974, p. 5.

13. *NASW News,* January 1977, p. 7.

14. 1976 Survey of "Information on Master of Social Work Programs with Health Care Content" as reported in E. Hooyman, Robert Schwanke, and Helen Yesner, "Social Work and Public Health: An Interdisciplinary Joint Degree Program" (University of Minnesota, Duluth), paper presented at annual CSWE Program Meeting, Phoenix, Ariz., March 1, 1977, pp. 3–4.

15. Edgar Perretz, "Social Work Education for the Field of Health: A Report of Findings from a Survey of Curricula," *Social Work in Health Care* 1, no. 3 (Spring 1976):357–66.

16. Robert Finney and Tony Matheis, "Educating Social Workers as Health Planners," manuscript submitted for publication, 1975.

17. National Institute of Mental Health, Division of Manpower and Training Programs, Social Work Education Branch, Rockville, Maryland, report issued February 21, 1975.

18. Finney, op. cit.

19. Neil Bracht and Scott Briar, "Relationship of Schools of Social Work to Academic Health Science Centers," paper presented at the annual program meeting of the Council on Social Work Education, Philadelphia, 1976.

20. Jane Collins, "Assessment of Social Services in a Large Health Care Organization: The Social Work Administrator's Perspective," in *Evaluation of Social Work Services in Community Health and Medical Care Programs,* 1973 Annual Institute, Berkeley, Calif. Public Health Social Work Program.

21. Lahe Mell, "Cost Containment as a Result of Social Services," *Journal of Long-Term Care Administration* 2, no. 4 (Fall 1974):4–10.

22. Frances Nason and Thomas Delbanco, "Soft Services: A Major Cost-Effective Component of Primary Health Care," *Social Work in Health Care* 1, no. 3 (Spring 1976):297–308.

23. Barbara Berkman and Helen Rehr, "Early Social Service Case Finding for Hospitalized Patients: An Experiment," *Social Service Review* 47 (June 1973):256–65.

24. Georgia Travis, *Chronic Illness in Children* (Stanford, Calif.: Stanford University Press, 1976).

25. Sylvia Sherwood, (ed) *Long-Term Care:* A Handbook for Researchers, Planners, and Providers, Holliswood, New York.

26. William Gordon and Harriett Bartlett, "Generalizations in Medical Social Work: Preliminary Findings," *Social Work* 4, no. 3 (July 1959):72–76.

27. David Hardcastle and Arthur Katz, "A Current Perspective on the Social Work Job Market and the Unemployed," paper presented at the Annual Program Meeting, Council on Social Work Education, Phoenix, Arizona, February 28, 1977, 43 pp.

28. Leo Simmons and Harold Wolff, *Social Science in Medicine* (New York: Russell Sage Foundation, 1954), p. 12.
29. George Rosen, *Medical Police to Social Medicine* (New York: Science History Publications, 1974), pp. 112–16.
30. Arthur E. Fink, *The Field of Social Work* (New York: Holt, 1942), p. 25.
31. Robert Lubove, *The Progressives and the Slums, Tenement House Reform in New York City 1890–1917* (Pittsburgh: University of Pittsburgh Press, 1962), and George Rosen, "The First Neighborhood Health Center Movement, Its Rise and Fall," *American Journal of Public Health* 61, no. 8 (August 1971):1620–37.
32. Gert Brieger, "The Use and Abuse of Medical Charities in Late 19th Century America," *American Journal of Public Health* 67, no. 3 (March 1977):264–67.
33. Report of the Committee on Local Authority and Allied Personal Services, London, 1968.
34. Rosen, op. cit., p. 297.
35. Richard Cabot, *Social Service and the Art of Healing* (New York: Moffat, Yard and Co. 1931), p. 180–82.
36. Shirley Wattenberg et al., "Comparison of Opinions of Social Work Administrators and Hospital Administrators Toward Leadership Tasks," *Social Work in Health Care* 2, no. 3 (Spring 1977):285–93.
37. George Silver and Charlotte Stiber, "The Social Worker and the Physician, Daily Practice of A Health Team," *Journal of Medical Education* 30, no. 5 (May 1957):324–30.
38. Margaret Dennis and Charles Goodrich, "Co-ordinated Medical Care for Public Welfare Clients: Implications for Medical Social Work Practice," *Social Casework,* January 1963, pp. 11–18.
39. Joel Alpert et al., "Attitudes and Satisfactions of Low Income Families Receiving Comprehensive Pediatric Care," *American Journal of Public Health* 60, no. 3 (March 1970):499–506.
40. Janice Paneth, "Deflation in an Inflationary Period: Some Current Social Health Need Provisions," *American Journal of Public Health* Vol. 62, no. 1 (January 1972):60–63.
41. Marc Lalonde, "A New Perspective on the Health of Canadians," *Information Canada,* cat. no. H31–1374, Ottawa, 1975, 75 pp. See also Nancy Milio, *The Care of Health in Communities: Access for Outcasts* (New York: Macmillan 1975).

SUGGESTED ADDITIONAL READINGS

Bartlett, Harriett. *50 Years of Social Work in the Medical Setting.* New York: NASW, 1957, p. 46

Becker, Dorothy, "Exit Lady Bountiful, The Volunteer and the Professional Social Worker," *Social Service Review* 38, no. 1 (March 1964):57–72.

Brogden, Margaret, "The Johns Hopkins Hospital Department of Social Services, 1907–31," *Social Service Review* 38, no. 1 (March 1964):88–98.

Butrym, Zofia. *Social Work in Medical Care.* London: Routledge and Kegan Paul Library of Social Work, 1967.

Cohen, Michael, "Some Characteristics of Social Workers in Private Practice," *Social Work,* April 1966, pp. 69–76.

Gentry, John, et al., "Promoting the Adoption of Social Work Services by Hospitals and Health Departments," *American Journal of Public Health* 63, no. 2 (February 1973):117.

Goldstein, Dora. *Expanding Horizons in Medical Social Work.* Chicago: University of Illinois Press, 1955.

Hirsch, Sidney, and Abraham Lurie, "Social Work Dimensions in Shaping Medical Care Philosophy and Practice," *Social Work,* April 1969, p. 75.

Hutter, M. J., G. E. Zakus, and C. I. Dungy, "Social Work Training of New Health Professionals," *Health and Social Work* 1, no. 2 (May 1976).

Nacman, Martin "Social Work in Health Settings: A Historical Review," *Social Work in Health Care*, 2, no. 4 (Summer 1977).

Randall, Ronald, "Ida M. Cannon: Pioneer in Medical Social Work," *Social Service Review* 49, no. 2 (June 1975).

Wittman, Milton, "Social Work Manpower for the Health Field," *American Journal of Public Health* 64, no. 4 (April 1974):370–75.

2/CONTRIBUTIONS TO
COMPREHENSIVE HEALTH CARE:
BASIC PREMISES

NEIL F. BRACHT

What exactly is the contribution of the social worker to health care programs? What can social workers cite as their contribution to comprehensive health care that is distinguishable from the contributions of other behaviorally related professions? How much professional autonomy is required for any health practitioner to achieve a distinct identity in complex multiprofessional health settings? These questions are addressed in this chapter.

Various conceptions of social work's role in comprehensive health care are found in the literature. Early in his expressed rationale to doctors for bringing social workers into hospitals, Cabot emphasized the "linkage" role between medical and environmental resources.[1] Morris reiterates much of the Cabot theme when he says social work should "handle the enlarged set of relationships between intricate networks of health and social services."[2] At the same time, Morris calls for a more distinct management role for social work in coordinating and operating that part of the health subsystem which deals with long-term care and handicapping conditions. Rehr has demonstrated that greater professional autonomy in hospitals is related to more active case finding and referral within the social service department itself, and that it produces greater benefit to patients and reduces hospital stay.[3] Hirsch and Lurie believe that "social work brings to the health field a methodology to reduce the incidence of social crises that aggravate health problems."[4] Palmiere has listed a set of characteristics and skills that make social work particularly relevant to the administration and community organization of medical care–social welfare services.[5,6] Nielsen stresses noninstitutional approaches and has shown that a home aid service can cut down hospital admissions and nursing home placements.[7] Cowen and Sbarbaro document successful use of social work in coordinating all aspects of a family-centered health care program.[8] Klein suggests that when attention is given to community outreach and follow-up efforts in a structured way, including psychosocial treatment, rehospitalization is less likely to occur.[9]

19

Can we distill from these differing perceptions and empirical findings a common set of premises that provide a rationale for social work practice in health settings? Fortunately, social work seems to have arrived at a point in its relatively young history of service to clients in the health care system at which its accomplishments are more visible and documentable. Although the availability of descriptive data and research information is limited in a few areas, overall a respectable accumulation of findings exist that support the need for and use of social services. This chapter sets forth a framework of five basic premises, supported in the literature, that undergird social work's practice contributions to health care. Prior to the discussion of the theoretical under-pinnings of specialty social work practice in health settings, two fundamental questions need to be addressed: (1) What is the nature of social work, and (2) what is the operational meaning of comprehensive health care?

According to the Pincus-Minahan model, social work "is concerned with the interactions between people and their social environment which affect the ability of people to accomplish their life tasks, alleviate stress and realize their aspirations and values."[10] As many authors have noted, social work differs from social welfare. Social welfare is seen as "an organized system of social services and institutions designed to aid individuals and groups to attain satisfying standards of life and health . . ."[11] Similarly, a recent United Nations publication views the field of social welfare as "a complex of institutions, services and processes delivered through specific programs to meet the needs of people in a manner that is socially satisfying and conducive to better social functioning . . . While other sectors or disciplines such as health and education may also lead to better social functioning, their immediate objectives are different from social welfare which is directly concerned with the sum of these activities"[12] Normative definitions of social welfare range from broadly conceived notions, in which social welfare is the very process of political and social responsibility for achieving a positive state of well-being, to a more restrictive view in which social welfare is narrowly viewed in terms of certain social services for the needy only.[13] (For a fuller discussion of various conceptions of social welfare, see R. M. Titmuss, "Developing Social Policy in Conditions of Rapid Change, The Role of Social Welfare," in *Proceedings 16th International Congress Conference on Social Welfare,* The Hague, The Netherlands, August 13–19, 1972, pp. 33–43.)

Increasingly the phrase "human services system" is used synonomously with "social welfare system." Under the human services "umbrella" a variety of local and state social, health, educational, economic, and rehabilitation programs are being administered and coordinated.

While the central 'business' of social work is social welfare, social work as a profession is clearly differentiated from the broader social welfare or human services system. The link between social work and social welfare is seen in the Pincus-Minahan description of the purpose of social work:[10]

   1. To enhance the problem-solving capacities of people.
   2. To link people with the systems that provide them with resources, services and opportunities.
   3. To promote the effective and humane operations of these systems.
   4. To contribute to the development and improvement of social policy.

The application of these generalized purposes of professional social work to specialty practice in health care will be described below under the operational definition of comprehensive health care.

Comprehensive health care for all Americans has been a persistent theme in the social-health legislation of the past decade. In a recent summary of thirty-five state health plans in the United States, "comprehensive system of care" was the most frequently mentioned goal.[14] Concern for the concept of comprehensive health care was reflected in a number of health care demonstrations following World War II.[15] In medical schools, comprehensive-care experiments were introduced in order to help medical students view people as physically and psychologically integrated "wholes" rather than as independently functioning "parts," and to help them become sensitive to the social and environmental aspects of illness and health. According to Weinerman, comprehensive health care is

the organized provision of health services to family groups, including a full spectrum of services from prevention to rehabilitation, continuity of care for the individual, emphasis upon the social and personal aspects of disease and its management, use of the health team concept including personal physician responsibility, and coordination of the diverse elements of modern scientific medical practice.[16]

In this definition the emphasis is on the delivery of personal health care services, in contrast to the broader definition of the World Health Organization, which states that "health is a state of complete physical, mental, and social well-being and not merely the absence of disease or infirmity." (For a more complete discussion of the concept of health, see Chapter 7.) In figure 2.1 a conceptualized scheme of a comprehensive health services delivery system is depicted. Access to primary care is through a variety of service modalities. Social workers are employed in all of these units.

   In a recent policy statement the American Public Health Association specifically lists medical-social services and mental health ambulatory care among some fifteen specific services to be included in comprehensive-care programs:[18]

   1. Health education and preventive services
   2. Primary health care
   3. Specialist care
   4. Hospitalization in short-term general hospitals

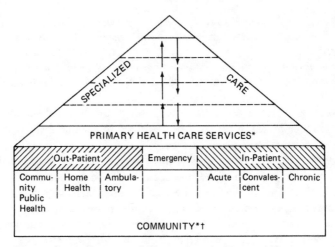

†Community constitutes accessibility to primary health care within time
constraint of one hour.
*Physical & mental health

Fig. 2.1 Conceptualized comprehensive health services delivery system.

Source: U.S. Department of Health, Education and Welfare, *Methodological Approaches to Determining Health Manpower Supply and Requirements*, vol. II, Health Resources Administration, Publication no. 76-14512 (Washington, D.C., 1976), p. 42. Adapted from U.S. Department of Health, Education, and Welfare, Division of Comprehensive Health Planning, *Guide to Comprehensive Health Planning*, prepared by Arthur Young & Company. Washington, D.C.: U.S. Government Printing Office, 1974.

5. Laboratory, radiological and other special diagnostic examinations
6. Ambulatory mental health service
7. Prescribed drugs
8. Suitable alternatives to care in a general hospital (skilled nursing homes or organized home care programs but not solely custodial in purpose)
9. Radiation therapy
10. Dental care exclusive of purely cosmetic
11. Rehabilitation service including physical, occupational speech therapy
12. Vision care including eye glasses
13. Prosthetic appliances
14. Ambulance services
15. Medical social services

The basic professional objectives and purposes of social work as listed by Pincus and Minahan are supportive of health care goals aimed at achieving comprehensive health care as discussed above. For example:

1. Social workers enhance the problem-solving capacities of people when they participate in comprehensive health care programs that assist patients and family with the social aspects of illness, disability, and recovery. Examples would be the fostering of self-help groups among former mastectomy or cancer

patients to deal with personal adjustment difficulties, or helping hospitalized renal patients and their families weigh the implications of home versus inpatient dialysis.

2. Social workers have long served as linkages for entry into the health care system. They also coordinate programs of comprehensive health and social care. In outreach programs social workers increase access to health facilities through health education programs and the use of trained indigenous workers. Social workers can improve the utilization of services.

3. Social workers in comprehensive health care programs also promote effective and humane operation of health care systems. Social workers were among the first leaders to assist in the development of ombudsman programs for hospitals and nursing homes. Social workers have led in the development of services to improve care in nursing homes and in the development of death-with-dignity programs, and in crisis intervention with families during medical emergencies. McNamara has described the development of a humanistic training program in a teaching hospital.[18]

4. Finally, social workers in health care have demonstrated their ability to contribute to the analysis and improvement of social policy and program development.[19] Social work studies of the effectiveness of home health services provide important research findings for policy decisions.[20] Studies of the health indexes of the poor[21] and their access to health services have been important contributions by social workers to overall social-health policy.

In summary, we can state that the general purposes of social work in the United States are compatible with a long-sought and significant social goal, that of comprehensive health care for all citizens.

BASIC PREMISES

Having addressed two preliminary questions, regarding the nature of social work and the nature of comprehensive health care, we now return to the more specific premises that underlie social work's specialty practice in the health care field. These premises provide a framework for viewing the contribution that social workers make in the wide range of health programs in this country. It is hoped that they may serve to unify the diversified roles, functions, and perceptions about social work mentioned at the beginning of this chapter. These premises are not all-inclusive, but they represent those that are well documented in the literature and provide a sound theoretical base from which social work intervention can proceed. (Social work and social science research supporting these premises is listed in Chart 2.1.)

FIVE BASIC PREMISES OF SOCIAL WORK PRACTICE IN HEALTH

1. Social, cultural, and economic conditions have a significant and measurable effect on both health status and illness prevention and recovery. A grow-

ing body of research suggests positive relationships between these variables and the development of illness conditions.

2. Illness-related behaviors, whether perceived or actual, frequently disrupt personal or family equilibrium and coping abilities. Illness conditions, whether acute, chronic, or terminal, can be exacerbated by the effects of institutionalization.

3. Medical treatment alone is often incomplete, and occasionally impossible to render, without accompanying social support and counseling services.

4. Problems in access to and appropriate utilization of health services are sufficiently endemic to our health care delivery system as to require concerted community action and institutional innovation.

5. Multiprofessional health team collaboration on selected individual and community health problems is an effective approach to solving complex sociomedical problems.

In order to familiarize the social worker with the research information on which these five premises are asserted, Chart 2.1 presents sociological, behavioral, and social work literature that is supportive of each premise. The use and efficacy of particular interventions that relate to the social conditions or need described in each premise are documented. Adjacent to the references a brief summary describing the outcome of selected interventions is presented.

PREMISES AND PROFESSIONAL AUTONOMY

The richly diverse knowledge that has supported and continues to support these basic premises provides a base for targeted professional social work interventions in the health care field. Just as the knowledge derived in support of these premises is not exclusively contributed by social workers, neither are the professional interventions or program developments flowing from these premises the exclusive domain of social workers. For example, social work alone cannot address longstanding problems of access and inappropriate utilization of health care; social work alone cannot ameliorate socioeconomic conditions that affect health status; social work alone cannot mandate all of the social supports needed in patient recovery and rehabilitation; and obviously, social work is but one of several participants in collaborative team processes related to complex sociomedical problems. One distinctive aspect of social work practice is that much of its *full-time professional activity* is related to improving the conditions and problems described in these premises. As Bartlett said, "The social worker is the only one in the [health] field with a consistent and central focus on social functioning."[22]

Since many professionals are concerned with activities and interventions related to these premises, questions of professional "turf" and autonomy do arise. While these are not new problems, there is growing concern and discussion about the increased blurring of role functions in the psychosocial aspects of patient care.[23] For example, the enlarged visibility of "psychosocial nurs-

CHART 2.1

Literature Supporting Five Basic Premises of Social Work Practice in Health.

PREMISE 1: Social, cultural, and economic conditions have a significant and measurable effect on both health status and illness prevention. A growing body of research suggests positive relationships between these variables and the development of illness conditions.

Social Work-Social Science Research References Supporting the Premise:

"Behavioral Factors Associated with the Etiology of Physical Disease," Six Papers on Disease Process and Relevant Social Conditions, *American Journal of Public Health* 64 (November 1974): 1033-55.

Bergum, Kathleen Holt, "Social and Psychological Factors in Congestive Heart Failure," *Social Work*, January 1969, p. 68.

Brenner, M. Harvey, "Economic Changes and Heart Disease Mortality," *American Journal of Public Health* 6, no. 3 (March 1971): 606-16.

Birch, Herbert, et al., *Mental Subnormality in the Community*. Baltimore: Williams & Wilkins, 1970.

Latham, Michael C. et al., "The Effects of Malnutrition on Intellectual Development and Learning," *American Journal of Public Health* 61, no. 7 (July 1971): 1307-24.

Pratt, Lois, "The Relationship of Socioeconomic Status to Health," *American Journal of Public Health* 61, no. 2 (February 1971): 281-90.

Watkins, Elizabeth, "Low Income Negro Mothers: Their Decision to Seek Prenatal Care," *American Journal of Public Health* 58, no. 4 (April 1968): 655-67.

Social/Health Interventions Related to Conditions Described in Premise:

Outcome Summary:

Gruenberg, Ernest, et al., "Social Breakdown Syndrome: Environmental and Host Factors Associated with Chronicity," *American Journal of Public Health* 63, no. 1 (January 1972): 91-94.

Incidence of social disability and malfunctioning reduced 50 percent through preventive reorganization of services.

Klein, Helen, et al., "Significant Social Variables in Favorable Community Adjustment of Schizophrenics: A 5-Year Follow-up," Public Health Briefs, *American Journal of Public Health* 64, no. 8 (August 1971): 813.

Carefully structured psychosocial treatment program substantially reduced rehospitalization of patients.

McGrath, Alaska Demonstration Project. *Making Health Education Work*. Washington, D.C., American Public Health Association, 1976, pp. 117-23.

Health education project improved physical status at significant measurable levels. Substantial changes in health knowledge and practices occurred.

Cunningham, Murray, et al., "Community Placement of Released Mental Patients: A Five-Year Study," *Social Work*, January 1969, pp. 54-60.

Delineates social and employment factors associated with veterans' successful community adjustment after discharge.

(continued)

CHART 2.1 (Continued)

PREMISE 2: Illness-related behaviors, whether perceived or actual, frequently disrupt personal or family equilibrium and coping abilities. Illness conditions, whether acute, chronic, or terminal, can be exacerbated by the effects of institutionalization.

Social Work–Social Science Research References Supporting the Premise:

Jaco, E. Gartly, ed. *Patients, Physicians and Illness*. New York: Free Press, 1972. See "Stages of Illness" (E. Suchman), chap. 11, and "Response Factors in Illness" (D. Mechanic), chap. 8.

Kaplan, D. et al., "Predicting the Impact of Severe Illness in Families," *Health and Social Work* 1, no. 3 (August 1976).

Killian, E., "Effect of Geriatric Transfers on Mortality Rates," *Social Work* 15 (1970):19-26.

Hudson, Kate, "Some Social and Emotional Implications of Dependence on Machinery," *British Journal of Social Work* 1, no. 2 (Summer 1971):149-95.

Rahe, Richard, et al., "Predictors of Illness Behavior and Failure in Stressful Training," *Journal of Health and Social Behavior* 14 (June 1973):134-43.

Stone, Olive, and Edith Shapiro, "Posthospital Changes in Role Systems of Patients," *Social Service Review* 42, no. 3 (September 1968):314-25.

Strauss, Anselm. *Chronic Illness and the Quality of Life*. St. Louis: C. V. Mosby, 1975.

Turk, J., "Impact of Cystic Fibrosis on Family Functioning," *Pediatrics* 34, no. 67 (1964).

Social/Health Interventions Related to Conditions Described in Premise:	*Outcome Summary:*
Linsk, N., "Behavioral Group Work in a Home for the Aged," *Social Work*, November 1975, pp. 454-63.	Increased resident participation in activities.
Kaplan, D., et al., "Family Mediation of Stress," *Social Work*, July 1973, pp. 60-68.	Provides data for organizing preventive and clinical programs that protect family's stress-mediating function.
Kaplan, Mary, et al., "Relocation Trauma Counseling for the Elderly." Paper presented to the Social Work Section, American Public Health Association Meeting, 1976, Miami.	Elderly relocated from inappropriate to appropriate facilities. Condition of over 90 percent remained stable or improved.
Clark, Eleanor, "Improving Post-Hospital Care for Chronically Ill Elderly Patients," *Social Work*, January 1969, pp. 62-67.	Aftercare planning improved, including five-day reduction in discharge delay.

(continued)

CHART 2.1 (Continued)

PREMISE 3: Medical treatment alone is often incomplete, and occasionally impossible to render, without accompanying social support and counseling services.

Social Work–Social Science Research References Supporting the Premise:

Battistella, Roger, "Factors Associated with Delay in the Initiation of Physician's Care Among Late Adulthood Persons," *American Journal of Public Health* 61, (June 1971):1348–61.

Kaplan, J., and C. S. Ford, "Rehabilitation for the Elderly: An Eleven-year Assessment," *Gerontologist* 15, no. 5 (October 1975):393–97. (Strong coordinating role of social work in high rate of return to community living.)

Starr, P., and K. Heiserman, "Factors Associated with Missed Appointments of Patients in a Cleft Lip and Palate Clinic," *Cleft Palate Journal* 12, no. 4 (October 1975):461–64.

Stewart, James, and William Hood, "Using Workers From 'Hard-Core' Areas to Increase Immunizational Levels," *Public Health Reports* 85 (February 1970):177–85.

Stimpert, Warren, et al., "A Description of Psychiatric Patients Five Years After Treatment," *Social Work*, July 1966, p. 78.

Thuyns, K., and R. Evans, "Comprehensive Health Care as a Function of Consumer-Provider Relationship," *Mental Health and Behavioral Science* 16 (August 1974):27–29.

Garson, J. Z., and Ruth Wolfe, "Social Problems of the Hospitalized Elderly," *Canadian Family Physician*, November 1975, pp. 85–93.

Social/Health Interventions Related to Conditions Described in Premise:

Outcome Summary:

Benedetto, R., "The 23-Hour Bed: Alternative to Hospitalization," *Health and Social Work* 2, no. 2 (May 1977):75–88.

Preadmission unit successful in returning clients to their homes. Inpatient hospitalization reduced by 38 percent.

Koonce, Geraldine, "Social Work with Mental Patients in the Community," *Social Work*, May 1973, pp. 30–34.

Close social work follow-up helps discharged patients function more independently in community.

Nielson, Margaret, et al., "Older Persons After Hospitalization: A Controlled Study," *American Journal of Public Health* 62, no. 8 (August 1972):1094–1100.

Significantly less institutionalization in the client group offered home aide service.

Hancock, Emily, "Crisis Intervention in a Newborn Nursery Intensive Care Unit," *Social Work in Health Care* 1, no. 4 (Summer 1976):421.

Social worker/doctor collaboration helps parents deal with birth of defective child.

Macdonald, Mary, et al., "Social Factors in Relation to Participation in Follow-Up Care of Rheumatic Fever," *Pediatrics* 62, no. 4 (April 1963):503–13.

Three general social factors associated with quality of family cooperation discussed.

(continued)

CHART 2.1 (Continued)

PREMISE 4: Problems of access to and appropriate utilization of health services are sufficiently endemic to our health care delivery system as to require concerted community and institutional innovation.

Social Work-Social Science Research References Supporting the Premise:

Hall, Julian, et al., "Delivering Mental Health Services to the Urban Poor," *Social Work*, April 1970, pp. 35-46.

Krell, George, "Overstay Among Hospital Patients: Problems and Approaches," *Health and Social Work* 2 no. 1 (February 1977):179.

Leopold, Edith, and L. Schein, "Missing Links in the Human Services Non-System," *Medical Care* 13, no. 7 (July 1975):595-606.

Moncure, Claribel, "Clinical Social Work Planning with 5,000 General Medical and Surgical Patients for Their Hospital Discharge," *Journal of Chronic Diseases* 11, no. 2 (February 1960):176-86. (67 percent able to return home)

Nemat, O. Borhani, et al., "Use of Health Services in a Rural Community," *Health Services Reports* 88 (March 1973):275.

Richardson, William, "Poverty, Illness and Use of Health Services in U.S.," *Hospitals* 43 (July 1969):249.

Sparer, Gerald, et al., "Evaluation of OEO Neighborhood Health Centers," *American Journal of Public Health* 61, no. 5 (May 1971):931-42.

Tessler, Richard, et al., "The Effect of Psychological Distress on Physician Utilization: A Prospective Study," *Journal of Health and Social Behavior* 17 (December 1976):353-64.

Social/Health Interventions Related to Conditions Described in Premise:	*Outcome Summary:*
Bates, T., A. Behr, et al., "The Place of Early Social Assessment in the Management of Surgical Patients," *Postgraduate Medical Journal* (England) 52 (February 1976):61-65.	Delays related to social factors in patient's (elderly, high-risk) discharge from the hospital were reduced 16 percent with regular help of social work.
Collins, Jane. "Assessment of Social Services in a Large Health Care Organization" In *Evaluation of Social Work Services in Community Health and Medical Care Programs*, Proceedings 1973 Institute, Public Health Social Work Program, Berkeley, California, 1973, pp. 57-67.	Social work intervention with high utilizers of emergency services reduced emergency room visits by 54 percent. Unnecessary ambulance "runs" were reduced by 68 percent.
Berkman, Barbara, and Helen Rehr, "Early Social Service Case Findings for Hospitalized Patients, An Experiment," *Social Service Review* 47 (June 1973):256-65.	Early identification and referral by Social Service Department reduced stay of elderly, on the average, by ten days.
Colombo, Theodore, et al., "The Integration of an OEO Health Program into a Prepaid Comprehensive Group Practice Plan," *American Journal of Public Health* 59, no. 4 (April 1969):641-50.	Large medically indigent population successfully integrated into an ongoing medical care system without serious problems.
Ravich, Ruth, et al., "Hospital Ombudsman Smooths Flow of Services and Communication," *Hospitals* 43 (March 1969):56-59.	Demonstrates advocacy role of social worker in improving patient care process.

(continued)

CHART 2.1 (Continued)

PREMISE 5: Multiprofessional health team collaboration on selected individual and community health problems is an effective approach to solving complex sociomedical problems.

Social Work–Social Science Research References Supporting the Premise:

Braham, S., et al., "Evaluation of the Social Needs of Nonhospitalized Chronically Ill Persons: Study of 47 Patients with Multiple Sclerosis," *Journal of Chronic Disease* 28, no. 7–8 (August 1975):401–20.

Houghton, L., and A. Martin, "Home vs. Hospital: A Hospital-Based Home Care Program," *Health and Social Work* 1, no. 4 (November 1976):88–103.

Kauffman, Margaret, and Anne Cunningham, "Epidemiologic Analysis of Outcomes in Maternal and Infant Health in Evaluating Effectiveness of Three Patient Care Teams," *American Journal of Public Health* 60, no. 9 (September 1970):1712–26.

Mannino, F., and M. Shore, "Demonstrating Effectiveness in an Aftercare Program," *Social Work*, May 1974, pp. 351–54.

Morse, A., et al., "Environmental Correlates of Pediatric Social Illness: Preventive Implications of an Advocacy Approach," *American Journal of Public Health* 67, no. 7 (July 1977):612–15.

Robinson, Derek, "Effectiveness of Medical and Social Supervision in a Multiproblem Population," *American Journal of Public Health* 58, no. 2 (February 1968):252–62.

Whittington, H. G., "Preliminary Evaluation of a Decentralized Community Mental Health Center," *American Journal of Public Health* 60, no. 1 (January 1970):64–78.

Social/Health Interventions Related to Conditions Described in Premise:

Outcome Summary:

Cowen, D., and J. Sbarbaro, "Family-Centered Health Care—A Viable Reality? The Denver Experience," *Medical Care* 10, no. 2 (March 1972):164.	Social Service Division responsible for coordinating successful family health care program.
Cowin, Ruth, et al., "Social Work in a Child Health Clinic: A Report of a Demonstration," *American Journal of Public Health* 55, no. 6 (June 1965):821.	Social worker brought special knowledge and skill additional to that of other staff.
Flomenhaft, Kalman, et al., "Avoiding Psychiatric Hospitalization," *Social Work*, October 1969, pp. 38–45.	Clinical team demonstrated that family crisis therapy was more economical and a less stigmatizing form of treatment than hospitalization.
Freeman, D., "Rehabilitation of the Mentally Ill Aging," *Social Work,* October 1959, pp. 65–71.	Successful multidisciplinary approach to returning patients to the the community.
Richter, Ralph, et al., "The Community Health Worker, a Resource for Improved Health Care Delivery," *American Journal of Public Health* 64, no. 11 (November 1974): 1056–61.	Use of indigenous health workers on interdisciplinary team increased "kept" appointments from 56 percent to 73 percent.

ing" as part of health and mental health care teams is a welcome event, long overdue. Nurses have frequent access to patients and opportunities for intervention that are not always available to social workers. Social work and nursing have a strong tradition of equal but interdependent collaboration. Their roots in "medicine" are of about equal depth. Compared with the present tensions between doctors and independent nurse practitioners concerning issues of role status, legal responsibility, and accountability, the differences between nurses and social workers are relatively mild. Potential differences in role functions between nurses and social workers could be greatly reduced by immediate and continuing dialogue among leaders representing these two professions at the national level. Regional workshops and discussions should be set in motion now—social work and nursing embrace many common values of health care and social betterment. Their combined force can be a powerful influence in implementing the reforms needed to achieve a truly comprehensive health care delivery system for all.

Social workers, in general, have been sanctioned by hospitals, health departments, and other governmental facilities to engage in professional practice with a major focus on social functioning, the development of coordinated community resources, and providing linkages to broader social welfare services. Professional autonomy does not mean professional isolation. Social work practice in a host setting is by its very nature interdependent and to an extent limited.[24] Social work autonomy develops in one sense from a strong research and demonstration base. Professional autonomy is achieved and can be strengthened by effective social work leadership. In addition to the Rehr study cited earlier, two recent research findings indicate that social work may be inhibited from achieving greater professional autonomy and leadership from within its own discipline. For example, a study of hospital administrators showed considerable agreement with several leadership functions for social workers in hospitals. However, social workers spend their time on such leadership functions less frequently than would be expected, given the general level of support from hospital administration.[25] Pfouts and McDaniel, in a survey of social work practice in twenty-eight teaching hospitals in the United States, conclude

that in some aspects of their practice, hospital social workers are more autonomous than myth would have it, but that in others, the opportunities to achieve greater autonomy [is] not grasped. The findings support our contention that it is not institutional forces alone, but the interaction of social workers and institution which determine the professional status of social work in the teaching hospital.[26]

As a young profession, social work is making progress toward more autonomous practice. Societal and professional changes call for flexibility in modes of practice. "Turf" problems are as old as the redwoods. Social workers are not alone in dealing with these issues. For example, professionally trained health educators were traditionally central to large public-information and health promotion campaigns. This is changing. Today many professionals such as physical therapists, nutritionists, nurses, and social workers participate in teaching activities centered on health education and health maintenance. This in no way extinguishes a central role for the professionally trained health educator in health education. The health educator should welcome these additional efforts in supporting his/her central role. In the same way, social workers can support the growing involvement of other professions in the psychosocial area. This can only benefit total patient care and assist social work in the fulfillment of its larger professional and societal goals, within and outside of the health care system.

A final question concerns the "location" of social workers in health settings. Do social workers have to be physically located in health settings in order to render the services that are essential to comprehensive health care? The British, for example, have recently moved social work out of health institutions and, for the most part, returned it to the general social service agencies, where social workers have medical caseloads and are responsible for working with other health professionals. Doran Teague, in recommending an innovative model for social work services to hospitals, describes a program in which the provision of such services is done on a contractual basis with an independent "social services enterprise."[27] For the immediate future it seems prudent to this author that the major aspects of social work practice that pertain to health care delivery remain strategically located within the health care institutions themselves. In future decades, as medical care becomes a more integral part of a broader human services system, there may be a need to reassess social work's location vis-à-vis health care.

NOTES

1. Richard Cabot, "Hospital and Dispensary Social Work," *Hospital Social Work* (1928).
2. Robert Morris, "The Place of Social Work in the Human Services," *Journal of Social Work* 19, no. 5 (September 1974):524. See also Robert Morris and Delwin Anderson, "Personal Care Services: An Identity for Social Work," *Social Service Review* 49, no. 2 (June 1975): 157–74.
3. Helen Rehr and Barbara Gordon Berkman, "Social Service Case Finding in the Hospital— Its Influence on the Utilization of Social Services," *American Journal of Public Health* 63, no. 10 (October 1973):857–62.
4. Sidney Hirsch and Abraham Lurie, "Social Work Dimensions in Shaping Medical Care Philosophy and Practice," *Social Work*, April 1969, p. 75.
5. Darwin Palmiere, "The Responsibilities of Social Work in Policy and Program Development," paper presented at the Regional Training Institute for Public Health Social Workers: The Changing Patterns of Social Work Services in the New Health Programs, East Lansing, Michigan, August 12–14, 1966.
6. See also Darwin Palmiere, "The Expanding Role of Social Work in Medical Care Settings," paper presented at the National Association of Social Workers Tenth Anniversary Symposium on Social Work Practice and Knowledge, Atlanta, May 21–23, 1965.
7. Margaret Nielsen et al., "Older Persons After Hospitalization: A Controlled Study of Home Aide Service," *American Journal of Public Health* 62, no. 8 (August 1972):1094–1100.

8. David Cowen and John Sbarbaro, "Family Centered Health Care—A Viable Reality? The Denver Experience," *Journal of Medical Care* 10, no. 2 (March-April 1972):164–72.

9. Helen Klein, D.S.W., et al., "Significant Social Variables in Favorable Community Adjustment of Schizophrenics: A Five Year Follow-up," *American Journal of Public Health* 64, no. 8 (August 1974):813.

10. Allen Pincus and Anne Minahan, *Social Work Practice: Model and Method* (Itasca, Ill.: F. E. Peacock, 1973).

11. H. L. Wilensky and C. N. Lebaux, *Industrial Society and Social Welfare* (New York: The Free Press 1958), p. 139.

12. United Nations, Department of Economic and Social Affairs, *Training for Social Welfare*, Fifth International Survey (New York, 1971), pp. 3–4.

13. V. D. Barnett, *Welfare in America* (Norman, 1960), p. 31.

14. *Baselines for Setting Health Goals and Standards*, Department of Health, Education and Welfare, Washington D.C. Health Resources Administration, no. 76-640, September 1976, p. 48.

15. P. Snoke and E. R. Weinerman, "Comprehensive Care Programs in University Medical Centers, *Journal of Medical Education* 40, (July 1965):625–57.

16. Ibid., p. 627.

17. American Public Health Association, "Health Maintenance Organizations: A Policy Paper," *American Journal of Public Health* 61, no. 12 (December 1971):2528–36.

18. James McNamara, "Social Work Designs a Humanistic Program to Enhance Patient Care," *Social Work in Health Care* 1, no. 2 (Winter 1975–1976):145–54.

19. Robert Morris and Elizabeth Harris, "Home Health Services in Massachusetts, 1971: Their Role in Care of the Long-Term Sick," *American Journal of Public Health* 62, no. 8 (August 1972):1088–93. See also Eleanor Clark, "Improving Post-Hospital Care for Chronically Ill Elderly Patients," *Social Work*, January 1969, pp. 60–66; Neil Bracht, "Health Maintenance Organizations: An Analysis," Continuing Education Series, National Association of Social Workers (Washington, D.C., November 1974), 31 pp.; Julian Hall et al., "Delivering Mental Health Services to the Urban Poor," *Social Work*, April 1970, pp. 35–46; Melvin Glasser, "Extension of Public Welfare Medical Care: Issues of Social Policy," *Social Work*, October 1965, pp. 3–9.

20. Debrah Merlin, "Home Care Project for Indigent Allows Dignified Care, Cuts Cost," *Hospitals*, Journal of the American Hospital Association, 49 (October 16, 1975). See also Morris and Harris, op. cit.

21. Elizabeth Watkins, "Low-Income Negro Mothers—Their Decision to Seek Prenatal Care," *American Journal of Public Health* 58, no. 4 (April 1968):655. See also Maurice Russell, "Social Work in a Black Community Hospital: Its Implications for the Profession," *American Journal of Public Health* 60, no. 4, (April 1970):704–12.

22. Harriet Bartlett, *Social Work Practice in the Health Field* (New York: NASW, 1961), p. 51

23. B. A. Moscato, "The Psychiatric Nurse as Outpatient Psychotherapist," *Journal of Psychiatric Nursing and Mental Health Services* 13, no. 5 (September-October 1975):28–36. See also Joan Mulaney et al., "Clinical Nurse Specialist and Social Worker—Clarifying the Roles," *Nursing Outlook* 22, no. 11 (November 1974):712–18.

24. Alexander Carr-Saunders, "Metropolitan Conditions and Traditional Professional Relationships," Robert M. Fisher, (Ed.) *Metropolis and Modern Life* (Garden City, N.Y.: Doubleday, 1955).

25. Shirley Wattenberg, Michael Orr, and Thomas O'Rourke, "Comparison of Opinions of Social Work Administrators and Hospital Administrators Toward Leadership Tasks," *Social Work in Health Care* 2, no. 3 (Spring 1977):285–94.

26. Jane Pfouts and Brandon McDaniel, "Medical Handmaidens or Professional Colleagues: A Survey of Social Work in the Pediatrics Departments of Twenty-Eight Teaching Hospitals," *Social Work in Health Care* 2, no. 3 (Spring 1977):275–84.

27. Doran Teague, "Social Service Enterprises: A New Health Care Model," *Social Work,* July 1971, pp. 66–77.

SUGGESTED ADDITIONAL READINGS

Baker, Frank, "From Community Mental Health to Human Service Ideology," *American Journal of Public Health* 64 no. 6 (June 1974):576–81.

Blum, Martin. *The Paradox of Helping.* New York: Wiley, 1975.

Brody, S. J., "Common Ground: Social Work and Health Care," *Health and Social Work* 1, no. 1 (February 1976):16–31.

Dana, Bess, "Health, Social Work and Social Justice: An Essay." Paper delivered to the Third Annual Symposium, NASW, New Orleans, 1972.

Gartner, Alan, "Four Professions: How Different, How Alike," *Social Work,* September 1975, pp. 353–58.

Gurman, Allen, "The Efficacy of Therapeutic Interventions in Social Work: A Critical Reevaluation," *Journal of Health and Social Behavior* 15, no. 2 (June 1974):136–41.

Rehr, Helen, ed. *Medicine and Social Work: An Exploration in Interprofessionalism,* published for the Doris Siegel Memorial Fund, Mt. Sinai Medical Center. New York: Prodist Publishing, 1974.

Stein, Herman, "Social Work's Developmental and Change Functions: Their Roots in Practice," *Social Service Review* 15, no. 1 (March 1976):1–10.

Wittman, Milton. "New Directions for Social Work Practice in Mental Health." In *Social Work Practice: Changing Patterns,* edited by Francine Sobey. New York: Columbia University Press (in press, 1976).

Part II

TRENDS IN HEALTH CARE DELIVERY

3/HEALTH CARE DELIVERY:

ISSUES AND TRENDS

NEIL F. BRACHT

Health services touch the lives of millions of Americans each day. The sheer size of the health industry is impressive. The total of examinations by physicians is now approaching 1 billion a year. The nation's 7,000 hospitals admit 33 million people each year. Visits to outpatient facilities total 181 million per year, and 2.7 million visits are made to mental health clinics.[1] Nearly one-tenth of the manpower in the health field is engaged in mental health services. By 1971, 609 community mental health centers were in operation in the United States. About 2,200 home health agencies participate in the Medicare program, and over 1 million people are treated in the country's 19,000 nursing homes. Health care is now the third-largest industry in terms of employment, containing over 5 percent of the labor force.

The spectrum of health care delivery services shown in Figure 3.1 indicates the different levels of care that are provided by the health care industry and clearly shows the relationship between social service delivery and health care delivery, particularly in restorative and continuing-care provider groups—for example, homes for unwed mothers, halfway houses for psychiatric patients, personal-care homes, and geriatric day care centers. As mentioned earlier, social workers are employed in nearly every facet or level of care. Knowledge of key issues and trends in health care can maximize social workers' professional contributions in health settings and provide an informed foundation for interprofessional collaboration in seeking health care delivery reforms.

Mechanic, who has studied health systems in several countries, comments:

The system of medical care in any country reflects the traditions of the past and the social priorities for the future. Health care is a vast industry and subsumes many groups with conflicting perspectives and interests. How these interests are weighed, negotiated, and resolved determines, in part, the organization of health services and the various priorities given to different aspects of health care.[2]

Because of these conflicting perceptions and multiple interests, the American health care system is full of paradoxes. For example, (1) "Medicine's high-powered technology and quick cure image differs considerably from the reality

37

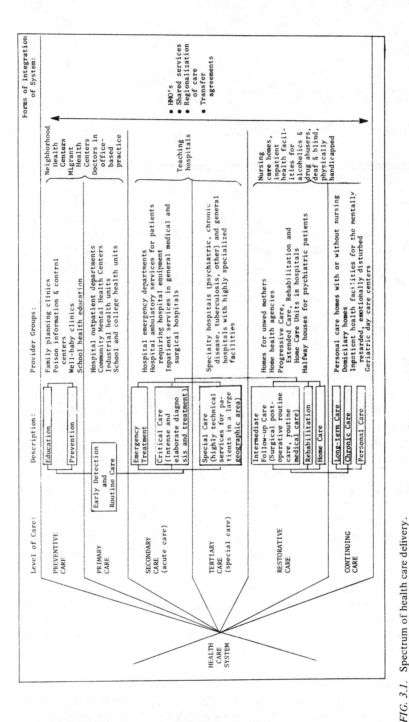

FIG. 3.1. Spectrum of health care delivery.

Source: U.S. Department of Health, Education and Welfare, *Trends Affecting U. S. Health Care System*, Publication no. 76–14503, (Washington, D.C., January 1976).

38

of what most needs to be done, that is, care of chronic illness, personal counseling services and social support networks."[3] Chronic illness and accompanying restoratory and rehabilitative care increase exponentially as new biomedical-engineering feats of medical science prolong life. (2) The entrepreneurial traditions of American medicine are reflected in an overemphasis on hospital reimbursement for acute-care problems and highly specialized surgical and medical techniques. Home care, self-care, and alternative health care services are not emphasized because "medicine as it is being practiced still focuses on repairs of the human machinery at a time when theoretical and empirical evidence indicates that health status is determined more by socio-environmental factors than by medical care services."[4] (3) Cost containment strategies for the health care field are uneven. Hospitals are asked to contain increases to 9 percent while no controls are suggested for the American drug industry, which enjoys one of the highest rates of profit among manufacturing corporations in the country. Adding to the overall costs of health care is the tendency of physicians to practice defensive medicine. In order to combat the potential of malpractice suits, they order more tests and seek more consultations than might normally be required. While the technical developments in American medicine have led to spectacular results and benefits, our society's ability to manage this technology in an organized and coordinated manner has not kept pace.

Health care for the poor continues to be a major problem in health services delivery. In Table 3.1 variations in the medical care received by different income groups are shown. While some improvement can be seen in access to hospital care for the poor, low-income children and the aged poor in 1973, as contrasted with earlier dates, were going to a doctor less often than those with high incomes. Only 65 percent of low-income children saw a doctor during 1973, and only 33 percent of those with low income had paid a visit to a dentist during the year. The comparable figure for people with high incomes was 59 percent. As Aday says,

the poor are still at a disadvantage, compared to the nonpoor. The poor with no private insurance coverage and no regular place to go for care, in fact, see a doctor the least often of any group, relative to their respective need for services.[5]

By the mid-1960s the problems in organizing and financing health services had become acute. The President's Commission on Health Manpower (1967) stated:

There is a crisis in health care, the indicators of such a crisis are evident to us as commission members and private citizens: long delays to see a physician for routine care; lengthy periods spent in the well-named "waiting room," and then hurried and sometimes impersonal attention in a limited appointment time; difficulty in obtaining care on nights and weekends, except through hospital emergency rooms; unavailability of beds in one

TABLE 3.1

Changing Differentials in Medical Care Received
by Different Income Groups: Selected Years 1957–1973

Age and Family Income[a]	Number of Physician Visits per Year per Person		% Seeing a Physician During a Year			Discharges from Short-Stay Hospitals per 100 Persons per Year		% Seeing a Dentist During a Year	
	July 1957–June 1959	1973	1963	1970	1973	July 1962–June 1963	1973	July 1957–June 1958	1973
All ages									
All family incomes	5.0	5.0	65%	68%	74.5%	12.4	13.9	40%	48.9%
Low income	{4.6					{12.5		{22	
	{4.6	5.7	56	65	73.8	{13.2	19.3	{31	32.8
Middle income	5.1	4.8	64	67	72.9	13.0	15.1	44	40.8
High income	5.7	5.0	71	71	76.4	11.5	11.7	58	59.0
Under 17 years[b]									
All family incomes	4.6	4.2	NA	NA	73.0%	6.5	7.0	NA	49.2%
Low income	{3.0					{4.8		{13%	
	{3.7	3.8	NA	51%	65.6	{6.9	9.5	{22	31.3
Middle income	5.0	3.8	NA	62	70.0	6.8	7.1	36	37.6
High income	5.7	4.5	NA	73	76.5	6.6	6.2	54	59.7
17–44 years[b]									
All family incomes	4.8	5.0	NA	NA	76.2%	15.5	15.6	NA	55.2%
Low income	{4.0					{16.2		{30%	
	{4.5	5.9	NA	NA	78.9	{17.5	19.8	{38	48.3%
Middle income	4.9	4.8	NA	NA	75.3	16.8	18.2	48	47.4
High income	5.5	5.1	NA	NA	76.9	13.0	13.6	59	61.1
44–64 years									
All family incomes	5.4	5.5	NA	NA	72.6%	13.9	16.6	NA	46.9%
Low income	{5.1					{12.5		{18%	
	{5.4	6.5	NA	NA	71.3	{13.3	22.5	{25	28.4
Middle income	5.4	5.6	NA	NA	70.5	15.6	17.9	33	38.1
High income	5.6	5.3	NA	NA	74.7	13.7	14.5	50	56.4
65+ years									
All family incomes	6.8	6.5	NA	NA	76.5%	17.0	23.8	NA	27.3%
Low income	{6.5					{15.2		{12%	
	{6.6	6.6	NA	73%	75.7	{16.5	25.0	{17	19.7
Middle income	6.9	6.5	NA	85	77.0	18.6	22.8	20	30.4
High income	8.7	7.1	NA	82	80.4	20.9	24.4	25	42.8

[a]Low income = Under $2,000 and $2,000–$3,999 in 1957–59, 1957–58, and 1962–63; under $5,000 in 1973; Middle income = $4,000–$6,999 in 1957–59, 1957–58, and 1962–63; $5,000–$9,999 in 1973; High income = $7,000+ in 1957–59, 1957–58, and 1962–63; $10,000+ in 1973; Income groups are not defined in 1963 and 1970.

[b]In 1957–59 and in 1962–63 two of the age groupings differed slightly from those given here; they were "under 15 years" (not "under 17 years") and "15–44 years" (not "17–44 years").

Note: NA =Not Available.

Sources: U.S. Congress, House of Representatives, Committee on Ways and Means, *National Health Insurance Resource Book* (Washington, D.C.: Government Printing Office, April 11, 1974), p. 263; U.S. Department of Health, Education and Welfare, Public Health Service, *Medical Care, Health Status and Family Income: United States*, Public Health Service Publication no. 1000–Series 10, no. 9 (Washington, D.C., May 1964); "Profile of American Health, 1973: Based on Data Collected in the Health Interview Survey," *Public Health Reports*, November-December 1974, pp. 504–24.

hospital while some beds are empty in another; reduction of hospital services because of a lack of nurses; needless duplication of certain sophisticated services in the same community; uneven distribution of care, as indicated by health statistics of the rural poor, urban ghetto dwellers, migrant workers, and other minority groups which occasionally resemble the health statistics of a developing country; obsolete hospitals in our major cities; costs rising sharply from levels that already prohibit care for some and create major financial burden for many more. Unless we improve the system *through which health care is provided, care will continue to become less satisfactory, even though there are massive increases in cost and in numbers of health personnel.*[6]

One year later the Blue Cross Association commissioned pollster Lou Harris to do an in-depth sampling of the American public to either validate or refute public criticism of the inadequacies of health insurance. Most of the respondents to the inquiry, whether poor or affluent, felt themselves isolated from good medical care. A majority reported that they would not know where to turn in the event of serious illness in the family. In his concluding statement about the survey findings, Harris said:

Now in the affluent '60s it can truthfully be said that over one-third of this nation feels ill cared for in its medical needs. Large segments of our population exhibit the deepest anxieties and frustrations when asked about the accessibility of good health care. Two-thirds of the general public feel that you can't get a doctor in an emergency. Forty percent of the general public and two-thirds of the poor worry that they will be unable to pay a doctor if they locate one and more than half of the general public and two-thirds of the poor told interviewers that they were terrified of serious illness which would disable the breadwinner and wipe out all family savings.[7]

Perhaps the most serious attack on our health care system is contained in a 1970 publication entitled "Our Ailing Medical System":

Our health care system stands on the brink of chaos. The time has come for radical change; the financial distortions, the inequalities and the managerial redundance in the system are of the kind that no competent executive can fail to see or would be willing to tolerate for long.[8]

Problems in health care delivery beset all countries regardless of level of organization and national financing mechanisms. Health planning, regionalization, and financing can improve access to and utilization of services. Social workers can participate in needed changes. A listing of key issues in health care delivery is provided here, followed by a detailed discussion of several of these issues, including possible solutions.

KEY ISSUES IN HEALTH CARE DELIVERY
• The rising demand for health care outstrips the ability of the medical care system to absorb this increase.

• Health care costs continue to rise dramatically, and incentives for cost containment are minimal.

• Inequality of access to health care still exists.

• Current patterns of health care delivery are not responsive to changing illness patterns. There is only a moderate focus on ambulatory, preventive, and home care services.

• Inefficiency in the management of health care programs remains a serious problem.

• Health services are not provided, for the most part, in a comprehensive and coordinated manner.

• There is a maldistribution of physicians and other health professionals, especially in rural and inner-city areas.

• Health planning processes have been deficient in activities to better coordinate *health* with *social* services at the community level.

• Strong consumer involvement in health care delivery and policy issues has not been broadly achieved.

THE ISSUE OF RISING DEMAND

A number of factors contribute to the increasing demand for medical care services. First, changes in the population and life expectancy have led to a significantly large aging population. In Table 3.2 projected changes in the population by age group show dramatic increases in the later age groups. The need, as well as the demand, for medical care increases among the elderly. The accumulated impact of chronic disease and rehabilitation efforts is staggering.

TABLE 3.2

Projected Changes in Population by Age Group (population in thousands)

	1974 Estimate	1985 Projection	2000 Projection	Percentage Change	
				1974–1985	1974–2000
All ages	211,090	234,067	262,494	+10.4	+23.9
0–4 years	16,304	19,785	18,364	+21.3	+12.6
5–17 years	50,960	44,768	52,714	−12.1	+3.4
18–44 years	79,501	99,012.	102,137	+24.5	+28.5
45–64 years	43,328	43,843	58,678	+1.2	+35.4
65–74 years	13,537	16,389	17,079	+21.1	+26.2
75 years & over	8,279	10,270	13,521	+24.0	+63.3

Source: Crane, Anabel Burgh "Prospects for the Future," in *Baselines For Setting Health Goals*, U.S. Department of Health, Education and Welfare Publication no. 76-640 (Washington, D.C., September 1976), p. 101.

The biomedical revolution has brought about technological advances that exert major influences on the health care system. The impact of such feats as control of genetic disorders, DNA discoveries, breakthroughs in reducing antigen rejection to allow for organ transplants, prevention of viral diseases and certain kinds of cancer, and the application of advances in space medicine to health maintenance (such as biofeedback machines and self-diagnosis consoles) all have major benefits for the American public. However, the most dramatic effect of these events is that they put further strains and stresses on an already fragmented system that is overloaded with technology directed toward acute-care conditions when chronic care and rehabilitation are overriding problems today.

Technology is both the handmaiden and the master of physicians. The increasing fear of malpractice claims causes many physicians to practice defensive medicine, thereby overutilizing costly diagnostic aids. Demand for access to new technological developments comes from both consumers and providers. Americans, placing a high value on health care, create pressure for access to new technology such as CAT (computerized axial tomography) scanners. Providers, on the other hand, wishing to enhance diagnostic and treatment interventions and at the same time improve their competitive status with other hospitals or health facilities, also seek the latest technology. While the new technology puts demand stresses on health care delivery, it is also a factor in spiraling health care costs, which will be discussed later.

Perhaps the most troubling problem in the demand for health services is the growing overdependence of the American public on medical care services. Several studies have corroborated the findings of Pratt and others that patients are poorly informed about the symptoms, etiology, and treatment of common diseases. On the other hand, it has been found that a majority of patients were given "isolated facts about their condition and few were given systematic explanation of either the etiology, prognosis, purpose of the test, test results, or treatment."[9] Providers and consumers of medical care services have overutilized drugs in the treatment of various illnesses, and too few people know how to make selective choices on when and when not to utilize medical care services.

POTENTIAL SOLUTIONS

Health care planners must increasingly take into consideration major population shifts and the increasing demand for restorative, rehabilitative, and continuing care of an increasingly elderly population. Alternative services for the elderly and those with chronic diseases must continue to be developed. Increasingly legislators, consumers, and providers must monitor technological developments in terms of their broad social effect and cost-benefit. Life-sustaining technology that may keep people alive unnecessarily must be tackled by federal, lay, and professional groups in order to arrive at acceptable community and ethical criteria for treating people with dignity in the terminal illness phase and giving individuals and families the right to die.

The single most important corrective action required to reduce excessive demand for health care is in the appropriate education of the American public regarding the use of medical treatment. Extensive efforts must be made to educate people regarding which symptoms need attention by physicians or nurse practitioners. Ways in which individuals can assume increasing responsibility for their own health maintenance must be accelerated. *Making Health Education Work,* the title of an important new book published by the American Public Health Association (1976), demonstrates how health education principles can be applied and provides suggestions for strengthening efforts where deficiencies must be overcome if health education is to realize its potential value. Social work's skills and experience in working with groups and communities can contribute to this most important area of health care.

HEALTH COSTS

The rapidly rising costs of health care are creating concern among consumers, providers, and government officials. During 1977, health care costs rose 16 percent. Looking at another fiscal indicator, the GNP, we find that in 1950, national health expenditures equaled 4.6 percent of the gross national product. By 1974, this figure had reached 7.7 percent. And by 1977, nearly 8½ percent of the gross national product was spent for health care. Federal passage of Medicare and Medicaid in the mid-1960s increased government expenditures to nearly 40 percent of the total of all health care funding.

The most dramatic increase in health care expenditures has been for hospital care. In 1950, this represented 30.7 percent of the total health care dollar as opposed to nearly 40 percent by 1974.

Drugs and sundries represent only about 10 percent of all health expenditures. However the continued use of trade brand names as opposed to generic prescription of drugs by physicians contributes to unnecessary costs for both consumer and government.

POSSIBLE SOLUTIONS

The dramatic rise in costs is related to numerous factors, including inflation, technology, increased consumer demand, ineffective management of hospital facilities, and patterns of insurance reimbursement (primarily acute conditions rather than the preventive and maintenance aspects of health care delivery). Regulatory commissions in the health care system are developing in an attempt to control utilization and monitor costs. Utilization review and PSRO requirements under Medicare are examples. Social workers participate in these efforts. At the state level, a number of hospital rate commissions are being established to review hospital budgets. Health Systems Planning Agencies now must issue certificates of need for facility construction or improvement. In a major experiment under way in the State of Washington in which prospective reimbursement is being used, hospitals have kept increases at a level below 10 percent. Current efforts to maintain hospital cost increases by the federal government seem realistic, but one must question whether maintaining ceilings in only one aspect of the health care industry is sufficient to reduce overall costs. Health professionals, including social workers, who want to make a more immediate impact on the direction of health care in the next decade will participate in the mushrooming regulatory apparatus of the health system. All professional groups need to set up peer review mechanisms to monitor the quality and appropriate utilization of services provided. Regulatory efforts must include a strong public-interest and consumer viewpoint but should not discourage innovation in health care delivery. A note of caution about regulatory commissions is in order:

It is not sufficient to assume because regulation sounds good on paper and seems to express high ideals, that it in fact operates in the public interest. . . . Historically, regulatory commissions have tended to behave as if they were under the influence of the regulated industry itself.[10]

OUTLOOK FOR NATIONAL HEALTH INSURANCE (NHI)

Economic controls will continue into the 1980s and have an impact on professionals and institutions alike. In all likelihood a national health insurance scheme, financed by both private and public funds, will emerge, but at first it may only insure against catastrophic and major illnesses. A national health insurance program based on current service delivery patterns and financing reimbursement would probably be "bankrupt" within a few years. An extended period of transition will be needed before comprehensive benefits under such a national health insurance program are achieved. National health insurance by itself is not a panacea for all of the financing and organizational problems in health care delivery. Careful analysis of the effects of NHI should be studied prior to its adoption.[11]

Two policy guidelines will be useful for social workers in deciding on which type of national health insurance proposal to support, if any. The policy statement on health care in the United States developed by the National Association of Social Workers (adopted by the 1971 Delegate Assembly) states the official viewpoint of the National Association. The *NASW News* has provided several analyses of national health insurance proposals, including summaries of testimony presented by NASW spokesmen at federal hearings (see especially November issue 1977). Anne Somers[12] has spelled out specific issues and questions that must be raised in respect to any national health insurance plan. For additional discussion of NHI see the Suggested Additional Readings at the end of this chapter.

ACCESS TO AND USE OF HEALTH SERVICES

Consumer access to medical services remains a serious problem. As noted by Aday (see above) and others, fifteen percent of the population in central cities and 12 percent of those living on farms have no regular source of medical care. Thirty-three percent of the population living in central cities must wait between 3 and 14 days for an appointment to see a doctor, and 14 percent must wait 15 days or more. Similarly high figures exist for those in rural areas.

POSSIBLE SOLUTIONS

Continued experimentation in service delivery patterns to the poor, the near poor, and rural residents should continue. The development of comprehensive neighborhood health centers during the 1960s was an effective approach in many ways to solving problems of access to and coordination of health care services. New professional worker groups developed in the last decade, such as family health workers, can continue to make a substantial contribution to health outreach programs.[13] National health insurance of and by itself cannot ensure access to health care. It can encourage structural changes in the system through incentive reimbursements. Financing has an important effect on the structure and style of health services delivery. For example, in 1972, 40 percent of all renal dialysis was carried out in the home. By 1975, less than 30 percent was performed in the home. This is partially related to increased incentives for inpatient dialysis units under the Medicare amendments of 1972.

ORGANIZATION OF SERVICES

The current organization of health services is not responsive to changing illness patterns. Only a moderate focus on ambulatory, preventive, and home care services can be observed in the health care industry. As Sylvia Clarke notes,

Progress in medical care is uneven. Scientific strides in the biological, physiological, chemical and pharmaceutical components in preventing and treating disease have not been matched with corresponding advances in psycho-social treatment and prevention of dysfunction. The ability to help with the psychological, sociological and physical consequences of illness has not kept pace with the technological ability to sustain and prolong life.[14]

Less than 1 percent of all Medicare funds is spent on home health care. Yet the need for such care continues to grow, and it is a preferred source of treatment for many. (See Frederick Seidl, Carol Austin, and Richard Green, "Is Home Health Care Less Expensive?" *Health and Social Work* 2, no. 2 (May 1977): 5–19.)

Health services are not delivered, for the most part, in a comprehensive and coordinated manner. The growth of specialization in medical practice as well as in other professions grows at the cost of increasing fragmentation and lack of coordination. While some models for coordinating health and social services are available, strong policy support backed up by legislative action is necessary. Mental health care is frequently uncoordinated with physical health care.

POSSIBLE SOLUTIONS

More emphasis on HMOs and the use of health teams, as well as continued experimentation with new delivery models that coordinate a complex range of health and social services, is required. Family medicine programs appear to be a step in the right direction. Social workers can increasingly take on roles as coordinators, managers, and planners of health care delivery systems. (See: *Family-centered Health Care—a Viable Reality?*)

OTHER ISSUES IN HEALTH CARE DELIVERY

Other issues include the following:

1. Inefficiency in the management of health care programs and new technology.

2. Maldistribution of physicians and other health professionals, especially in rural and central-city areas.

3. Inadequate health planning and coordination between health and social services.

4. Lack of strong consumer involvement in health care delivery and policy issues.

Efforts are under way to correct some of these longstanding problems as well. The development of the Health Systems Agencies with consumer and provider boards is clearly a step in the right direction. Maldistribution of physicians and other key health professionals will continue unless there is a national effort to provide incentives for physicians to locate in underserved medical areas. Tighter restrictions on some specialty residency programs is probably forthcoming.[15]

CONCLUSION

Major issues in health care delivery have been summarized and their implications discussed. Some possible solutions and trends have been highlighted. Social workers can play an important role in joining with others to plan for the best solutions to these perplexing problems. Health care delivery problems will not go away. Policy decisions affecting day-to-day social work practice in health settings must be influenced by a strong national social work voice. The National Association of Social Workers is one such voice, and increasingly its legislative activities, in coalition with other professional groups, are having an impact. Just as social workers must participate in needed reforms of the nation's social-welfare system, so also their contributions need to be felt in health care systems.

NOTES

1. *Building a National Health Care System* (New York: Committee for Economic Development, 1973), pp. 31–51.
2. David Mechanic, "Ideology, Medical Technology, and Health Care Organizations in Modern Nations," *American Journal of Public Health* 65, no. 3 (March 1975):242.
3. Thomas Arie, "Community Medicine," *New Society* 5 (June 1975).
4. Rick Carlson, "Health in America: What Are the Prospects?" *Center Magazine* 5 (November-December 1972):46.
5. LuAnne Aday, "The Impact of Health Policy on Access to Medical Care," *Health and Society*, Milbank Memorial Fund Quarterly, Spring 1976, pp. 215–32.
6. *Report of the President's Commission on Health Manpower* (Washington, D.C.: Department of Health, Education and Welfare, 1967).
7. *Sources*, A Blue Cross Report on the Health Problems of the Poor (Chicago, 1968), pp. 22–36.
8. *Fortune*, January 1970.
9. Lois Pratt et al., "Physician's Views on the Level of Medical Information Among Patients," *The American Journal of Public Health* 47 (October 1957):1277–83.
10. Clark Havighurst, "The Hazards of Regulation and Less Hazardous Alternatives," in National Health Council, *The Changing Role of Public and Private Sectors in Health Care in New York*, (1975), pp. 34–49. For a related but slightly different focus on regulations, see Norris E. Class, "The Regulatory Challenge to Social Work: An Historical Essay on Professional Policy Formulation," in *Continuing Education Series* (National Association of Social Workers, Washington, D.C.: 1974).
11. Robert Eilers, "National Health Insurance: What Kind and How Much," *New England Journal of Medicine* 284, no. 17 (April 29, 1971):881–984. See also Joseph Newhouse et al., "Policy Options and the Impact of National Health Insurance," *New England Journal of Medicine* 290, no. 24 (June 13, 1974):1345–59. See also Thompson R. Fulton, "Not Just 'Some Kind' of National Health Insurance," *Proceedings of the Social Welfare Forum*, 1976, National Conference on Social Welfare (New York: Columbia University Press, 1977), pp. 175–91.
12. Anne Somers, "Specific Issues for Investigation in Relation to Any Proposed National Health Insurance Program," in *Health Care in Transition: Directions for the Future* (Chicago: Hospital Research and Educational Trust, 1971), Appendix B.
13. Torrey Fuller et al., "The Family Health Worker Revisited, A Five Year Follow-up," *American Journal of Public Health* 63 (January 1973):71–78.
14. Sylvia Clarke, "The Humanization of Health Care: A Statement of Scope and Credo of Social Work in Health Care," *Social Work in Health Care* 1, no. 1 (Fall 1975).
15. See Robert Ebert, "The Medical School," *Scientific American* 229 (September 1973):148.

SUGGESTED ADDITIONAL READINGS

Bracht, Neil, "Health Care: The Largest Human Service System," *Social Work* 19, no. 5 (September 1974):532–42.
Bracht, Neil, "Testimony on National Health Insurance," presented on behalf of the National Association of Social Workers to H.E.W. Secretary Joseph Califano, Oct. 4, 1977. Copies available from NASW, Washington D.C.
Davis, Karen, *National Health Insurance, Benefits, Costs and Consequences*, Washington D.C., Brookings Institution, 1975.
Fulton, Tom, "National Health Insurance Success will be determined by Federal Role," Washington D.C., National Association of Social Workers *News*, Nov. 1977, p. 11.

Leopold, Edith, and Loren Schein, "Missing Links in the Human Services Non-System," *Medical Care* 13, no. 7, (July 1975):595–606.

Newman, Edward, and Harold Demone, "Policy Paper: A New Look at Public Planning for Human Services," *Journal of Health and Social Behavior* 10, no. 2 (June 1969):142–49.

Roemer, Milton. *Rural Health Care.* St. Louis: C. V. Mosby, 1976.

Sparer, Gerald, and Joyce Johnson, "Evaluation of OEO Neighborhood Health Centers," *American Journal of Public Health* 61, no. 5 (May 1971):931–42.

Weaver, Jerry L. *National Health Policy and the Underserved: Ethnic Minorities, Women and the Elderly.* St. Louis: C. V. Mosby, 1976.

Stewart, James, and Lottie Lee Crafton. *Delivery of Health Care Services to the Poor, Findings from a Review of the Current Periodical Literature with a Key to 47 Reports of Innovative Projects,* Human Services Monograph Series no. 1. Austin: University of Texas, 1975, 71 pp.

4/HEALTH MAINTENANCE ORGANIZATIONS: A MODEL FOR COMPREHENSIVE HEALTH AND MENTAL HEALTH CARE DELIVERY

NEIL F. BRACHT

A health maintenance organization (HMO) is an organization that operates or manages an organized health services delivery system on a prepaid basis for an enrolled population. It is designed to provide comprehensive health care economically and effectively. Coverage includes doctor visits, laboratory, and pharmacy costs as well as hospital services. Periodic health checkups, immunizations, health education, and other prevention services, including continuity of care, are emphasized. Expanded professional roles for social workers are developing in this area, especially following the 1973 HMO Act, which required medical social services as part of the comprehensive services offered to enrollees.

While the phrase "health maintenance organization" is relatively new, the concept is not. The first organized private medical group clinic in the United States (the Mayo Clinic) was established in 1914. In Canada, the Calgary Clinic was developed in 1919. The first successful *prepaid* group practice in the United States (Ross-Loos) was organized in 1929. At the national level, the Committee on the Costs of Medical Care presented, in 1935, favorable arguments for the organization of health services on a group prepaid basis. The Kaiser Permanente Foundation Plans, Group Health Cooperative of Puget Sound (Seattle), and Group Health Plan of Minnesota are examples of prototype HMOs. Restrictive state laws have until recently inhibited the growth of prepaid group plans. Early prepaid health plans employing doctors were viewed by some as "socialized medicine programs."

CURRENT DEVELOPMENTS

Currently it is estimated that over 7 million Americans receive their medical care through HMOs. There has been an increase in prepaid group practice plans (approximately 200 now operating) during the past 5 years (see Figures 4.1 and 4.2). Approximately 200 additional HMOs were in some stage of planning and development by 1975. Some priority is given to HMOs serving medically underserved areas. Essentially, four indexes are used to determine and specify a medically underserved area: (1) the ratio of primary-care physicians to population, (2) the infant mortality rate, (3) the percentage of the

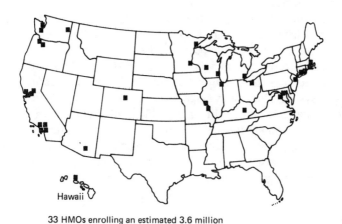

33 HMOs enrolling an estimated 3.6 million

FIG. 4.1. Sites of prototypes of health maintenance organizations before February 1971.
Source: *Public Health Reports* 90, no. 2 (March-April 1975): 101.

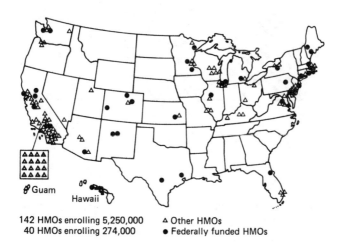

142 HMOs enrolling 5,250,000   △ Other HMOs
40 HMOs enrolling 274,000   ● Federally funded HMOs

FIG. 4.2. Sites of federally funded and other health maintenance organizations, October 1974.
Source: *Public Health Reports* 90, no. 2 (March-April 1975): 101.

population that is age 65 or over, and (4) the percentage of the population with family incomes below the poverty level.

Prepaid groups still represent a small percentage of the total of medical groups in the country. The advantages of delivering quality health services on an organized, prepaid group basis with a full range of medical and related services available to consumers have been discussed for many years.[1,2,3,4] In Figures 4.3 and 4.4 the HMO emphasis on preventive and ambulatory care is contrasted with traditional medical plans.

There are interesting similarities between the enthusiasm and growth of neighborhood health centers in the 1960s and the HMO developments of the 1970s. Both have articulate advocates and encourage consumer involvement. At least one-third of the policy board of an HMO must consist of enrollees. HMOs appear to tackle head on the deficiencies of the present fragmented health care system. But just as neighborhood health centers have not been the hoped-for panacea for the health care problems of low-income groups and the disadvantaged (owing to the inability to resolve basic structural and economic problems of the system), so some caution must accompany the development of HMOs for the general population in light of unresolved national health policy and financing issues.

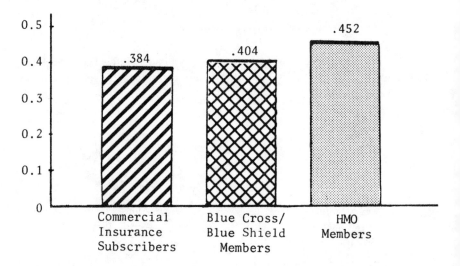

FIG. 4.3. Amount of preventive care received by subscribers to three types of health care plans.

Note: The University of California School of Public Health compiled a "preventive service index" accounting for such services as Pap smears, chest X-rays, blood tests, routine rectal examinations, and immunizations. The results were placed on a range of zero to one, and are illustrated above.

Source: U.S. Department of Health, Education and Welfare, *Trends Affecting U.S. Health Care System*, Health Resources Administration, Publication no. 76–14503 (Washington, D.C., 1976) p. 226.

Health Care Plan	Doctor Visits Per 1,000 Per Year (a)	Hospital Days Per 1,000 Per Year (b)	Ratio (a):(b)
Commercial Insurance	3,104	864	3.6
Blue Cross/Blue Shield	3,984	1,109	3.6
Prepaid Group Practice (HMO)	3,324	526	6.3

FIG. 4.4. Doctor visits versus hospital days with three types of health care plans.
Source: Milton Roemer and William Shonick, "HMO Performance: The Recent Evidence," *Health and Society* (Milbank Memorial Fund Quarterly), Summer 1973, p. 291. Reprinted with permission of the Milbank Memorial Fund.

HMOs by themselves cannot change the residual elements of resistance in an acute-care-oriented health care industry overnight. They cannot radically change health manpower distribution inequities. With all of the focus on and discussion of the potential of health maintenance, medicine has yet to demonstrate its ability to perform in this area. "Except for those doctors involved in the automated multiphasic screening program or other aspects of preventive medicine, the typical medical attitude toward disease prevention is one of skepticism, with the obvious exception of immunizations."[5] While preventive efforts are difficult to measure, Breslow believes that

professionals in health care are beginning to understand that it is now possible to maintain systematic surveillance over at least five parameters of health [immunological, anatomical, chemical, physiological, and behavioral] in which finding and remedying largely asymptomatic deviations can prevent much disability and premature death.[6]

HOW HEALTH MAINTENANCE ORGANIZATIONS WORK

What are the major features of an HMO? There are four basic principles involved in health maintenance organizations. An HMO is (1) a managing organization that assumes legal, fiscal, public, and professional accountability in order to (2) provide or arrange for a set of comprehensive health maintenance and treatment services, including primary care through rehabilitation; (3) enroll a defined population of individuals or groups who voluntarily join through a contract arrangement; and (4) prepay their medical care costs on a fixed periodic payment basis. In linking prepayment with the responsibility to organize and arrange for services, HMOs represent a definite and constructive departure from traditional approaches.

For the most part, health services are today

delivered by units that are both too small and too specialized. Frequently, only informal mechanisms exist for referring the patient from one specialist to another, for helping him get preventive care, for guiding his use of the clinic, or hospital, and for keeping his medical history. When there were fewer people and fewer services, the family doctor performed this function. Now it is necessary to find other methods to bring together all the services needed to keep a consumer healthy and to assure him that services will be available to him when needed. At present medical organizations that take responsibility for defined populations on an enrolled or geographic basis are rare. Payment of services is based upon the number of physician contacts and hospital days used. The consumer, unable to judge his own treatment needs, pays for whatever he is told he needs. Market mechanisms such as competition and informed consumer demand, which might provide a check on the provision of unnecessary services, inflation and inequitable distribution, do not exist in the health industry.[7]

While HMO sponsors have never claimed that these "new" organizations will solve all of the problems of health care delivery, HMOs do reverse some longstanding ills in the provision of services. HMOs are attractive to consumers. They provide "one-step" medical care for all kinds of conditions. Twenty-four-hour service for the entire family is readily available. Laboratory, X-ray, pharmacy, and specialty referral are usually housed in one major convenient location. Prepayment of medical costs eliminates financial worries and fosters early care. There is better continuity between inpatient and outpatient care. Families can usually choose one health professional as their primary-care coordinator-manager.

On the other hand, it is important to remember that traditional (entrepreneurial) medical practice retains a remarkably strong, respectful, and sympathetic popular constituency. A patient's "freedom" may be lessened when he/she joins a bureaucratic organization that seeks to maximize the efficient deployment of physician and other ancillary services.

Sponsorship of HMOs can include a wide variety of groups:

Type	*Example*
1. Profit-making corporations	California prepaid health plans (PHPs) serving "Medi-Cal" patients
2. Nonprofit corporations/foundations	Kaiser Permanente Foundation Plans
3. Associations and foundations	Physicians Association of Clackamas County (Oregon)
4. Consumer cooperatives	Group Health Cooperative of Puget Sound (Seattle)
5. Partnerships	Palo Alto Clinic (California)
6. Hospitals–medical schools	Columbia Medical Plan

While there are advantages to the heterogeneity of organizational approaches in the governing of HMOs, important policy questions must be raised about a large percentage of HMOs being run by profit-making corporations. California Medicaid recipients experienced considerable problems in obtaining care from new HMOs.[8] On the other hand, many established HMO plans serve Medicaid recipients very well and at less cost than standard medical fees.[9,10] In Table 4.1 the effect of HMO performance on health status is illustrated.

SOCIAL WORK IN HMOs

Medical social services are required under the 1973 HMO Act (PL-222) in Section 1301(C)(9) of the *basic* health services to be provided to enrollees. This section states that "each health maintenance organization shall provide for its members health education services, education in the appropriate use of health services and education in the contribution each member can make to the maintenance of his own health." Social work and related professions are vital to obtaining the HMO goals of health maintenance and promotion. Healthiness is difficult to achieve when there is a major disequilibrium between the

TABLE 4.1

Effect of HMO Performance on Health Status (prematurity and mortality)

Health Status Indicator	HMO	Traditional Mode	HMO as % of Traditional Mode
Premature Births Per 100 Live Births			
White	5.5	6.0	92%
Non-white	8.8	10.8	81
Infant Mortality Per 1,000 Births			
White	22.7	27.3	83
Non-white	33.7	43.8	77
Annual Mortality of Elderly Population (18 Months or More After Plan Membership)	7.8%	8.8%	89

Note: Data standardized for age, sex, income, residence, and where appropriate, age of mother.

Source: Sam Shapiro, Harold Jacobjiner, et al., "Further Observations on Prematurity and Prenatal Mortality in a General Population of a Prepaid Group Practice Medical Care Plan," *American Journal of Public Health*, September 1960, pp. 1304–17, and Sam Shapiro, Josephine Williams, et al., "Patterns of Medical Use by the Indigent Aged Under Two Systems of Medical Care," *American Journal of Public Health*, May 1967. Reprinted with permission of the American Public Health Association, Inc.

human organism's psychological, biological, and ecological components. The impact of perceived or actual illness is rarely confined within biological parameters. Social techniques may eliminate requests for unnecessary medical procedures or enhance compliance with medical regimens (see Chapter 19). Sociobehavioral changes such as attitudes, living arrangements, and satisfying work may not only be a more productive approach to health but may even modify illness perceptions and lead to positive preventive behaviors (e.g., change of dietary habits).

For social work practitioners the HMO framework can provide an attractive professional employment situation. The HMO as a central organization with defined responsibility for comprehensive services to a target population is generally supportive of social work-related health services. Follow-up services and monitoring can be more carefully controlled within a defined population. Issues of "ability to pay" and associated means tests are essentially removed for those covered by the HMO plan. Health maintenance and health education efforts require specific linkages with a wide range of community resources. Social work has demonstrated expertise in such a facilitating and coordinating role.[11]

A most interesting practice change foreseen in the HMO strategy is the significant reversal of institution-based practice to a more family-centered, outpatient, and preventive-service orientation.[12,13,14] New programs in consumer relations and health education could very well be directed by social workers. It is probable that additional management positions[15] as coordinators or directors of specialized programs in HMOs (such as Home Care, Community Relations, Mental Health Services, and Outreach Division) will be staffed by social workers. The development of HMOs requires specialized marketing skills, demographic analysis, and community organization and public-information efforts. While social work personnel do not customarily think of themselves as being in the "marketing" business, they may have to reorientate their thinking to play a different role in the community development aspects of HMOs.

The integration of preventive mental health services in HMOs offers new opportunities for social work personnel.[16,17] At the Santa Clara Medical Center in California (Kaiser-Permanente), mental health screening is being integrated with annual physical checkups. Under a 1974 grant from the National Institute of Mental Health (MH 24109), a project entitled "Systems Approach to Mental Health Care in an HMO Model" has been operationalized on a voluntary basis for enrollees. Essentially, the screening program identifies potential mental health problems through self-administered psychological questionnaires. Among the measurement scales employed are the Heimler Social Functioning Scale and the Holmes Life Change Scale. Some early data results are particularly interesting regarding the enrolled population that is frequently described as "worried-well" (at the Oakland Kaiser-Permanente this group accounts for some 20 percent of the 220,000 plan members).

The "worried-well" group frequently presents complaints not validated by laboratory tests and medical diagnostic procedures. At the Santa Clara Medical Center, for example, it was found that some 25 percent of the "worried-well" identified themselves as having sexual problems. It is interesting also to note that people who scored high on the Holmes Life Change Scale made more frequent visits to the health center compared with members of a control group. The reader may recall that the Holmes Scale identifies a series of life changes and suggests that there is a risk of acquiring some kind of physical illness once the total score reaches a certain level. At the Santa Clara Medical Center a series of educational courses in "more effective living" (e.g., sexual functioning) has been developed with a local community college, and enrolled members who have no medical symptoms yet seek help at the HMO are referred to these courses. A social worker is involved in the project.

While a few social workers have practiced in prepaid group health plans for several years,[18] their numbers are likely to increase. The following guidelines on social work functions in HMOs were recommended by the New York Ad Hoc NASW Committee in 1974:*

- Assistance in adjustment to illness.
- Assistance in understanding and following medical care recommendations.
- Assistance with personal and behavioral problems that adversely affect the health of the individual or family.
- Help in preserving family ties.
- Helping the individual and family utilize their strength and resources in maintaining health and overcoming illness.
- Evaluation of the effects of medical conditions and guidance in the use of community resources necessary to the individual and family in coping with the results of illness.
- Facilitating the referral of patients to appropriate resources.
- Assistance in establishing eligibility for other programs.
- Help in coordinating necessary rehabilitative services, including provision for obtaining appropriate appliances.
- Assistance in effecting appropriate connections with job and occupation resources in the community.
- Assistance in locating appropriate housing arrangements.
- Following up broken appointments when social and emotional factors are believed to be involved.
- Helping determine nonmedical needs of patients and families relating to the maintenance of their health.

---

*Committee chaired by Gerald Beallor, director of social services, Montifiore Hospital, New York City.

• Assisting the health care team in defining whether the presenting problem is medical, emotional, or social.

• Providing mental health services, including crisis intervention, brief treatment, and referral for longer-term psychiatric treatment.

• Providing in conjunction with health educators, family life education programs.

• Providing supplemental services.

• Developing and carrying out research related to the social and emotional aspects of health care.

• Participating in interdisciplinary activities related to planning as well as provision of health care.

• Providing training, recruitment, and organization of consumer participation.

• Assistance in setting up grievance machinery for consumers.

• Discharge planning services for hospitalized enrollees.

SOCIAL WORK PRACTICE IN HMOs—CASE ILLUSTRATIONS

In order to illustrate how social work staff are used differentially in HMOs, Bell and Gorman describe and assess social work roles in several different types of HMO plans. One plan is described as follows:[19]

This urban HMO serves a large blue-collar population of approximately 50,000 members. The health plan is based in an urban community hospital with three additional satellite ambulatory clinics in suburban areas.

EVOLUTION AND ORGANIZATION

In 1967 the health plan hired one social worker to deliver casework services to inpatients upon physician referral. Social services became a department in 1970, with the original social worker as department head and a staff of one. The social service staff submitted grant applications and was awarded state and foundation grants for alcoholism and drug abuse services. The department was expanded to five MSW's, three case aides, and two psychologists to provide services under the grant; a social worker retained direction of the department.

Social services is a separate department within the hospital having status on a par with other medical staff with the same authority as physicians. Social service aides assist the social workers by performing intake, transportation, and clerical duties. Interestingly, psychiatrists are in a separate department specializing in the treatment of acute psychiatric disturbances.

FUNCTION

The Social Service Department's major function is to direct and implement three special programs: alcoholism, drug abuse and home health. The social service staff develops treatment plans, coordinates all services to health plan members and their families in the alcoholism and drug addiction programs. Under the home health program, the department coordinates health care and community resources for homebound patients which include traditional casework services.

The Social Service Department also engages in traditional casework with inpatients and outpatients referred by health plan physicians. Services initiated in the hospital continue on an outpatient basis as needed.

In the emergency room social workers perform a triage function in concert with nursing personnel. (Triage is the timely assignment of unscheduled patients to the appropriate provider or providers of services.) There is social work coverage 24 hours a day to facilitate problem identification and appropriate referrals to the social services and mental health departments. Social workers also conduct aggressive case finding through union meetings, special mailings, and consumer education programs. Health plan members can request help directly from the Social Service Department on an outpatient basis.

EDUCATION AND TRAINING

The majority of social workers in this health plan were previously employed in a social service department of a community hospital.

The inservice training program for social workers . . . emphasizes HMO orientation and alcoholism and drug abuse treatment. The program includes lectures and on-the-job training.

ASSESSMENT

The Social Service Department legitimized its activities and expanded its staff by taking the initiative in submitting proposals to funding sources external to the parent organization. This illustrates the direct influence that social workers can have upon the development of services within their organization, even beyond the constraints of budget limitations and allocations. By generating funding for their own programs and by administering their own department, social workers were able to determine and define their own objectives consistent with social work principles, values, and abilities.

Social workers can take the responsibility to create services for which they perceive a need. In this instance, they identified persons who were not adequately served by the traditional health system and developed programs and an innovative strategy for identification and treatment that involved social work triage and outreach. The problems they addressed were uniquely suited to social workers in medical settings because they encompassed both social and medical aspects of health.

The social worker thus bridged the gap between social, psychological, and medical practice areas.

This case illustration shows that while significant opportunities exist for social workers in HMOs, the profession must not lose sight of the troubling policy questions involved in HMO developments and must continually try to bring about needed changes.[20,21] The question of whether the HMO strategy can be readily incorporated into rural areas remains a major issue.*

Many organizers of new HMOs state that offering comprehensive health services is too expensive. If this is true, then the "fault" remains the lack of an adequate national health insurance "floor" to support basic comprehensive *health* coverage in HMOs. Major gaps will still occur for HMO members on public assistance as their eligibility requirements change and they are left without adequate health protection. People who are not employed regularly will also fall through the "cracks."

Social workers need to be especially concerned about (1) ensuring strong consumer representation and grievance procedures in HMOs; (2) developing new models for the integration of HMOs with other community mental health and rehabilitation[22,23] resources; (3) designing ways in which new HMO population groups can be selected so as not to discriminate by income, race, or geography; and (4) outlining the special problems of HMO coverage for low-income individuals and those who are seasonally employed.

In conclusion, social work's current major locus of employment in acute-care facilities has lessened the profession's experience and research development with large ambulatory-care populations. Many social workers need to relearn the tools of early case finding and health promotion that have been applied effectively in past preventive and public health demonstration and research programs.[24,25,26] HMOs can help the profession regain much of its historical role in health promotion and preventive medicine.

NOTES

1. Avedis Donabedian, "An Evaluation of Prepaid Group Practice," *Inquiry* 6, no. 3 (September 1969).
2. P. L. Bashshur, C. A. Metzner, and A. Worden, "Consumer Satisfaction with Group Practice," *American Journal of Public Health* 57 (November 1967).
3. Elliot Freidson, "The Organization of Medical Practice and Patient Behavior," *American Journal of Public Health* 51 (January 1961).
4. U.S. Department of Health, Education and Welfare, Public Health Service, Division of Medical Care Administration, "Selected References on Group Practice" (Washington, D.C.: Government Printing Office, 1967).
5. Greer Williams, "Kaiser, What Is It, How Does It Work, and Why Does It Work?," reprinted from *Modern Hospital,* February 1971, p. 89.
6. Lester Breslow, "Consumer-Defined Goals for Health Care Systems in the 1980's," in Morris Collen, ed., *Technology and Health Care Systems,* U.S. Department of Health, Education and Welfare Publication no. 73–3016 (Washington, D.C., 1972), p. 121.
7. Doman Lum, "The Health Maintenance Organization," *Social Work* 18, no. 5 (September 1973):16–25.

*See for discussion "Why Some HMOs Develop Slowly," *Public Health Reports* 91, no. 6 (November-December 1976):497–503.

8. For discussion see Carol Deonofrio and Patricia Mullen, "Consumer Problems with Prepaid Health Plans in California," *Public Health Reports* 92, no. 2 (March-April 1977):121–34.

9. Merlyn Greenlick et al., "Comparing the Use of Medical Care Services by a Medically Indigent and a General Membership Population in a Comprehensive Prepaid Group Practice Program," *Medical Care* 10, no. 3 (May-June 1972):187.

10. U.S. Department of Health, Education and Welfare, Medical Services Administration, Social Rehabilitative Service, *Medicaid HMO-Type Contracts* (Washington, D.C., March 1972). See also John Kidneigh, *Health Care for the Poor: A Study of Patterns of Use and Cost Factors in Two Group Practice Prepayment Plans.* (Minneapolis, Minn.: Group Health Plan, January 1973).

11. Archie Golden et al., "Non-Physician Health Teams for Health Maintenance Organizations, *American Journal of Public Health* 63, no. 8 (August 1973):732–36.

12. David Cowen and John Sbarbaro, "Family Centered Health Care—A Viable Reality? The Denver Experience," *Medical Care* 10, no. 2 (March-April 1972).

13. E. J. Hobson and P. W. Grayburn, "Social Work in Group Medical Practice," *Group Practice* 18, no. 6 (1969).

14. Samuel Wolfe and Genevieve Teed, "A Study of the Work of the Medical Social Worker in a Group Medical Practice," *Canadian Medical Association Journal* 96, no. 11 (November 1967).

15. Harold L. Light and Howard J. Brown, "Social Worker as Lay Administrator of Medical Care Plan," *Social Casework,* April 1964.

16. I. Goldberg et al., "Effect of a Short-Term Outpatient Psychiatric Therapy Benefit on the Utilization of Medical Services in a Prepaid Group Medical Practice," *Medical Care* 8, no. 5 (September-October 1970).

17. W. Follette and Nicholas Cummings, "Psychiatric Services and Medical Utilization in a Prepaid Health Plan Setting," *Medical Care* 5, no. 1 (January-February 1967):25.

18. T. B. Litherland, "Social Services a Group Medical Practice Should Provide," *Group Practice,* 9 (June 1960):770–75. Also, E. Alt, "Social Work Consultation in a Prepayment Medical Care Plan," *American Journal of Public Welfare* 49 (March 1959):350.

19. Cynthia Bell and Laurel Gorman, "The HMO's: New Models for Practice," *Social Work in Health Care* 1, no. 3 (Spring 1976):325–36.

20. James Vohs, Richard Anderson, and Ruth Straus, "Critical Issues in HMO Strategy," *New England Journal of Medicine* 286, no. 20 (May 1972).

21. "Health Maintenance Organizations: A Policy Paper," American Public Health Association, *American Journal of Public Health* 61, no. 12 (September 1971):2528–36.

22. Richard Morrill, "A New Mental Health Services Model for the Comprehensive Neighborhood Health Center," *American Journal of Public Health* 62, no. 8 (August 1972):1178.

23. Roberta Gonzalez, John Thomas, James Alden, and Karl Herrenkohl, "Symbiosis in Planning and Operation of a Comprehensive Health Center and Community Mental Health Program in Philadelphia," *American Journal of Public Health* 62, no. 8 (August 1972):1175.

24. *Public Health Concepts in Social Work Education,* proceedings of seminar held at Princeton University, March 4–9, 1962 (New York: Council on Social Work Education, 1962), p. 227.

25. William Neser et al., "The Host-Agent Model in Social Work Research," *Social Work,* April 1968, pp. 96–100.

26. *The Family Health Maintenance Demonstrations: A Controlled Long Term Investigation of Family Health,* proceedings of 1953 Round Table (New York: Milbank Memorial Fund, 1954).

SUGGESTED ADDITIONAL READINGS

Bracht, Neil. *Health Maintenance Organizations: An Analysis,* NASW Continuing Education series. Washington, D.C., 1974.

————, "Medical Plans and Health Care: Consumer Participation in Policy Making, A Book Review," *Social Service Review,* March 1968.

Christian, Ethel, Ann Gullion, and Alice Varela. "Social Work Program in a Prepaid Group Practice Plan." Paper delivered at the Annual Meeting of American Public Health Association (Social Work Section) Chicago, November 1975. (Describes HIP Plan in New York.)

Freidson, Elliot. *Patients' Views of Medical Practice.* New York: Russell Sage Foundation, 1961, pp. 226–27.

Freidson, Elliot, and John H. Mann, "Organizational Dimensions of Large Scale Group Medical Practice," *American Journal of Public Health* 61, no. 4 (April 1971).

Garfield, Sidney, "The Delivery of Medical Care," *Scientific American* 222, no. 4 (April 1970).

"Health Maintenance Organizations, Emphasis on Preventive Medicine, Corporate Organization and Community Involvement," *Journal of the American Hospital Association* 35 (March 16, 1971).

"HMO's—A Special Section," *Public Health Reports* 90, no. 2 (March-April 1975):99–139.

Lorish, C. C., "Can HMOs Improve Health Care for the Poor?" *Health and Social Work* 1, no. 2 (May 1976):52–67.

Lum, D., "The Social Service Health Specialist in an HMO," *Health and Social Work* 1, no. 2 (May 1976):30–50.

McNamara, Mary, and Clifford Todd, "A Survey of Group Practice in the U.S.," *American Journal of Public Health* 60, no. 7 (July 1969):1303.

Part III

ENTERING HEALTH CARE SYSTEMS

5/ORIENTING SOCIAL WORKERS TO HEALTH CARE SETTINGS: A TRAINING MODEL

CINDY COOK WILLIAMS

REG ARTHUR WILLIAMS

NEIL F. BRACHT

Did you ever sit through an orientation program bored stiff? Or perhaps, as a new social work employee or student, been subjected to a barrage of agency policies that were ill-timed in their presentation and confusing to learn? Like many individuals, you may not have been oriented at all; instead, you were expected to provide professional services in a work setting that you knew little about and that knew little about you. These are typical experiences often encountered by new practitioners and students who enter health care settings.

This chapter is designed to assist social work trainers and educators in orienting new staff and students to health agencies. First, the importance of providing an effective orientation is discussed. Second, several principles of adult learning, such as assessing learning needs and establishing realistic goals, are defined with an emphasis on how to plan a training program. A teaching model for a hospital orientation will then be provided, including practical illustrations on how to familiarize people with this type of medical setting. The conclusion of the chapter discusses the organizational factors that are inherent in coordinating an orientation, as well as guidelines for conducting program evaluations and future inservice education endeavors.

THE IMPORTANCE OF ORIENTING NEW SOCIAL WORKERS AND STUDENTS

Social work's increasing involvement in health care is documented in Chapter 1. To meet the educational needs of new practitioners entering the field, schools of social work need to incorporate more health care content into their curriculum. Although academic preparation is improving (see Chapter 22), few students focus exclusively on a health care track or pursue all the educational resources available within and outside the schools for entry into the field. Too often new workers lack the basic knowledge essential to function as health

65

care practitioners. For example, the new social worker may have no awareness that the behavior of an uncontrolled diabetic can be inaccurately diagnosed as a functional psychosis. The staff of the health agency frequently must acquaint new workers and students to the special knowledge base, the unique attributes of the agency, and the general characteristics of the health care delivery system. Integrating the knowledge and skills required for practice is a sizable task. An effective orientation program can assist in this important process.

Due to the rapid changes in medical technology and the accelerated pace of medical care, new staff and students are expected to know more, to have advanced skills, and to understand the complex dynamics of an agency in a relatively short period. Unfortunately, the following norm is often established: "If you don't know what you are doing, pretend that you do." A trial-and-error approach to learning about the agency and one's professional responsibilities can seriously jeopardize patient care and is an unnecessary stress for the new worker. In addition, the lack of clarity about social work responsibilities and contributions perpetuates the confusion among other health care disciplines concerning the role of social workers in medical settings.[1]

APPLYING PRINCIPLES OF ADULT LEARNING TO ORIENTATION PROGRAMS

One frequent difficulty with orientation programs is the trainer's assumption that the learners know either too much or too little. As an example, the trainer might present a detailed outline of medical diseases or a treatise on laboratory tests for the hospitalized patient; both topics may have little current value for the new worker who is struggling to become acquainted with the work environment. On the other hand, the trainer must guard against treating the learners as if they have neither the life experience nor the intelligence for independent thinking. While information dissemination is important in the orientation process, the application of adult learning principles is equally critical.

Two different educational approaches, pedagogy and andragogy, have been employed in the instructional process. *Pedagogy* has come to mean the general art and science of teaching. The term is derived from the Greek root *ped*, meaning child, and *agogue*, meaning to lead. However, many of the traditional methods of teaching children are not appropriate in educating the adult learner. The term *andragogy* has recently been adopted to encompass adult education; the root *andra* means adult. Ingalls defined andragogy as a "process for problem finding and problem solving in the present; it is an orientation to the discovery of an improvable situation, a desired goal, a corrective experience, or a developmental possibility in relation to the reality of the present situation."[2] In other words, andragogy is a problem-centered approach rather than a subject-centered approach.

Knowles proposed four basic assumptions of adult learning. They include (1) self-identity, (2) life experiences, (3) learning readiness, and (4) mental set.[3] Bryant added a fifth dimension, the physiological conditions involved in adult learning.[4] How can these assumptions be applied to an orientation program? A brief description of each category and their application follows.

SELF-IDENTITY

Most adults perceive themselves as mature, self-directed people, and they desire a learning experience that is congruent with this self-concept.[5] They wish to be actively involved in the learning process rather than "talked down to" or "lectured to." Many adults, however, have experienced primarily pedagogical learning, in which the participant is the passive receptor of the instructor's wise words. Consequently the trainer must be prepared for a degree of resistance and skepticism when asking adults to assume the initiative and responsibility for much of their own learning.[6] Bryant suggested that in training programs the classroom atmosphere should be eliminated as much as possible and "a physical environment provided in which the adult feels at ease and free to express opinions without fear of ridicule or judgement."[4] In addition, capitalizing on the learner's problem-solving abilities can enhance his self-image.

LIFE EXPERIENCES

The life experiences of adults directly contribute to their problem solving in new situations. These experiences are valuable and can be brought out through microlabs and various group techniques. The participatory experiential teaching techniques "shifts the emphasis from mere transmittal methods to ways which allow new or creative solutions to appear."[4] The effective trainer recognizes the importance of life experiences and uses them in fulfilling the educational objectives of the orientation program.

LEARNING READINESS AND MENTAL SET

The information dicussed in an orientation program may fall on deaf ears if it is not targeted to the immediate learning needs of the new worker or student. Programs should avoid abstract, philosophical content and focus on the practical concerns of the group, such as role expectations and work space. As an example, a presentation by the hospital director might be delayed until the learners have actually experienced the effect of hospital policies and have specific concerns. Knowing that the hospital is a regional center for burn patients may not be as important initially as knowing the location of the dictating equipment.

PHYSIOLOGICAL CONDITIONS

In an orientation program there is a need for varied stimulation in the learning activities. A presentation conducted by one speaker in a monotone without audio-visual aids can inhibit the sensory stimulation that is essential to effective adult learning. Group discussions, films, and well-timed coffee breaks are helpful in maintaining participant interest. The normal ritual of a grand hospital tour for all new employees might be replaced by a series of short tours closely associated with specific educational objectives, such as visiting the emergency room following a discussion of the use of crisis intervention techniques in health settings.

Awareness of these five underlying assumptions of adult learning is essential for good educational programming. Additional readings on this topic are suggested at the end of the chapter.

ASSESSMENT OF LEARNING NEEDS

One of the first steps in planning a successful adult orientation experience is assessing the learning needs of the participants. In Figure 5.1 a model assessment form used in hospitals is illustrated. The questionnaire, with modifications based on the particular agency, should be sent to the participants at least six weeks in advance of the training program. This period allows sufficient time for return of the questionnaires, as well as compiling data, contacting resource people, and designing the orientation schedule.

If a preassessment survey is not possible, the trainer may wish to employ the Delbecq method of group needs assessment.[7] This technique can be employed on the first day of the orientation to determine individual and group learning needs. In brief, all the participants' learning needs are listed on a blackboard or newsprint tablet and then categorized. As an example, 20 ideas might fit into 5 or 6 major topics. Even if the preassessment questionnaire has been utilized, the Delbecq method can be useful in helping the learners determine their combined learning needs as a group.

In a complex health setting such as a hospital, the number of things a new worker or student needs to know can be staggering. Some topics that the authors consider important in a hospital orientation are listed in Table 5.1. Corresponding pages and chapters in this book that address these topics or provide resources in the literature are included next to each category. Trainers can also use this list as part of the learning needs assessment questionnaire described previously.

DEVELOPING LEARNING GOALS AND MEASURABLE OBJECTIVES FOR AN ORIENTATION PROGRAM

Assessing the learner's current level of knowledge indicates "what is," whereas the goals of an orientation program delineate "what should be." The goal statements offer a general idea of what needs to be accomplished; they define the general purpose of the teaching endeavor. As an example, the trainer might receive the completed learning assessment questionnaires with the following topics given highest priority as learning needs: (1) knowledge of medical terms and abbreviations, (2) reading a medical chart, (3) common disease states and their social implications, and (4) use of crisis intervention techniques with hospitalized patients. The new employees and students may also have com-

LEARNING NEEDS ASSESSMENT FORM

Welcome to our hospital. We are developing an orientation that will assist you in becoming familiar with our health care setting. Through the following questionnaire, your response will be combined with those of other new social work employees and students to formulate an individualized introduction to our facility.

The first section of the questionnaire asks for basic demographic information, while the second part requests that you indicate those topics which would be most helpful in acquainting you with the social work role in a hospital system.

An immediate response to this inquiry would be appreciated. Enclosed is a stamped self-addressed envelope for its return. Your response to the questionnaire is important for your orientation to our agency. Thank you.

Name _____

Section I

1. Please mark the highest degree you have acquired.
   _____ Associate degree
   _____ Baccalaureate degree
   _____ Master's degree
   _____ Other, please describe _____
   _____

2. Was any of your educational training in a health concentration or setting?
   _____ No
   _____ Yes, please describe _____
   _____

3. What is your age?
   _____ years

4. How many years have you been employed as a social worker? (If you have *not* been employed as a social worker, please skip question 5.)
   _____ years

5. In what type of agency/agencies were you employed as a social worker?
   _____
   _____
   _____

6. What type of volunteer work have you done?
   _____
   _____

7. What professional and/or personal experience have you had with hospitals or other types of health care facilities?
   _____
   _____
   _____
   _____

(Continued)

69

Section II

Section II includes a list of topics that other social workers have found helpful in their clinical practice at our hospital. Some topics may also be useful for you as a new employee or student; others will not.

Please indicate your need to acquire more knowledge about the various topics as follows:
    1 = that topic which you have the *greatest* need to learn about
    2 = your second-greatest learning need, down to
    13 = the least helpful topic to learn about
Be sure to place a separate number by each topic listed. Do not assign the same number to more than one category.

Blank spaces have been included on the list for any topics you might want to add. Please indicate the order of importance of these categories along with those suggested by our staff.

_____ A. Common medical terminology used in health settings
_____ B. Interdisciplinary health care teams
_____ C. Organization of hospital and patient rights
_____ D. Common medical abbreviations
_____ E. How to read and interpret a patient's hospital record
_____ F. Common disease states and social implications
_____ G. Problem-oriented medical recording (POMR)
_____ H. Ethnic and cultural differences in illness perception
_____ I. _____
_____ J. _____
_____ K. _____
_____ L. _____
_____ M. _____

(Other topics can be added or substituted based on the unique attributes of the health care agency.)

Thank you for completing this questionnaire. The first day of the orientation program will be _____. We will meet in Room _____ at _____ .

A map is enclosed showing the location of parking space, the building, and the room. Information on public transportation is also included.

FIG. 5.1. Hospital orientation: assessment of learning needs.

mented on how much they look forward to their experiences in the hospital but mentioned that they feel apprehensive about their new role responsibilities. Based on these hypothetical responses, the following general goals might be formulated for the orientation:

1. Acquiring additional knowledge and skills necessary to function as a social worker in a hospital.

2. Reducing apprehension concerning new role as hospital social worker.

After the statement of goals, the specific training objectives can be designed. An educational objective, as defined by Mager, is "an *intent* communicated by a statement describing a proposed change in a learner—a statement of what the learner is to be like when he has successfully completed a learning experi-

TABLE 5.1

Hospital Orientation Topics

Topic	Relevant Section of Book
1. Common medical terminology used in health settings	p. 73–8 and Appendix A
2. Interdisciplinary health care teams	Chapter 6 in entire
3. Organization of hospitals	p. 166–70 and 297–9
4. Common medical abbreviations and symbols	Appendix A
5. Social Work Research contributions in health settings	Chapters 18–19 in entire and chart 2.1
6. Common disease states and social implications	Chapters 8 and 9 in entire and p. 73–8
7. Problem oriented medical recording (POMR)	p. 121–3 and p. 310
8. Ethnic and cultural differences in illness	p. 103–6, p. 112–4, and p. 262–4
9. Social Work Roles in hospitals	Chapter 11 in entire and p. 23–30
10. Models of social-medical diagnosis	Chapter 8 in entire
11. Social treatment of selected diseases and their family impact	Chapters 9 and 10 in entire
12. Use of crisis/emergency care techniques with hospitalized patients	pp. 145, 148, and 151
13. Health maintenance and illness prevention	Chapters 4 and 13 in entire, p. 9–10, p. 101–8, and p. 249–52
14. Ethical implications of social work practice in hospitals	p. 145
15. Community consultation and planning activities	p. 233–7 and p. 253–60
16. Accountability system for social work department	Chapter 21 in entire, and p. 175–9
17. Delivery and financing of health care programs	Chapter 3 in entire
8. Poverty and illness	p. 9–12 and p. 103–6
19. Discharge planning	p. 174–5 and p. 308
20. Women's health care	Chapter 17 in entire

ence."[9] If the change cannot be observed or measured, it would be difficult to evaluate how effective the training program was in its attempt to meet the objectives. A written objective, then, must describe what the learner will be doing to achieve the proposed change outlined in the objective. Using the hypothetical results of the learning assessment questionaire described earlier, the measurable objectives might include the following:

1. Be able to identify at least two sources of apprehension and anxiety concerning new role as hospital social worker.

2. Be able to use medical dictionaries and the prefix-suffix model to interpret medical terms found in a simulated patient record.

3. Be able to list four principles of crisis intervention in a patient record that is role played by two learners.

4. Be able to identify and use available resources to identify social implications of a given disease state.

With clearly defined objectives, a sound basis is provided for implementing the training design and evaluating its success. The importance of defining clear objectives cannot be overemphasized.

DESIGNING A HOSPITAL ORIENTATION PROGRAM

This section discusses several preliminary considerations helpful to the trainer in designing and coordinating an orientation program. An example of a teaching model for a hospital orientation is provided, including an illustration of how two topics might be presented on the first day of the program.

PRELIMINARY CONSIDERATIONS

While the learning needs of new employees and students should be an integral part of the orientation, the needs of the institution must also be considered. As an example, more interest may be expressed in learning about crisis theory than in acquiring an understanding of how to complete a statistical caseload count for accountability purposes. Yet, as discussed in Chapters 18 and 21, a department's statistical records are a valuable source of information for justifying the need for new staff positions or obtaining the funds to keep present positions. An accurate statistical system requires the cooperation and understanding of each member of a social service department; consequently this topic needs to be discussed at some point in the orientation program. It may not fit the learner's concept of what he needs or wants to learn, but it is a vital accountability measure for the department and the institution. How this content could be incorporated into the program might be discussed with the participants themselves. Their ideas and doubts might then be elicited and discussed as a group endeavor.

The degree of clinical experience among the learners may vary greatly in an orientation program. The resources of the more experienced learners could actively be used to facilitate the learning process of the other participants. Although circumstances may dictate special orientations for students and advanced practitioners, there are no inherent problems in mixing the two groups. In fact, as previously discussed, distinct advantages exist if the trainer applies the principles of andragogy in the program.

Another recommendation in designing the program is using the resources of other social work staff. Too often trainers fail to capitalize on the teaching skills of colleagues within their own profession. It seems pointless to have another discipline conduct a seminar when a departmental colleague has the same or perhaps a better level of knowledge. As an example, discussion of the emotional reactions of patients who are placed in nursing homes might be less informative when conducted by a physician as compared to an experienced hospital social worker. Some topics, on the other hand, might be more appropriately taught by members of other professions. Consideration might also be given to using community resource people (consumers and providers) whose view of the hospital and its services may be especially enlightening.

A questionnaire designed to assess the areas of teaching expertise among social workers and other disciplines is given in Figure 5.2. Not only can participation be a valuable teaching experience for staff; it also provides varied stimulation for the learners and visibility for the department among other professions.

DESIGN OF HOSPITAL ORIENTATION

This section provides an example of a hospital orientation program for new social work staff and students. Although the format is one of many models, it has the potential to be modified according to the unique attributes of one's agency. Table 5.2 illustrates a proposed schedule for the first two days of the program. The design of two seminars conducted on the first day is discussed in depth; other topics, previously mentioned, that could be included in the program are listed in Table 5.1.

TEACHING DESIGN: SEMINAR ON MEDICAL TERMINOLOGY

Assuming that understanding medical terminology is a high-priority learning need for new social workers, the objectives and teaching design must be determined. It is evident that *all* medical terminology cannot be dealt with in the limited time frame of an orientation program. However, it is realistic to acquaint the learners with the most common terms and offer them an instructional technique for interpreting medical terms in the future. The following objective for the seminar could be, "Be able to use medical dictionaries and the prefix-suffix model to interpret medical terms found in a simulated patient record."

After some group discussion of common problems encountered in deciphering medical terms, the learners would be acquainted with the medical dictionaries, such as *Taber's Cyclopedic Dictionary*[10] or *Dorland's Illustrated Medical Dictionary*.[11] These references provide definitions as well as lists of the basic prefixes and suffixes of terms. Having copies of these books available as teaching aids, plus a handout of common prefixes and suffixes (Table 5.3), would facilitate the teaching design.

Using the model shown in Figure 5.3, the learners would be acquainted with how to break down specific medical terms into their prefix-suffix components and then combine them to formulate a meaning. Small-group practice sessions can be used in applying the model using a simulated patient record. Prior to the orientation the trainer could construct the medical record to include the

Our department will be orienting new social work staff and students to the hospital beginning on _____ . Any assistance you can provide in the planning and/or teaching of topics for the orientation program would be helpful.

Please complete the following questionnaire and return it to _____ in Room _____ as soon as possible. If you have any questions, please contact _____ . Thank you.

Name: _____

Profession: _____

Clinical Assignment: _____

Telephone Extension: _____

1. Are you interested in assisting with the orientation program for new social work staff and students?

    _____ Yes (If yes, please answer the remaining questions.)

    _____ No

2. In which of the following areas would you like to provide your assistance? (Mark as many as apply.)

    _____ Presenting one or more lectures, discussions, or seminars

    _____ Conducting a tour of your own clinical area

    _____ Assisting with the overall planning of the teaching design

    _____ Other, please describe _____

    _____

3. Mark the topic(s) you have interest and/or expertise in presenting during the orientation?

    _____ A. Common medical terminology used in health settings

    _____ B. Interdisciplinary health care teams

    _____ C. Organization of hospital and patient rights

    _____ D. Common medical abbreviations

    _____ E. How to read and interpret a patient's hospital record

    _____ F. Accountability system for social work department

    _____ G. Problem-oriented medical recording (POMR)

    _____ H. Common disease states and social implications

    _____ I. Ethnic and cultural differences in illness perception

4. Please list topics, *other than the above*, that you have the interest and/or expertise in teaching.

    A. _____

    B. _____

    C. _____

    D. _____

5. Please list topics that you think would be important in orienting new social work staff and students.

    A. _____

    B. _____

    C. _____

    D. _____

Thank you. I will be in contact with you personally if you have expressed an interest in assisting with our orientation program.

FIG. 5.2. Assessment of staff teaching interests and resources.

TABLE 5.2

Two-Day Schedule of Hospital Orientation

First Day:	
9:00 A.M.	Introduction of staff and new employees/students; coffee
9:30 A.M.	Housekeeping items, i.e., hours, office space, parking, cafeteria facilities, questions
10:15 A.M.	Discussion of learning needs based on results of learning assessment questionnaire; modifications in schedule
11:00 A.M.	Coffee break
11:15 A.M.	"Understanding Medical Terminology: It Isn't All That Tough!"
12:30 P.M.	Lunch
1:30 P.M.	Small-group exercise: how to read and interpret medical terminology used in simulated patient chart
2:45 P.M.	Coffee break
3:00 P.M.	"Common Disease States and Social Implications"
4:30 P.M.	General discussion; plans for next day
Second Day:	
9:00 A.M.	Tour of hospital library; introductions to resource people and references available to investigate disease states and their social implications
10:15 A.M.	Coffee break
10:30 A.M.	"Problem Oriented Medical Recording"
11:30 A.M.	"Accountability System for Social Work Department"
Noon	Lunch
1:00 P.M.	"Social Work's Role in Hospitals"
2:00 P.M.	Free time to use available resources to investigate one disease state and its social implications
3:15 P.M.	Coffee break
3:30 P.M.	Small-group discussion of chosen disease state and related social factors
4:45 P.M.	Plans for next day

diagnoses and treatment of common disease states. Examples might include cardiovascular and respiratory difficulties. The record can also be used as a teaching aid for learning abbreviations, treatment modalities, and medications. Reading the simulated chart brings the learners closer to what they will actually be doing in clinical practice while simultaneously providing an opportunity to measure what they have learned. This might also be an appropriate time to discuss issues of patient confidentiality and access to medical records, including the appropriate procedures for making social work notations on the chart.

TEACHING DESIGN: SEMINAR ON DISEASE STATES AND SOCIAL IMPLICATIONS

Again, it is not possible to list all common diseases and accompanying social implications in an orientation program. A realistic objective would include

TABLE 5.3

Example of Handout: Common Prefixes and Suffixes*

Meaning of Prefix		Meaning of Suffix	
a-	negative	*-aemia*	blood
ab-	away from	*-aethesia*	sensation
acou-	hear	*-agra*	catching; seizure
ad-	toward	*-ase*	enzyme
aden-	gland	*-cele*	tumor; cyst; hernia
adip-	fat	*-cide*	causing death
aer-	air	*-cyst*	bladder; bag
alg-	pain	*-cyte*	cell
alve-	channel; cavity	*-dynia*	pain
amb-	both, on both sides	*-ectomy*	a cutting out
an-	negative; up; positive	*-emesis*	vomiting
angio-	related to blood or lymph vessels	*-emia*	blood
ante-	before	*-esthesia*	sensation
anti-	against; counter	*-ferent*	bear; carry
arter-	artery	*-form*	form
arthr-	joint	*-fuge*	drive away
articul-	joint	*-gram*	write; record
aur-	ear	*-graphy*	a writing; a record
bil-	bile	*-iasis*	condition; pathological state
blephar-	eyelid	*-ism*	condition; theory
brachi-	arm	*-itis*	inflammation
brachy-	short	*-ize*	to treat by special method
bronch-	windpipe	*-kinesis*	motion
bucc-	cheek	*-lite*	stone; calculus
calc-	stone; heel	*-lith*	stone; calculus
carcin-	cancer	*-logy*	science of; study of
cata-	down	*-lysis*	setting free; disintegration
cath-	down	*-megaly*	large; great; extreme
caud-	tail		
cephal-	head		
cer-	wax		
cervic-	neck		

*This list represents the format that could be used. Additional prefixes and suffixes need to be included to complete the handout.

having the learners use available hospital and staff resources to identify the social implications of any given disease process, such as hypertension, myocardial infarctions, or cancer. The teaching design would include familiarizing the new social workers and students with selected references in the literature on the social aspects of illness.[12] Chapter 9 (social treatment of selected illnesses), as well as Chapters 7 and 8 (social and behavioral components of health and illness), will be helpful to the trainer in delineating the social dimensions of illness, disability, and recovery.

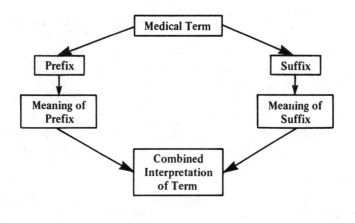

Example #1

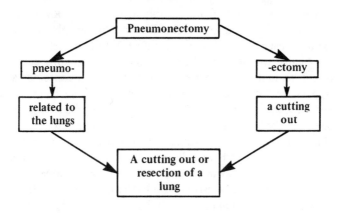

Example #2

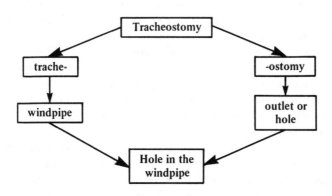

FIG. 5.3 Interpreting the meaning of medical terms from their prefixes and suffixes.

77

One method developed by the authors in teaching the social aspects of illness involves an extension of the prefix-suffix model discussed previously. As illustrated in Figure 5.4, the learners can be helped to ascertain what part of the body's normal functioning has changed as a result of the disease process. The subsequent changes in social functioning can then be determined. Application of the model using the example of a colostomy is also shown in Figure 5.4. Using another example, cancer of the larynx, the group could begin discussing the social implications based on the following guidelines: Patients with cancer of the larynx often undergo a laryngectomy, which includes removal of the voice box and the structuring of a permanent tracheostomy. The learners would be questioned about the psychosocial difficulties inherent in the inability of a person to communicate verbally with others. In the realm of employment, an individual whose occupation includes frequent interactions with people may be forced to make major adjustments. The social worker's role might include assisting the patient in negotiating with his employer or possibly initiating a referral for vocational rehabilitation or job placement if these negotiations are unsuccessful. Financial difficulties often are a result of employment problems, and of course these can have a devastating effect on both the patient and his family. The patient may also feel self-conscious about the cosmetic appearance of a tracheostomy. Ways of making one's appearance more acceptable can be recommended, such as using scarves or high-collar shirts. In the realm of sexual interactions, the male laryngectomy patient may have difficulties in adjustment to sexual functioning. The social worker can conduct sexual counseling. Changes in recreation may be another concern. If a patient has always enjoyed swimming, he will no longer be able to participate in this sport since water can be aspirated into the lungs through the tracheostomy. Social work intervention might include problem solving with the patient in an attempt to identify other enjoyable sources of recreation. Community resources should be recommended to enhance involvement in these alternate activities.

Using this example, each learner can choose a disease state that is common in his new work area. Two additional sources of information on disease processes and their social implications need to be mentioned. These resources include nurses and staff physicians, who are usually willing to teach social workers about illness patterns, as well as the patients themselves, who can provide a wealth of information on the personal implications of their own diseases. With an introduction to the resources available, the learners can then gather data on their chosen disease and present their findings to the group later in the orientation.

This section concludes the discussion of the two seminars presented on the first day of the orientation program. The final part of the chapter describes the organizational and evaluative activities necessary in training programs, as well as the relationship of an orientation to inservice education programing.

ORGANIZATIONAL AND EVALUATIVE ACTIVITIES IN AN ORIENTATION PROGRAM

The organizational aspects of planning an orientation have been discussed briefly throughout the chapter. Key elements in organizing the program include the following:
1. Mutual planning with learners prior to orientation.
2. Assessing staff members' teaching expertise and availability.
3. Developing realistic goals, objectives, and teaching designs.
4. Printing a schedule and securing room space.
5. Developing a learning climate based on the principles of adult learning.
6. Securing audio-visual resources and handout materials.

Trainers often find the use of a checklist helpful in coordinating the many details of the program.[13] Securing adequate space in a hospital setting may require advance planning. Conference rooms are frequently overbooked and must be scheduled early. Small rooms with inadequate ventilation and lighting can be disruptive to the learning climate. If space outside the agency is required, the budget for the orientation program will have to cover this expense. The financing of the program is another organizational consideration. An orientation is not a cost-free endeavor and must be planned as a legitimate item in the department's annual budget request.

One final note regarding the training program is the need to maintain organizational flexibility in both the teaching design and the content of the program. Training models can be developed for an intensive one to five days; on the other hand, training can be interspersed throughout the initial months of the new worker or student's assignment. One model is not always best for all situations. The trainer must consider the model that best meets the needs of the learners and the agency.

Evaluation is also an inherent part of the entire learning process. Assessing the effectiveness of the program is difficult without clearly stated objectives defining what new knowledge or skills the learners were expected to attain. An evaluation form (Figure 5.5) illustrates one method of measuring the overall reaction to the program and the degree to which the objectives were achieved. In addition, it can elicit information on new learning needs that can be addressed in the future. Other modes of evaluation that can be used are described in Ingalls' *A Trainers Guide to Andragogy*.[2] While evaluation following the program is important, the trainer must also be receptive to verbal and nonverbal feedback from the participants throughout the orientation.

THE RELATIONSHIP OF ORIENTATION TO INSERVICE EDUCATION PROGRAMMING

Inservice training for departmental staff is closely related to the activities of the orientation program. All the topics identified by new workers as learning interests cannot possibly be incorporated into a time-limited orientation pro-

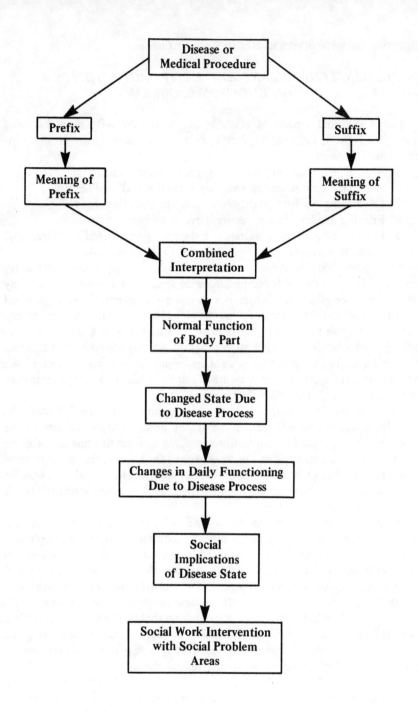

FIG. 5.4 Model for determining social implications of disease states.

Example: Colostomy

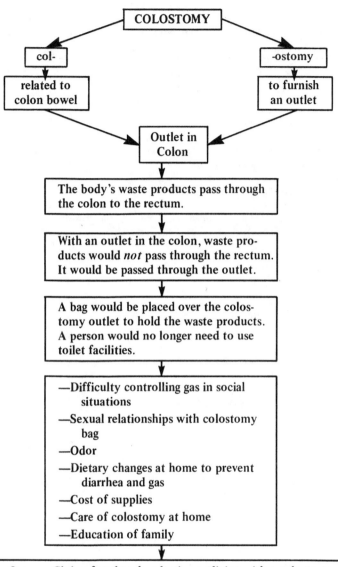

COLOSTOMY

col- → related to colon bowel

-ostomy → to furnish an outlet

→ Outlet in Colon ←

The body's waste products pass through the colon to the rectum.

With an outlet in the colon, waste products would *not* pass through the rectum. It would be passed through the outlet.

A bag would be placed over the colostomy outlet to hold the waste products. A person would no longer need to use toilet facilities.

—Difficulty controlling gas in social situations
—Sexual relationships with colostomy bag
—Odor
—Dietary changes at home to prevent diarrhea and gas
—Cost of supplies
—Care of colostomy at home
—Education of family

—Ostomy Club referral re. handy tips on living with a colostomy
—Sexual counseling
—Visiting nurse referral re. stoma care, dietary management at home, etc.
—Financial assessment and assistance re. cost of supplies

FIG. 5.4 (Continued)

This questionnaire asks for your evaluation of the orientation program as well as your assessment of how well you attained the learning objectives. It will also provide information on which topic areas could be included in our staff development/inservice education seminars in the future.

Please complete the questionnaire and return it to ＿＿＿＿＿ as soon as possible. Thank you.

Section I

Evaluation of Orientation Program and Future Educational Needs

1. What aspects of the orientation program were *most* helpful for you?

2. What aspects of the program were *least* helpful?

3. What changes would you propose in making the orientation program more helpful for other new social work employees and students?

4. What topics would you like included in our staff development/inservice education seminars that would be beneficial to your clinical practice at our hospital?

Section II

Attainment of Orientation Learning Objectives

This section includes your evaluation of how well you attained the program objectives. Please place the number that best describes your situation next to each objective.

1 = can accomplish this in the future without further assistance.
2 = accomplished this during the orientation, but will need further assistance.
3 = unable to attain the objective during the orientation program. (Please describe the reason in the comments section below.)

＿＿＿＿＿ A. Be able to use medical dictionaries and prefix-suffix model to interpret medical terminology in simulated patient hospital chart.

＿＿＿＿＿ B. Be able to use available resources in the hospital to identify the social implications of a given disease state.

＿＿＿＿＿ C. Be able to identify the sources of anxiety and apprehension concerning new role as hospital social worker.

＿＿＿＿＿ D. Be able to complete statistical caseload count from one staff member's record of clinical work during a given month.

＿＿＿＿＿ E. Be able to discuss the major role responsibilities of six health care professionals in the hospital.

＿＿＿＿＿ F. Be able to make social work entry into simulated hospital record based on POMR model.

(Other measurable objectives can be substituted or added based on the learning needs and unique attributes of the health care facility.)

Comments:

FIG. 5.5. Evaluation of orientation program.

gram. Some of these topics may also be of mutual interest to more experienced staff; hence, including these topics in an ongoing inservice education program can serve to enhance the knowledge base of both new and experienced employees. In a study conducted by Estes, mental health professionals preferred inservice programs that focused on improving individual skills.[14] They desired further training that was short, intense, problem-oriented, and related to difficulties in clinical practice.

SUMMARY

Developing an orientation program for new social work staff and students sets the stage for effective professional practice in health care. A training model for orienting social workers to these settings has been the primary focus of this chapter. Assessment of learning needs, development of goals and measurable objectives, and suggestions for the design of a hospital orientation program have been discussed. A list of major topics frequently included in training programs has been provided; corresponding sections of this book that address these topics are highlighted for the trainer's convenience. Examples of various assessment tools and teaching aids have also been included. The importance of an effective evaluation is addressed, and its use as an instrument to identify future inservice education needs for new and experienced staff is emphasized.

NOTES

1. Katherine Olsen and Marvin Olsen. "Role Expectations and Perceptions of Social Workers in Medical Settings," *Social Work* 70 (July 1967):78.
2. John D. Ingalls, *A Trainers Guide to Andragogy* (Waltham, Mass: Data Education, Inc., May 1973).
3. Malcom S. Knowles, *The Modern Practice of Adult Education* (New York: Association Press, 1975).
4. Vernon E. Bryant, "Andragogy: Fresh Concepts for Staff Development," paper presented for the Conference on Professional Assessment and Development: Theory and Practice, Lake Wilderness Education Center, Seattle, Washington, 1975.
5. Beulah Rothman, "Perspectives on Learning and Teaching in Continuing Education," *Journal of Education for Social Work* 9, no. 2 (Spring 1973):39–52.
6. Bernard Gelfand et al., "An Andragogical Application to the Training of Social Workers," *Journal of Education for Social Work* 11 (Fall 1975):55–61.
7. A. Delbecq and Van De Ven, "A Group Process Model for Problem Identification and Program Planning," *Journal of Applied Behavioral Sciences* 7 (1971):466.
8. H. Atwood and Mason, "Diagnostic Procedure in Adult Education," *Community Teamwork* 19 (March 1967):2ff.
9. Robert F. Mager, *Preparing Instructional Objectives* (Belmont, Calif.: Lear Siegler/ Fearon Publishers, 1972).
10. Clarence Wilbur Taber, *Taber's Cyclopedic Medical Dictionary,* 10th ed. (Philadelphia: F. A. Davis, 1965).
11. *Dorland's Illustrated Medical Dictionary*, 24th ed. (Philadelphia: W. B. Saunders, 1968).
12. "Behavioral Factors Associated with the Etiology of Physical Disease," six papers on disease process and relevant social conditions, in *American Journal of Public Health* 64 (November

1974):1033–55. See also B. Cobb, *Medical and Psychological Aspects of Disability* (Springfield, Ill.: Charles C. Thomas, 1973).
13. Eva Schindler-Rainman and Ronald Lippitt, *Taking Your Meetings Out of the Doldrums* (Columbus, Ohio: Association of Professional Directors, 1975), pp. 29–34.
14. R. J. Estes, "Learning Style Preferences of Community Mental Health Professionals," *Community Mental Health Journal* 11 (Winter 1975):450–61.

SUGGESTED ADDITIONAL READINGS

Ash, Joan, and Michael Stevenson. *Health: A Multimedia Source Guide*. New York: R. R. Bowker, 1976.

Bertino, Laura, and Robert Jackson, eds. *Social Workers as Trainers in Health Programs*. Proceedings, 1971 Annual Institute for Public Health Social Workers, Berkeley, California, 1972.

Dunn, Patricia, and Ernest Krall "A Model for Developing Basic Training Skills." Paper presented at Annual Program Meeting, Council of Social Work Education, Phoenix, Arizona, 1977.

Frenay, Sister Agnes Clare. *Understanding Medical Terminology* 5th ed. St Louis, Mo.: Catholic Hospital Association, 1975.

Liang, Matthew H., "An Introductory Course in Prescription Drugs for Community Health Workers Developed by a Systems Approach," *American Journal of Public Health* 66, no. 3 (March 1976):290–93.

Society for Hospital Social Work Directors. *Social Work Staff Development for Health Care*. Chicago: American Hospital Association, 1976, p. 27.

U.S. Department of Health, Education and Welfare, Health Resources Administration, Bureau of Health Manpower. *Costs of Hospital-Sponsored Orientation and Inservice Education for Registered Nurses,* Publication no. 77-25. Washington, D.C., 1977.

6/THE INTERPROFESSIONAL TEAM
AS A SMALL GROUP*
ROSALIE A. KANE

Human services are increasingly planned, delivered, and evaluated by inter-professional teams; the team is often cited as the ideal mode of service in a complex system in which "no professional is an island" and all are interdependent. Teamwork is deemed necessary to ensure competent, coherent, unfragmented, and comprehensive services to people who need help.

Too often, interprofessional teams are battlegrounds for rivalrous factions, struggling for power, speaking separate languages, or perhaps not speaking at all to teammates of other professions. Alternately, teams may be divided nations in which each profession conducts its function within its own territory, with communiqués taking the place of real communication and joint decision making. Recently the value of interprofessional teamwork has been questioned by critics who see the team as cumbersome, ceremonious,[1] tending to conservatism,[2] or an evasion of individual responsibility.[3]

Viewed another way, the interprofessional team is a small face-to-face group, subject to the same laws and tendencies as any primary group. Although the various helping professions have some familiarity with group dynamics, the team is seldom discussed in terms of group phenomena. Yet the professional's behavior on an interprofessional team is a product of group process as well as the interaction of professional roles and statuses.

SOURCES FOR UNDERSTANDING THE TEAM AS A GROUP

Much of the data about groups is applicable to the interprofessional team; however, the synthesizer finds overlapping concepts couched in language distinctive to the background of its originator. Thus terms such as *sub-actualized heterogeneity,*[4] *ascribed and achieved authority,*[5] and *functional and substantive rationality*[6] have each been used in recent articles about interprofessional teamwork. This turmoil of terminology from the social psychologist, the soci-

*Reprinted with permission of the author from *Social Work in Health Care* 1, no. 1 (Fall 1975).

ologist, the social group worker, and the management theorist confuses the reader in search of common themes.

A rich resource for understanding the small group is the group dynamics literature. The large volume of laboratory research conducted on the workings of the small group has been compiled by scholars into a fairly coherent body of laws and principles.[7-11] The related work emanating from the T-group movement may also be applied to the interprofessional team.[12] The National Training Laboratory sponsored specific study of the interprofessional research team,[13, 14] reaching insights pertinent to other kinds of teamwork.

In the last decade social group work, an applied discipline, has evolved theory more characteristically its own[15, 16] that touches upon the formation of groups, stages of group development, and the nature of the problem-solving process. This theoretical resource is often neglected in application to the interprofessional team.

In the health field, discovery that teams have been dysfunctional has led to the employment of management consultants[17, 18, 19] or to detailed examination of teams in action.[20, 21] Some studies of actual team processes have been undertaken in mental hospitals and comprehensive mental health centers.[22, 23] These research efforts are difficult because of the multiplicity of variables and perplexities of measurement but are helpful in adding to understanding of the team.

Yet another source, particularly available to the social worker, is the growing literature describing the hierarchical intraprofessional team within the social work profession.[24, 25] Although the hierarchical team's goals are derived from the values of a single profession, it resembles the interprofessional team in its concern with establishing a harmonious and productive work group.

The remainder of the paper assembles data from these diverse sources under eight interrelated topics, namely, (a) the individual in the group, (b) team size, (c) group norms, (d) democracy, (e) decision making and conflict resolution, (f) communication and structure, (g) leadership, and (h) harmony and productivity.

THE INDIVIDUAL IN THE GROUP

Team members are first individuals, then professionals, and even later members of interprofessional teams. Individual characteristics, including age, sex, ethnicity, and geographic origin, may be peripheral to the selection of the team member yet may influence his/her behavior and the behavior of others toward him/her.[26] Some professions are associated with a particular sex or social class, making it difficult to judge whether the professional or personal attributes most explain behavior. In addition, the individual brings to the team the repertoire of roles he/she has played in other groups to which he/she has belonged.

Although science is imprecise on the subject of selecting compatible individuals to compose a team, some writers have tried to predict how a given individual might interact with specific teams. A study of the selection of mental hospital teams concluded that the personality of the staff member, the formal demands of the position, and the strivings for authority of the individual should be balanced in team selection.[5] For example, a psychiatrist with a low need for authority might be combined with a social worker with a high interest in leadership. The authors suggest that application of their rather difficult criteria could result in conflict-free teams.

A similar but more cynical conclusion was reached in Rushing's[27] detailed study of mental hospital personnel. Noting that psychiatrists tended to expect "a testing function" from psychologists and a "welfare function" from social workers and that these role definitions were unacceptable to high-caliber professionals, he suggested that the organization might find it preferable to hire the average or mediocre individual. When the goals of a professional role are clearly articulated at a minimal level, a less competent individual might perform the job adequately and experience more satisfaction.

SIZE OF THE TEAM

Most commentators indicate a preference for a rather small team. Referring to the social work team, Brieland, Briggs, and Leuenberger[24] propose five or six full-time members as ideal. Luszki[13] suggests that the interdisciplinary research team should remain rather small and not attempt to incorporate too many disciplines so that conflicting views may receive expression.

Research suggests that as the size of a group increases, greater demands are placed on the leader but the group tolerates direction from the leader better, the more active members tend to dominate the group, and the more passive members withdraw from participation. Also, the larger the group, the less intimate the atmosphere, the more anonymous the actions, the longer it takes to reach decisions, the more acceptable become unresolved differences, the more subgroups form, and the more formalized are the rules and procedures of the group.[9]

This commonsense catalogue of differences related to increasing size has applications to the interprofessional team. Critics who consider the team too large may be reacting to some properties of large groups such as increased formality and anonymity which lead to diffusion of commitment to and responsibility for actions. On the other hand, all advantages do not rest with the larger group; in the smaller team unresolved differences would be less tolerated, yet differences must be permitted to exist if individual professional perspectives are brought to bear on a problem. Perhaps the team should be just large enough to include individuals with all the relevant skills for problem solving. There is some tendency to window-dress the interprofessional team (particularly if ample funding is available) so that it includes representatives of as many professions as possible.

GROUP NORMS ON THE INTERPROFESSIONAL TEAM

Norms are the standards of behavior and belief that a group imposes on its membership. When an individual is caught between groups with conflicting norms, he becomes uncomfortable and moves to resolve the conflict in favor of the group to which his ties are strongest.[9] It is unclear whether, in the interests of service, it is preferable for the major loyalty of the team member to lie with the team or with the member's profession. An excessive attachment to a professional reference group could render the team member inflexible and unresponsive in a work situation, yet excessive team attachment might prevent the member from applying the distinctive professional viewpoint that justifies interprofessional teamwork in the first place.

Certain norms are probably not conducive to good interprofessional teamwork. Norms against conflict or against praise are both dysfunctional; the former impedes team members from making professional judgments while the latter denies members the support they should derive from the group. Another harmful norm is one that calls for a physician to automatically become team leader.

An individual's adherence to norms is linked to his/her status in the group, and status may be associated with professional affiliation. The more eager an individual is to belong to a group, the more he/she will conform to group norms.[9] Thus the profession aspiring for a place on a team may become a conforming profession. The highest ranking and most secure members of a group are willing to disagree with the group publicly and privately, the lowest ranking members tend to disagree privately and conform in public, and middle-ranking members tend to conform both in public and in private. This rule of group dynamics suggests the value of increasing the sense of security of the lower ranked members of the team.

The flexibility of a group is also related to group norms. The less definite outside standards (such as science, religion, or morality) are about a matter, the more free a group is to exact its own standards.[9] Perhaps this accounts for the team that is strongly committed to an ideology with little evidence to support the stand. As long as no definite opposing standards exist and as long as the group is cohesive, the team is free to exact demands on its membership. When there is no objective basis for judgment and no group standard either, judgments tend to be unstable, and much more group time is required for interaction.[9] It almost seems that the group norms can become a shorthand to group process.

The more stable a group's membership, the more established are its norms, the more attached members are to the group, and the harder it is for the group to shift activities.[9] Since the team must be a responsive instrument as well as a smooth-functioning one, frequent turnover of personnel may be helpful in preventing group norms from solidifying. But the newcomer on the team faces difficulties. Although social workers are very aware that the new member of a treatment group will require help and support, often it is assumed that a new member of an interprofessional team can take the place of a former member as if he/she were an interchangeable part. Such a view ignores the fact that the new member brings unique individual qualities to the group and that the group has already established norms for behavior that cannot be known to the neophyte. Orientations to the team are neglected as a subject in the literature, yet knowledge of group process suggests that they are important.

What of the team with dysfunctional norms? One is reminded of Kurt Lewin's dictum that it is more feasible to change an entire group than an individual within it.[28] Perhaps the problem is best handled through team discussion, reeducation, and shared decision to change than through efforts to supervise and influence individual members.

DEMOCRACY AND TEAM PROCESSES

A troublesome ideology of the interprofessional team, which is at times its pride and at times its nemesis, is the democratic ideal which pervades the literature. Many writers[29, 30, 31] take for granted that the team should be a community of equals, each member possessing a vote, as it were, in the deliberations of the team. The democratic ideal shapes the nature of group process in the team, including decision making and communication, and therefore must be examined. Although the official ideology of many teams minimizes status differences between professions, research indicates that both the patients[21] and the team members themselves[32] accurately perceive where the power lies in the team hierarchy.

Democratic leadership, as opposed to authoritarian or laissez-faire leadership, has been considered the preferred leadership style. In terms of research results[9] the advantages of the democratic style are durability, ability to pursue a task in the absence of the leader, more satisfaction to members, and possibly better productivity. It is also reported that the more people associate together on equal terms, the more they share values and norms and come to like each other.

A democratic process, although slow and producing few decisions, seems to reassure team members during early phases of group development. Later, the "town meeting" approach becomes unsatisfactory, and members crave clearer role delineation so they can proceed with their work.[33] Luszki,[13] referring to research teams, insists that at the very least each team member requires explicit recognition of status differences in the hierarchy. Bartlett[34] also opts for role clarity in pointing out that one of social work's tasks on the health team is to "recognize the middle-level status of social work."

Group work theorists[35] recognize a struggle around equality as a stage in the development of the small group. It is argued that most groups go through an early period in which power and control are crucial issues, and in which problems of status, ranking, and influence are paramount. This stage ends in a period of intimacy and a feeling of belonging, and from there moves to a stage of differentiation, in which group members are able to appreciate each other's uniqueness. Perhaps teams that constitute themselves as miniature democracies attempt to short-circuit the natural stages of group development known to social group work theorists. Perhaps, too, many interprofessional teams are in a state of "arrested group development" and never leave the stage of grappling over power and control.

It is useful to differentiate between political democracy, which implies time-limited delegation of powers, and social democracy, which concerns making judgments on the basis of the merits rather than the status of the speaker.[36] The team is not a political democracy, and, ironically, a social democracy should accentuate inequalities. If all have a right to speak, individuals will produce ideas of varying merit.

One cannot argue against a team process that facilitates participation according to ability and treats each member with courtesy and respect; the use of democratic slogans, however, often leads to a confusion of team processes with political processes and rights. The ambiguity, and sometimes inaccuracy, of the term *democracy* as applied to the interprofessional team complicates clear, open communication from the outset; probably the term should be abandoned.

DECISION MAKING AND CONFLICT RESOLUTION

In an interprofessional team, several people may have input into any given decision. A common problem, however, is the absence of any planned process for decision making. In a milieu that glorifies the importance of the group, this deficit may lead to premature decisions based on an apparent rather than a genuine consensus.

There is some evidence that a group decision is superior to decisions of individuals working separately, especially if the group receives instruction on how to work toward a consensus.[37] A group's decision-making skills can, it seems, be learned and improve with practice. In some instances, however, group decisions may be less accurate or perceptive than those of one group member uninfluenced by colleagues. Janis[38] coined the term *groupthink* to designate a phenomenon he noted in policy-making groups at a high governmental level. Characterized by strong norms and a firm bond between members, such groups may become impervious to new insights and fail to question the assumptions of an original policy, even when that policy is not working. Interprofessional teams, too, are subject to groupthink as they struggle to implement programs that do not appear to be meeting service needs.

As guidelines for reaching decisions on teams, Rubin and Beckhard[18] suggest that in each instance it must be determined who has the necessary information to make the decision, who must be consulted before the decision is made, and who must be kept informed after the fact. Most analysts would concede that work groups do not require unanimity on decisions, nor do they require participation of the whole group on all matters. Noting that each member is limited in decision-making participation by the three factors of time, interest, and competence, Binner[36] advocates a procedure by which each team member feels a responsibility to actively express dissenting views. With this understanding, a leader who hears no opposition can safely assume general agreement.

A useful rule of thumb holds that the entire team should participate in the decisions that affect the entire group.[39] These might include formulation of new policies or procedures or the hiring of a new team member. Technical decisions should be made by those with expertise and responsibility for that aspect of the work. To help a team reach wise decisions, a leader might borrow techniques from the social group worker;[40] leaders can help members recognize the issues, stimulate a search for tentative solutions, form subgroups to ensure full participation, and ensure that conclusions are evaluated. The team itself should, of course, have real power to make decisions; teams are hamstrung if they need to refer to an external authority, even in the same organization, for day-to-day decisions.

A decision-making procedure must take into account a way of managing the inevitable conflicts that will (and should) occur. Northern[41] put it well when she stated that conflict and cooperation are part of the same phenomenon. Both are aspects of problem solving, and the group is a problem-solving medium. Much of the literature on the interprofessional team is concerned with decreasing tensions and disagreements to arrive at an integrated group. This emphasis on cooperation may, unfortunately, have obscured the fact that honest disagreement is not only permitted but necessary on the team.

From the perspective of social group work Bernstein[15] has described conflict and its possible resolutions. Rather than compromise or subjugation of opposition, he calls for forging a new and acceptable synthesis. His catalogue of levels of conflict resolution ranges from physical violence to respect for differences. Although the latter is the preferable way to deal with conflict, many of the intervening patterns such as verbal violence, search for allies, diversionary tactics, and appeal to authority are well known to interprofessional teamworkers.

It may be argued that the complexities that make the team necessary at all also necessitate role differentiation of members and make conflict inevitable. Eichhorn[4] evolved a theoretical framework for this differentiation process which she conceptualized in three stages. First, differences are suppressed, conflict minimized, and teams fail to utilize their full range of problem-solving potential. In the second stage, conflict occurs as individuals identify their own interests and needs. Efforts are made to evolve a new structure to accommodate the differences which lead to the final stage when differences are legitimized and utilized as a resource.

COMMUNICATION AND STRUCTURE ON THE TEAM

Communication, in all its forms, verbal and written, formal and informal, structured and unstructured, is the vehicle through which the team members interact and the work gets done. In a broad sense, the term encompasses the kinds of messages transmitted and received, the people involved in various communications, the language employed, and the structural arrangements that guide the flow of information and feeling.

Ongoing communication is a process requiring a commitment of time and energy. To enhance communication, a good secretarial system, a single record, and physical proximity of offices are all useful. Brieland et al.[24] advocate that members of the social work team share a large office with small adjoining rooms available for interviewing. Such an arrangement sacrifices members' status needs but encourages accurate communication. Moreover, mutual observation of each other's work accentuates the ideal of team responsibility to both team members and clients.

It has been suggested that team members should not report upward to professional departments,[17] contrary to established practices of professions such as nursing or social work. Although professions may have compelling reasons for retaining a strong tie to a professional department, departmentalization does dilute the team focus. The social work practice of providing supervision for a neophyte by means of a worker outside the team has also been shown to be detrimental to team solidarity.[20, 21]

Elimination of esoteric language also fosters communication. Each professional should be able to express plans in a straightforward way that is comprehensible to other team colleagues. Lack of trust sometimes underlies the reluctance to part with jargon.[42] Certain systems of record keeping[43] have been suggested as a format that enables all team members to utilize the same record in language all can understand. These records are likely to be resisted until the various professions are willing to remove some of the mystique from their practice.

Research findings[9] indicate that one-way communication, as opposed to mutual communication, is less accurate and engenders lack of confidence; feedback increases accuracy. Centralized communication through a single point produces satisfaction at the center of the group but not at the periphery, permits task efficiency and coordination of efforts, clearly identifies the leader, and diminishes member criticism of the group. With centralized communication error is more likely, and there is less chance to correct mistakes. Both the centralized and decentralized patterns have advantages and disadvantages. Centralized communications helps clarify structure and coordinate the task;

it establishes the leader in a way consistent with role clarity for teams that do have a designated leader. Yet without safeguards, a team with centralized communication is prone to miscommunication and error. A solution is to structure centralized channels of communication but build in opportunity for feedback; one analyst recommends that each team designate a team manager through whom information might flow.[17] The manager would ensure that communication be mutual and two-way, as well as clear and accurate.

LEADERSHIP ON THE TEAM

Leadership, a complex subject that has been studied extensively,[8] is here defined as any conscious act of influence over the behavior of others. A given group, then, includes many members who exercise leadership in addition to the designated leader. In order to influence behavior, a leader must understand human motivation. On the other hand, the leader must also understand the task in which the team is engaged and exercise judgment about proposed actions. Leadership ability in the sense of persuasive interpersonal skills may be worse than no leadership at all if exercised on behalf of an ill-judged cause.[44]

Leadership is a combination of goal-oriented and interpersonal skills. Research suggests that leaders are followed more faithfully if they satisfy the members' need for guidance as well as for harmony and acceptance.[9] In other words, both an intellectual and a social leadership is required for a group, and these two facets are rarely equally well fulfilled by a single individual.

Team reformers recognize that automatic physician leadership has not enhanced team processes on medical or psychiatric teams. In reaction, other professions have been thrust into titular leadership without preparation for the task. One group, for example, designated public health nurses as team leaders only to find that they were not prepared to assume that responsibility.[45] A better suggestion is to choose the leader, not on the basis of professional affiliation, but on understanding of and skill in utilizing the group process on behalf of team goals. A designated leader handles the group process in such a way as to encourage contributions and leadership of others—this is the role of the suggested team manager. It appears that the leaderless team is a myth, and that it is more accurate that many acts of leadership are performed by members of a group at different times, according to the issues facing the team. The titular leader, or team manager, should be able to facilitate each member's leadership abilities.

Clearly many interprofessional teams are in violation of what is so far known about leadership. Responsibility for team process often rests with the most educated member, who also may carry legal responsibility for the task. Sometimes the team is constituted with the fiction that there will be no leader. But Rittenhouse[23] examined leadership on such teams only to find that leadership actually resided in the same person across a variety of tasks. It apparently is insufficient to declare that all members shall be leaders in their own sphere unless a manager-leader facilitates a process that encourages that result.

HARMONY AND PRODUCTIVITY: TASK AND PROCESS ON THE TEAM

Much discussion of communication and decision making on the team is predicated on the view that the team will perform its task better in a congenial working environment. Some small-group research does suggest that both the effectiveness and the satisfaction of a group increase when members find their personal goals are met.[9] Further, it has been suggested that groups with a high degree of intrateam friendships will be motivated to work harder and be more productive.[11] Commentators on the team have tended to support the view that a harmonious team spends less energy on conflict and more on goal-directed activity.

Certainly a group must attend to its own processes as well as completion of its tasks,[7] but too much attention to group maintenance is counterproductive. Drawing an analogy to the maintenance of a car, some routine servicing makes the car run better and prevents future breakdown, but when the car is constantly being maintained, its effectiveness for transportation is reduced.

Berrien[46] has developed operational definitions for formal achievement (FA) and group need satisfactions (GNS), suggesting that an optimum balance between FA and GNS produces a homeostasis associated with an effective group. Some indicators of this homeostasis are group cohesiveness, satisfaction with the leader's interpersonal relationships, satisfaction with the leader's technical skills, satisfaction with tangible rewards, and member pressure to remain in the group.

The data on harmony in relationship to productivity are, unfortunately, somewhat contradictory. Certainly a group that places harmony above its task cannot be effective. Underscoring this point, Bass[8] evokes the familiar situation of the meeting that postpones complex issues and tackles simple agenda items only: "Solution of these simple items gives a sense of task accomplishment, although the major success occurred in achieving satisfying interaction."

In harmonious work groups, the danger of groupthink[38] is ever present. Groups with this problem are characterized by lack of contingency plans, imperviousness to outside input, and inability to reconsider original premises; instead the members are overly supportive of each other. Remedies to avoid this sterile situation call for leader activity in providing outside experts, playing the devil's advocate, postponing decisions, and refraining from lending his/her weight to early solutions. Such leader behaviors are necessarily geared toward goal achievement rather than group need satisfaction.

The scant empirical research regarding team morale is inconclusive. One study[22] found a high association between good morale and time spent in patient interviews and admission workups. Different findings emerged from the Midway study of intraprofessional teams in public assistance[47] which found that high productivity in terms of frequent client contact and home visiting was not associated with job satisfaction. A profile analysis of the productive group indicated that they were young, newly employed, and not interested in a career in the agency; the authors concluded that such workers are better able to resist group norms toward a leisurely pace.

DISCUSSION

A number of interrelated components of group process pertinent to the interprofessional team have been discussed. Although more variables might have been considered, the list is already long enough to create practical problems in reaching conclusions about a team's process. Choice of meaningful variables is a dilemma for the student of small groups; Golembiewski[10] challenged researchers with this problem some years ago: "A considerable volume of future work must be accomplished in two general areas. The first area is the clarification of existing concepts and operations and the determination of the degree of overlap of existing variables allegedly tapping the same or similar phenomena. The second area requires that the variables utilized be pared down to a small number. . . . If small-group analysis is not to bog down in a morass of variables, research tastes must change."

Analysis of interprofessional teams is at an early stage and might profit from Golembiewski's caution. Study of the team must include variables of profession and team purpose as well as process elements, and the more the latter can be consolidated, the more readily practical conclusions can be drawn. Currently there is little basis for eliminating variables. The present exercise in examining the team as a small group is only a first step. In some ideal future, professional students may be taught to analyze teamwork in its group process dimensions so that they may approach their professional careers with some confidence about what makes teamwork work.

NOTES

1. Paul Ellwood, "Can We Afford So Many Rehabilitation Professions?" *Journal of Rehabilitation* 34 (1968):21–22.
2. Bernice Eiduson, "Intellectual Inbreeding in the Clinic," *American Journal of Orthopsychiatry* 34 (1964):714–21.
3. A. F. Rae-Grant and Donald Marcuse, "The Hazards of Teamwork," *American Journal of Orthopsychiatry* 38 (1968):4–8.
4. Suzanne Eichhorn, *Becoming: The Actualization of Individual Differences in Five Student Health Teams* (The Bronx, N.Y.: Institute for Health Team Development, 1973).
5. Sydney Bernard and Toaru Ishiyama, "Authority Conflicts in the Structure of Psychiatric Teams," *Social Work* 5 (1960):77–83.
6. Peter Kong-Ming New, "An Analysis of the Concept of Teamwork," *Community Mental Health Journal* 4 (1968):326–33.

7. Robert Bales, *Interaction Process Analysis* (Cambridge, Mass.: Addison-Wesley Press, 1950).
8. Bernard Bass, *Leadership, Psychology, and Organizational Behavior* (New York: Harper & Row, 1960).
9. Bernard Berelson and Gary Steiner, *Human Behavior: An Inventory of Scientific Findings* (New York: Harcourt, Brace & World, 1964).
10. Robert Golembiewski, *The Small Group* (Chicago: University of Chicago Press, 1962).
11. A. Paul Hare, *Handbook of Small Group Research* (New York: Free Press of Glencoe, 1962).
12. Fred Odhner, "Group Dynamics of the Interdisciplinary Team," *American Journal of Occupational Therapy* 24 (1970):484–87.
13. Margaret Luszki, *Interdisciplinary Team Research* (New York: National Training Laboratories, 1958).
14. Muzafer Sherif and Carolyn Sherif, *Interdisciplinary Relationships in the Social Sciences* (Chicago: Aldine, 1969).
15. Saul Bernstein, *Explorations in Group Work* (Boston: Boston University School of Social Work, 1965).
16. Robert Vinter, *Readings in Group Work Practice* (Ann Arbor: Campus Publications, 1965).
17. Richard Beckhard, "Organizational Issues in the Team Delivery of Comprehensive Health Care," *Milbank Memorial Fund Quarterly* 50 (1972):287–316.
18. Irwin Rubin and Richard Beckhard, "Factors Influencing the Effectiveness of Health Teams," *Milbank Memorial Fund Quarterly* 50 (1972):317–35.
19. Harold Wise, Richard Beckhard, Irwin Rubin, and Aileen Kyte, *Making Health Teams Work* (Cambridge, Mass.: Ballanger, 1974).
20. H. David Banta and Renie C. Fox, "Role Strains of a Health Care Team in a Poverty Community," *Social Science and Medicine* 6 (1972):697–722.
21. George Silver, *Family Medical Care,* 2d ed. (Cambridge, Mass.: Ballanger, 1974).
22. Brenda Dickey, "Team Morale, Time Utilization, and Treatment Effectiveness," *Journal of the Fort Logan Mental Health Center* 1 (1963):103–16.
23. Joan Rittenhouse, "The Application of a Modified Balesean Paradigm to the Study of Psychiatric Team Interaction," *Journal of the Fort Logan Mental Health Center* 4 (1967): 59–74.
24. Donald Brieland, Thomas Briggs, and Paul Leuenberger, *The Team Model of Social Work Practice* (Syracuse: Syracuse University School of Social Work, 1973).
25. David Gill, "Social Work Teams," *Child Welfare* 44 (1965):442–46.
26. John Horwitz, *Team Practice and the Specialist* (Springfield, Ill.: Charles C. Thomas, 1970).
27. William Rushing, *The Psychiatric Professions* (Chapel Hill: University of North Carolina Press, 1964).
28. Margaret Hartford, *Groups in Social Work* (New York: Columbia University Press, 1972).
29. Maurice Connery, "The Climate of Effective Teamwork," *Journal of Psychiatric Social Work* 22 (1953):59–60.
30. Joseph Eaton, "Social Processes of Professional Team Work," *American Sociological Review* 16 (1961):707–13.
31. Frederick Whitehouse, "Professional Teamwork," in *Proceedings of the National Conference on Social Welfare,* 1957.
32. Boyd Oviatt, "Role Convergence in a Therapeutic Community," *Journal of the Fort Logan Mental Health Center* 2 (1964):117–29.
33. David Kaplan, "The Continuous Workshop: A Forum of Interdisciplinary Research," *Social Work* 5 (1960):78–82.
34. Harriet Bartlett, *Social Work Practice in the Health Field* (New York: NASW, 1961).
35. James Garland, Hubert Jones, and Ralph Kolodony, "A Model for Stages of Development in Social Work Groups," in *Explorations in Group Work,* edited by Saul Bernstein (Boston: Boston University School of Social Work, 1965).

36. Paul Binner, "The Team and the Concept of Democracy," *Journal of the Fort Logan Mental Health Center* 4 (1967):115–24.
37. J. Hall, "Decisions, Decisions, Decisions," *Psychology Today* 5 (1971):51.
38. Irving Janis, "Groupthink," *Psychology Today* 5 (1971):43.
39. Thomas Briggs and Evert Van Voorst, "Teaching and Learning about Interprofessional Teamwork," paper read at the 17th International Congress of Schools of Social Work, June 1974, Addis Ababa, Ethiopia.
40. Louis Lowy, "Decision-Making and Group Work," in *Explorations in Group Work,* edited by Saul Bernstein (Boston: Boston University School of Social Work, 1965).
41. Helen Northern, *Social Work with Groups* (New York: Columbia University Press, 1969).
42. Anita K. Bahn, "A Multi-Disciplinary Psychosocial Classification Scheme," *American Journal of Orthopsychiatry* 41 (1971):830–35.
43. Rosalie Kane, "Look to the Record!" *Social Work* 19 (1974):412–19.
44. Daniel Katz and Robert Kahn, *The Social Psychology of Organizations* (New York: John Wiley & Sons, 1966).
45. David Cowan and John Sbarbaro, "Family-Centered Health Care—A Viable Reality," *Medical Care* 10 (1972):164–72.
46. F. K. Berrien, "Homeostasis Theory of Groups," in *Leadership and Interpersonal Behavior,* edited by Luigi Petrullo and Bernard Bass (New York: Holt, Rinehart & Winston, 1961).
47. C. Anderson and Thomas Carlson, "The Midway Project on Organization and Use of Public Assistance Personnel," in *Manpower Research on Utilization of Baccalaureate Social Workers,* edited by Robert Barker and Thomas Briggs (Washington, D.C.: United States Government Printing Office, 1971).

SUGGESTED ADDITIONAL READINGS

Bassoff, Betty Zippin. Interdisciplinary Education for Health Professionals: Issues and Directions, *Social Work in Health Care* 2, no. 2 (Winter 1975):219–28.
Bracht, Neil. "Community Fieldwork Collaboration Between Medical and Social Work Students." *Social Work in Health Care* 1 Fall (1975):7–18.
Mason, Elizabeth J. and Parascandola, John. "Preparing Tomorrow's Health Care Team." *Nursing Outlook* 20 (1972):728–31.
Mullaney, Joan Ward, Fox, Ruth Ann, and Liston, Mary F. "Clinical Nurse Specialist and Social Worker—Clarifying the Roles." *Nursing Outlook* 22 (1974):712–18. (November)
Pluckhan, Margaret L. "Professional Territoriality: A Problem Affecting the Delivery of Health Care." *Nursing Forum* 11 (1972):302.
Tuhy, M. (ed.), *"Health Care Teams: An Annotated Bibliography."* Praegar, 1974.

Part IV

SOCIAL AND BEHAVIORAL COMPONENTS OF HEALTH AND ILLNESS

7/LIFE STYLE, POVERTY, AND

CHANGING ILLNESS PATTERNS   NEIL F. BRACHT

Health is a troubling concept to define and to operationalize. The term *health* has normative connotations that invite differing interpretations. Is health to be defined broadly so that it is indistinguishable from well-being, happiness? How does wellness differ from illness, and can the two be measured? Some medical leaders who feel that medical care can play only a limited role in people's health wish to narrow the definition of medicine:

In proposing that there is an area of health which falls outside of the area of avoiding or combating illness, the WHO definition, I believe, expresses the important truth; but at the same time I doubt that this non-illness related area of health should be or can be the particular object of medicine.[1]

This narrowing of the scope of medicine is both welcome and problematic. For example, the increased emphasis on individual responsibility for altering habits (smoking) injurious to health is much desired. If, however, the social action and/or resources required to assist people to stop smoking are not seen as an integral responsibility of health care, then 'holistic' approaches to human health and social care are threatened. Dana sees this potential pulling away from an enlarged conception of health by the medical care industry and comments as follows:

The prevention of disease and disability whether physical or mental is intimately con-nected with the conditions of human life. Thus a retreat from the vigorous pursuit of a social mission for health and medical care delivery is a denial of both science and society.[2]

NEW APPROACHES TO HEALTH

For some time the World Health Organization's definition of health has been widely used by health professionals. Without retreating from the "social well-being" mission implied in this longstanding definition, Terris suggests that perhaps some modification of the definition is needed:

Clearly the word "complete" should be deleted since health is not absolute; there are degrees of health. The term disease needs to be replaced by "illness" since health and disease are not mutually exclusive (a large proportion of the adult population carries the disease of atherosclerosis, yet only a small percentage gives evidence of illness. Cancer of the cervix is found by cytological examination in numerous healthy women). Finally health needs to be defined in functional as well as subjective terms. A revised WHO definition would thus read as follows: Health is a state of physical, mental and social well being and ability to function and not merely the absence of illness or infirmity.[3]

The inclusion of the phrase "ability to function" by a respected health researcher is important to social workers who have long been concerned with the social-functioning aspects of medical care. Attention to the social dimension of health and illness is clearly present in the first three premises underlying social work's contribution to health care as described in Chapter 2. Current research measuring both perceptions of well-being and social dysfunctioning related to sickness are encouraging trends.[4] Traditional measures such as life expectancy, death rates, morbidity rates, physician visits, and hospital stays are also limited measures of the health status of individuals.

Since social work's primary concern is with the interactions between people and their social environment, the profession brings special expertise to these nonmedical aspects of health. Social work's accumulated knowledge and values recognize the basic unity of human behavior and the interrelationships among biological, psychological, and social factors. Social work's primary focus in human behavior has been on social functioning in general and on rehabilitation and prevention in particular. Social work's linkage function to other aspects of social welfare provides a way for the health care system to address nonmedical aspects of personal care, which may not be its central focus.

Acknowledging that this kind of activity (nonmedical) may fall more into the province of psychologists and sociologists, Terris[5] believes that epidemiologists and other health workers can make important contributions by directing studies to four important areas. These include:

1. Studies of the capacity for performance.
2. Studies measuring impediments to performance.[6]
3. Measurement of performance.[7]
4. Studies of subjective feelings regarding the degree of physical, mental, and social well-being.

Some beginning social work research in the area of subjective feelings has been attempted. Nielsen was able to measure differences in the change in contentment among older people following hospitalization.[8] Self-health appraisals by elderly people have been shown to be effective.

While social work has long been concerned with issues of social functioning, it has been slow to identify the variables that contribute to optimal social functioning. Some research has been done in this area. In a recent hospital study of the effectiveness of postdischarge follow-up, Mannino and Shore showed how marital status, family stage, family type, and family position have an interactive effect that produces less favorable outcomes for patients discharged from a state hospital.[9] Robert Perkins and his associates summarize for social workers the task that lies ahead:

> If social, economic conditions do, indeed, exert an influence on an individual's state of health, it would be illogical to assume, a priori, that this influence is unidirectional and exists only in the direction of being pathogenic. The literature, in fact, contains evidence to support the opposite contention. The morbidity rates of certain diseases under certain socioeconomic conditions are sufficiently low to suggest a possible prophylactic quality in the socioeconomic condition. ... If social work is to continue its significant and unique contributions to health care, it must develop a sound theoretical base that demonstrates the relevance of social and emotional factors to illness.[10]

LIFE STYLE AND ILLNESS TRENDS

The life style of contemporary Americans has an enormous effect on the health status of the population and consequently on the way people use medical services:

> The epitome of the problem is an American having a third martini while puffing a cigarette as he unwinds from a day at a stressful job and contemplates a too-rich dinner. In brief, America drinks too much, smokes too much, worries too much and eats unwisely. ... The result is higher rates of alcoholism and liver damage, lung cancer, mental illness, heart disease, stroke, overweight and high blood pressure, not to mention hepatitis, emphysema and diabetes.[11]

These are the diseases of an affluent industrial society. Smoking is clearly a social disease, and it has been shown that a social climate of acceptance or rejection of such behavior has strong implications for its reduction.[12] In addition to the strong underlying social and psychological factors in the etiology of each of these illnesses, they have in common the potential for chronicity in terms of limitation of activity, disability, and marked increase in utilization of medical resources.[13] The accumulated individual and family impact of "new" social illnesses coupled with increasing life span and the prevention of early death through medical intervention represents one of the most pressing problems in modern industrial society.

POVERTY AND ILLNESS

The "new" social diseases of the affluent not only "attack" the poor but do so in a much more devastating way. Health data on the U.S. population

> support the conclusion that the poor in the United States are sicker than the non-poor and use fewer ambulatory health services. If anything, however, these crude value mea-

sures of utilization applied to a national sample tend to understate both the severity and the complexity of the problem.[14]

The striking relationship between poverty and health problems, especially those causing activity limitation, is shown in Figure 7.1. White summarizes his data on family income and health problems in the following way:

Those with less than $2,000 family income report more than four times as many heart conditions as those in the highest income group, six times as much mental or nervous trouble; six times as much arthritis and rheumatism; six times as many cases of high blood pressure; over three times as many orthopedic impairments; and almost eight times as many visual impairments. The income level, less than $2,000, is heavily weighted for the aged, but the contrast at the next lowest level is still great, although not quite as dramatic.[15]

It is interesting to note that in several surveys of people living in poverty, health is ranked as one of their highest priorities. For too long their access to appropriate health education and treatment resources has been deficient. Table 7.1 illustrates the impact of income on the need for health care and shows how the poor suffer from a larger percentage of limitations on major activity due to chronic conditions. Once they are given access to health resources their need for hospitalization may be greater and their average length of stay increases. The early periodic screening, diagnosis, and treatment program (EPSDT) authorized by the 1967 Social Security amendments (staffing for the program, which could serve some 11.5 million eligible children, did not start until 1974) has reported that 45 percent of the children screened require treatment for severe dental problems, inadequate immunizations, vision problems, and upper-respiratory ailments.

Socioeconomic conditions are related to the health status of minorities of ethnic color: 38.3 percent of American Indians have income below the poverty level; 35 percent of American blacks and 23.5 percent of Hispanics live below the poverty level. Data from the National Health Survey program (annual interviews on some 42,000 households in the United States) have consistently shown race-related differences in the utilization and receipt of health services for these groups. For example, in 1967 the average number of physician visits by nonwhite children under the age of 15 was only 1.9 annually while for white children in higher-income groups the average number of visits was 4.2. Fewer visits by the poor have also been reported for dental care and other preventive services.

Health statistics for the American Indian, while improving gradually, have long been a disgrace in this affluent nation. The infant mortality rate among Indians is nearly double the rate for the white population. The 1965 maternal mortality rate of 6.3 deaths for every 1,000 live births among Indian mothers was three times the rate for white mothers. The life expectancy of Indians is

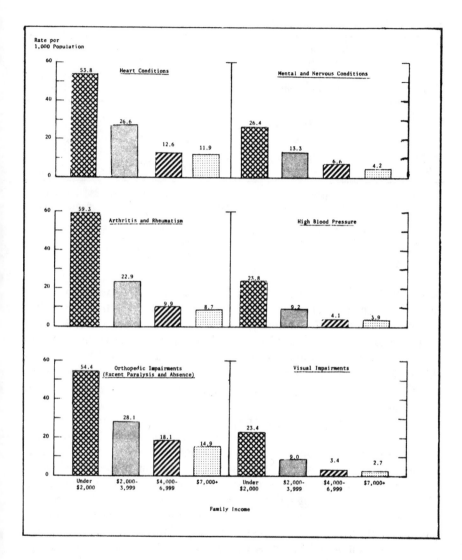

FIG. 7.1. Relationship between family income and health problems causing activity limitation: July 1962–June 1963 (rate per 1,000 population).

Source: U.S. Department of Health, Education and Welfare, National Center for Health Statistics, *Medical Care, Health Status, and Family Income,* Public Health Service Publication no. 1000–Series 10, no. 9 (Washington, D.C., May 1964), p. 60.

105

TABLE 7.1

Impact of Income on Need for Health Care: 1973

Family Income Level	% of Population with Limitation in Major Activity Due to Chronic Conditions[a]	Number of Short-Stay Hospital Discharges per 100 Persons per Year	Average Length of Stay (in days) for Discharges from Short-Stay Hospitals
All family income levels	10.2%	13.9	8.1
Under $5,000	22.9%	19.3	9.8
$5,000–$9,999	10.7	15.1	8.3
$10,000 and over	5.6	11.7	6.9

[a] Among these chronic conditions are such things as heart conditions, high blood pressure, arthritis and rheumatism, orthopedic impairments, visual impairments, and mental and nervous conditions.

Source: "Profile of American Health, 1973: Based on Data Collected in the Health Interview Survey," *Public Health Reports*, November-December 1974, pp. 504–523.

approximately seven years less than that of the white population. Infectious diseases continue to cause greater mortality among Indians than among the rest of the population. Interestingly, the rate of cardiovascular diseases among Indians is lower. One of the most serious health problems of Indians remains alcoholism, which constitutes a major cause of death and disability among them. Cirrhosis of the liver is the seventh leading cause of death among Indians, that is, 38.9 per 100,000 as contrasted with 14.1 per 100,000 for the U.S. population.[16]

Chicanos and other Hispanics show higher mortality and morbidity rates than similar Anglo-American populations and communities.[17] Migrant health clinics provide some additional access to medical care services for this group. Use of the *curandero* healer in Mexican-American communities (see Ari Kiev, *Curanderismo, Mexican-American Folk Psychiatry* [New York: Free Press, 1968]) represents differing cultural approaches to health and illness. Similar cultural variations exist in Asian American groups. Socialization patterns, diet, and stress-reducing activities seem to account for significantly lower rates of heart disease among Japanese-American males.[18] Health professionals must be aware of these differences if effective and mutual planning for health programing is to occur in minority communities.

SOCIAL WORK AND THE "NEW SOCIAL DISEASES"

Life style, poverty, and affluence all contribute to changing illness patterns in American society. Today there are an increasing number of chronic, disabling conditions that have a major impact on families and one's productive capacity. The "old" social diseases such as VD and TB are clearly outnumbered by the "new" social diseases of postindustrial society: hypertension, alcohol and drug abuse, heart disease, obesity, auto accidents. Some 20 million nonfatal injuries occur in home accidents each year. Nearly 400,000 children are affected by lead poisoning annually. Recently the National Research Council of the National Academy of Sciences noted that traumas and associated disabilities are the "neglected epidemic of modern society." Although much attention has been given to accidents involving motor vehicles, these account for fewer than 2 of every 100 people suffering accidents. Household accidents occur five times more frequently. Finally, mental illness ranks fourth among the conditions causing days of bed disability in the United States.

These new "social diseases" have, in large part, social causes that are amenable to intervention and behavioral change. Cassel presents four general principles derived from animal analogue experiments as a basis for further epidemiologic research on illness and social/behavioral factors:

1. *Social or familial disorganization,* one result of overcrowding, has been linked to increased rates of tuberculosis, mental disorder, death from stroke, and hypertension.

2. *Domination and subordination:* Differences in the susceptibility of individuals in a group to the effects of disorganization have been observed. Those having the most status are less vulnerable and have lower morbidity and mortality rates.

3. The concept of *social buffers* is concerned with the degree to which an individual is insulated from the consequences of social disorganization by the presence or absence of social-familial support systems. For example, epidemiologic studies on tuberculosis have shown a higher incidence of the disease in people who lack social contacts.

If these three principles, or hypothesis, were correct, it would imply that the health consequences of social disorganization will not be universal, affecting all people in the same manner. A more adequate formulation would hold that such consequences would be dependent on:

- *The importance or salience of the relationships that become disordered under conditions of social disorganization.*
- *The position of the individuals experiencing such disordered relationships in the status hierarchy.*
- *The degree to which the population under study has been unprepared by previous experience for this particular situation (i.e., has had insufficient time to adapt).*
- *The nature and strength of the available group supports.*

4. *The ability to anticipate illness* under certain conditions of social disorganization. Animal studies tend to support the conclusion that "variations in group relationships, rather than having a specific etiological role, would enhance succeptibility to disease in general."

Presumably, then, the causes of disease may vary under different conditions. In preindustrial societies, living in small, tightly organized communities, the exposure to highly potent disease agents may account for the major part of disease causation. Under these circumstances variations in susceptibility due to social processes may be of relatively little importance. With increasing culture contact, populations become increasingly protected from such disease agents but simultaneously exposed to ... social processes.... Variations in susceptibility now assume greater importance in the etiological picture and the concomitant changes in such factors as diet, physical activity, and cigarette smoking will facilitate the emergence of new manifestations of such susceptibility.[19]

A social-intervention technology is developing.[20] Professional skills in behavioral-change strategies are aimed at helping individuals develop the motivation to change deleterious health habits or comply better with medical regimens (see Chapter 19). While behavioral-change strategies aimed at increasing positive health habits among large population groups may be a desirable public health goal, some writers on the subject raise questions about the potential intrusion of government support (and perhaps control) in this realm of health care. Lalonde comments:

The ultimate philosophical issue raised by the concept is whether, and to what extent, government can get into the business of modifying human behavior, even if it does so to improve health. The marketing of social change is a new field which applies the marketing techniques of the business world to getting people to change their behavior, i.e. eating habits, exercise habits, smoking habits, driving habits, etc. It is argued by some that proficiency in social marketing would inevitably lead government into all kinds of undesirable thought control and propaganda. The dangers of governmental proficiency in social marketing are recognized but so are the evident abuses resulting from all other kinds of marketing. If the siren song of coloured television, for example, is creating an indolent and passive use of leisure time, has the government not the duty to counteract its effects by marketing programs aimed at promoting physical recreation? As previously mentioned, in Canada some 76% of the population over age 13 devote less than one hour a week to participation in sports while 84% of the same population spends four or more hours weekly watching television. This kind of imbalance extends to the amount of money being spent by the private sector on marketing products and services, some of which, if abused, contribute to sickness and death. One must inevitably conclude that society, through government, owes it to itself to develop protective marketing techniques to counteract those abuses.[21]

Lalonde's view is open to debate and further discussion. Protection of client rights, privacy, and full disclosure of treatment effects are values long supported by the social work profession. Potential abuse by government or any other group in society must be guarded against. At the same time, social workers can be an instrumental force in reshaping the health care system by helping to shift the focus from cure to care and from illness treatment to health promotion. While the new behavioral strategies seem promising, it is important for social workers to remember that no amount of behavioral change aimed at better personal health habits will offset the weight of longstanding racial discrimination, substandard housing, and inferior education, which have contributed in large part to the poor health of low-income and minority groups. These "unhealthy" social conditions cannot be cured by a shot of penicillin. Many of the solutions to these problems lie beyond the medical care system.

NOTES

1. Peter Steinfels, "The Concept of Health," *Hastings Center Studies* 1, no. 3 (1973):4.
2. Bess Dana, "Health, Social Work, and Social Justice," in Bernard Ross and Charles Shireman, eds., *Social Work Practice and Social Justice* (Washington, D.C.: National Association of Social Workers, 1973), p. 123.
3. Milton Terris, "Approaches to an Epidemiology of Health," *American Journal of Public Health* 65, no. 10 (October 1975):1038.
4. Betty Gilson et al., "The Sickness Impact Profile: Development of an Outcome Measure of Health Care," *American Journal of Public Health* 65, no. 2 (December 1975):1304–14.
5. Terris, op. cit., p. 1038.
6. F. E. Viteri, "Considerations on the Effect of Nutrition on the Body Composition and Physical Working Capacity of Young Guatemalan Adults," in N. S. Scrimshaw and A. M. Altschul, eds., *Amino Acid Fortification of Protein Foods* (Cambridge, Mass.: M.I.T. Press, 1971), pp. 350–75.
7. U.S. Department of Health, Education and Welfare, Public Health Service, *Total Loss of Teeth in Adults, United States, 1960–1962,* National Health Survey, ser. 11, no. 27 (Washington, D.C.: Government Printing Office, 1967) and *Prevalence of Selected Impairments, United States, July 1963–June 1965,* National Health Survey, ser. 10, no. 48 (Washington, D.C.: Government Printing Office, 1968).
8. Margaret Nielsen et al., "Older Persons After Hospitalization: A Controlled Study of Home Aide Service," *American Journal of Public Health* 62, no. 8 (August 1972):1094–1100.
9. Fortune Mannino and Milton Shore, "Demonstrating Effectiveness in an Aftercare Program" (Brief Notes), *Social Work,* May 1974, p. 352.
10. Robert Perkins et al., "Multiple-Influence Paradigms in Illness," *Social Casework,* November 1975, pp. 531–37.
11. *What You Should Know About Health Care* (Washington-Alaska Blue Cross Association, 1972).
12. Ralph Buncher, "Cigarette Smoking: Social Disease in an Intolerant Social Climate," *American Journal of Public Health* 65, no. 11 (November 1976):1107.
13. Neil Bracht, "The Social Nature of Chronic Illness and Disability," Margaret Brogden Symposium, Johns Hopkins Hospital (Baltimore: September 30, 1977).
14. William Richardson, "Poverty, Illness, and the Use of Health Services in the United States," *Hospitals* 43, (July 1969):249.
15. E. White, "Age and Income Differentials in Selected Aspects of Morbidity, Disability and Utilization of Health Services," *Inquiry* 5, no. 1 (March 1968):18–20.
16. U.S. Department of Health, Education and Welfare, *Health of the American Indian,* Publication no. 73-51118 (Washington, D.C.: April 1973), 30 pp.
17. Robert Aranda, "The Mexican-American Syndrome," *American Journal of Public Health* 61, no. 1 (January 1971):104–09.
18. Y. Scott Matsumoto, "Social Stress and Coronary Heart Disease in Japan," in Hans Peter Dreitzel, ed., *The Social Organization of Health,* (New York: McMahon, 1971), pp. 123–49.

19. John Cassel, "An Epidemiologic Perspective of Psychosocial Factors in Disease Etiology," *American Journal of Public Health* 64 (November 1974):1040–43.
20. R. Stuart, "A Three Dimensional Program for the Treatment of Obesity," in Katz and Zlutnick, eds., *Behavior Therapy and Health Care,* (New York: Pergamon Press, 1975), pp. 585–99.
21. Marc Lalonde, *A New Perspective on the Health of Canadians: A Working Document* (Ottowa: Information Canada, 1975), p. 36.

SUGGESTED   ADDITIONAL   READINGS

Bell, Daniel. *The Coming of Post Industrial Society: A Venture in Social Forecasting.* New York: Basic Books, 1973.

Carlson, Rick, "Health in America: What Are the Prospects?" *Center Magazine* 5 (November-December 1972):47.

Coe, Rodney, and Albert Wessen, "Social-Psychological Factors Influencing the Use of Community Health Resources," *American Journal of Public Health* 55, no. 7 (July 1965):1022–31.

Farber, Arthur, "The Peckham Experiment Revisited: Cultivating Health," *Health and Social Work* 1, no. 3 (August 1976):28–38.

Graham, Saxon, "Studies of Behavior Change to Enhance Public Health," *American Journal of Public Health* 63 (April 1973):327–34.

Grinnell, Richard, and Nancy Kyte, "Environmental Modification: A Study," *Social Work* 20, no. 4 (July 1975):313–18.

Katz, Alfred. "The Social Causes of Disease." In *The Social Organization of Health,* edited by Hans Peter Dreitzel. A recent sociology no. 3, New York: McMahon, 1971, pp. 5–14.

Lewis, Ronald, and Ho Mankeung, "Social Work with Native Americans," *Social Work,* September 1975, pp. 379–82.

Maruyama, Magoran, "Yellow Youth's Psychological Struggle," *Mental Hygiene* 55, no. 3 (July 1971).

Mayfield, William G., "Mental Health in the Black Community," *Social Work* 17, no. 3 (May 1972):106–110.

Sisson, Daniel, "Social Futures Related to Health Care Delivery," *Center Report* 6, no. 1 (February 19, 1973):14–16.

Somers, Anne. *Health Care in Transition: Directions for the Future.* (See esp. chap. 2, "The Patient.") Hospital Research and Educational Trust, 1971, 161 pp.

8/ASSESSING THE PSYCHOSOCIAL EFFECTS OF ILLNESS

DONA LANSING BRACHT

~~~~~~

The will to live is not a theoretical abstraction, but a physiologic reality with therapeutic characteristics . . . I was incredibly fortunate to have as my doctor a man who knew that his greatest job was to encourage to the fullest the patient's will to live and to mobilize all the natural resources of body and mind to combat disease.

—Norman Cousins

In Chapter 7 the relationship between contemporary illness patterns and community demographic and cultural factors was discussed. In this chapter focus is directed more specifically at variables that need to be considered before an individualized psychosocial treatment plan is developed. In addition to knowledge of the somatic malady affecting the patient (as discussed in Chapter 5), "assessment" of the physically sick individual takes into account the social, personal, familial, and economic aspects of his/her life that bear on recovery and/or adjustment to illness. As such, the task involves an analysis of (1) the patient's unique personal history, (2) individual strengths and weaknesses, (3) the social/environmental milieu, (4) the medical system in which the patient finds himself/herself, (5) economic resources, (6) the individual's reaction to the illness problem, and (7) changes in life style brought about by illness—both immediate and long term.

The primary objective of a professional assessment is the organization of pertinent information toward an individual treatment plan. This provides baseline information against which treatment interventions can be measured. Such information, clearly stated, is useful not only to social workers but also to other members of the health care team. This is especially true in utilizing the problem-oriented medical record system.[1] Clarity and specificity are essential prerequisites for the needed improvement of social work information and accountability systems. As mentioned in Chapter 2, professional autonomy depends to a large extent on the ability to demonstrate and document one's effectiveness.

In working with a patient and his/her family throughout various phases of illness, the social worker uses relationship skills in tandem with objective criteria. The diagnostic process becomes one of balancing the patient's environmental and personal strengths against the debilitating forces of disease. An important question involves *what* to assess and to *what* degree. Thus before discussing several approaches to assessment that lend themselves to practice in health settings it seems appropriate to consider the spectrum of effects and reactions that the patient and family are likely to experience during various phases and kinds of illness and treatment. Special attention will be given to the concept of "sick role" in understanding individual responses to illness. Life style and stress as both cause and effect of illness will be discussed as critical assessment foci. Following a brief description of the common reactions to illness, selective assessment tools derived from differing theoretical perspectives (behavioral, dynamic, etc.) will be presented. Suggested additional readings for the practitioner are also listed.

SICK ROLE

Much of our theoretical understanding regarding the motivations and behaviors related to illness episodes have evolved out of social science research aimed at validating the Parsonian model of the "sick role." First introduced by Talcott Parsons in 1951, the concept of sick role was described as an institutionalized expectation system with two major rights and two major obligations. The occupant of the sick role is
   1. not responsible for his/her illness as it is beyond his/her control.
   2. exempt from normal social role obligations.
   3. under obligation to seek technically competent help.
   4. expected to cooperate in the process of getting well.
According to Parsons, "the element of exemption from ordinary role-obligations may be interpreted as permissiveness for temporary relief from the strains of trying hard to achieve. The patient is permitted to indulge his dependency needs under strictly regulated conditions, notably his recognition of the conditional legitimacy of his state, and exposure to the therapeutic task."[2] As Kassebaum and Bauman have noted, "the normative expectations do not preclude the fact that a patient may enjoy various secondary gains due to illness, but these are purchased at a steep price, and accompanied by the obligation to cooperate actively toward his cure and subsequent resumption of usual role-obligations."[3] While accepting the applicability of the sick-role concept in a general sense and, especially, in the case of acute illness episodes, Kassebaum and Bauman have used it as a point of departure in investigating variations in sick-role norms and expectations. The usefulness of the sick-role concept in the psychosocial assessment process derives from the results of such studies, which address the varieties of reactions that people of different social, cultural and subcultural, economic, and educational backgrounds have to illness of varying kinds and severity. Also significant are studies that identify the stages through which the sick person "travels" from the symptom experience stage to the recovery or rehabilitation stage.[4] In practice terms the social

worker who renders service to the sick individual first seeks to understand the meaning that illness in general has for him or her. The social worker must then assess the unique implications of a particular illness for the patient throughout the several stages of illness.

Reactions to a medical diagnosis may be highly subjective and unrelated to the realities of the medical prognosis and physical ramifications of the illness. For example, the "dependent woman" who learns she is suffering from a chronic deteriorating condition such as rheumatoid arthritis might react in a way that manifests her characteristic tendency to be dependent on others. The active, independent woman who faces a hysterectomy might abhor the idea of being "surgically assaulted" and look for alternative treatments. Another patient facing the same operation may delight in belaboring every detail of her symptomotology, complain woefully to family and friends about minor discomforts, and prolong her recovery by indulging in too much bed rest and little or no exercise.

Patients who value independence and self-sufficiency also vary in their response to disability. The often-used idiom "will to live" or "will to get well" may defy applicability in some cases; for example, the "self-sufficient" businessman who suffers a severe heart attack may give up and become dependent on his significant others, feeling that the limitations imposed by his illness render him useless. A similar patient with a history of independent achievement might deny that he is seriously ill and reject all gestures of concern and outside efforts necessary for rehabilitation.

A study by Overs and Healy[5] suggests that aspects of a patient's value system may be important predictors of his/her reaction to illness and subsequent recovery. The study, which focused on stroke patients and their families, found that "certain values held by patients which prior to the stroke may have been adaptive or at least minimally impairing became maladaptive after the stroke." These factors were as follows:

1. Maintaining the rigidity of one's values as a virtue.

2. Keeping up appearances more important than solving problems.

3. For men, holding a job is necessary to maintain self-respect until after retirement age is reached.

4. For women, self-respect is earned only by doing housework.

5. Dependence on people outside the family is undesirable even in a reciprocal arrangement where something is contributed by the stroke victim's family.

The Kassebaum and Bauman study mentioned earlier surveyed reactions by four groups of chronically ill people (patients with (1) arteriosclerotic heart disease, (2) diabetes, (3) psychoneurosis, or (4) multiple diagnoses) to their illness. Findings indicated that sick-role attitudes differed according to such variables as age, sex, ethnicity, education, occupation, and diagnosis. Regarding the latter variable, the authors poignantly conclude that "sick role expectations are influenced not only by the patient's accustomed roles but by the effects of his particular diagnosis on his capacity for performing them." For example, diabetics were found to be less inclined to deny their illness than people with multiple diagnoses. Older patients and blue-collar workers were found to have more concern about role performance than other groups.

A common theme running through the Parsonian sick-role model and research aimed at further development of the concept suggests the importance of individual predisposition toward dependence and/or independence (prior to illness onset) as an important assessment variable. The individual's tendencies to adopt or reject aspects of the sick role in varying degrees may interact dynamically with his/her perceived or actual loss of independence and desire to become more dependent or obtain relief from independent achievement. As previously stated, the behavior of individuals who characteristically value independence may or may not reflect an orientation toward self-sufficiency during an illness episode. In the same light, patients whose previous patterns of coping with stress suggest extreme dependence on others may insist on "doing things for themselves" and deny that they are ill.

In summary, a broad spectrum of reactions and attitudes toward illness are within the realm of possibility. The concept of sick role is limited to the degree that it ascribes a common set of expectations and behaviors to all sick people. It is useful to the degree that it helps the practitioner understand variation in human response to illness. Increasingly, emphasis is being placed on the psychological aspects of illness, especially as reflected in the patient's will to survive. Unexplained medical recoveries do occur, and in what medical or social context do we explain them? "Natural resources" do exist in each patient that, if activated, can bring together the forces needed for adaptation and recovery.

LIFE STYLE, STRESS, AND SICKNESS

The role of an individual's life style in the etiology of disease and the rehabilitation process is a subject that has been studied from several vantage points. The following perspective draws heavily upon a chapter by Edward Sachar entitled "The Current Status of Psychosomatic Medicine," which can be found in *Psychological Care of the Medically Ill,* by Strain and Grossman.[6] According to Sachar, the question of just how specific and nonspecific life stress leads to somatic disease has been a central focus of psychosomatic research over the past twenty years. Many diseases, such as peptic ulcer, ulcerative colitis, neurodermatitis, and rheumatoid arthritis, are currently seen as "psychosomatically unresearchable." This is due largely to the fact that the actual medical nature of the primary disorders has yet to be identified. In other words, "How can one study the pathways by which emotional states lead to flare-ups of rheumatoid arthritis if one does not know what system is basically awry in that illness? Is rheumatoid arthritis an autoimmune disease, a latent viral infection, an enzymatic defect of the synovial membrane cells, or a collagen disease? The strategies of psychosomatic research would be quite different in each instance." As a result psychosomatic research has turned away from studies of complex disease entities and toward somatic systems that are influenced by psychological variables and whose responses are measurable. Sachar gives a few examples of such systems and describes some of these new research directions:

1. *Autonomic nervous system:* Studies applying principles of instrumental conditioning to autonomic responsivity suggest that it is possible to "learn" autonomic response patterns. Original observations showed that animals and people could be "trained" to raise and lower blood pressure, alter vascular flow, change pulmonary resistance, and so forth. Biofeedback experiments along these lines continue.

2. *Neuroendocrine system:* Psychological stimuli are known to have important influences on neuroendocrine control mechanisms that regulate the secretion of anterior pituitary hormones such as ACTH, cortisol, growth hormone, prolactic, testosterone, and perhaps TSH and thyroxin. "Because this group of hormones from the pituitary and its target glands affect virtually every biochemical process in the body, it is obvious that the neuroendocrine system could play a significant role in somatic disease."

3. *Psychophysiology:* Research in this area operates on the premise "that just as there appear to be critical periods in development when psychological patterns can be imprinted, there also may be critical periods for the imprinting of physiological response patterns. . . . In the human neonate, developmental psychophysiological research has focused on identifying some of the inborn constitutional differences between infants in psychophysiological responsivity, traits that may someday help account for the differences between people in their susceptibility to certain illnesses."

4. *Cardiovascular physiology:* Research with mice has demonstrated that alteration of the psychosocial environment affects blood pressure. "With increasing crowding, social disorganization and confrontations over dominance, the mice develop hypertension with pathological consequences—experimental observations that might make the urban dweller uncomfortable indeed."

5. *Gastrointestinal system:* Experiments altering the nature of conditioned psychological stress and range of coping devices available to the animal increased and decreased the amount of gastric ulceration produced.

A final quote from Sachar rings a note of cautious optimism to the mental health practitioner in the health field:

There is every reason to believe that with increased medical understanding of the pathogenesis of diseases such as atherosclerosis and rheumatoid arthritis, a linkage will eventually be made between the two growing spheres of research. When and if this occurs, we can look forward to the development of a true science of psychosomatic medicine. In the interim, the liaison psychiatrist will wisely refrain from excessive psychologizing in his approach to patients with peptic ulcer or rheumatoid arthritis, but he will be more aware than ever of the vulnerability of every patient's physiology to the stresses and strains of everyday life.[7]

One particularly important work in the area of life stress and illness is the development by Holmes and Rahe[8] of the Social Readjustment Rating Scale, which may be used to measure an individual's predisposition toward illness. Numerical values are assigned to certain life events (see Table 8.1) that have been identified (empirically) as stressful in and of themselves. People who score within a certain range on the scale or have experienced several stressful events in proximity are said to be more vulnerable to illness, a viable response to stress. As such, illness is both a stressor that renders an individual vulnerable to more illness and a result of several stressful life events that predispose one to sickness. Within this context stress becomes a primary conceptual target in the assessment process. The social worker might ask, "What events such as loss of job, death in the family, overwork, financial problems, and the like might have contributed to the particular illness of the patient? Which interventions will be most effective with that particular patient in ameliorating causative stress and resultant strain and preventing a recurrence?" Of particular importance is an evaluation of the individual's characteristic ways of dealing with stress (e.g., what are the typical behaviors employed to "unwind" from a "bad" day at the office or at the assembly line?). Perhaps the stressful event is of less concern than the patient's reaction to it. Assessment of the resultant strain brought on by the exigencies of illness is important in an immediate and anticipatory sense. Reducing environmental complications that exacerbate the stressful impact of illness will greatly enhance the recovery process. A mother who has had a difficult childbirth and is experiencing postpartum exhaustion may need to find child care for the other children in the home simply to reduce the amount of stimulation in her environment. On the other hand, a similar patient may find that having her children at home maintains the domestic status quo, which for her is less stressful than "peace and quiet."

   Helping a patient redesign his/her life style to avoid another medical crisis or to manage current symptoms often requires ingenuity and resourcefulness on the parts of all involved—patient, social worker, family, physician, and friends. A review of the literature on alterations in life style as a result of illness points to the increasing prevalence of this often neglected aspect of illness. Ferguson and McPhail reported that 20 percent of the patients in their study required drastic alteration in their living arrangements after discharge from the hospital.[9] Suchman[10] found that one out of five patients reported that their current medical diagnosis and treatment called for changes in their eating, drinking, and smoking habits. Thirty percent had restrictions on their household duties and social activities. Patients in this study listed their first concerns as those related to the seriousness of their illness and the likelihood of recovery. Their second concerns were social in nature and included the following:

TABLE 8.1

Social Readjustment Rating Scale

Life Events	Mean Value
Trouble with boss	23
Change in sleeping habits	16
Change in eating habits	15
Revision of personal habits	24
Change in recreation	19
Change in social activities	18
Change in church activities	19
Change in number of family get-togethers	15
Change in financial state	38
Trouble with in-laws	29
Change in number of arguments with spouse	35
Sex difficulties	39
Death of close family member	63
Death of spouse	100
Death of close friend	37
Gain of new family member	39
Change in health of family member	44
Change in residence	20
Minor violations of the law	11
Jail term	63
Business readjustment	39
Marriage	50
Divorce	73
Marital separation	65
Outstanding personal achievement	28
Son or daughter leaving home	29
Retirement	45
Change in work hours or conditions	20
Change in responsibilities at work	29
Fired at work	47
Change in living conditions	25
Wife begins or stops work	26
Mortgage over $10,000	31
Mortgage or loan less than $10,000	17
Foreclosure of mortgage or loan	30
Vacation	13
Change in schools	20
Change to different line of work	36
Begins or ends school	26
Marital reconciliation	45
Pregnancy	40
Personal injury or illness	53

Source: T. H. Holmes and R. H. Rahe, "The Social Readjustment Rating Scale," *Journal of Psychosomatic Research* 11 (August 1967):213–18. Reprinted with permission of Pergamon Press, Inc.

- 50% concerned about carrying on normal activities
- 22% concerned about loss of independence
- 37% concerned about the cost of treatment
- 30% concerned about loss of work
- 15% concerned about the interruption of previously made plans

Shanas found that 14 percent of those 65 or over suffered important functional loss requiring additional social supports.[11]

Two important areas (see Table 8.2) to consider when anticipating possible life style changes for patients include (1) the changing of daily living habits in order to manage a medical regimen and (2) the changing of deleterious living habits that may have been causal factors in the illness. Strauss, in his excellent book entitled *Chronic Illness and the Quality of Life,* offers the health worker many rich insights into the life style adjustments of the chronically ill. He notes that

major redesigning can involve moving to a one-story house, buying clothes that cloak disfigurement, getting the boss to assign jobs that require less strength, and using crutches

TABLE 8.2

Assessment Checklist for Evaluating Possible Life Style Changes
Related to Illness and Recovery

I. Changing of daily living habits in order to manage a medical regimen
  A. Compliance with medication schedules
  B. Arrangement of social life so as not to interfere with regimen
  C. Changes required on the part of other family members in order to comply with regimen
  D. Restructuring physical surroundings (housing, temporary convalescent care)
  E. Management of home care protocol, e.g., renal dialysis
  F. Frequent transportation to medical facilities
  G. Dietary changes that require planning and special preparation
  H. Increase or restriction in daily exercise
  I. Changes in sexual activity
  J. Restricted travel
  K. Need for outside help in management of medical regimen or domestic chores, e.g., specialized nursing and/or meals on wheels
  L. Changes in occupational role and/or routine brought on by illness
  M. Need for specialized vocational-educational or rehabilitative programs

II. Changing deleterious living habits that may have been causal factors in illness
  A. Smoking
  B. Nutritional habits (overeating, poor diet)
  C. Excessive or moderate drinking
  D. Ineffective relaxation and/or rest behaviors
  E. Reduction of stressful occupational and/or social activity
  F. Increase or decrease in physical exercise
  G. Interpersonal conflict within family or social milieu
  H. Other psychological/behavioral disturbance(s)

or other aids to mobility. Some of the alternative possibilities are more unusual; they are based on the ingenuity of the sufferer or on his stumbling on a solution.[12]

In the future, assisting patients with the requisite personal skills as well as necessary community supports for life style changes will become a major aspect of social work in health care. Frequently these efforts will require the combined contributions of the interdisciplinary team. The social work component of helping clients comply with medical and health promotion regimens is discussed by Levy in Chapter 19. The challenge to social work to contribute new knowledge to our understanding of the relationship between environmentally stressful events and the development of disease has never been more promising.

REACTIONS TO AND EFFECTS OF ILLNESS AND INSTITUTIONALIZATION

Any attempt to explain and/or categorize emotional reactions to a particular illness will of necessity appear to the practicing social worker as an oversimplification. Descriptions of feeling states associated with illness fall short of revealing the complexity, intensity, and individual variation in such reactions. To those involved in the illness experience of a single individual, his/her behaviors and attitudes are expressions of his/her comfort or discomfort as an occupant of the patient role. The more compliance and cooperation the patient demonstrates, the easier he/she makes it for those directly involved with his/her care. The social worker needs to be aware of "good patient" behaviors that may mask certain fears and insecurities brought on by insitutionalization and illness. Some patients may demonstrate such feelings overtly, often through some form of noncompliance. It is safe to assume that the most cheerful and willing of patients experience some realistic concern related to the nature and severity of their diagnosis. Past experiences with regard to illness or other experiences in which the patient learned to trust or distrust others, as well as culturally entrenched beliefs and attitudes, may predispose the individual to certain apprehensions and expectations with regard to the care he/she receives. A medically knowledgeable patient cannot help but wince at futuristic machines, implements, and sophisticated gadgetry essential to his/her diagnosis and treatment. Patients are under obligation to surrender their bodies to the expertise of a strange environment. They forfeit the sense of predictability that their world heretofore held for them. Some excerpts from a study by Tagliacozzo and Mauksch[13] in which eighty-six cardiovascular and gastrointestinal patients were interviewed highlight the patient's view of his hospital experience:

They directly expressed their awareness of their inability to control those who are in charge of their care. Patients felt that they were subject to rewards and punishment and that essential services can be withheld unless they make themselves acceptable. Some of these patients were dependent upon intimate forms of physical assistance, and their points of view reflected their awareness of this dependence upon others.

A male patient with gastrointestinal illness expressed his fear as follows:

When you are really sick, you are at the mercy of the hospital staff. In my opinion, you've got to have luck on your side. You've got to be lucky enough to get key people in the hospital who are really alert and wish to do a job; and have someone on the shift at the time you need them who wants to give the service or you are just out of luck. I think you could die in one of these hospitals of a heart attack before anybody came in to help you. Perceptions of the patient role make it unlikely that such fears will be openly expressed by many patients. It is one of the obligations of a patient to have "trust and confidence" in those who care for him. The expression of these concerns could thus be interpreted as a failure to conform to these obligations.

For a detailed account of characteristic reactions and coping behaviors associated with specific illnesses, the reader is directed to Chapter 9, which provides a bibliographical reference to psychosocial treatment with over sixty illness categories. Two common categories of reactions to illness deserve comment and further elaboration here.

GRIEF AND DEPRESSION

Grief reactions are distinguished here from depression, although the terms are often used interchangeably. According to Sachar, the affect and mental preoccupations of the depressed patient are generally out of proportion to reality, whereas grief is a reaction to a loss or disappointment and generally occurs in proximity to a precipitating event.[14] Depressed patients often exhibit sad affect and low activity levels that are independent of external events, while the medical patient is expected to express some disappointment and sadness over loss of health and its multiple consequences. Strain and Grossman list some of the emotional precursors to grief during an illness episode:[15]

1. separation from loved ones for several days or weeks of hospitalization
2. loss of ability to work
3. fear of loss of functions and of an independent way of life
4. fear of losing the esteem of family and colleagues who perceive him/her as an impaired or vulnerable person
5. change in self-image
6. fear of loss of control of developmentally achieved functions, e.g., bowel or bladder control, speech, sexuality
7. fear of loss or injury to body parts
8. fear of strangers in whom care is entrusted and to whom patient has no personal ties
9. fear of loss of life itself

It should be emphasized here that the possibility of severe depression following or precipitating illness should be considered. A patient who exhibits prolonged depressive symptoms in spite of an improved physical condition may require treatment for the depression itself. When assessing a medical patient who has a history of depressive illness, the diagnostician must be careful to differentiate between symptoms. Specificity is required in tracking the onset and course of depression, and an assessment tool that deals exclusively with its antecedents and characteristics may be indicated. This is further complicated by the presence of certain physical symptoms in some illnesses that resemble those found in depressed patients, for example, fatigue, anorexia, and the like. The experienced worker will also take into account the effects of medication on the mood, level of physical energy, and mental alertness of his/her patients.

DENIAL

The term *denial* is commonly used in a psychological context, but clarity and consistency in its definition are not found in the literature. Depending on the orientation of the clinician, "denial" connotes "a flagrant escape from reality" or, less alarming, "difficulty in accepting the seriousness of a given diagnosis or situation."

Depending on the seriousness of the illness, many patients experience an initial reaction in which they find it difficult to believe that "it could happen to them." To be suddenly informed by a relative stranger (albeit expert) that he/she is at once vulnerable invokes in the individual a need to fight back and set things right again. A mild form of denial or "hope" for a new cure or surgical technique can sometimes function as a source of strength for the patient (and family) suffering from an incurable illness. However, a prolonged belief in the certainty of an unlikely cure may prevent the patient from following through with necessary life-sustaining treatments. In this case the therapist will have to decide (based on assessment of the patient's strengths and coping abilities) if it is prudent to confront him/her (or the family) with the medical realities.

THE PROCESS OF ASSESSMENT

The following section presents selected assessment approaches for use in the health setting. Special attention is given to the problem-oriented record (POR) and the behavioral assessment model as each is a relatively recent addition to the health care field and offers the clinician a more structured way of monitoring and evaluating treatment efforts.

THE PROBLEM-ORIENTED RECORD

The POR was developed by Weed as a solution to the lack of continuity and clarity characteristic of long and cumbersome medical records.[16] According to

Kane, "It provides a framework of organization that permits even long records to become coherent, usable and goal oriented."[17] The POR is increasingly being utilized in the hospital setting, private medical practice, community mental health settings, and psychiatric wards. Recommendations for its use are intended in part to answer criticisms leveled against social workers for their inadequate means of record keeping and accountability systems. Four major components form the basis of the POR and relate to four areas of problem solving: (1) acquisition of a data base, (2) problem identification, (3) development of a plan related to each identified problem, and (4) implementation of the plan.

The development of the data base varies according to the type of agency, the kinds of client populations served, and the nature of the interventions used. For purposes of establishing an adequate baseline, data base requirements must be consistent in amount and depth:

Too frequently within a single agency, and even within the work of a single practitioner, there is variation in the amount of background material that is recorded. Such material may range from long and detailed to short and skimpy and seems to be dictated solely by mood and convenience. But if records are to be reviewed in terms of prognosis or effectiveness of intervention, the initial data must be uniformly collected and transcribed.[18]

The problem list (not to be confused with "diagnosis") allows the worker to list observed behaviors and problems systematically and without inference as to causes and prognosis:

The problem list of the POR forces the recorder to avoid jargon or sweeping categories and to indicate problems at the highest level of understanding supported by the available data.[19]

As information about the particular problem increases, the problem may be redefined. The renamed problem retains the same identifying number as the original one, thus allowing the worker to trace the course of a single problem via the record. For example, "inability to hold a job" might later be reclassified as "mental retardation" or "lack of requisite job skills."

Once the data base and problem list have been established, the worker begins to formulate a plan for problem resolution. Two basic rules form the guidelines for this aspect of the POR: (1) Subsequent entries in the POR must refer to a previously identified problem, and (2) the rationale and basis for all decisions and information must be recorded. Four categories of information, Subjective, Objective, Assessment, and Plan (SOAP), govern the context of future POR entries. Subjective entries are based on information gained from the client or family. Objective information is gleaned from clinical observation, tests, referral data, census data, and so forth. Assessments and conclusions are based on the available data. The rationale for the treatment plan is clearly stated in terms of previously recorded information.

The Action portion of the POR records and describes the client's progress and responses throughout treatment. Again, subjective and objective entries are made in the record with notes regarding current assessments and plans that correspond to the ongoing information.

THE BEHAVIORAL ASSESSMENT MODEL

Behavior therapy is becoming increasingly visible in the health care setting both as a mode of direct practice and as a strategy for research efforts. Many health problems that stem from poor health habits and/or self-control (e.g., obesity) have been shown to be especially amenable to behavioral interventions. Behavioral techniques have been used to teach patients to control such disease symptoms as enuresis, irregular heart rates, high blood pressure, seizures, migraine headaches, and asthma. One particular advantage of behavior therapy is that treatment interventions are continually monitored and measured against baseline information gathered during the assessment phase of treatment. In fact it is the empirical nature of behavioral therapy that differentiates it from more traditional forms of therapy and information-gathering systems. The behavioral therapist records and tallies the frequency, intensity, and duration of maladaptive behaviors prior to initiating treatment. Thus his/her change efforts are put to an empirical test and the success or failure of intervention remains visible throughout treatment. As such, behavior therapy is a self-correcting methodology based strongly on principles of accountability. As an outgrowth of social learning theory, behavior therapy focuses primarily on observable, learned behaviors—their antecedents and consequences for the individual. During assessment the therapist is interested in an individual's past only to the extent that he/she may have *learned* maladaptive behaviors, feelings, and attitudes. In contrasting behavioral therapy with traditional therapies, Bandura states:

> *Most theories of maladaptive behavior are based on the disease concept, according to which abnormalities in behavior are considered symptoms of an underlying neurosis or psychic illness. Today many psychotherapists are advancing the view that behavior that is harmful to the individual or departs widely from accepted social and ethical norms should be viewed not as some kind of disease but as a way—which the person has learned —of coping with environmental demands. Treatment then becomes a problem of "social learning." The abnormal behavior can be dealt with directly, and in seeking to modify it the therapist can call on principles of learning that are based on experimentation and subject to testing and verification.[20]*

In situations in which a minor or major life style change is indicated following an illness, a behavioral assessment may give rise to creative solutions involving changes in the patient's physical surroundings, habitual sources of pleasure and relaxation, and material or social reinforcements. Rather than searching for evidence of repressed conflicts, the behavior therapist analyzes with the patient the behaviors that are troublesome and the personal-environmental factors that cue and maintain them. For example, in a behavioral self-control program the obese patient who seeks to lose fifty pounds is the coengineer of his/her treatment plan. He/she helps monitor caloric intake and records incidents that provoke excessive eating. The patient may utilize cognitive methods of self-control and be the primary dispenser of reinforcers throughout treatment.[21] In lieu of placing responsibility for his/her condition on some puzzling psychological conflict, and hence on the therapist for the solution, the patient takes control of his/her problem using the expertise of a skilled clinician.

Major categories and steps involved in a behavioral assessment include the following:

1. Observation, specification, and definition of target behaviors.
2. Measurement of the frequency, intensity, and duration of target behaviors.
3. Recording the antecedents and consequences of target behaviors (i.e., the relationship of the behavior to environmental determinants).

According to Katz and Zlutnick, important questions to be asked include the following:

A. What are the consequences of change for the patient and others in his social milieu? Will it expedite his recovery or improve upon management of his problems?

B. Under what conditions does the troublesome activity occur? i.e., what are the discriminative stimuli that occasion troublesome behavior that may be altered to effect behavioral change?

C. What are the reinforcing consequences for the behavior that might also be altered to produce corresponding change?

D. What alternative behaviors are available to the patient that might take the place of troublesome activity?

E. What operations are needed to assist the patient to learn these appropriate behaviors?[22]

4. Specification of treatment plan and method of evaluation.

Much of the information necessary for a complete problem assessment can be obtained from interviews with the patient and/or his/her family. For a more detailed account of behavioral assessment procedures the reader is referred to *Behavioral Assessment, a Practical Handbook,* by Hersen and Bellack (New York: Pergamon Press, 1976). Measurement procedures are explained in *Single Case Experimental Designs,* by M. Hersen and D. Barlow (New York: Pergamon Press, 1976); *How to Do Psychotherapy and How to Evaluate It,* by J. M. Gottman and S. R. Leiblum (New York: Holt, Rinehart and Winston, 1974); and *Behavior Modification in Applied Settings,* by Alan E. Kazdin (Homewood, Ill.: Dorsey Press, 1975).

THE MEDICAL-SOCIAL DIAGNOSIS MODEL

Doremus[23] has developed a "social system review" model that focuses on roles, reactions, relationships, and resources in making a medical-social diagnosis. Briefly, role review consists of an analysis of social functioning both prior to and at onset of illness. Assessment of reactions to illness includes (1) feelings about the illness that affect the patient's role and self-concept; (2) the patient's stage of adjustment, including shock, denial, depression, or beginning integration; (3) reactivation of any prior social dysfunction or psychiatric crisis; and (4) the patient's motivation for coping with the problem. The relationships of the patient to family and significant others are assessed according to their nature and the effect of the illness on them. Knowledge about the patient's resources includes (1) financial, (2) environmental, (3) institutional, and (4) personal information. This model is depicted in Figure 8.1.

Diagnostic data obtained from this model can be adapted to many record-keeping systems. Doremus shows in Figure 8.2 how the "four Rs" can be utilized with the problem-oriented medical record.

THE SICKNESS IMPACT PROFILE (SIP)

The SIP, developed by faculty at the University of Washington, is a "scaled measure of health related dysfunction designed for use in conjunction with other kinds of assessment in evaluation of health care services and particularly of comprehensive health care programs. It is a behavioral measure, independent of diagnostic criteria, which relies solely on an individual's perception of the impacts of sickness on his usual daily activities."[24] One advantage in the use of the SIP approach is that it relies neither on clinical diagnoses nor on subjective feeling states as a measure of illness impact. Rather, the SIP focuses on the behavioral-performance dimension of sickness as perceived by the individual patient. This instrument, while still in a developmental phase, shows promise in measuring congruence between provider and consumer perceptions related to illness and patient needs. (See Table 8.3.)

BEHAVIORAL SCALE—GERIATRIC PRACTICE

A final example of assessment approaches comes from the field of geriatric research. Developed by Jorgensen and Kane,[25] the Behavioral Scale was used with nursing home patients and describes fifteen categories of normal and abnormal behavior. This or similar models could be useful to social workers in monitoring patient progress and reactions to institutionalization. (See Table 8.4.)

SUMMARY

A major purpose of this chapter has been to orient the new worker to the process of assessment as an essential prerequisite to social treatment and evaluation in health settings. The concept of sick role was presented as one theoretical framework for understanding the range and variability of attitudes

I. **Individualization of the Patient:** value considerations (considerations of him or her as a whole person, a unique individual)

II. **Analysis of the Patient's Illness or Disability**
   A. Technical information (diagnosis or prognosis: possible
   permanent impairment)
   B. Socioethnic cultural influences
   C. Social implications (visibility, criticality, chronicity,
   predictability)

III. **Analysis of the Psychosocial Impact of the Illness on the
Patient and His Social Milieu**
   A. The patient's or his family's perception of his problems
   and goals
   B. The social system review
      1. *Roles* and prior social functioning: life-style (who
      he or she is: background, capacities, prior perfor-
      mance)
      2. *Reactions* to illness and life situation: feelings, atti-
      tudes, motivation for coping
      3. *Relationships* within his or her social milieu (who
      they are; nature of relationships)
      4. *Resources* for coping with his or her problems
         a. Financial (sources of payment for care; source
         of support)
         b. Environmental (community and housing; physical
         and emotional security)
         c. Institutional (vocational, educational, religious,
         social agencies)
         d. Personal: family, friends, affiliations (that influ-
         ence behavior or experiences; coping ability)

IV. **Medical-Social Diagnosis** (Impression and Plan)
   A. Assessment of the problem presented through the four
   Rs
   B. Medical, personal, interpersonal, practical (Impression)
   C. The range of interventive measures to be instituted and
   by whom (Plan)

FIG. 8.1. A conceptual model for a medical-social diagnosis.

Source: Bertha Doremus, "The Four R's: Social Diagnosis in Health Care," *Health and
Social Work* 1, no. 4 (November 1976): 127. Reprinted with permission of the National
Association of Social Workers.

and responses to illness. Individual life style, with special emphasis on life
stress, was highlighted as a major consideration in understanding the causes
and impact of illness. Several physical and emotional factors that can cause
fear, grief, depression, and noncompliance during hospitalization and/or illness were outlined. The "process" of assessment was described, beginning with

Social Work Data Base:
Problem No. and Title:
Source of Referral and Reason:
Sources of Data: How Obtained:
Family Constellation:

S   SUBJECTIVE
The patient's (or family's) perception of the problem and expectations
Reported data
  1. The patient's current roles identified; recent social functioning and pertinent background data
  2. Nature of his or her significant relationships
  3. Resources (financial, environmental, institutional, personal) of significance reported as available or lacking

O   OBJECTIVE
The social worker's professional evaluation of the patient's (and family's)
  4. Reactions—attitude, behavior, motivation, capacities; i.e., positive or negative reactions and interpersonal relationships observed.
Specific objective social data that is validated and of current significance

A   ASSESSMENT (The Medical-Social Diagnosis)
The social worker's assessment and listing of those problems that require intervention in regard to the patient's role functioning, interpersonal relationships, resources or reactions to the problems in his life situation

P   PLAN
Specific plans for intervention (social treatment or environmental services) or recommendations for interdisciplinary action

---

FIG. 8.2. The conceptual model for medical-social diagnosis applied to the problem-oriented medical record.

Source: Bertha Doremus, "The Four R's: Social Diagnosis in Health Care," *Health and Social Work* 1, no. 4 (November 1976): 136. Reprinted with permission of the National Association of Social Workers.

a focus on the problem-oriented record and followed by a discussion of the behavioral approach. Selected examples of other approaches were presented to provide the reader with a broader perspective. Throughout the chapter emphasis has been placed on the importance of clarity, specificity, and validity in gathering and recording assessment data. Whatever the worker's orientation, it is clear that the assessment process is fast becoming a critical element of quality assurance in the health care field. Social workers will be held more

128

TABLE 8.3

Categories and Selected Items of the Sickness Impact Profile

Category	Items Describing Behaviors Involved in or Related to	Selected Items	Scale Values
A	Social Interaction	I make many demands, for example, insist that people do things for me, tell them how to do things	7.7
		I am going out less to visit people	5.2
B	Ambulation or Locomotion Activity	I am walking shorter distances	3.3
		I do not walk at all	9.2
C	Sleep and Rest Activity	I lie down to rest more often during the day	4.6
		I sit around half asleep	8.1
D	Taking Nutrition	I am eating no food at all, nutrition is taken through tubes or intravenous fluids	12.3
		I am eating special or different food, for example, soft food, bland diet, low salt, low fat foods	5.6
E	Usual Daily Work	I often act irritable toward my work associates, for example, snap at them, give sharp answers, criticize easily	7.1
		I am not working at all	8.6
F	Household Management	I have given up taking care of personal or household business affairs, for example, paying bills, banking, working on budget	6.9
		I am doing *less* of the regular daily work around the house that I usually do	3.9
G	Mobility and Confinement	I stay within one room	9.9
		I stop often when traveling because of health problems	4.2

H	Movement of the Body	I am in a restricted position all the time	13.6
		I sit down, lie down, or get up only with someone's help	10.4
I	Communication Activity	I communicate only by gestures, for example, moving head, pointing, sign language	11.3
		I often lose control of my voice when I talk, for example, my voice gets louder, starts trembling, changes pitch	6.4
J	Leisure Pastimes and Recreation	I am doing more physically inactive pastimes instead of my other usual activities	3.9
		I am going out for entertainment less often	2.8
K	Intellectual Functioning	I have difficulty reasoning and solving problems, for example, making plans, making decisions, learning new things	8.3
		I sometimes behave as if I were confused or disoriented in place or time, for example, where I am, who is around, directions, what day it is	11.2
L	Interaction with Family Members	I isolate myself as much as I can from the rest of the family	8.9
		I am not doing the things I usually do to take care of my children or family	6.8
M	Emotions, Feelings, and Sensations	I act irritable and impatient with myself, for example, talk badly about myself, swear at myself, blame myself for things that happen	5.4
		I laugh and cry suddenly for no reason	8.1
N	Personal Hygiene	I dress myself, but do so very slowly	4.6
		I do not have control of my bowels	11.2

Source: Betty S. Gilson et al., "The Sickness Impact Profile, Development of an Outcome Measure of Health," *American Journal of Public Health* 65, no. 12 (December 12) pp 1304–10. Reprinted with permission of the American Public Health Association, Inc.

TABLE 8.4

Behavioral Scale Utilized in Geriatric Practice

Instructions: In using this rating form, observers should adhere to the following guidelines:

1. Circle the one statement that most accurately describes the individual as you have usually observed him.

2. Focus on what you have seen the individual do in the last week. Several examples have been provided to indicate the kinds of activity that constitute each category. In selecting the most accurate descriptive statement, base your decision, whenever possible, on such indices as the frequency with which the activity occurs, its intensity, or its duration.

3. Rate all individuals on each item before moving on to the next item.

4. Be objective and don't let personal feelings bias your ratings.

5. An individual may have both favorable and unfavorable ratings in different areas. Judge each category independently of all others.

Behavior Category	*Signs*

1. *Complains* of physical problems
  a. More than once a day
  b. At least once a day
  c. Less than once a day
  d. Almost never
	Spontaneously or upon inquiry complains of such problems as pain, sleeping problems, fatigue, or restlessness.

2. *Eats* all of prepared meals
  a. Almost never
  b. At least once a day
  c. More than once a day
  d. Nearly always
	Consumes all of the prepared meal except for occasional food dislikes.

3. *Sleeps* well
  a. Less than once a week
  b. About four times a week
  c. Almost every night
	Sleeps uninterrupted throughout the night.

4. Is *pleasant* in dealings with others
  a. Usually very grouchy
  b. Most often grouchy
  c. Most frequently pleasant
  d. Almost always pleasant
	Gives friendly answers when spoken to; gets along with others; is neither irritable nor grouchy.

5. Is *sullen* or *depressed*
  a. Always sullen
  b. Most frequently sullen
  c. Rarely sullen
  d. Most often cheerful
	Nonresponsive to others; preoccupied with gloomy thoughts; talks or moves sluggishly.

6. Is *hostile* or *irritable*
  a. Always hostile
  b. Usually hostile
  c. Rarely hostile
  d. Usually friendly
	Gives abrupt or unfriendly answers when spoken to; is demanding or complaining.

7. Is *excited*
  a. Always very excited
  b. Usually excited
  c. Rarely excited
  d. Almost never excited
	Talks quickly and frequently, changes the subject; flighty; unable to sit still for longer than a few minutes.

TABLE 8.4 *(Continued)*

8. Is *suspicious*
   a. Very frequently suspicious
   b. Often suspicious
   c. Rarely suspicious
   d. Almost never suspicious

States that others are out to get him or pick on him, or have prevented him from attaining certain goals; reacts strongly to slight and unintended injury.

9. Is *disoriented* or *confused*
   a. Always very disoriented
   b. Usually disoriented
   c. Rarely disoriented
   d. Signs of disorientation not observed

Makes inaccurate statements about happenings in the home; cannot perform routine tasks without becoming "lost"; cannot participate in back and forth conversation; does not know his name.

10. Shows signs of *poor memory*
    a. Always very forgetful
    b. Usually forgetful
    c. Rarely forgetful
    d. Poor memory not observed

Forgets to carry out routine assignemtns as well as names of patients and staff around him; requires frequent reminding.

11. Shows signs of *impaired thinking*
    a. Never really understands
    b. Understands some of the time
    c. Usually understands
    d. Immediately grasps what he is told

Requires repeated explanation before grasping things that are told to him. (Exclude difficulty attributable to hearing loss.)

12. Is *withdrawn* socially
    a. Very withdrawn--will not speak
    b. Moderately withdrawn—interacts only when encouraged by others
    c. Frequently talks with others and initiates functional activity on his own

Sits alone most of the time; rarely talks or moves around.

13. *Appearance* is
    a. Almost always disorderly
    b. Frequently disorderly
    c. Rarely disorderly
    d. Almost never disorderly

Appearance includes dress, hair, and beard for males.

14. Shows *independent action*
    a. Almost always dependent on others
    b. Usually dependent on others
    c. Occasionally dependent on others
    d. Usually behaves independently of others

Does things that are *expected of him* without having to be told how and when to do it; does not rely on others to perform tasks he could do himself.

15. Engages in *activities*
    a. Almost never
    b. Infrequently
    c. Sometimes
    d. Regularly

Has hobbies, plays games, watches TV, reads, attends functions away from the nursing home, etc.

Source: Lou Ann B. Jorgensen and Robert L. Kane, "Social Work in a Nursing Home: A Need and an Opportunity," *Social Work in Health Care* 1, no. 4 (Summer 1976):480-81.

131

accountable for the outcomes of their interventions. The art of social work will continue to be refined through scientific validation. Finally, it should be noted that in the last analysis it is the patient who gives direction to the process.

NOTES

1. Rosalie Kane, "Look to the Record," *Social Work* 19, no. 4 (July 1974):412–19.
2. Talcott Parsons, "Definitions of Health and Illness in the Light of American Values and Social Structure," in E. G. Jaco, ed. *Patients, Physicians and Illness* (New York: Free Press, 1958), p. 183.
3. Gene Kassebaum and Barbara Bauman, "Dimensions of the Sick Role and Chronic Illness," in E. G. Jaco, ed., *Patients, Physicians and Illness* (New York: Free Press, 1958), pp. 141–42.
4. Edward Suchman, "Stages of Illness and Medical Care," in E. G. Jaco, ed., *Patients, Physicians and Illness* (New York: Free Press, 1958), pp. 155–70.
5. Robert Overs and John Healy, "Stroke Patients: Their Spouses, Families and Community," in A. Beatrice Cobb, ed., *Medical and Psychological Aspects of Disability* (Springfield, Ill.: Charles C Thomas, 1973), pp. 87–117.
6. Edward Sachar, "The Current Status of Psychosomatic Medicine," in James Strain and Stanley Grossman, ed., *Psychological Care of the Medically Ill: A Primer in Liaison Psychiatry* (New York: Appleton-Century-Crofts, 1975), pp. 54–63.
7. Ibid., p. 61.
8. T. H. Holmes and R. H. Rahe, "The Social Readjustment Rating Scale," *Journal of Psychosomatic Research* 11 (August 1967):213–18.
9. Thomas Ferguson and A. N. MacPhail, *Hospital and Community* (London: Oxford University Press, 1954).
10. Suchman, op. cit., p. 165.
11. Ethel Shanas, "Health Status of Older People: Cross-National Implications," *American Journal of Public Health* 64, no. 3 (March 1974).
12. Anselm Strauss, *Chronic Illness and the Quality of Life* (St. Louis: C. V. Mosby, 1975), p. 36.
13. Daisy Tagliacozzo and Hans Mauksch, "The Patient's View of the Patient's Role," in E. G Jaco, ed., *Patients, Physicians and Illness* (New York: Free Press, 1958), pp. 172–85.
14. Edward Sachar, "Evaluating Depression in the Medical Patient," in James Strain and Stanley Grossman, eds., *Psychological Care of the Medically Ill* (New York: Appleton-Century-Crofts, 1975), pp. 64–75.
15. James Strain and Stanley Grossman, *Psychological Care of the Mentally Ill* (New York: Appleton-Century-Crofts, 1975), pp. 26–28.
16. Lawrence L. Weed, *Medical Records, Medical Education, and Patient Care* (Cleveland: Case Western Reserve University Press, 1969).
17. Kane, op. cit., p. 413.
18. Ibid., p. 414.
19. Ibid.
20. A. Bandura, "Behavioral Psychotherapy," *Scientific American* 216 (March 1967):78.
21. Alan S. Bellack and Jeffrey S. Schwartz, "Assessment for Self-Control Programs," in Michael Hersen and Alan Bellack, *Behavioral Assessment, a Practical Handbook* (New York: Pergamon Press, 1976), pp. 111–42.
22. Roger C. Katz and Steven Zlutnick, *Behavior Therapy and Health Care, Principles and Applications* (New York: Pergamon Press, 1975), p. 30.
23. Bertha Doremus, "The Four R's: Social Diagnosis in Health Care," *Health and Social Work* 1, no. 4 (November 1976):120–39.

24. Betty S. Gilson et al., "The Sickness Impact Profile, Development of an Outcome Measure of Health Care," *American Journal of Public Health* 65, no. 12 (December 1975):1304–10.
25. Lou Ann B. Jorgensen and Robert L. Kane, "Social Work in a Nursing Home: A Need and an Opportunity," *Social Work in Health Care* 1, no. 4 (Summer 1976):480–81.

SUGGESTED ADDITIONAL READINGS

Doremus, Bertha, "The Four R's: Social Diagnosis in Health Care," *Health and Social Work* 1, no. 4 (November 1976):120–39.

Franklin, Paula A., "Impact of Disability on the Family Structure," *Social Security Bulletin,* May 1977, pp. 3–18.

Fried, Marc. "Social Differences in Mental Health." In *Poverty and Health.* Cambridge, Mass.: Harvard Press, 1969, chap. IV, p. 114.

Grandstaff, Netta W. "The Impact of Breast Cancer and Mastectomy on the Family." In *Family Health Care: Health Promotion and Illness Care.* Berkeley, Calif., Public Health Social Work Program, 1976, pp. 145–55.

Gunderson, Eric, and Richard Rahe, eds. *Life Stress and Illness.* Springfield, Ill.: Charles C Thomas, 1974.

Hudson, Kate, "Some Social and Emotional Implications of Dependence on Machinery," *British Journal of Social Work,* 1, no. 2 (Summer 1971):149–95.

Ince, Laurence. *The Rehabilitation Medicine Services.* Springfield, Ill.: Charles C Thomas, 1974.

Katz, Roger, and Steven Zlutnick. *Behavior Therapy and Health Care, Principles and Applications.* New York: Pergamon Press, 1975.

Kosa, John, and Leon Robertson. "The Social Aspects of Health and Illness." In *Poverty and Health.* Cambridge, Mass.: Harvard Press, 1969, p. 35.

Lawton, M. P., and E. M. Brody, "Assessment of Older People's Self-Maintaining and Instrumental Activities of Daily Living," *The Gerontologist* 9, no. 3 (Autumn 1969):179–86.

Litman, T. J., "The Family as the Basic Unit in Health and Medical Care: A Social Behavioral Overview," *Social Science and Medicine* 8, (September 1974):495–519.

Picken, B., and G. Ireland, "Family Patterns of Medical Care Utilization: Possible Influence of Family Size, Role and Social Class in Illness Behavior," *Journal of Chronic Disease* 22 (August 1969):181.

Pratt, L. *Family Structure and Effective Health Behavior: The Energized Family.* Boston: Houghton Mifflin, 1975.

Strauss, Anselm M. *Chronic Illness and the Quality of Life.* St. Louis: C. V. Mosby, 1975. (See esp. chap. 1, "Problems of Living with Chronic Illness," and chap. 2, "Specific Chronic Conditions and Their Implications.")

Thomas, E. J. "Bias and Therapist Influence in Behavioral Assessment." In *Behavior Modification Procedures: A Sourcebook,* edited by E. J. Thomas. Chicago: Aldine, 1974, pp. 163–69.

Part V

PSYCHOSOCIAL INTERVENTIONS WITH HEALTH PROBLEMS

9/SOCIAL TREATMENT OF SELECTED ILLNESSES: A REFERENCE LISTING

NEIL F. BRACHT

Approaches to understanding and assessing the psychosocial effects of illness were discussed in Chapter 8. In this chapter a reference guide to treatment interventions with selected illnesses and health conditions is provided, including an introductory perspective on social treatment. The bibliographical listing that follows (p. 141) is presented to facilitate the clinician's or new student's familiarity with social work and/or behavioral science practice with specialized health problems. It is not a comprehensive guide to all aspects of a particular illness. Many medical and nursing references pertinent to illness or health conditions are not cited, simply because of their voluminous nature. In developing the guide, diversity of methodological as well as professional perspectives was a key criterion. The guide emphasizes social, psychological, and environment-related interventions. Social work practitioners will find the *Selective Bibliography of Current Literature,* which appears quarterly in *Social Work in Health Care,* an excellent source for keeping up to date with recently published professional literature from the fields of social work, medicine, health care, gerontology, nursing, occupational therapy, rehabilitation, psychology, sociology, and mental health. Another resource is "Index to Current Abstracts," in *Community Mental Health Review,* published bimonthly by The Haworth Press, New York.

What is social treatment? Whittaker defines it as "an approach to interpersonal helping which utilizes direct and indirect strategies of intervention to aid individuals, families and small groups in improving social functioning and coping with social problems."[1] The variety of practice modalities possible is important to social workers in the health field, who must use a wide range of treatment strategies and techniques. For example, in emergency room practice crisis intervention techniques[2] will be more appropriate than behavioral-change strategies[3] employed in pain or obesity clinics. Task-centered brief casework models[4] may be more appropriate on medicine and surgery wards than in outpatient medicine and psychiatry units. Group work techniques can be very useful in rehabilitation programs and nursing homes.[5] Social change

137

and community development techniques are used in many of the new programs of outreach consultation, planning, and prevention, as discussed in Chapters 15, 16, and 17. The references contained in the following pages focus on remedial and rehabilitative aspects of social work practice as opposed to broader developmental-change functions. As Stein notes,

The major difference between the developmental function (in social work) and the system maintenance function is that the latter focuses on remedial and rehabilitative operations usually involving the most vulnerable sectors of the population whereas the developmental function aims at broader social coverage and . . . at the strengthening of social institutions to make them more capable of meeting aspirations of the population.[6]

System change, in contrast to either the system maintenance or the developmental function of social work, aims at directly changing significant elements in the social structure and challenges existing values or organizational investments in the status quo. (See Chapter 17, "Organizing Nonsexist Health Care Services for Women.")

Social workers in health settings usually specialize in direct clinical treatment modalities but frequently are required to combine social change and advocacy strategies. In a study by Taber and Vattono it was found that the so-called opposing orientations of "clinical" and "social" did not necessarily predominate as a realistic division in a sample of some 821 practicing social workers. The study suggests that the escalation of a clinical-versus-social controversy in the literature has little meaning to social workers who coordinate both functions in their daily work.[7] The social worker's holistic approach to the patient and family entails a dynamic process of weighing intrapsychic, institutional, and socioenvironmental factors prior to developing a treatment plan.

Siporin,[8] in an interesting article entitled "Social Treatment: A New-Old Helping Method," believes social work practice theory must be eclectic and evolve links for the operational use of both personality and social system theories. He further comments:

In social treatment the social worker serves as a system change agent for both personality and social systems. He seeks to be active and effective at several levels of intervention, choosing targets and entry points in individual, family, group, organizational, community, and institutional structures and domains of functioning. . . . The social worker is, as always, expected to be an expert troubleshooter who can intervene in severe crises, mediate violent disputes, negotiate and find innovative resolutions for impossible difficulties. But high value is accorded the provider and coordinator of social supports and community resources needed for the client's development and problem-solving adaptation. As resource person and procedural guide the worker actively uses intergroup community processes within the unofficial, natural helping system of the client's social network. Or he deals directly with the official social welfare community and bureaucracies to make available to the client varied social provisions and social utilities such as financial aid, day care, and homemaker and medical care services.[9]

Reflected in the bibliographical references that follow is the rich variety of social treatment modalities of social workers and other sociobehavioral disciplines in helping with the crises of illness and disability. In all of our professional helping experiences, it is important to encourage and allow patients and families to use the strengths they have to solve problems. Kress provides an illustration of this basic principle:

A 50-year-old research director had traveled widely, cared for an elderly parent, and led an active and competent life while avoiding close relationships. Confronted with the crisis of regular dialysis, he directed people to check insurance policies, collect information on dialysis centers in Europe in case he wanted to travel, and, in general, acted in an officious, directive way. Some of the unit staff reacted with resentment to the patient's imperious manner, until his behavior was seen as his characteristic way of relating to people and mastering situations. Knowing that he was coping this way, the team was able to respond to this patient on his own terms. He was able to feel in control of his own life again.[10]

Social work has acquired many of the characteristics of a profession, namely, a professional association, standards of practice, a set of values and code of ethics, and increased recognition through licensure. One earmark of a profession, a scientifically validated and replicable knowledge base, has been an elusive goal. Theories of personality and human development are often abstract and vague and do not offer the specificity desired by students or new workers. Their search is for an understanding of which treatment interventions "work" with certain client populations, and with what exceptions. As Epstein notes, "We cannot remain satisfied with this state of affairs; and we cannot depend upon theories of human development and personality functioning to provide usable answers to what and how to do social treatment. We need to develop treatment models which strive for specificity."[11] Since social workers in health settings operate within policy structures that are not always in accord with their values and treatment goals, the necessity to more clearly specify client population needs as well as the outcomes of treatment intervention becomes a paramount thrust of future social work practice in health care.

N O T E S

1. James Whittaker, *Social Treatment: An Approach to Interpersonal Helping* (Chicago: Aldine, 1974), p. 49.

2. Howard J. Parad, *Crisis Intervention: Selected Readings* (New York: Family Service Association of America, 1965).

3. Richard Stuart, "A Three-Dimensional Program for the Treatment of Obesity," in Katz and Zlutnick, eds., *Behavior Therapy and Health Care: Principles and Application* (New York: Pergamon Press, 1975), pp. 585–600.

4. William Reid and Laura Epstein, *Task-Centered Casework,* (New York: Columbia University Press, 1972).

5. Cinnie Henkle, "Social Group Work as a Treatment Modality for Hospitalized People with Rheumatoid Arthritis," *Rehabilitation Literature* 36, no. 11 (November 1975):334–41. See

also N. Linsk, "Behavioral Group Work in a Home for the Aged," *Social Work,* November 1975, pp. 454–63.

6. Herman Stein, "Social Work's Developmental and Change Functions: Their Roots in Practice," *Social Service Review* 15, no. 1 (March 1976):1–10.
7. M. A. Taber and Vattano, A. J. "Clinical and Social Orientations in Social Work: An Empirical Study," *Social Service Review* 44, no. 1 (March 1970):34–43.
8. Max Siporin, "Social Treatment: A New-Old Helping Method," *Social Work,* July 1970, pp. 22–23.
9. Helene Kress, MSW, ACSW, "Adaptation to Chronic Illness: A Two-Way Street," *Social Work in Health Care* 1, no. 1 (Fall 1975):40–44.
10. Laura Epstein, "Task-Centered Casework: A Model of Planned Short-Term Treatment," in Mary M. Lewis, ed., *Social Work Services in Pediatric Hospitals,* proceedings of the meeting of directors of social work departments in pediatric hospitals, James Whitcomb Riley Hospital for Children, Indianapolis, 1972.

SUGGESTED ADDITIONAL READINGS

Briar, Scott, "The Casework Predicament," *Social Work,* January 1968, pp. 5–11.

Davis, Inger. "Social Treatment Process Research: Some Thoughts and Viewpoints," Occasional Paper no. 7. University of Chicago, School of Social Service Administration, December 1976, pp. 1–14.

Kiestler, Donald. *The Process of Psychotherapy: Empirical Foundations and Systems of Analysis.* Chicago: Aldine Press, 1973.

Pasewark, Richard A., and Dale Albert, "Crisis Intervention: Theory in Search of a Program," *Social Work* 17, no. 2 (March 1972):70–77.

Thomas, Edwin, "Selected Sociobehavioral Techniques and Principles: An Approach to Interpersonal Helping," *Social Work,* January 1968.

Whittaker, James, "Models of Group Development: Implications for Social Group Work Practice," *Social Service Review* 44, no. 3 (September 1970):308–21.

REFERENCE GUIDE TO SOCIAL TREATMENT INTERVENTIONS WITH SELECTED ILLNESSES

AGED–IMPAIRED

Austin, Michael J., "A Network of Help for England's Elderly." *Social Work,* March 1976, pp. 114–19.

Brody, Elaine N., Charlotte Cole, and Miriam Moss, "Individualizing Therapy for the Mentally Impaired Aged," *Social Casework* 54, no. 8 (October 1973).

Gason, J. Z., and Ruth Wald, "Social Problems of the Hospitalized Elderly," *Canadian Family Physician,* November 1975, pp. 85–93.

Linsk, N., Michael W. Howe, and Elsie M. Pinkston, "Behavioral Group Work in a Home for the Aged," *Social Work,* November 1975, pp. 454–63.

Locker, R. "Elderly Couples and the Institution," *Social Work* 21, no. 2 (March 1976):149–50.

Yawney, Beverly A., and Darrell L. Slover, "Relocation of the Elderly," *Social Work,* May 1973, pp. 86–95.

ALCOHOLISM

Corrigan, Eileen M., "Linking the Problem Drinker with Treatment," *Social Work,* March 1972, pp. 54–60.

Fewell, Christine, "The Social Work Role in an Inpatient Alcoholism Treatment Team," *Social Work in Health Care* 1, no. 2 (Winter 1975):155–66.

Littman, Gerard, "Alcoholism, Illness, and Social Pathology Among American Indians in Transition," *American Journal of Public Health* 60, no. 9 (September 1970):1769–78.

Miller, P. "The Use of Behavioral Contracting in the Treatment of Alcoholism: A Case Report." In *Behavior Therapy and Health Care,* edited by Roger C. Katz and Steven Zlutnick. New York: Pergamon Press, 1975, pp. 561–66.

Mueller, John F., "Casework with the Family of the Alcoholic," *Social Work,* September 1972, pp. 79–85.

National Institute on Alcohol Abuse and Alcoholism. *Special Report to U.S. Congress on Alcohol and Health,* Department of Health, Education and Welfare Publication no. 72-9099. Washington, D.C. 1971.

ANOREXIA NERVOSA

Azerrad, J., and R. Stafford. "Restoration of Eating Behavior in Anorexia Nervosa Through Operant Conditioning and Environmental Manipulation." In *Behavior Therapy and Health Care,* op. cit., pp. 121–30.

AMPUTATION (ADJUSTMENT TO)

Lane, Helen J., "Working with Problems of Assault to Self-Image and Life Style," *Social Work in Health Care* 1, no. 2 (Winter 1975-1976):191–98.

Thomas, K. R., et al., "Correlates of Disability Acceptance in Amputees," *Rehabilitation Counseling Bulletin* 19, no. 3 (March 1976):508–11.

ARTHRITIS

Henkle, Cinnie, "Social Group Work as a Treatment Modality for Hospitalized People with Rheumatoid Arthritis," *Rehabilitation Literature* 36, no. 11 (November 1975):334–41.

Randar, Mary Ann T., "Expanding Role of the Social Worker in the Health Field," *American Journal of Public Health* 62, no. 8 (August 1972):1102–04.

ASTHMA-ALLERGIES

Barmettler, Donna, and Grace L. Fields, "Using the Group Method to Study and Treat Parents of Asthmatic Children," *Social Work in Health Care* 1, no. 2 (Winter 1975):167–76.

Levine, M. I., "The Social Worker's Interview in Chronic Urticaria," *Annals of Allergy* 35, no. 5 (November 1975):278–80.

Travis, Georgia. "Asthma." In *Chronic Illness in Children.* Stanford, Calif.: Stanford University Press, 1976, chap. 6, pp. 164–94.

BATTERED CHILD-ABUSE

Cook, JoAnn, and Sharrell Munce. "Group Treatment for Abusive Parents: Creating a New Family System." In *Family Health Care: Health Promotion and Illness Care,* Proceedings 1975 Institute for Public Health Social Workers, edited by Robert Jackson and Jean Morton. Berkeley: University of California, School of Public Health, Public Health Social Work Program, 1976.

Elmer, Elizabeth. "Social Workers' Double Bind: Conflicting Roles of the Social Worker in Working with the Child, Parents, and the Community in Relation to Child Abuse." In *Approaches to Health Care, Proceedings of the 1976 Medical Social Consultants Annual Meeting,* edited by Roger B. White. Baltimore: Johns Hopkins University, School of Hygiene and Public Health, Department of Maternal and Child Health.

Lapicki, Lee. "Child Abuse—The Parent's View." In ibid.

Martin, Harold, ed. *The Abused Child: A Multidisciplinary Approach to Developmental Issues and Treatment.* Cambridge, Mass: Ballinger, 1977.

BLINDNESS

Minkoff, H., "Integrating the Aging Visually Handicapped into Community Groups in New York City," *New Outlook for the Blind* 9 (November 1975):396–98.

Negrin, S., "The Advocacy Role of the Social Worker in Blind Services," *New Outlook for the Blind* 70, no. 1 (January 1976):30–33.

Vander-Kolk, C. J., "Counseling and Psychotherapy with the Visually Impaired: An Annotated Bibliography," *Outlook for the Blind* 70, no. 3 (March 1975):109–15.

BREAST CANCER-MASTECTOMY

Burdick, Caniel, "Rehabilitation of the Breast Cancer Patient," *Cancer* 36, no. 2 (August 1975): 645–48.

Grandstaff, Netta W. "The Impact of Breast Cancer and Mastectomy on the Family." In *Family Health Care,* op. cit, pp. 145–56.

Schain, W. S., "Psychosocial Issues in Counseling Mastectomy Patients," *The Counseling Psychologist* 6, no. 2 (1976):45–49.

(For additional references see Chapter 17.)

BURN

Cowin, Ruth, "Social Factors in Treating Burned Children," *Children* 2, no. 6 (November-December, 1964):229–33.

Breslin, P. W., "The Psychological Reactions of Children to Burn Traumata: A Review—Part II," *Illinois Medical Journal* 148, no. 6 (December 1975):595–602.

Broadland, G. A., and N. Andreasen, "Adjustment Problems of the Family of the Burn Patient," *Social Casework* 55, no. 1 (January 1974):13.

Granite, U., and S. B. Goldman, "Rehabilitation Therapy for Burn Patients and Spouses," *Social Casework* 56, no. 10 (December 1975):593–98.

Talabere, L., and P. Graves, "A Tool for Assessing Families of Burned Children," *American Journal of Nursing* 76, no. 2 (February 1976):225–27.

CANCER

(See also Breast Cancer; Leukemia; Terminal Illness)

Bahnson, C., "Psychologic and Emotional Issues in Cancer: The Psychotherapeutic Care of the Cancer Patient," *Seminars in Oncology* 2, no. 4 (December 1975):293–310.

Evans, A. E., "Practical Care for the Family of a Child with Cancer," *Cancer* 35, supp. 3 (March 1975):871–75.

Harper, B. C., "Social Aspects of Cancer Recovery," *Cancer* 36, no. 1, supp. (July 1975):271–75.

Kagan, L., "Use of Denial in Adolescents with Bone Cancer," *Health and Social Work* 1, no. 4 (November 1976):70–87.

O'Neill, Marcella P., "Psychological Aspects of Cancer Recovery," *Cancer* 36, no. 1, supp. (July 1975):271–73.

Peebler, D., "How Patients Help Each Other," *American Journal of Nursing* 75, no. 8 (August 1975):1354.

Sheldon, A., C. P. Ryser, and M. J. Krant, "An Integrated Family Oriented Cancer Care Program: The Report of a Pilot Project in the Socio-Emotional Management of Chronic Disease," *Journal of Chronic Diseases* 22, no. 11 (November 1970):743–55.

Stone, R. W. "Employing the Recovered Cancer Patient," *Cancer* 36, no. 1, supp. (July 1975): 277–78.

CEREBRAL PALSY

Arnold, G. G., "Problems of the Cerebral Palsy Child and His Family," *Virginia Medical Monthly* 103, no. 3 (March 1976):225–27.

Nielsen, H. H., "A Follow-up Study of Young Cerebral Palsied Patients: Some Psychological, Education and Vocational Aspects," *Scandinavian Journal of Psychology* 16, no. 3 (March 1975):217–24.

CHILDREN'S ILLNESSES–FEARS

Burton, Lindy. *The Family Life of Sick Children.* London and Boston: Routledge and Kegan Paul, 1975.

Gorman, Joanna, F., ed. *Social and Health Needs in Childhood and Adolescence,* Proceedings of the 1970 Annual Institute for Public Health Social Workers. Berkeley: University of California, Program in Public Health Social Work, 1972.

Gurney, Wilma, "Building a Collaborative Network," *Social Work in Health Care* 1, no. 2 (Winter 1975-1976):185–89.

Romano, Mary D., "Preparing Children for Parental Disability," *Social Work in Health Care* 1, no. 3 (Spring 1976):309–15.

Sheridan, Mary S., "Children's Feelings About the Hospital," *Social Work in Health Care* 1, no. 1 (Fall 1975):65–70.

Townsel, Lee E., John Irving, and Hans H. Stroo, "Mobile Consultation: An Integrative Approach to Mental Health Service to Children," *Social Work in Health Care* 1, no. 1 (Fall 1975):81–92.

Travis, Georgia. *Chronic Illness in Children.* Stanford, Calif.: Stanford University Press, 1976.

CLEFT PALATE

Smyth, Wilma, "Preventive Aspects of Medical Social Work Consultation in a Rural State," *Social Work,* July 1960, pp. 91–96.

Starr, Phillip, and Kitty Heiserman, "Factors Associated with Missed Appointments of Patients in a Cleft Lip and Palate Clinic," *Cleft Palate Journal* 12, no. 4 (October 1975):461–64.

Starr, P., and E. Zirpoli, "Cleft Palate Patients—The Social Work Approach," *Health and Social Work* 1, no. 2 (May 1976):105–12.

COMMUNICATION DISORDERS

Gray, S., and H. R. Konrad, "Laryngectomy: Postsurgical Rehabilitation of Communication," *Archives of Physical Medicine and Rehabilitation* 57, no. 3 (March 1976):140–42.

Sampson, Norma, MSW, "Family Therapy for the Child with a Communicative Disorder," *Journal of Communication Disorders* 5, no. 2 (July 1972):205–11.

Spink, Diane, "Crisis Intervention for Parents of the Deaf Child," *Health and Social Work* 1, no. 4 (November 1976):140–60.

CHRONIC ILLNESS

Clark, Eleanor, "Improving Post-Hospital Care for the Chronically Ill Elderly Patient," *Social Work,* January 1969, pp. 62–66.

Bayrakal, S., "A Group Experience with Chronically Disabled Adolescents," *American Journal of Psychiatry* 132, no. 12 (December 1976):1291–94.

Hall, Julian C., and Anna K. Bradley, "Treating Long-Term Mental Patients," *Social Work,* September 1975, pp. 383–86.

Sherwood, Sylvia, ed. *Long-Term Care: A Handbook for Researchers, Planners, and Providers.* New York: Halstead Press, Spectrum Publications, 1975.

Strauss, Anselm L. *Chronic Illness and the Quality of Life.* Saint Louis: C. V. Mosby, 1975.

Travis, Georgia, *Chronic Illness in Children.* Stanford, Calif.: Stanford University Press, 1976.

CYSTIC FIBROSIS

Burnett, B. A., "Family Adjustment to Cystic Fibrosis," *American Journal of Nursing* 75, no. 11 (November 1975):1986–89.

Grossman, M. L., "The Psychosocial Approach to the Medical Management of Patients with Cystic Fibrosis," *Clinical Pediatrics* 14, no. 9 (September 1975):830–33.

Travis, Georgia, op. cit., chap. 9.

DEPRESSION

Beck, A., and M. Kovacs, "A New Fast Therapy for Depression," *Psychology Today,* January 1977, pp. 94ff.

Lewinsohn, P. M., A. Biglan, and A. N. Zeiss. "Behavioral Treatment of Depression." In *Behavioral Management of Anxiety, Depression and Pain,* edited by P. O. Davidson. New York: Brunner/Mazel, 1976, pp. 91–146.

Pehm, Lynn P. "Assessment of Depression." In *Behavioral Assessment, a Practical Handbook,* edited by Michael Hersen and Allen Bellack. New York: Pergamon Press, 1976, pp. 233–59.

Stuart, Richard B., "Casework Treatment of Depression Viewed as an Interpersonal Disturbance," *Social Work* 12, no. 2 (April 1967).

Weismann, Myrna M., "The Depressed Woman: Recent Research," *Social Work* 17, no. 5 (September 1972).

DEVELOPMENTAL DISABILITY

(See also Handicap—Disability; Mental Retardation)

McGrath, Francis, et al. *Social Work Education in the University Affiliated Facility: Instructional Manual and Evaluation Guide* (MCH Project Grant no. 903). Miami: Mailman Center for Child Development, June 1976.

Selan, Betta H., "Psychotherapy with the Developmentally Disabled," *Health and Social Work* 1, no. 1 (February 1976):73–84.

DIABETES

Guthrie, D. W., and R. A. Guthrie, "Diabetes in Adolescence," *American Journal of Nursing* 75, no. 10 (October 1975):1740–50.

Randar, Mary Ann T., "Expanding Role of the Social Worker in the Health Field," *American Journal of Public Health* 62, no. 8 (August 1972):1102–04.
Small, D., "Special Needs of the Geriatric Diabetic Patient," *Journal of Practical Nursing* 26, no. 11 (November 1976): pp. 25–27.

DISASTER RELIEF
Feld, Allen, "Reflections on the Agnes Flood," *Social Work,* September 1973, pp. 46–51.
Grossman, Leona, "Train Crash: Social Work and Disaster Services," *Social Work,* September 1973, pp. 38–44.
Parad, Howard J., ed. *Crisis Intervention: Selected Readings.* New York: Family Service Association of America, 1974.

EMERGENCY CARE
Bergman, Anne Sturmthal, "Emergency Room: A Role for Social Workers," *Health and Social Work* 1, no. 1 (February 1976):32–44.
Epperson, Margaret, "Families in Sudden Crisis," *Social Work in Health Care* 2, no. 3 (Spring 1977):265–74.
Getz, William L., Diane C. Altman, William C. Berleman, and David B. Allen, "Paraprofessional Crisis Counseling in the Emergency Room," *Health and Social Work* 2, no. 2 (May 1977): 58–73.
Sadler, Alfred, Blair Sadler, and Samuel Webb. *Emergency Medical Care: The Neglected Public Service.* Cambridge, Mass.: Ballinger, 1976.
Strinsky, C., "Medical Social Work: Valuable Asset to Emergency Room Staff-Hospitals," *Hospitals* 44 (May 1970):58–60.

EMPHYSEMA
Parry, Joan K., and Nancy Kahn, "Group Work with Emphysema Patients," *Social Work in Health Care* 2, no. 1 (Fall 1976):55–64.

ENURESIS
Mowrer, O. H., and W. M. Mowrer, "Enuresis—A Method for Its Study and Treatment." In Katz and Zlutnick, op. cit., pp. 41–104.

EPILEPSY
Livingston, Samuel, "What Hope for the Child with Epilepsy?" *Children* 12, no. 1 (January-February 1965):9–13.
Randar, Mary Ann T., op. cit.
Thomas, Madison, "Levels of Progress in Prevention of Seizures and Restoration of the Person with Epilepsy," *National Spokesman,* July-August 1974, pp. 6–7.

ETHICAL DECISIONS IN ILLNESS–RESEARCH
Berg, P., D. Baltimore, S. Brenner, et al., Asilomar Conference on Recombinant DNA Molecules," *Science,* 188, no. 4192 (June 6, 1975):991–94.
Brody, Howard. *Ethical Decisions in Medicine.* Boston: Little, Brown, 1976. (Copyright: Michigan State University, College of Human Medicine.)
Healey, Joseph, "The Quinlan Case and the Mass Media," *American Journal of Public Health* 66, no. 3 (March 1976):295–96.
Jonsen, A. R., et al., "Critical Issues in Newborn Intensive Care: A Conference Report and Policy Proposal," *Pediatrics* 6 (June 6, 1975):756–67.
Kohlsaat, Barbara. "The Social Worker (Ethical Dilemmas in Health Care Practice)." In *Approaches to Health Care,* Proceedings 1976 Medical Social Consultants, edited by Roger B.

White. Baltimore: Johns Hopkins University, School of Hygiene and Public Health, Department of Maternal and Child Health, 1976, p. 113.

Roycroft, E. B., "Letter: Confidentiality in Social Work," *Lancet* 1, no. 7910 (April 5, 1975):797.

Shore, Milton F., and Stuart E. Golan, eds. *Current Ethical Issues in Mental Health,* based on a workshop at the 47th Annual meeting of the American Orthopsychiatric Association, San Francisco, California, March 1970. Rockville, Md.: NIMH.

U.S. Congress, Senate, Committee on Labor and Public Welfare. *Quality of Health Care—Human Experimentation, hearings,* 92nd Cong., 2nd sess., 1973. Washington, D.C.: Goverment Printing Office, 1973.

See also *Bibliography of Society, Ethics and the Life Sciences,* issued annually by Institute of Society, Ethics and the Life Sciences, 623 Warburton Avenue, Hastings-on-Hudson, New York.

FAMILY–IMPACT OF ILLNESS

Breslin, Ruth L. Newborn Special Care Units: Special Care to Families. In *Family Health Care Health Promotion and Illness Care,* Proceedings 1975 Institute for Public Health Social Worker, edited by Robert Jackson and Jean Morton. Berkeley: University of California, School of Public Health, Public Health Social Work Program, 1976, pp. 99–118.

David, Ann C., and Elizabeth H. Donovan, "Initiating Group Process with Parents of Multihandicapped Children," *Social Work in Health Care* 1, no. 7 (Winter 1975–1976):177–84.

Glass, Lora, and Martha Hickerson, "Dialysis and Transplantation: A Mothers' Group," *Social Work in Health Care* 1, no. 3 (Spring 1976):287–96.

Gogan, J. L., et al., "Impact of Childhood Cancer on Siblings," *Health and Social Work* 2, no. 1 (February 1977):42–56.

Maddox, George. Families as Context and Resource in Chronic Illness. In *Long Term Care,* edited by Sylvia Sherwood. New York: Spectrum Publications, 1975, pp. 317–48.

Morse, J., "Family Involvement in Pediatric Dialysis and Transplantation," *Social Casework* 55 (April 1974):216–23.

Rice, Nancy, Betty Satterwhite, and I. B. Pless, "Family Counselors in a Pediatric Specialty Clinic Setting," *Social Work in Health Care* 2, no. 2 (Winter 1976–1977):193–204.

GENETIC DISEASES–COUNSELING

Griffin, Margaret, et al., "Genetic Knowledge, Client Perspectives and Genetic Counseling," *Social Work in Health Care* 2, no. 2 (Winter 1976):171–80.

Kiely, Lynn, Richard Sterne, and Carl J. Witkop, "Psychosocial Factors in Low-Incidence Genetic Disease: The Case of Osteogenesis Imperfecta," *Social Work in Health Care* 1, no. 4 (Summer 1976):409–20.

Murray, Robert F., "Psychological Aspects of Genetic Counseling," *Social Work in Health Care* 2, no. 1 (Fall 1976):13–24.

Schild, S., "Social Work with Genetic Problems," *Health and Social Work* 2, no. 1 (February 1977):59–76.

Weiss, Joan O., "Social Work and Genetic Counseling," *Social Work in Health Care* 2, no. 1 (Fall 1976):5–12.

GERIATRIC DAY CARE–AFTERCARE

Allen, K. S., "A Group Experience for Elderly Patients with Organic Brain Syndrome," *Health and Social Work* 1, no. 4, (November 1976):61–69.

Austin, Michael J., Jordan I. Kosbert, James Hermans, and Gilbert McDaniel, "The Sub-acute Center: A Proposal for Relocating Elderly Mental Patients." *Social Work in Health Care* 1, no. 2 (Winter 1975–1976):199–212.

Bradshaw, B. A., "Community-Based Residential Care for the Minimally Impaired Elderly: A Survey Analysis," *Journal of the American Geriatric Society* 24, no. 9 (September 1976):423–29.

Keith, P., "Evaluation of Services for the Aged by Professionals and the Elderly," *Social Service Review* 49, no. 2 (June 1975):271–78.

Mehta, N., and C. Mack, "Day Care Services: An Alternative to Institutional Care," *Journal of the American Geriatric Society,* 23, no. 6 (June 1975):280–83.

Rathbone-McCuan, Eloise, and Martha Warfield Elliott, "Geriatric Day Care in Theory and in Practice." *Social Work in Health Care* 2, no. 2 (Winter 1976–1977):153–70.

HANDICAP-DISABILITY

Allen, John E., and Louis Lelchuck, "A Comprehensive Care Program for Children with Handicaps," *American Journal of Diseases of Children* 3 (March 1966):229–35.

Cobb, Beatrix. *Medical and Psychological Aspects of Disability.* Springfield, Ill.: Charles C Thomas, 1973.

Holmes, H. A., and F. F. Holmes, "After Ten Years, What are the Handicaps and Life Styles of Children Treated for Cancer?" *Clinical Pediatrics* 14, no. 9 (September 1975):819–29.

Millet, John A. P., "Understanding the Emotional Aspects of Disability," *Social Work,* October 1957, pp. 16–21.

The Role of Maternal and Child Health and Crippled Children's Programs in Evolving Systems of Health Care, Conference Proceedings, Towsley Center for Continuing Medical Education. Ann Arbor: University of Michigan Medical Center, March 23–25, 1970.

Travis, Georgia. "A Conceptual Foundation for Work with Handicapped Children." In *Chronic Illness in Children,* op. cit., chap. 2, pp. 10–41.

HANSEN'S DISEASE (LEPROSY)

Cannon, Willard E., "Social Casework for Patients with Hansen's Disease," *Public Health Reports* 79, no. 3 (March 1964):193–99.

HEART DISEASE

Brown, J., and M. Rawlinson, "The Morale of Patients Following Open-Heart Surgery," *Journal of Health and Social Behavior* 17, no. 2 (June 1976):134–44.

Brown, Elliot C., "Casework with Patients Undergoing Cardiac Surgery," *Social Casework* 52, no. 10 (December 1971):611–16.

Geiger, Jack, and Norman Scotch, "The Epidemiology of Essential Hypertension: A Review with Special Attention to Psychologic and Sociocultural Factors," *Journal of Chronic Diseases* 16, (1963):1170ff.

Hesse, K. A., "Meeting the Psychosocial Needs of Pacemaker Patients," *International Journal of Psychiatry and Medicine* 6, no. 3 (March 1975):359–72.

Richman, Harold A., "Casework with a Child Following Heart Surgery," *Children* 2, no. 5 (September-October 1964):183–88.

Sokol, B. "The Clinical Social Worker as a Member of the Health Team in a Coronary Care Unit." *Clinical Social Work Journal* 4, no. 4 (Winter 1976) p. 269–75.

Travis, Georgia. "Congenital Heart Disease." In *Chronic Illness in Children,* op. cit., chap. 8, 233–68.

Wegner, M., J. A. Ruiz, and L. D. Caccamo, "The Social Worker in the Private Practice of Internal Medicine," *Archives of Internal Medicine* 118, no. 4 (October 1966):347–50.

HOME CARE

Houghton, Lisbeth, and Anita E. Martin, "Home VS Hospital: A Hospital-Based Home Care Program," *Health and Social Work* 1, no. 4 (November 1976):88–103.

A. V. Hurtado. *Integration of Home Health and Extended Care Facility Services into a Prepaid Comprehensive Group Practice Plan,* Portland, Ore.: Kaiser Foundation Research Institute, 1970, 410 pp. Report no. PB 196021.

Seidl, Frederick, et al., "Is Home Health Care Less Expensive?" *Health and Social Work* 2, no. 2 (May 1977):5–19.
Ullmann, Alice, "Social Work in a Home Care Program," *Journal of Chronic Diseases* 15 (September 1961):925–34.

HUNTINGTON'S DISEASE
Miller, Eunice, "The Social Work Component in Community-Based Action on Behalf of Victims of Huntington's Disease," *Social Work in Health Care* 2, no. 1 (Fall 1976):25–39.
Wise, T. N., "Psychiatric Involvement with Huntington's Chorea," *Psychosomatics* 16, no. 3 (March 1975):135–37.

HEMOPHILIA
Jones, Peter. *Living with Hemophilia.* Philadelphia: F. A. Davis, 1974.

HYPERTENSION
Benson, H., et al., "Decreased Systolic Blood Pressure Through Operant Conditioning Techniques." In Katz and Zlutnick, op. cit., chap. 16, pp. 223–28.
Cobb, Sydney, and Robert Rose. "Hypertension, Peptic Ulcer and Diabetes in Air Traffic Controllers." In *Health and the Social Environment,* edited by Rudolf Moos and Paul Insel. Stanford U. Press, Palo Alto, Ca. 1974. pp. 73–80.
Peters, Ruanne, et al, "Daily Relaxation Response Breaks in a Working Population: Effects on Blood Pressure." *American Journal of Public Health* 67 no. 10 (October 1977) pp. 954–65.

ILEOSTOMY
Moser, S., "Social Worker's Role in Ileostomy," *Journal of the Association of Operating Room Nurses* 23, no. 1 (January 1976):58–59.

INTENSIVE CARE
Benfield, D. G., et al., "Grief Response of Parents After Referral of the Critically Ill Newborn to a Regional Center," *New England Journal of Medicine* 294, no. 18 (April 1976):975–78.
Cole, C., "Social Work in an Intensive Care Unit," *Injury* 7, no. 3 (February 1976):244–45.
Hancock, Emily, "Crisis Intervention in a Newborn Nursery Intensive Care Unit," *Social Work in Health Care* 1, no. 4 (Summer 1976):421–32.
Sheridan, M., and D. Johnson, "Social Work Services in a High-Risk Nursery," *Health and Social Work* 1, no. 2 (May 1976):87–102.
Sokol, B., "The Clinical Social Worker as a Member of the Health Team in a Coronary Care Unit," *Clinical Social Work Journal* 4, no. 4 (Winter 1976):269–75.
Williams, Cindy, et al., "The Intensive Care Unit: Social Work Intervention with the Families of Critically Ill Patients," *Social Work in Health Care* 2, no. 4 (Summer 1977).

KIDNEY
Association of Nephrology Social Workers. *White Paper: Positions of Nephrology Social Workers on Public Law 92–603, Title II, Section 2991* (chronic renal disease). Judith Kari, et. al., Ad Hoc Committee, Minneapolis: VA Hospital, 1973, 9 pp.
Cain, Lillian Pike, "Casework with Kidney Transplant Patients," *Social Work* 8 (July 1973): 76–83.
Fox, Renee C., and Judith P. Swazey. *The Courage to Fail: A Social View of Organ Transplants and Dialysis.* Chicago: University of Chicago Press, 1974. (pp. 94–98 describe the role of social work)

Hudson, Kate, "Some Social and Emotional Implications of Dependence on Machinery," *British Journal of Social Work* 1, no. 2 (Summer 1971):149–95.

Kress, Helene, "Adaptation to Chronic Dialysis: A Two-Way Street," *Social Work in Health Care* 1, no. 1 (Fall 1975):41–46.

Leff, Barbara, "A Club Approach to Social Work Treatment Within a Home Dialysis Program," *Social Work in Health Care* 1, no. 1 (Fall 1975):33–40.

Whatley, L., "Social Work with Potential Donors for Renal Transplant," *Social Casework* 53, no. 7 (July 1972):399.

LEUKEMIA

(See also Cancer)

Kaplan, David, et al., "Predicting the Impact of Severe Illness in Families," *Health and Social Work* 1, no. 3 (August 1976):71–81.

Knapp, Vrinda, et al., "Helping Parents of Children with Leukemia," *Social Work*, July 1973, pp. 70–75.

MENTAL HEALTH–MENTAL ILLNESS

Burns, Brenda, "The Use of Play Techniques in the Treatment of Children," *Child Welfare*, Vol. XLIX no. 1 (January 1970).

Caplan, G., "Patterns of Parental Response to the Crisis of Premature Birth: A Preliminary Approach to Modifying the Mental-Health Outcome," *Psychiatry* 23, no. 4 (1960):365–74.

Gottesfeld, Harry, "Alternatives to Psychiatric Hospitalization," *Community Mental Health Review* 1, no. 1 (January-February 1976):1.

Kaplan, D. M., "A Concept of Acute Situational Disorder," *Social Work* 7, no. 2 (1962):15–23.

Klugman, David J., Robert E. Litman, and Carl J. Wold, "Suicide: Answering the Cry for Help," *Social Work* 10, no. 4 (October 1965).

Koonce, Geraldine, "Social Work with Mental Patients in the Community," *Journal of Social Work* 18, no. 3 (May 1973):30–35.

Morrill, Richard G., "A New Mental Health Services Model for the Comprehensive Neighborhood Health Center," *American Journal of Public Health* 62, no. 8 (August 1972):1108–11.

Raphling, D. L., et al., "Patients with Repeated Admissions to a Psychiatric Emergency Service," *Community Mental Health Journal* 6, no. 4 (1970):313–18.

Regester, David, "Community Mental Health—For Whose Community?" *American Journal of Public Health* 64, no. 9 (September 1974):886–93.

Satir, Virginia. *Conjoint Family Therapy.* Palo Alto, Calif.: Science and Behavior Books, 1967.

Schulberg, Herbert C., Ph.D., "The Mental Hospital in the Era of Human Services," *Hospital and Community Psychiatry* 24, no. 7 (July 1973):467–72.

Sherman, Sanford, "Socio-psychological Characteristics of Family Group Treatment," *Social Casework* 45, no. 4 (April 1964):195–201.

Shore, Milton, and Fortune Mannino. *Mental Health and the Community—Problems, Programs and Strategies.* New York: Behavioral Publications, 1969.

Stein, Bradley, "Social Work and Liaison Psychiatry," *Social Work in Health Care* 1, no. 4 (1976):483–88.

Turner, Harriet, "A Therapeutic Community for Chronic Mental Patients," *Health and Social Work* 1, no. 3 (August 1976):96–112.

MENTAL RETARDATION

Borenzweig, H., "Social Group Work in the Field of Mental Retardation: A Review of the Literature," *Social Service Review* 44, no. 2 (June 1970):177–83.

Dittman, Laura L., "The Family of the Child in an Institution," *American Journal of Mental Deficiency* 66, no. 5 (March 1962):759–65.

Gershen, J. A., "Galactosemia: A Psycho Social Perspective," *Mental Retardation* 13, no. 4 (August 1975):20–23.

Grass, Constance, and Richard Umansky, "Problems in Promoting the Growth of Multi-Disciplinary Diagnostic and Counseling Clinics for Mentally Retarded Children in Nonmetropolitan Areas," *American Journal of Public Health* 61, no. 4 (April 1971):698–710.

Koch, Richard, and James C. Dobson, eds. *The Mentally Retarded Child and His Family: A Multidisciplinary Handbook.* New York: Brunner/Mazel, 1976, 546 pp.

Oberman, William J., et al., "A Program for Mentally Retarded Children in a Child Health Clinic Setting," *Clinical Proceedings, Children's Hospital, Washington, D.C.*, 22, no. 5 (May 1966): 129–39.

Scheerenberger, R. C., "Generic Services for the Mentally Retarded and Their Families," *Mental Retardation* 8, no. 6 (December 1970):10–16.

Segal, Arthur, "Worker's Perceptions of Mentally Disabled Clients," *Social Work* 15, no. 3 (July 1970).

The Social Sciences and Mental Retardation: Family Components, Report of a Conference, January 8–9, 1968, National Institute of Child Health and Human Development, Bethesda, Maryland. Washington, D.C.: Department of Health, Education and Welfare, 1968.

Sterns, C. R., "Mental Retardation Content in the Curricula of Graduate Schools of Social Work," *Mental Retardation* 14, no. 3 (June 1976):17–19.

MUSCULAR DYSTROPHY

Travis, Georgia. "Muscular Dystrophy: Duchenne's Form." In *Chronic Illness in Children,* op. cit., chap. 15, pp. 403–31.

MIGRAINE

Mitchell, K., and D. Mitchell. "Migraine: An Exploratory Treatment Application of Programmed Behavior Therapy Techniques." In Katz and Zlutnick, op. cit., pp. 343–54.

NEUROLOGICAL DISEASES

Lambert, Gladys, "Patients with Progressive Neurological Diseases," *Social Casework,* March 1974, pp. 154–59.

OBESITY

Flack, R., and E. D. Grayer, "A Consciousness Raising Group for Obese Women," *Social Work* 20, no. 6 (November 1975):484–87.

Maddox, George, and Veronica Liederman, "Overweight as a Social Disability With Medical Complications," *Journal of Medical Education* 44 (March 1969):214–20.

Stuart, R. "A Three-Dimensional Program for the Treatment of Obesity." In Katz and Zlutnick, op. cit., pp. 585–600.

OBSTETRICS AND GYNECOLOGY

The First National Workshop on the Delivery of Hospital Social Work Services in Obstetrics/ Gynecology and Services to the Newborn. New Haven, Conn.: Yale-New Haven Medical Center, 1974.

Schinke, Steven, and Lewayne Gilchrist, "Adolescent Pregnancy: an Interpersonal Skill Training Approach to Prevention," *Social Work in Health Care* 3, no. 2 (Winter 1978). (in press)

Wallace, Helen M., et al., "A Study of Services and Needs of Teenage Pregnant Girls in the Large Cities of the United States," *American Journal of Public Health* 63, no. 1 (January 1973):5–16.

Wessel, Morris A., "The Unmarried Mother: A Social Work-Medical Responsibility," *Social Work* (January 1963):66–71.

OMBUDSMAN–PATIENT ADVOCACY

Quinn, Nancy, and Anne R. Somers, "The Patient's Bill of Rights—The Consumer Revolution," *Nursing Outlook* 22, no. 4 (April 1974):240–44.

Ravich, Ruth, and Helen Rehr, "Ombudsman Program Provides Feedback," *Journal of the American Hospital Association* 48 (September 16, 1974).

Terry, M., "Those Who Speak Up," *Mental Hygiene,* Summer 1975.

Thompson, F., A. Limon, R. Reneck, and J. Foloesman. "Patient Grievance Mechanisms in Health Care Institutions." In Secretary's Commission on Medical Malpractice, Department of Health, Education and Welfare, Washington, D.C., 1972.

PAIN
(See Chapter 10)

PEDIATRICS–ADOLESCENTS

Coleman, Jules V., Marcia L. Lebowitz, and Frederick P. Anderson, "Social Work in a Pediatric Primary Health Care Team in a Group Practice Program," *Social Work in Health Care* 1, no. 4 (Summer 1976):489–98.

Comfort, R. L., and M. S. Kappy, "Pediatrician and Social Worker as a Counseling Team," *Social Work* 19 (July 1974):486–89.

Cyr, Florence E., and Shirley H. Wattenberg. "Social Work in a Preventive Program of Maternal and Child Health." In *Crisis Intervention: Selected Readings,* edited by Howard J. Parad. New York: Family Service Association of America, 1965, pp. 88–99.

Gentry, Martha E. *Early Detection and Treatment: Social Worker and Pediatricians in Private Practice.* Paper presented at the 104th Annual Meeting, American Public Health Association, Social Work Section, Miami Beach, Florida, October 14–21, 1976, (to be published in *Social Work in Health Care*)

Key, Glenn Shelton, ed. *Delivery of Social Work Services in Pediatric Hospitals,* Proceedings of a workshop held at Essex Inn, Chicago, April 13–18, 1970, Cosponsored by The Children's Memorial Hospital, Chicago, and Maternal and Child Health Service, Department of Health, Education and Welfare. Chicago: Children's Memorial Hospital, 1971.

Kornels, J. W., "Social Work Assistance in Private Pediatric Practice," *Social Casework,* November 1973, pp. 537–44.

Le Pontois, Joan, "Adolescents with Sickle-Cell Anemia Deal with Life and Death," *Social Work in Health Care* 1, no. 1 (Fall 1975):71–81.

Soroker, Eleanor, "An Analysis of Pediatric Outpatient Care," *Health and Social Work* 2, no. 2 (May 1977):89–103.

Wishingrad, L., J. T. Shulff, and A. Sklansky, "The Role of a Social Worker in a Private Practice of Pediatrics," *Pediatrics* 32 (July 1973):125–29.

PREGNANCY, ADOLESCENT
(See Obstetrics and Gynecology)

PSYCHOPHYSIOLOGICAL ILLNESSES

Jeffress, Elizabeth J. *Psychosomatic Medicine: Current Journal Articles.* New York: Medical Examination Publishing Company, 1977.

Sachar, Edward J. "The Current Status of Psychosomatic Medicine." In *Psychological Care of the Medically Ill,* edited by James J. Strain and Stanley Grossman. New York: Appleton-Century-Crofts, 1975, chap. 5, pp. 54–63.

Sargent, J., E. Walters, and E. Green. "Psychosomatic Self-Regulation of Migraine Headaches.", In Katz and Zlutnick, op. cit., chap. 26, pp. 385–402.

RAPE

Anonymous, "Rape—A Personal Account," *Health and Social Work* 1, no. 3 (August 1976): 83–95.

Kaufman, Arthur, et al., "Impact of a Community Health Approach to Rape," *American Journal of Public Health* 67, no. 4 (April 1977):365–68.

McCombie, S., "Characteristics of Rape Victims Seen in Crisis Intervention," *Smith College Studies in Social Work* 46, no. 2 (March 1976):137–57.

Williams, Cindy Cook, and Reg Arthur Williams. "Rape: A Plea for Help in the Hospital Emergency Room," in *The Rape Victim,* Deanna R. Nass (ed.)., Dubuque, Iowa: Kendall/Hunt Publishing Company, 1977.

REHABILITATION

Abrams, Ruth D., and Bess S. Dana, "Social Work in the Process of Rehabilitation," *Social Work,* October 1957, pp. 10–15.

Breedlove, James, "Casework in Rehabilitation," *Social Work,* October 1957, pp. 32–36.

Freeman, David, "Rehabilitation of the Mentally Ill Aging," *Social Work,* October 1959, pp. 65–71.

Ince, Laurence P., ed. *The Rehabilitation Medicine Services.* Springfield, Ill.: Charles C Thomas, 1974. (See esp. chap. 17, "Social Work Service," pp. 467–86.)

Wilbur, J. R., "Rehabilitation of Children with Cancer," *Cancer* 36, no. 2, supp. (August 1975): 809–12.

SELF-HELP

Levin, L. S., A. H. Katz, and E. Holst, eds. *Self Care: Lay Initiatives in Health.* Neale Watson, New York: Academic Publications, 1976.

Lurie, A., and H. Ron, "Self Help in an Aftercare Socialization Program," *Mental Hygiene* 55, no. 4 (October 1971):467–72.

Mantell, J. E., E. S. Alexander, and M. A. Kleiman, "Social Work and Self Help Groups," *Health and Social Work* 1, no. 1 (February 1976):86–100.

Vickery, Donald M., and James F. Fries. *Take Care of Yourself. A Consumers Guide to Medical Care.* Reading, Mass.: Addison-Wesley, 1976.

SEXUAL DYSFUNCTION IN ILLNESS

Bloch, A., "Sexual Problems After Myocardial Infarction," *American Heart Journal* 90, no. 4 (October 1975):536–37.

Gochos, Harvey L., "Sexual Problems in Social Work Practice," *Social Work* 16, no. 1 (January 1971).

McKevitt, Patricia M., "Treating Sexual Dysfunction in Dialysis and Transplant Patients," *Health and Social Work* 1, no. 3 (August 1976):132–56.

Sobrero, A. J., and K. L. Kohli, "Two Years' Experience of an Outpatient Vasectomy Service," *American Journal of Public Health* 65, no. 10 (October 1975):1091–94.

Woods, Nancy Fugate. *Human Sexualtiy in Health and Illness.* Saint Louis: C. V. Mosby, 1975.

SICKLE CELL ANEMIA

Alleyne, Sylvan I, Eleanor Wint, and Graham R. Serjeant, "Psychosocial Aspects of Sickle Cell Disease," *Health and Social Work* 1, no. 4 (November 1976):104–18.

Gary, Lawrence, "The Sickle Cell Controversy," *Social Work,* May 1974, pp. 263–72.

Le Pontois, Joan, op. cit., Pediatrics—Adolescents

Olafson, Freya, and Alberta Parker, eds. *The Neglected Disease: Community Approaches to Combating Sickle Cell Anemia.* Berkeley: University of California, University Extension, 1973, p. 109.

White, Joanna C., "Screening Programs for Sickle Cell Disease," *Social Work*, May 1974, pp. 273–78.

SPINA BIFIDA
Travis, Georgia, op. cit., chap. 17.

SPINAL CORD INJURY
Evans, R. L., "Multidisciplinary Approach to Sex Education of Spinal Cord Injured Patients," *Physical Therapy* 56, no. 5 (May 1976):541–45.
Ghatti, A. Z., and R. W. Hanson, "Outcome of Marriages Existing at the Time of a Male's Spinal Cord Injury," *Journal of Chronic Disease* 28, no. 7–8 (August 1975):383–88.
Richards, B., "An Evaluation of Home Care After Spinal Cord Injury," *Paraplegia* 12, no. 4 (February 1975,):263–67.
Travis, Georgia, op. cit., chap. 18, "Spinal Cord Injury."
Wheeler, Doris, et al., "Emotional Reactions of Patients, Family and Staff in Acute Care of Spinal Cord Injury (pt. 1)," *Social Work in Health Care* 2, no. 4 (Summer 1977):369–78.

STRESS
Brown, Barbara. *Stress and the Art of Biofeedback.* New York: Harper & Row, 1977.
Gunderson, Eric, and Richard Rahe. *Life Stress and Illness.* Springfield, Ill.: Charles C Thomas, 1974.
Kaplan, David, et al., "Family Mediation of Stress," *Social Work,* July 1973, pp. 60–69.
Selye, Hans. *The Stress of Life.* New York: McGraw-Hill, 1956.
Ullmann, Alice, "Teaching Medical Students to Understand Stress in Illness," *Social Casework,* November 1976, pp. 568–74.

STROKE
Singler, Judith, "Group Work with Hospitalized Stroke Patients," *Social Casework* 56, no. 6 (June 1975):348–54.
Branson, H. K. "Helping the Stroke Victim and His Family," *Nursing Care* 10, no. 3 (March 1977):32–36.

SURGERY
Bates, T., et al., "The Place of Early Social Assessment in the Management of Surgical Patients," *Postgraduate Medical Journal* (London) 52 (February 1976):61–65.
Brown, Julia, and May Rawlinson, "The Morale of Patients Following Open-Heart Surgery," *Journal of Health and Social Behavior* 17 (June 1976):135–45.
Sime, A. M., "Relationship of Preoperative Fear, Type of Coping, and Information Received About Surgery to Recovery from Surgery," *Journal of Personality and Social Psychology* 34, no. 4 (October 1976):716–24.
Strozier, A., and W. F. Ballinger, "The Social Worker and the Surgeon," *Surgery* 78, no. 2 (August 1976):128–29.

TERMINAL ILLNESS
Burton, Lindy, ed. *Care of the Child Facing Death.* London and Boston: Routledge and Kegan Paul, 1974.
Christopherson, L. K., "Cardiac Transplant: Preparation for Dying or for Living," *Health and Social Work* 1, no. 1 (February 1976):58–72.
Cowin, R., "Problems of Impending Death: The Role of the Social Worker," *Physical Therapy* 48, no. 7 (July 1968):743–48.

Glasser, Barney. "Disclosure of Terminal Illness." In *Patients, Physicians and Illness,* 2d ed., edited by E. Jaco. New York: Free Press, 1972.

Hackett, T. P., "Psychological Assistance for the Dying Patient and His Family," *Annual Review of Medicine* 27 (1976):371–78.

Illich, Ivan, "The Political Uses of Natural Death," *Hastings Center Studies* 2, no. 1 (January 1974):3–20.

Kobryzcki, P., "Dying with Dignity at Home," *American Journal of Nursing* 75, no. 8 (August 1975):1312–13.

Krieger, G. W., and L. O. Bascue, "Terminal Illness: Counseling with a Family Perspective," *Family Coordinator* 24, no. 3 (July 1975):351–54.

Kubler-Ross, Elizabeth. *Death: The Final Stage of Growth.* Englewood Cliffs N.J.: Prentice-Hall, 1975.

Matse, J., "Reactions to Death in Residential Homes for the Aged," *Omega: Journal of Death and Dying* 6, no. 1 (January 1975):21–32.

Stubblefield, Kristine, "A Preventive Program for Bereaved Families," *Social Work in Health Care* 2, no. 4 (Summer 1977):379–89.

Wald, F. S., "Hospice Care for Dying Patients," *American Journal of Nursing* 75, no. 10 (October 1975):1816–32.

10/THE CHRONIC-PAIN EXPERIENCE: CASE ILLUSTRATIONS

MARGO G. WYCKOFF

Every year over 10 million Americans endure a particular brand of suffering that has been termed *chronic pain*. Hospitals, private physicians' offices, health clinics, and family agencies are frequently contacted by chronic-pain patients and their families requesting treatment for this phenomenon. Yet, primarily because the chronic-pain experience demands both physiological and psychological investigation, many patients both are frustrated by and frustrate professionals who employ a one-dimensional diagnostic framework.

The greatest success in diagnosing and treating chronic pain is generally accepted to result from a multidisciplinary approach utilizing medical and behavioral health care practitioners. Evidence for this is seen in the recent emergence of "pain clinics," not only in the United States but also internationally.[1] Clinical services for pain care are most frequently provided in hospitals but can also be obtained by means of referral to appropriate medical and social work practitioners who have expertise in dealing with this patient population. Social workers equipped with specific assessment and treatment skills, including a reasonable understanding of disease processes, are and can be an integral part of any multidisciplinary pain diagnosis and treatment group. Specific social work approaches will be discussed later. First let us explore the definition and meaning of chronic pain.

WHAT IS CHRONIC PAIN?

Pain patients have one outstanding common denominator, and that is the presentation of suffering in *physiological* terms. Whether a lesion is found to be present or not, the expression of hurting is almost always described in terms of unpleasant bodily sensations. The chronic-pain syndrome is differentiated from acute pain in terms of longevity, over six months' duration being generally accepted as a reasonable time frame. Both medical and sociobehavioral professionals have attempted to define and explain pain by utilizing their own terminology and vocabulary. Mersky states that "pain is an unpleasant experi-

155

ence which we primarily associate with tissue damage or describe in terms of tissue damage or both."[2] Szasz takes a perceptual stance toward pain and sets forth the notion that the individual experiencing pain is actually experiencing his or her perception of the pain's impact upon the body rather than definitive lesion.[3] Some psychologists take the view that within the chronic-pain response are learned behaviors that can remain after tissue repair is effected and then can be the dominant feature of the pain experience. Perhaps the vernacular definition of pain is the most perplexing and yet the most understandable— "pain is where it hurts."

If one accepts the latter definition and also the premise that "hurting" is detrimental to the integrity of the emotional and physical well-being of the individual, whether it be caused by tissue damage, emotional suffering, or learned behaviors, then one can appreciate and understand the different approaches required to diagnose and treat this difficult population. As Sternbach notes,

this approach honors the integrity of the patient's pain experience. It does not imply, as does the traditional view, that he is "imagining" his pain, or that it is not real, or that it is not really pain. That is, description in parallel languages assumes what clinical experience in fact suggests, that there is a single phenomenon—pain—and not two phenomena—"painful pain" and "painless pain."[4]

The newly divorced patient with an aching shoulder for which no tissue damage can be observed is often unable to express the anguish of social trauma experienced during the disintegration of the marriage. Even though the physician cannot locate specific tissue damage to treat, the patient's expression of suffering, through physiological language, must be recognized as being valid for that person. Nothing will block communication with these patients more surely than that oft-repeated phrase, "Your pain is all in your head." Even if one believes that the patient's pain etiology can be more realistically described with psychological language, the patient still perceives unpleasant sensation in the shoulder. Forthright attempts to verbally remove or make invalid the organic "legitimacy" of the pain will be met with hostility, manipulative behavior, despair, and probably failure.

Samuel Mines quotes Dr. Benjamin R. Crue as saying, "In 99-plus percent of the functional pain problems we get there's a reason why it's in the left face or the left shoulder instead of the right. There's an old injury there—there's underlying pathology. Almost always. But it's being potentiated, exaggerated, consciously or subconsciously, and that is your chronic pain syndrome."[5] A more radical medical view is set forth by Dr. John Loeser, a neurosurgeon, who states that "most people with chronic non-cancer pain have essentially emotional illness masquerading as a health care problem. A lot of people are suffering, lonely, anxious. But a patient can't walk into a doctor's office and say, 'Nobody loves me, nobody needs me.' He can say, 'My back hurts.' It's not malingering, not conscious.'"[6]

THE SOCIAL WORK ROLE

Social workers are invaluable to the initial diagnostic procedures with this population in that they are trained to observe, diagnose, and report on the social and psychological stresses that contribute to human dysfunction. Whether one's preferred modality is ego psychology, social learning theory, or existential or transactional analysis, the social work practitioner can utilize the range of treatment techniques necessary in an etiologically complex problem.

Social workers need not overly concern themselves with taking a quasi-medical history—this only replicates the function of the physician and prevents the patient from fully expressing what the chronic pain experience has done to his or her life style and family system.

Recent attention to the "illness behavior model" indicates that patients often adhere to and form attachment behaviors toward and around a proscribed medical diagnosis.[7] Continuing attention to medical-illness labeling rather than the psychosocial elements of patients' lives may tend to inhibit the social worker's evaluation of social behaviors that might be reinforcing the "illness role."

Recent research conducted at the University of Washington Hospital (Pilowsky, Chapman, Bonica) indicates that *denial of psychosocial problems is a salient feature of the chronic-pain population*. The authors state:

Since these patients present us with a complex array of physical and psychological problems, it is often quite possible for only one aspect of their disturbance to receive attention. The nature of the difficulty, however, makes a total psychological, social, and somatic evaluation mandatory and emphasizes the need for collaborative interdisciplinary efforts in the management of chronic pain.[8]

INTERVIEWING AND ASSESSMENT APPROACHES

In the initial interview an approach found to be successful is, "Hello, Mr. X, my name is Ms. Y and I'm a social worker. I routinely see all patients referred for diagnosis because we know that your pain experience has probably made changes in your life. I'd like to talk with you about what life was like for you before the onset of your pain and what it is like now."

With this introduction the worker can take a social history, paying special attention to parental attitudes toward illness, actual illness experienced by family members during the patient's childhood, and general and specific questions relating to psychosocial growth and development. A goodly number of chronic-pain patients come from families in which chronic pain has been experienced by parents or siblings, giving credence to the "learned behaviors" theory. As this portion of the interview is conducted one can get a sense of what rewards and attitudes surround the patient's perceptions of "wellness" or "illness."[9]

Nonverbal messages are of importance, as chronic-pain patients usually present with a sad and woeful or angry affect. It is interesting to note affective changes during the interview, with special attention to the part of the body that expresses the pain. Often an interviewer observes patients using the part of the body that is affected by pain more freely as the interviewer touches on more positive aspects of their lives.

Of crucial importance in the interview is ascertaining what, in terms of life stresses, was occurring just before or around the time of onset of pain. Often professionals find that the pain experience began when the individual experienced life changes such as divorce, loss of employment, or children leaving home.[10] The anger and/or grief associated with these life changes may become translated into anger at physical incapacity and eventually toward the medical profession for not being able to effect a cure. Some case examples are as follows:

1. Mrs. B was referred to the pain clinic for extreme pain in her legs consequent to a fall three years prior to admittance. She had been to eight different physicians, was addicted to her pain medication and could not walk more than one block, necessitating that her son and daughter-in-law do her grocery shopping and housework. No physical findings were observable. Upon further examination it was determined that Mrs. B had taken her fall when climbing the church steps to her son's wedding. She admitted to despising her daughter-in-law and to grief at the reality of her son's leaving the family home to marry. A combination of physical therapy and behavioral counseling aided this woman toward regaining her physical and emotional health.

2. Mr. S was referred after five years of intractable shoulder pain. Because he had first noticed the pain while lifting at work, he was receiving workmen's compensation and remaining at home. Further interviews revealed that near the time of the injury his father had died and his wife had had an affair with his brother. To add insult to injury, the brother had also been left with the major share of their father's estate. The patient admitted receiving perverse pleasure at staying at home and "making my wife's life miserable." Subsequent marital counseling helped this patient make small but important changes in his familial relationships.

Chronic pain obviously leads to a certain amount of reactive depression and anxiety or dysphoria. Another phenomenon associated with chronic pain is *addiction to pain medication*. The usual response to onset of pain is to prescribe drugs that can usually alleviate the pain during the early stages (i.e., acute pain) of the experience. However, in the case of addictive drugs the longer the patient takes them, the less relief he or she will receive. "In addition, the medications prescribed may have a confusing effect on the higher mental functions, so often this regimen in this type of patient leads to continuation and even magnification of the pain complaints. This can result in self-administration of medicine and can continue on to habituation and addiction."[11]

Further, if the patient's social situation has become especially "painful," continued use of addictive medications makes the world a little more "fuzzy" and less threatening. The vicious circle is completed as the patient must produce more pain in order to receive more medications. Any suggestion by the physician or social worker that the patient is drug addicted in every sense of the word leads to vehement anger on the part of the patient. Needless to say, very little can be done for chronic-pain patients until they are withdrawn from their drugs, a process that usually takes two to three weeks and must be managed by a skilled physician, preferably in a hospital setting. During this process the social work professional can take a supportive stand; however, intense interviewing or therapy would seem ill advised. After the withdrawal, further investigations into the family structure can be carried out.

IMPACT OF THE FAMILY SYSTEM

The family system is almost always affected in some way by the chronic-pain experience, and this effect is usually detrimental in nature. Sexual functioning is decreased; children are often required to assume care of the home; and the social activities of the family unit are curtailed. Family members are frustrated, angry, and bitter, but are usually unable to express these feelings initially because they feel that these responses to someone "in pain" would be unacceptable and cruel. The professional can help family members talk out their feelings and help effect more honest communication within the family circle.

Occasionally the social worker will chance upon a situation in which the chronic-pain patient is being kept in that role for the benefit of the rest of the family. A case example is as follows:

Mrs. T was referred to the pain clinic for treatment of leg pains resultant from diabetic neuropathy. Although some pain would be expected with this diagnosis, the severity of her suffering was far beyond what is considered reasonable. Upon interviewing the entire family the social worker found the following family dynamic to be operating: Mrs. T's husband had moved her mother into the home to take care of her, thus making the mother feel happy, needed, and dominant over her daughter once again. The husband had then set up housekeeping in the basement and came and went as he liked. He finally admitted to having a homosexual orientation that he was loath to speak of for fear that it would ruin his standing in the community and within his family. The 16-year-old son had a lot of freedom and was unwilling to be disciplined by either mother or grandmother. Consequently he spent a good deal of time away from the home.

As one can readily see, this family had made Mrs. T the scapegoat of their dysfunctioning. Two years of psychotherapy ensued before she was able to take an active hand in determining her own daily routine and became strong enough emotionally to confront the issues that had been prominent in keeping her bedridden.

Many chronic-pain patients are also victims of what has been referred to as the "great green poultice" syndrome. This poultice is our system's disability compensation program. Because people who are injured on the job can receive almost three-quarters of their former salary tax free there may be little incentive to get well, especially if the former employment was not satisfactory.

Studs Terkel writes in the introduction to his classic book, *Working*:

For the many there is hardly concealed discontent. The blue collar blues is no more bitterly sung than the white collar moan. "I'm a machine," says the spot welder, "I'm caged," says the bank teller and echoes the hotel clerk. "I'm a mule," says the steel worker. "A monkey can do what I do," says the receptionist. "I'm less than a farm implement," says the migrant worker. "I'm an object," says the high-fashion model. Blue collar and white call upon the identical phrase, "I'm a robot."[12]

Too often, little effort is made or can be made owing to the lack of funds to retrain patients who can no longer engage in their former work. Or, if the effort is made, the alternative job possibilities are unacceptable to the patient's self-concept and perhaps may bring home less income than the disability payments. Quite frankly, this situation is most difficult for all involved, especially physicians who are called upon to make judgements on ability for work strictly on the basis of physical evidence. The patient is often left in the limbo of still feeling pain yet having to return to a job he or she feels physically and emotionally incapable of performing.

Another area of the diagnosis of chronic pain involves being attentive to different cultural expressions of pain. With the advent of national health insurance, social workers attached to pain clinics will undoubtedly be seeing a greater cross-section of our population and will have to familiarize themselves with the variety of pain manifestations that have traditionally been handed down in cultural groups.[13]

It has often been remarked by social work professionals and medical personnel that the chronic-pain population is one of the most difficult populations to work with. Those involved in treatment often have to be satisfied with very small gains over a long period. However, the frustrations experienced in dealing with the chronic-pain population are most definitely exceeded by its rewards. To observe a bedridden patient begin to function again, to watch family members begin to strengthen and rediscover each other, is indeed a challenging and satisfying professional experience.

NOTES

1. John J. Bonica, founder of the first multidisciplinary pain clinic (University of Washington) and author of *The Management of Pain* (Seattle: Lea and Febiger, 1953).
2. J. Mersky and F. G. Spear, *Pain, Psychological and Psychiatric Aspects* (London: Bailliere, Tindall and Cassell, 1967), p. 21.

3. T. S. Szasz, *Pain and Pleasure, A Study of Bodily Feelings* (New York: Basic Books, 1957).
4. Richard Sternbach, *Pain Patients, Traits and Treatment* (New York: Academic Press, 1974), p. 21.
5. Samuel Mines, *The Conquest of Pain* (New York: Grosset and Dunlap, 1974), p. 33.
6. "Pain Under Attack at the University of Washington Clinic," *Seattle Times*, December 5, 1976, Magazine Section.
7. David Mechanic, "Response Factors in Illness: The Study of Illness Behaviours," in E. Garely Jaco, *Patients, Physician and Illness* (New York: Free Press, 1972).
8. USPHS Grant GM15991, DHEW Grant MB00184.
9. Wilbert E. Fordyce et al., "Some Implications of Learning in Problems of Chronic Pain," *Journal of Chronic Diseases* 21 (1968):179–90; Wilbert E. Fordyce, *Behavioural Methods for Chronic Pain and Illness*, (St. Louis: Mosby Press, 1977).
10. Thomas Holmes and Minoru Masuda, "Life Change and Illness Susceptibility," in Dohrenwend and Dohrenwend, *Stressful Life Events* (New York: Wiley, 1974).
11. Richard G. Black, *The Management of Pain in the Office Practice*, (Seattle: University of Washington, 1975).
12. Studs Terkel, *Working*, (New York: Pantheon Books, 1972), p. xi.
13. B. B. Wolff and S. Langley, "Cultural Factors and the Response to Pain: A Review," *American Anthropologist* 70 (1968):494–501; M. Zborowski, "Cultural Components of Pain," *Journal of Social Issues* 8 (1952):16–30.

SUGGESTED ADDITIONAL READINGS

Berne, E. *Games People Play.* New York: Grove Press, 1964.

Fordyce, W. D., R. S. Fowler, Jr., J. F. Lehmann, and B. J. DeLateur, "Some Implications of Learning in Problems of Chronic Pain," *Journal of Chronic Disease* 21 (1968):179–90.

Kenyon, F. E., "Hopochondriasis: A Clinical Study," *British Journal of Psychiatry* 110 (1964): 478–88.

Lesse, S., "The Multivarient Masks of Depression," *American Journal of Psychiatry* 124 (1968): 35–40.

Mechanic, D., "Social Psychologic Factors Affecting the Presentation of Bodily Complaints," *New England Journal of Medicine,* 286 (1972):1132–39.

Merskey, H., "The Characteristics of Persistent Pain in Psychological Illness," *Journal of Psychosomatic Research* 9 (1965):291–98.

Pilowsky, I., "Dimensions of Hypochondriasis," *British Journal of Psychiatry* 113 (1967):89–93.

——"The Diagnosis of Abnormal Illness Behaviour," *Australian and New Zealand Journal of Psychiatry* 5 (1971):136–38.

Szasz, T. S. *Pain and Pleasure: A Study of Bodily Feelings.* New York: Basic Books, 1957.

——"The Psychology of Persistent Pain: A Portrait of L'homme Douloureux." In *Pain,* edited by A. Soulairac, J. Cahn, and J. Charpentier. New York: Academic Press, 1968.

Wolff, B. G., and S. Langley, "Cultural Factors and the Response to Pain: A Review," *American Anthropologist* 70 (1968):494–501.

Woodforde, J. M., and H. Merskey, "Personality Traits of Patients with Chronic Pain," *Journal of Psychosomatic Research* 16 (1972):167–72.

Zborowski, M. *People in Pain.* San Francisco: Jossey-Bass, 1969.

Part VI

SOCIAL WORK PRACTICE IN HOSPITALS AND NURSING HOMES

11/SOCIAL WORK PRACTICE IN HOSPITALS: CHANGING DIRECTIONS AND NEW OPPORTUNITIES

NEIL F. BRACHT

The hospital occupies a central and prestigious role in the delivery of health services in many American communities. In addition to the highly specialized and sophisticated medical services offered within its own walls, the hospital is increasingly involved in regional networks of community health services. For nearly three decades the hospital has been a focal point in discussions about improving the delivery of health care services. Issues of concern that surround the hospital include professional and institutional needs versus community needs, geographic variations in the quality of care, acceleration of operational costs, shared services between hospitals, regional planning to avoid costly overbedding, and legal and ethical uncertainties regarding new life-sustaining technologies. More recently peer review and utilization review along with other forms of accountability and cost control have been in the forefront of these prolonged discussions. In describing the hospital as the technological center of the health care world, Somers also speaks of the plight of the modern community hospital:

Internally, the hospital has not been able to resolve the deep-rooted conflict between medical staff and lay administration, resulting in diffuse management and numerous inefficiencies. Externally, the hospital's role in the evolving health care system is challenged both by those who would turn the clock back to pre-institutional medicine and those who claim the center of the evolving system should not be the hospital but some type of primary care unit, apart from the hospital. Forced to carry multiple and ever growing responsibilities, with these two major issues unresolved, the hospital's costs spiral ever upward and in turn add fuel to the fire of public criticism.[1]

Social workers who practice in hospitals are not immune from the changing forces that swirl about them in hospital settings. As Nacman notes, "The

165

establishment and development of a social work program within a given health organization is therefore influenced by the policies formulated by political, economic, and professional elite, both governmental and private, who influence national health policies and those who supervise and control a specific health institution."[2]

In this chapter we look at how social workers are responding to the changing hospital system and describe ways in which the profession's practice innovations are contributing solutions to complex patient service questions. Areas of program leadership in prehospital, in-hospital, and after-hospital care are highlighted. This is preceded by a discussion of the hospital's organizational structure and social work decision making.

HOSPITAL STRUCTURE AND SOCIAL WORK DECISION MAKING

In 1970 the Joint Commission on the Accreditation of Hospitals adopted the principle that social services "must be available to patients accepted for care, as well as to their families, in order to promote optimal social functioning of the patient." This has included a standard under which every hospital shall have a well-defined plan for providing social services to the patient with social problems, including supervision of the delivery of such services by a qualified social worker. Approximately half of all American hospitals have social service departments. Ways of further promoting the adoption of hospital social services have been described in a study by Gentry and his associates.[3] Once established by a hospital, a social service department's success will be influenced by a number of factors, such as the size and location of the hospital, receptivity to the social component on the part of professional (other) disciplines, the quality and leadership ability of the social work staff, budget and reimbursement patterns, and last but not least, the social structure of the hospital itself.

A number of social work authors have described approaches to influencing social work program directions and patient services in hospital settings. Hallowitz describes a process of social work intervention in interdepartmental relations as one possible way of improving communication with non-social work hospital staff.[4] Lurie and Rosenberg discuss the administrative skills required to influence both the internal and the external systems of the hospital.[5] McNamara has provided a description of a process for humanizing patient care through staff training.[6] Nacman, utilizing a systems analysis approach, sees the social worker practicing in the health setting

as being in an advantageous position to become an advisor to administration and other staff. . . . Social workers gain influence as they assist other employees in the resolution of organizational and administrative problems that are crucial to fellow health care professionals.[7]

Wax analyzes a hospital's power structure and provides suggestions for ways social work can bring about changes within the setting.[8] Weiner says that social work makes an impact on the health care system

to the degree that it is clear about what its function is. Not to the extent that it has a marvelous value system which identifies with the disadvantaged. . . . The resource of social work power is expertise. Without professional competence, we have nothing. With it, not necessarily much more, unless we are able to build coalitions with nurses, dietitians, families, relatives, communities and really work at the political strategy.[9]

All of these authors point to the need to better understand both hospital structure and decision making if social work leadership and program development are to be successful.

ORGANIZATIONAL HIERARCHY—IMPLICATIONS FOR DECISION MAKING

Social workers practicing in hospitals need to be aware of hierarchical structures and inherent organizational complexities that can enhance or impede intraprofessional and interprofessional practice. Figure 11.1 is a typical organizational diagram of a hospital. Of course not all hospitals are alike. They differ in size, goals, location (rural or urban), and whether or not they are affiliated teaching hospitals. Coe believes that the social structure of most hospitals has three major characteristics.[10] These include (1) a dual authority system, (2) an extreme division of labor, and (3) an authoritarian nature. As can be seen from the diagram, there are two distinct lines of authority. The broken-line relationship among the board (which legally appoints physicians to the hospital staff), hospital administrators, and staff physicians is clearly different from the direct-line relationship of the hospital administrator to the service department heads, including social work. In hospitals where physicians are not salaried members of the hospital staff or under the supervision of a full-time salaried chief of staff, physicians essentially operate "freely" within the hospital, coming and going as they perceive their private patients' needs. While in the hospital, they give direction to line staff over whom they do not technically have administrative authority. For example, the ward nurse may be given a directive by the hospital administrator to economize as much as possible on certain supplies. Unaware of this problem, the physician may prescribe a medically justified treatment regimen that is not conducive to the nurse's need to economize. More serious problems in patient care policy can arise under this dual accountability system. For example, the social work department may gain approval from the hospital administrator to initiate a plan involving automatic (nonphysician) referral of certain high-risk patients, only to have this "approval" reversed by a more powerful medical staff that is unwilling to move in this direction.

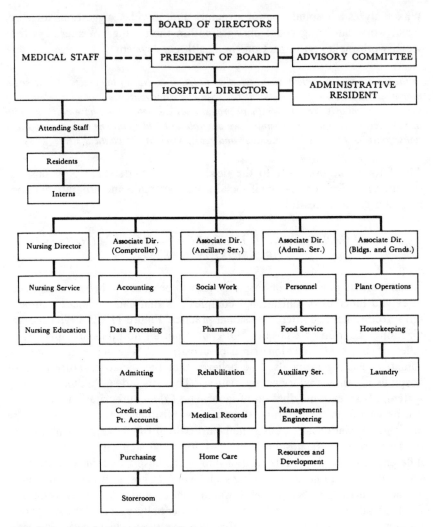

FIG. 11.1. Organization of the hospital.

Source: R. Coe, *Sociology of Medicine* (New York: McGraw-Hill, 1970), p. 270. Used with permission of McGraw-Hill Book Company.

This dual authority system, coupled with the division of labor characteristic of hospitals, can create problems for patients as well. In one well-known study of patient care in a hospital, the authors concluded that "the central purpose of the hospital—the care of patients, especially the personal aspects of that care —was not controlled directly or effectively by the hospital or by anyone."[11] One study is not a general indictment of all hospitals. Social workers, however, who have for many years been witness to countless problems in the coordination of hospitalized care for patients, will not find these results surprising. The extreme division of labor in hospitals, while required for modern management of highly sophisticated medical services, leads easily to fragmented care, which at times is unresponsive to the personal aspects of care. Greater autonomy for nursing departments in the exercise of authority over patient care is a trend with potential benefits to both patients and administration.

The physician's authority in the hospital rests primarily on his/her monopoly over medical knowledge and skill. Hospitals would not survive without the physician's input. On the other hand, other professionals have skills and expertise regarding the personal- and social-care aspects of medical treatment that is equally vital to the hospital's service responsibility.* In the hospital study cited earlier it was found that

although patients and physicians focused upon physical disease, personal and social attributes produced disability as great as that caused by physical disease. Of the 155 patients discharged alive, 14 percent were not disabled, 24 percent were disabled from physical disease, 44 percent were disabled from psychosocial disturbances, and 18 percent were disabled from a combination of these causes.[12]

Unless the social work staff and/or director can clearly elucidate these social and community factors of illness through appropriate planning and policy groups in the hospital, their recognition and "treatment" will succumb to the more powerful or better-articulated interests of other services and disciplines. Schoenfeld, a hospital administrator, believes that because there is a lack of understanding of the value of certain social work functions, the hospital does not always receive the full benefit of the expertise of the social worker or of a social medicine philosophy.[13]

A hospital's value orientations, as reflected in formal board and medical-staff policies as well as through a host of informal ward processes and mechanisms, can obviously have a significant impact on social work operations and autonomy in the hospital:

The number of social work department staff hired, the qualifications of these staff members, the nature and extent of the program to be developed, and the relationship of the social work program to other hospital programs are strongly influenced by the value judgments of lay and medical administrators who determine the organization's basic commitment to psychosocial treatment and their acceptance of non-medical practitioners. This state of affairs has resulted in much frustration for social workers but also a serendipitous gain. It offers incentive for social workers to acquire an understanding of the politics of the organizations in which they work and to learn how to deal with the system.[14]

---

*"Psychosocial Aspects of Health Care: The Hospital's Responsibility," Statement of the American Hospital Association, 1976.

This latter point is extremely important. Social workers, as noted previously, are learning how to deal with and influence complex health care organizations. Hospitals are not monolithic institutions; not all issues are viewed in the same way. Some physicians may be as committed to the psychosocial and community aspects of care as are social workers. It must be remembered that no one in the hospital has absolute authority. Practically everyone in the hospital is dependent on another person for the fulfillment of his/her own role or function. Each medical service has its own particular formal and informal decision-making apparatus. Value conflicts and role relationship problems can be anticipated;[15, 16] patient care processes can be improved;[17, 18] and program innovations can be accomplished.[19, 20]

When social workers perceive their influence in patient care programs to be minimal, it may be tempting and consoling to blame the hospital bureaucracy or the "powerful medical staff" as the "villain." Recent studies of social work leadership in hospitals suggest another culprit—the social work department itself.

Wattenberg, in a study of social work leadership tasks, compared the opinions of social work administrators and hospital administrators in a midwestern health-planning area.[21] In Table 11.1 we see that there is considerable congruence between hospital directors and social work directors regarding the appropriateness of certain leadership tasks. Wattenberg's study indicated, however, that in actuality these tasks were performed only occasionally or seldom. It would appear that some social work directors either do not have the inclination or have not been well prepared to exercise skillful decision making and program leadership. Clinical program orientations at the administrative and supervisory levels must be complimented by a systems or community-wide perspective on health needs and modes of planning and intervention.[22, 23] Such orientations and associated strategies are discussed in more detail in Part IX of this book, which deals with "Organizing and Planning Community Health Services," and in Part XI, which discusses "Administration and Accountability in Social Service Programing." The suggested additional readings at the ends of these chapters are also a resource for further study.

THE NATURE AND CHANGING CHARACTERISTICS OF SOCIAL SERVICES IN HOSPITALS

The range of social work services provided in hospitals and related institutions comprises three major programatic areas of patient care: preadmission, inpatient, and discharge–aftercare. During the past decade social work services have expanded into many new facets of hospital care, adapting to new technological developments in medicine (e.g., kidney dialysis) and changing community demands for hospital services (e.g., child abuse and sexual assault centers). The premises on which the need for and use of social work services in hospitals

TABLE 11.1

Comparison of Attitudes of Social Work Administrators and
Hospital Administrators Toward Importance of Leadership Tasks*

Task	Social Work Administrators		Hospital Administrators		t-Value	2-Tailed Probability
	$\overline{X}$	s.d.	$\overline{X}$	s.d.		
Develop inservice training programs	6.17	.63	6.31	.79	−.55	.59
Act as advocate ombudsman for patient/family	6.17	.81	5.56	1.60	1.38	.18
Interpret hospital policies and services	6.06	.79	5.93	1.03	.40	.69
Participate in planning committee regarding improvement of care	6.06	.57	6.47	.72	1.80	.08
Participate in development committee regarding long-range planning	5.83	.94	5.54	1.96	.45	.65
Participate in community councils representing hospitals	5.73	1.03	5.00	1.51	1.51	.14
Policy planning for hospital personnel health and welfare	5.50	1.02	5.50	1.01	0	1.00
Participate in review of utilization services (PSRO)	5.50	.73	5.81	1.68	−.91	.37
Formal teaching (lecture) to other health disciplines	5.38	.96	5.63	1.02	−.62	.54
Clinical teaching to other health professions	5.33	1.49	5.64	1.08	−.63	.53
Clinical teaching to medical students/resident interns	5.27	1.62	5.13	1.96	.18	.85
Formal teaching (lecture) to medical students/resident interns	5.00	1.00	5.67	1.21	−.82	.44

* Range of importance: 7 = extremely important; 6 = quite important; 5 = slightly important; 4 = neither important or unimportant; 3 = slightly unimportant; 2 = quite unimportant; 1 = extremely unimportant.
Source: Shirley Wattenberg, et al., "Comparisons of Opinions of Social Work Administrators and Hospital Administrators Toward Leadership Tasks," *Social Work in Health Care* 2, no. 3 (Spring 1977).

are based were discussed in Chapter 2. The specific types of services usually provided by social workers in hospitals include the following:[24]

1. Assessment of need for social work service
2. Case finding, outreach, and high-risk population identification, and services to such groups
3. Counseling to patients and families related to reaction to illness and disability, and facilitation of a treatment plan
4. Discharge-planning service
5. Preadmission planning
6. Provision of continuity of care
7. Information and referral service
8. Consultation to staff and outside agencies
9. Institutional services planning
10. Community liaison services
11. Community planning and coordination activity
12. Collaboration with physicians and other staff

PREADMISSION SERVICES

Preadmission services are becoming an increasingly important aspect of social services. With shortened hospital stays, early assessment of psychosocial factors that may complicate medical treatment or prolong hospitalization is necessary. High-risk populations (e.g., elderly, single-parent families) require prompt identification and contact, involving coordination between the medical and nursing staffs and the hospital admission office. Outreach planning with families prior to surgery for care of children or follow-up care after discharge can be initiated much earlier. In order to be effective at both the preadmission and the in-hospital phase of the patient care process, social work departments need more autonomy in identifying and selecting patients for treatment or referral.

Historically social workers operating in a "host" agency such as the hospital have waited for or depended on medical and nursing staff referral of patients. Physician referral has been the dominant source of social worker–patient contact. Several studies[25] of the referral process show that doctor-initiated referrals range from 40 percent to 71 percent of all referrals; 14–20 percent of referrals are initiated by patients or their families. For many patients several days elapse after admission before they are referred to social services. Two consequences of such referral patterns are delay in referral of complex psychosocial problems requiring prolonged treatment activities and potential biases operating in the process by which patients are selected for social work services. Berkman and Rehr have shown that when social work develops its own professional criteria and initiates its own referrals, the benefits to both patient and hospital are considerable.[26] In a controlled study of hospitalized elderly, early intervention by social workers reduced the hospital stay of these patients by an average of ten days.

The definition of what constitute *preadmission* activities by social workers and members of other disciplines must be expanded in terms of the changing role of the hospital and its community responsibility. Health education and preventive work in the community should be seen as a legitimate function of the hospital's broader input into improving community health. Efforts to prevent hospitalization are as legitimate as efforts to coordinate hospital discharge of patients.[27]

Involvement of social work staff in community-wide planning efforts to improve community facilities and services and facilitate communication between health and social services[28] are as important as utilizing social workers for in-service training to improve interviewing skills of admission office workers. Special outreach efforts to the poor and medically underserved by social workers can help eliminate problems faced by hospitals such as inappropriate use of hospital emergency rooms[29] and missed outpatient department appointments.[30] Health professionals should not lose sight of a consistent finding in a number of empirical research studies:

The primary explanation for poor people's limited participation in the majority of health care programs is not their lack of motivation but the way in which these health services have generally been structured.[31]

INPATIENT-RELATED SOCIAL SERVICES

Inpatient-related social services comprise the largest array of professional interventions provided by social workers in hospitals. A review of social treatment modalities with selected illness conditions or program areas (e.g., intensive-care units) as described in Chapter 9 (pp. 141–154) will indicate the expansiveness of social work's contribution to nearly all facets of hospital patient care, teaching (see Chapter 15), and research (see Chapters 18 and 19). Social work has demonstrated its relevance to patient care in all medical services, from anesthesiology to surgery. Most specialty services, both inpatient and outpatient, utilize social workers. These include

1. admissions office—prescreening, intake
2. burn clinics, pain centers, and seizure clinics
3. developmental disability–retardation clinics
4. emergency room social work and critical-care units
5. genetic counseling clinics
6. hospital-based home care
7. hospital-based day care programs
8. intensive care (coronary)
9. kidney dialysis centers
10. medical–surgery units
11. mental health–psychiatric inpatient and outpatient clinics
12. neurology and orthopedics
13. ombudsman–patient advocacy programs and offices

14. rehabilitation
15. newborn nurseries and pediatric wards
16. extended-care units
17. outreach clinics for the underserved

Social workers are heavily involved in utilization and peer review and are especially critical in discharge and aftercare planning. They have provided leadership in program development for hospital care; for example, social work was in the forefront of the development of patient representative or ombudsman programs, which have done much to improve the patient care process and to prevent more serious communication problems between the hospital and the community.[32] Social work has been particularly effective in new programs for patients or families experiencing sudden crisis (e.g., accident victims, sexual abuse) as seen in the emergency room.[33] New programs to integrate volunteer services with the social work department can avoid unnecessary duplication of effort in some areas. Crisis counseling in newborn and other types of intensive- or critical-care units can be especially helpful with families and parents. A trend toward more twenty-four-hour hospital coverage by social workers is under way and can be expected to grow.[34]

DISCHARGE PLANNING–AFTERCARE ACTIVITIES

Discharge planning–aftercare activities are central to one of social work's distinct practice functions, that of linking the patient to appropriate community resources. As Lurie and Tuzman note, the development of an effective and efficient discharge-planning program requires the concerted effort of the health care team:

The discharge planning process is an integral component of the medical center's philosophy of patient care and at the same time reflects the Patient's Bill of Rights. This philosophy indicates that the patient is entitled to health care that is comprehensive and personal, that respects him as an individual, that takes into consideration not only immediate problems but also its consequences and that provides for continuity of treatment. The informed patient is the central component of an effective discharge planning process.[35]

This latter point is especially crucial to discharge planning in psychiatric facilities, where there has been some tendency "of hospital personnel to take over all decision making [for patients]."[36]

Social work's role in discharge planning has had significant effects on unnecessary delays in leaving the hospital. Clark has reported delays reduced by five days in a discharge project coordinated by the social service department.[37] As chronic conditions increase in the patient populations, social work must exercise increasing responsibility for well-coordinated patient referral and relocation to appropriate community resources (e.g., home health care).

This includes follow-up and monitoring techniques to ensure that initial placements or referrals are in keeping with the overall treatment plan.[38]

A discharge plan should contain the following essential elements:[39]

1. Early identification of patients requiring discharge planning.

2. Integration of discharge planning with admitting procedures, with the focus on the physician identifying the patient's expected need upon discharge—at the point when hospitalization is indicated and at any point during the patient's stay at the hospital.

3. Development and implementation of preadmission and admission screening of all patients admitted to the hospital.

4. Centralization of activities and responsibilities and standardization of procedures.

5. Coordination of discharge planning with utilization review.

6. Developing a mechanism for review of specific discharge plans and for periodic review of the discharge-planning program.

7. Greater understanding by all professional staff of the goals of effective discharge planning.

HOSPITAL TRENDS AND NEW PROGRAM OPPORTUNITIES

Major trends having an impact on the delivery of health services in the United States were discussed in Chapter 3. Similar forces and trends are at work in hospitals and are influencing programatic efforts and pointing to new opportunities for social workers. These include the following:

1. New patient care programs involving highly sophisticated equipment that can be frightening to patients while hospitalized or require planning for a permanent life style adjustment (e.g., home dialysis).

2. As a result of these technological advances, social workers find themselves increasingly involved in many of the knotty ethical and legal aspects of life-sustaining procedures and ultimately the question of the right to die with dignity.

3. Increased concern for quality assurance through peer review has seen the development of quality assurance protocols in social service departments (see Figure 11.2).

4. Concern over utilization and increasing costs have resulted in stepped-up accountability efforts, which are leading to improved information systems and *cost-finding techniques*. Kahn describes the essential components in the cost finding process as follows:

Cost finding involves the identification of costs for social work (or any) programs and relating such costs to specific services and units of services received by patients. Ideally it involves determining the costs of the input relative to the units of benefit, that have effect on the patient. Currently, at best, we determine the cost of input effort relative to the product or units of output. For social work that could mean, for example, the cost of having an MSW function an eight-hour workday.

I. Criteria for referral to social worker
   (one of the following is sufficient justification for referral)
   A. Patient in need of additional community resources, including medical assistance, financial assistance, follow-up counseling
   B. Patient and/or family having difficulty understanding disease and treatment, with resultant lack of adherence to treatment program
   C. Patient and/or family requests contact with social worker
   D. Patient having personal or interpersonal problems that interfere with treatment of disease
   E. Patient having difficulty adjusting to disease symptomatology, including pain, fatigue, decreasing mobility
   F. Patient having functional pain
II. Protocol
   A. Assessment
      1. Description of patient, disease, length of time patient has had disease, general condition, prognosis, other illnesses
      2. Patient's general attitude about and adjustment to disease, that is, denying, accepting, depressed
      3. Patient's family composition, response to disease, employment status of household members, health of family members, financial constraints, division of labor at home
      4. Patient's employment status, potential for employability, and desire to work
      5. Patient and family's usual response to pain and stress
   B. Goal setting
      1. List of problems as seen by patient, family, physician, and other staff
      2. Goals established with patient and relevant staff
   C. Implementation of plan
      1. Make recommendations to patient regarding appropriate community resources
      2. Reinforce medical information and need for particular treatment with follow-up on questions. Refer to other medical personnel when appropriate
      3. Provide counseling to patient and/or family members or refer to community agency when family lives too far away or clinic visits are infrequent
   D. Recording
      1. Summary of assessment and treatment plan in chart
      2. Progress toward goals noted in chart
      3. Documentation of recommendations to patient regarding community resources in chart
III. Unexpected complications
   A. Patient's refusal of service
   B. Patient discharged prior to being seen by social worker
IV. Criteria for termination
   A. Cases will be terminated when goals have been reached or
   B. When it appears that goals cannot be achieved

FIG. 11.2. Illustration of social work protocol used at the University of Michigan Hospital.

Source: Kris Ferguson et al., "Initiation of a Quality Assurance Program for Social Work Practice in a Teaching Hospital," *Social Work in Health Care* 2, no. 2 (Winter 1976–1977): 212-14.

There are available models of statistical accountability systems which effectively measure the cost of services, * though they may fall short of dealing with benefits to the patient. This paper mainly will attempt to deal with specific issues for cost finding in a conceptual sense. As one thinks of cost finding, one realizes immediately that a viable system needs to be based upon an instrument which permits description and measurement of the impact of service inputs upon the patient.

Major issues for cost finding include making a decision regarding units for service to be used for charging for direct, indirect and supporting services. Time is often seen as the most manageable unit in terms of figuring costs of services. Yet, for fee setting, it is necessary also to have a system which permits weighting according to the complexity of the task performed during a given contact period. Thus, assigning unit values to tasks, and procedures as does Blue Cross, with a given value assigned to the unit, may serve to differentiate cost wise between professional and nonprofessional services, and between complexities of tasks performed by personnel with different levels of competence.

If the standard unit of service were a personal contact with a patient or on his behalf, that unit could be assigned a monetary value, (1) according to level of staff and problem solving tasks involved per contact, (2) according to cost per case figured on the basis of actual number of contact units counted at the end of service, with monetary value assigned according to level and complexity of problem, or (3) according to cost of a service package, which can also be done, by assigning monetary values according to complexity and level of competence of staff. The following are issues which should be kept in mind when thinking about the development of a rate for social work services which may be included in health insurance premiums:

1. It is necessary to establish the total cost of the program of the department. This refers to direct and indirect services, and overhead costs, such as rent, utilities, in addition to salaries. How much of the cost for indirect services (community work education, research, etc.) may be charged beyond the cost to produce a service (input) must be determined by each social work services provider. However, rates must reflect efficiency, effectiveness, and economy.

2. In insurance language, fees upon which the premium is to be based must be usual, customary and reasonable (the UCR principle). That is, fees should be at a reasonable level and in line with what most members of the profession are charging in a given community.

3. The relative value approach to personal contact needs to be considered as an alternative in cost finding. The question is whether all contacts are to have a fixed price, or whether they will be given unit values according to the complexity of the contact, which in turn can be translated into dollars and cents.

4. A decision needs to be made whether the entire cost per encounter is to be paid through the insurance, or whether there is to be patient participation, or insurance riders.

5. Possible limits for services provided under the coverage in terms of number of contacts in a given time period is another important consideration. Specifically, this

---

*One of the most comprehensive and functional ones known to the writer in terms of accountability is in use at the Department of Clinical Social Work at the UCLA Center for Health Sciences, Mrs. Eleanor Klein, Director.

means thinking about limits on monetary benefits to be paid for services within a given time, for instance a year.

6. Cost for service depends in large part upon salary budget. Therefore, the following factors need to be considered:

- *Staff/enrollee ratio*
- *Staff salary levels by type of personnel providing social services (technicians, B.A. social workers, M.S.W.'s, D.S.W.'s and Ph.D.'s)*
- *At risk assignments, odd shifts, etc. Staffing patterns must reflect enrollee needs and wishes within limitations of safety from the point of view of services required. In some neighborhoods, for example, consumers may prefer neighborhood health aides to professional staff.*
- *Wise differential use of staff would make much difference cost wise. Therefore, it is of great importance to sort tasks in their professional and nonprofessional aspects more responsibly so that the most reasonable rate for services may be developed.*

There is no doubt that some benefits to the patient may be lost when the professional person does not render the entire service. There will be some loss of judgment and some fragmentation. However, experience in both social work and nursing suggests that the end justifies the means, and that there is little choice.

7. Projection of service unit output. In considering the matter of costs and fee setting, one must remember that costing out services according to contacts and total overhead budget, figured within certain time limits is only part of what needs to be done. It addition it is necessary to be able to predict how many service units—personal contacts—will be needed to perform a variety of service tasks which may be needed to provide a complete service, and how many of these will be needed for the total population of a given health plan.

8. Cost of success. To determine the cost of a service unit or of a completed service is one thing, to determine cost of a successful service is quite another. How is a success unit to be defined, how much time, what kind of staff time does it take? These questions may seem simple. However, again we are back with the issue of how to measure what difference social work services make in health care. *

5. The consumer–patient rights movement is requiring more sensitivity to joint planning and mutual decision making in the delivery of professional services in many health care settings.[40] Community and self-care alternatives to institutionalization are also an important theme in the consumer movement. These trends and others require an increased effort to develop social work practice innovations, new styles of administration based on improved management techniques,[41] and continuing advocacy efforts for improving hospital care for the community.

Social work practice in hospitals is still hampered by restrictive state and federal insurance reimbursement patterns, which in many instances do not

---

*Source: Elsbeth Kahn, "Issues and Problems in Cost Finding in Social Services," in W. Hall and G. St. Denis, eds., *Quality Assurance in Social Services in Health Programs for Mothers and Children*, (Pittsburgh: University of Pittsburgh, School of Public Health, 1975), pp. 81–93.

recognize social work units of service as valid components of overall patient care operating costs. Various methods of payment for social work have been discussed.[42] Frequently social services are paid for through the hospital's administrative costs. This is not an adequate cost-accounting solution for the long run. The insurance industry as well as governmental reimbursement programs must be continually petitioned for a reversal in their longstanding discriminatory practice of not reimbursing specified professional social services. Why should a physician be reimbursed for caring for an abused child in the emergency room and a social worker not be reimbursed for his/her efforts in counseling both child and family including time-consuming referral and follow-up activities with child protective services? Assertive political action in unison with consumer and professional groups will be required to win full vendor status and reimbursement for professional health care provider services. Five states now have "freedom of choice" legislation requiring social work inclusion in all insurance programs.

Hospital practice will remain an important arena for the professional social worker. Much of social work's leadership in the health field has come from hospital-based practitioners, including the Veterans Administration hospitals.[43] The leadership of hospital social workers in responding to the new challenges of institutional care will be even more important in the future.

Schoenfeld sees several major areas of leadership for social-work functions in a hospital setting.[44] These include the following:

1. Social improvement of the hospital organization.

2. Assisting the hospital administration and medical staff in developing new ways to implement the external changes that have taken place and will take place in the health field.

3. Improving both patient and community understanding of hospital objectives.

4. Helping to develop the social policies of boards of trustees and becoming part of long-range planning committees.

5. Participating in the education of general staffs of hospitals, which could include employee orientation to improve the understanding of the psychology of the sick and to initiate advocacy programs for patients.

In facing these and other new opportunities, the hospital social worker should not be naive about the realistic obstacles to change in organizations. On the other hand, he/she cannot be reluctant to "take the necessary risks that come in designing new programs and new organizational structures."[45] Social workers must continue to increase their understanding of how organizational change occurs.[46] Equally important is the need to improve skills in program planning, budgeting, and evaluation. (Loeb has developed a nine-step process of relating program needs to expected results and costs.[47]) For the staff social worker who feels "powerless" to influence large organizations, Pruger offers one kind of advice:

*The employee in a bureaucracy needs to acquire a competence needed by the organiza-
tion. The competencies I refer to here are those which are increasingly required by modern
service organizations but for which no formal training is readily available. Such skills
include proposal writing, or the ability to bridge the gap between the organization and
the community, or a knowledge of modern budgeting and training techniques.*[48]

The skilled and energetic social worker—hospital practice requires considerable stamina—has many opportunities to contribute innovative solutions to
complex organizational and patient care problems. In addition, as hospitals
become more integrated with community health and welfare services, including health care planning agencies, social workers can enlarge their historical
linkage function between hospital and community. By helping to guide collaborative efforts between the institution and the broader community, social
workers facilitate coordinated networks of social and health services in our
ever-evolving human services system.

NOTES

1. Anne Somers, *Health Care in Transition: Directions for the Future* (Chicago: Hospital Research and Educational Trust, 1971), p. 36.
2. Martin Nacman, "A Systems Approach to the Provision of Social Work Services in Health Settings—Parts I and II," *Social Work in Health Care* 1, nos. 1 and 2 (Fall 1975):48.
3. John Gentry el al., "Promoting the Adoption of Social Work Services by Hospitals and Health Departments," *American Journal of Public Health* 63, no. 2 (February 1973):117.
4. Emanuel Hallowitz, "Innovations in Hospital Social Work," *Social Work* 17 (July 1972): 89–97.
5. Abraham Lurie and Gary Rosenburg, "The Current Role of the Hospital Social Work Director," Reference Article, American Hospital Association (Chicago, June 1973), 12 pp.
6. James McNamara, "Social Work Designs: A Humanistic Program to Enhance Patient Care," *Social Work in Health Care* 1, no. 2 (Winter 1975–1976):155–66.
7. Nacman, op cit., p. 139.
8. John Wax, "Developing Social Work Power in a Medical Organization," *Social Work* 13 (October 1968):62–71.
9. Hyman J. Weiner, "Workshop on Administration," in Mary M. Lewis, ed., *Social Work Services in Pediatric Hospitals,* Proceedings of the Directors of Social Work Departments in Pediatric Hospitals, James Whitcomb Riley Hospital for Children, Indianapolis, 1972, p. 17.
10. R. Coe, in *Sociology of Medicine,* McGraw-Hill, 1970, pp. 268–73.
11. Raymond Duff and August Hollingshead, *Sickness and Society* (New York: Harper and Row, 1968), p. 378.
12. Ibid., p. 377.
13. Harvey Schoenfeld, "Opportunities for Leadership for the Social Worker in Hospitals: An Administrator's Expectations," *Social Work in Health Care* 1, no. 1 (Fall 1975):93–96.
14. Nacman, op cit., pp. 48–49.
15. Ronald Bohr et al., "Value Conflicts in a Hospital Walk-Out," *Social Work,* October 1971, pp. 33–42.
16. Joan Ward Mullaney et al., "Clinical Nurse Specialist and Social Worker—Clarifying the Roles," *Nursing Outlook* 22 (November 1974):712–18.
17. Ruth Ravich et al., "Hospital Ombudsman Smooths Flow of Services and Communication," *Hospitals* 43 (March 1969):56–59.

18.- Carl Harm and Joseph Golden, "Group Workers' Role in Guiding Social Process in a Medical Institution," *Social Work,* April 1961, pp. 44–51.

19. Debrah Merlin, "Home Care Project for Indigent Allows Dignified Care, Cuts Cost," *Hospitals* 49 (October 16, 1975).

20. Margaret Chambers, "Administrative Considerations in Programming for Specific Services," in Glen Shelton Key, ed., *Delivery of Social Work Services in Pediatric Hospitals,* Proceedings of workshop held at Children's Memorial Hospital, Chicago, 1971.

21. Shirley Wattenberg et al., "Comparisons of Opinions of Social Work Administrators and Hospital Administrators Toward Leadership Tasks," *Social Work in Health Care* 2, no. 3 (Spring 1977):285–94.

22. Maurice Russell, "Social Work in a Black Community Hospital: Its Implications for the Profession," *American Journal of Public Health* 60, no. 4, 704–11.

23. Robert Morris, "Basic Factors in Planning for the Coordination of Health Services—Parts I and II," *American Journal of Public Health,* February 1963, pp. 20–31, and March 1963, pp. 32–42.

24. "Standards for Hospital Social Services," National Association for Social Workers *News,* June 1977, p. 12–13.

25. Alice Ullman and Gene Kassebaum, "Referrals and Services in a Medical Social Work Department," *Social Service Review* 35, no. 3 (September 1961):258. See also *Social Work Practices in Hospitals,* U.S. Public Health Service Publication no. 519, Washington, D.C., 1956, and Barbara Gordon and Helen Rehr, Selectivity Biases in Delivery of Hospital Social Services," *Social Service Review* 43, no. 1 (March 1969):35–41.

26. Barbara Berkman and Helen Rehr, "Early Social Service Case Finding for Hospitalized Patients: An Experiment," *Social Service Review* 47 (June 1973):256–65.

27. Kalman Flomenhaft et al., "Avoiding Psychiatric Hospitalization," *Social Work,* October 1969, pp. 38–45.

28. Edith Leopold and Lawrence Schein, "Missing Links in the Human Services Nonsystem," *Medical Care* 13, no. 7 (July 1975):595–606.

29. Jane Collins, "Assessment of Social Services in a Large Health Care Organization," in *Evaluation of Social Work Services in Community Health and Medical Care Programs,* Proceedings 1973 Public Health Social Work Institute Program, Berkeley, 1973, pp. 57–67.

30. Ralph Richter et al., "The Community Health Worker, a Resource for Improved Health Care Delivery," *American Journal of Public Health* 64, no. 11 (November 1974): 1056–61.

31. James C. Stewart and Lottie Lee Krafton, eds., *Delivery of Health Care Services to the Poor: Findings from a Review of the Current Periodical Literature* (Austin: University of Texas, Graduate School of Social Work, Center for Social Work Research, 1975), p. 11.

32. Ravich, op cit. See also Tery Mizrabi Madison, "Those Who Speak Up," *Mental Hygiene,* Summer 1975, pp. 28–31.

33. Anne Sturmthal Bergman, "Emergency Room: A Role for Social Workers," *Health and Social Work* 1, no. 1 (February 1976):32–44.

34. G. I. Krell, "Hospital Social Work Should Be More Than a 9 to 5 Position," *Hospitals* 50, no. 10 (May 1976):99–104.

35. Abraham Lurie and Leonard Tuzman, "Social Work Program Responsibilities in Health Care Discharge Planning," Paper delivered to Social Work Section, Annual Public Health Association Meeting, Miami, October 19, 1976, p. 2.

36. Dorothy McGriff, "A Coordinated Approach to Discharge Planning," *Social Work,* January 1965, pp. 45–50.

37. Eleanor Clark, "Improving Post Hospital Care for Chronically Ill Elderly Patients," *Social Work,* January 1969, pp. 62–67.

38. Lurie and Tuzman, op. cit., p. 9.

39. Ibid, p. 10.

182   NEIL F. BRACHT

40. Donald Snook "Patient Rights," *Hospitals* 28(April 1974), and Nancy Quinn and Anne Somers, "The Patient's Bill of Rights—The Consumer Revolution," *Nursing Outlook* 22 no. 4 (April 1974).
41. Robert Spano and Sander Lund, "Management by Objectives in a Hospital Social Service Unit," *Social Work in Health Care* 1, no. 3 (Spring 1976):267–76.
42. Elsbeth Kahn, "Issues and Problems in Social Services Costfinding," in William Hall and Gerald St. Denis, eds., *Proceedings, Quality Assurance in Social Services in Health Programs for Mothers and Children,* Public Health Social Work Program, University of Pittsburg, 1975, pp. 81–93. See also James Lyon "Social Services Coverage in Health Settings: Prospects and Issues," in Robert Jackson and Jean Morton, eds., *Evaluation of Social Work Services in Community Health and Medical Care Programs,* Proceedings, 1973 Institute for Public Health Social Workers, 1973, Berkeley pp. 139–54.
43. Veterans Administration Advisory Committee, *Final Report, Role and Function of the Social Work Service,* Study and Review of the Social Work Veterans Administration Program by the Chief Medical Directors, (Washington, D.C., April 1973), 64 pp.
44. Schoenfeld, op. cit., p. 95.
45. Robert Veninga, "The Management of Organizational Change in Health Agencies," *Public Health Reports* 90, no. 2 (March–April 1975):149–53.
46. Rino Patti and Herman Resnick, "Changing the Agency from Within," in Ralph M. Kramer and Harry Specht, eds., *Readings in Community Organization Practice* 2nd Edition (Englewood Cliffs, N.J.: Prentice-Hall); See also Hyman Weiner, "Toward Techniques for Social Change," *Social Work,* April 1961, pp. 26–35.
47. A. Loeb, "Planning for Programs and Evaluation: Management by Objectives," in: *Evaluation of Social Work Services in Community Health and Medical Care Programs,* R. Jackson and J. Morton (eds), 1973 Proceedings, Public Health Social Work, U. Of California, Berkeley, 1973, pp. 136–37.
48. Robert Pruger, "The Good Bureaucrat," *Social Work,* July 1973, p. 26.

SUGGESTED ADDITIONAL READINGS

Bryant, John H., M.D., et al. *Community Hospitals and Primary Care.* Cambridge, Mass.: Ballinger, 1976.
Carmody, Francis, Jr., "Planning Social Work Services for an Army General Hospital," *Military Medicine,* March 1976, pp. 172–76.
Catts-Levy, Sandra, "Triggering Change: A Case Study of Innovations," *Social Work in Health Care* 2, no. 3 (Spring 1977):319–28.
Elling, Ray, and Ollie Lee, "Formal Connections of Community Leadership to the Health System," *Milbank Memorial Fund Quarterly* 44 (July 1966):294–306.
Hirsch, Sidney, and Abraham Lurie, "Establishing a Hospital Social Service Department," *Social Work,* April 1959, pp. 86–93.
"Hospital Social Work Consumers' Critique," *Health Perspectives,* Consumers Commission on the Accreditation of Health Services, 3, no. 6 (November–December 1976):1–4.
Light and Brown, "Social Worker as Lay Administrator of a Medical Care Plan," *Social Casework,* April 1964.
Lurie, Abraham, "Staffing Patterns: Issues and Program Implications for Health Agencies," *Social Work in Health Care* 2, no. 1 (Fall 1976):85–94.
Pfouts, Jane, and Brandon McDaniel, "Medical Handmaidens or Professional Colleagues: A Survey of Social Work Practice in the Pediatrics Department of Twenty-eight Teaching Hospitals," *Social Work in Health Care* 2, no. 3 (Spring 1977):275–84.
Smith, Carole, "Social Workers in Hospitals: Misplaced Intruders or Essential Experts?" *British Medical Journal* 25 (August 1973):443–44.

Thompson, F., et al., "Patient Grievance? Mechanisms in Health Care Institutions," in Department of Health, Education and Welfare, *Secretary's Commission on Medical Malpractice* (Contract no. HEW OS-72-159 with Fry Consultants, Inc., Report no. SCMM-FC-PG), *Appendix of Commission Report* (Washington, D.C., 1973), pp. 758–836.

Vielhaber, David P. and Nancy A. Irvin, Accounting For Social Work Services in Discharge Planning, in: *Proceedings, Quality Assurance in Social Services in Health Programs for Mothers and Children,* William Hall and Gerald St. Denis (eds), Public Health and Social Work Program, U. of Pittsburg School of Public Health, Pittsburgh, 1975.

Weed, L. L. *Medical Records, Medical Education and Patient Care: The Problem-Oriented Record as a Basic Tool.* Chicago: Press of Case Western Reserve University, 1969.

12/UNMET SOCIAL SERVICE NEEDS IN SKILLED NURSING FACILITIES*

LU PEARMAN
JEAN SEARLES

Elderly citizens represent an increasing segment of the population in the United States. In the early 1900s, persons over 65 represented only 4% of the population (about 3 million), whereas by 1970 their numbers had grown to represent 9.5% (about 20 million) of the population. It is estimated that they will number 28.2 million by the year 2000.[1] Nursing homes, a new phenomenon of the 1930s,[2] have been increasingly seen as the major answer to unmet health needs for elderly citizens.** "According to the U.S. Public Service data, about 90% of the population over 65 institutionalized for chronic illness received their care in nursing homes,"[2] this population percentage varying significantly from state to state.[3]

The low status currently ascribed to elderly people in our society has tended to allow nursing care facilities to operate at levels less than desirable. Professional staff have not been attracted to working in these facilities, which too often are seen as the final residences of elderly people where little can be done other than meeting their physical needs. Social workers, until recently, have seldom been found on the full-time or consultant staff in nursing facilities. This has been partially due to: (a) a lack of regulatory requirements that mandate social services;[4] (b) the lack of a well-developed reimbursement scale that recognizes social services on a fee-for-service basis (comparable to physical and occupational therapy, etc.);[5] (c) authority conflicts with the medical profession

*Reprinted with permission of the authors from *Social Work in Health Care* 1, no. 4 (Summer 1976).

**Although this study focuses on those residents of long-term care facilities who are over 65 years of age, the authors recognize that there are also younger groups of residents with specialized needs resulting from chemical dependency, mental retardation, physical disability, mental illness, or social and cultural deprivation. This study did not address the appropriateness of their placement in the long-term care setting.

that have perpetuated a defensive posture of social service deliverers;[6, 7] (d) the limitations of the social service profession in developing measurable outcome objectives of social work services;[6] and (e) paternalism and political passivity of the social service profession that have led to ineffective advocacy.[8]

In spite of past trends, there is a current movement toward defining social work responsibilities in the following areas of service:

1. *Social services to the resident,* which include traditional casework, group work, and discharge planning services, as well as an advocacy posture to assist the resident in assuring appropriate placement and in retaining his basic human rights once in a nursing facility.

2. *Social services to families,* which include assisting them to express their feelings toward the relative's disability and to resolve these feelings so they are better able to participate with the staff in meeting the needs of the family member in the nursing home.

3. *Social service involvement in staff training* that is specifically related to the interpretation of residents' social and emotional needs and basic rights.

4. *Social service involvement in policy development* within the facility to promote the residents' rights to humane and individualized care.

5. *Social service outreach to the community,* which includes efforts to increase public awareness of the needs of elderly persons in nursing facilities in order to develop community programs and resources for nursing home residents.[4, 9-15]

In order to identify further the responsiblity of social workers in the previously defined areas of service, a study was undertaken, and measurable objectives for social services in long-term care facilities were developed. In addition, a program specification was developed to indicate the rationale behind these objectives and to illustrate their relationship to total integrated care in the long-term care setting (see Figure 12.1). This program specification suggests that the advocacy role of the social worker as the resident's representative is inherent in all social services delivered. In long-term care, the goal is to enable the older person to maximize himself in a normal developmental stage of his lifetime. This includes development of individual potential and the prevention of unnecessary impairment through a comprehensive, planned approach rather than only crisis intervention. Total integrated care includes meeting the physical, social, emotional, and spiritual needs of the elderly resident through coordinating internal programs with the surrounding community.

THE STUDY

In February 1974, the authors contracted with the Planning Office of the Minnesota Department of Health to study social service delivery in the 51 skilled nursing facilities in Hennepin County, a metropolitan area with a

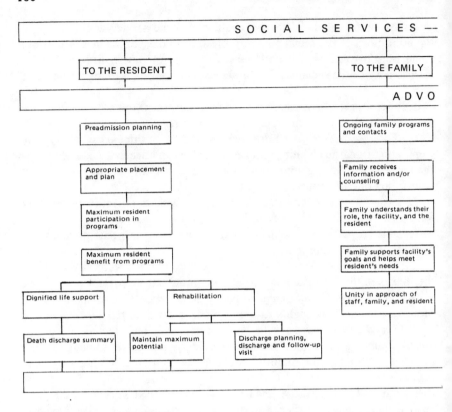

FIG. 12.1. Program specification.

population of approximately 981,000. All proprietary and nonproprietary skilled nursing facilities were studied including freestanding and extended care units attached to acute care hospitals.

The purpose of this study was: (a) to provide data on the number, educational background, and length of employment of social service staff; (b) to provide a measure for practitioners and administrators in long-term care facilities, for ongoing assessment of social service delivery; (c) to identify existing social service needs for institutions educating and training professionals for long-term care facilities; and (d) to provide a data base for the Minnesota Department of Health, state and federal legislators, and community agencies to facilitate their response to social service needs in long-term care facilities. The research project included plans for wide circulation of data findings to all of these sectors.

The following five categories of service were identified to be measured in the study. They are process oriented rather than directed at the outcome effects on the individual resident:

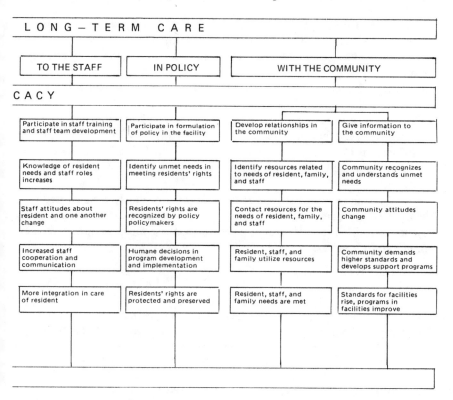

1. *Social services to the resident:* (a) preadmission resident contact is completed by a staff member for evaluating the admission plan; (b) medical, nursing, and social information is received for evaluation by staff prior to admission; (c) social history and social assessment are completed on each resident; (d) a plan is implemented for facilitating access to and/or use of personal spending money by residents; (e) individual and group counseling services are available to residents; (f) predischarge resident assessment is completed by a staff member for evaluating the discharge plan; and (g) postdischarge resident contact is completed by a staff member for evaluating the placement plan.

2. *Social services to the family or interested person:* (a) preadmission family contact is completed by a staff member for evaluating the admission plan; (b) individual and group counseling services are available to the family or interested person; (c) a structured group orientation program is available to the family or interested person; and (d) predischarge family contact is made by a staff member for evaluating the discharge plan.

3. *Social services to the staff:* (a) a plan is developed for the ongoing assessment of the discharge potential of residents; (b) an in-service program is implemented for staff relating to the social and emotional needs of residents; (c) an in-service program is implemented for staff relating to resident rights; and (d) interdisciplinary team conferences are structured to plan and develop individualized programs for residents.

4. *Social services in policy development:* (a) a staff member is designated to represent residents in policy decisions; (b) there is structured time for the education of residents on the "Patient Bill of Rights"; and (c) a structure is developed for utilizing community resources in resolving resident grievances.

5. *Social services with the community:* (a) relationships are structured with the community agencies, which are resulting in utilization of community resources; and (b) time is structured for promoting the development of new community resources.

METHOD

Interviews were conducted with administrators and/or social work staff over a 5-week period. Administrators were the initial contact in all facilities. In the 21 facilities without social work staff, the administrator was interviewed alone. In the 30 facilities with social work staff, some administrators preferred to complete the interview with the social worker present, some were interviewed alone, and some referred the interviewer to the social worker. Three questions were asked on each social service measured using an understanding-performance-satisfaction trichotomy. The *understanding* question assessed the respondent's awareness level of the nature and importance of that service. (Example: "Is it useful to have a system in your facility to handle resident grievances?") The *performance* question assessed the facility's input and output in that social service. (Example: "Do you have a system to handle resident greivances at this time?") The *satisfaction* question measured the respondent's attitude toward the current service delivery. (Example: "Are you covering what you would like to do about resident grievances within your facility?")

The understanding-performance-satisfaction trichotomy provided a data base that can indicate which was more predominant in each social service measured: the respondent's general knowledge, the facility's performance structures, or the respondent's attitudes and values. This trichotomy also indicated the interrelatedness of these three factors.

Responses were entered by the interviewees on a high-medium-low scale according to specific predetermined criteria (see Table 12.1). Data were coded, and frequency distributions were run to tabulate the level of understanding, performance, and satisfaction in each social service measured. A statistical analysis (Mann-Whitney Test) was done to determine if there was a significant difference in responses made by facilities with and without social service staff.

The following intervening variables may have affected data results: (a) varying characteristics and locations of the skilled nursing facilities; (b) staff turnover rate; (c) varying attitudes, education, and experience of social workers; (d) varying attitudes, education, and experience of administrators; (e) degree of community support offered to the facilities; (f) differing interviewing techniques; and (g) state regulating agency sponsorship of the study.

FINDINGS

Study findings confirmed the increasing utilization of qualified social workers in the skilled nursing facilities. Over 50% of the facilities had full-time social work staff, and 50% of those facilities had acquired this staff within the last 2 years (see Table 12.2). No attempt was made in this study to determine if there was a difference in responses related to the educational background of social work staff. This was not feasible because social workers were not always designated to be interviewed.

The individual social services measured varied considerably in the level of understanding, performance, and satisfaction.

SOCIAL SERVICES TO THE RESIDENT

Understanding of preadmission contact was almost three times higher than performance, and motivation to improve service delivery was low. There was no statistical difference in facilities with social service staff.

TABLE 12.1

Criteria for Scoring Understanding-Performance-Satisfaction
Social Services in Long-Term Care

	Low	Medium	High
Understanding Questions	Denial of usefulness or relevance of the service; confusion about it.	Neutrality about the service; neither denial or affirmation.	Affirmation of the usefulness or relevance of the service.
Performance Questions	No delivery; no organized plan for delivery; staff person designated has other major priorities.	Plan or procedure being developed; two or more staff designated, but with other major priorities.	Organized plan for delivery; staff designated has high priority for this service.
Satisfaction Questions	Dissatisfied with current performance; motivation to improve was expressed.	Mixed or contradictory statement of satisfaction; uncertain motivation to improve.	Satisfied with current performance; no motivation to improve.

TABLE 12.2

Summary Data on Social Work Staff

Number of Social Workers		Educational Level		Length of Employment	
Number of Facilities	Social Work Staff	Number of Facilities	Education of Social Work Staff	Number of Facilities	Length of Employment
13	1 part-time or consultant	2	PhD in social work	7	Less than 1 year
9	1 full-time	11	MSW	9	1-2 years
3	2 full-time	12	BSW	5	3-5 years
2	3 full-time	1	Bach. other	9	more than 5 years
3	More than 3 full-time	4	Other		
30	Total with social service staff	30		30	
21	Total with no social work staff				

    Facilities scored higher in understanding and performance in collecting preadmission referral information than in other services to the resident. There was no significant difference in facilities with social service staff.

    Although the understanding of the need for collecting social history information and completing a social assessment was high, performance was low. Almost half of the facilities indicated motivation to improve service delivery in this area. There was no significant difference in facilities with social service staff.

    The need for some plan to facilitate the use of personal funds to meet individual resident needs is less clearly understood than other social services to the residents. Higher satisfaction in facilities with social service staff was significant (.01). However, performance levels in these facilities did not justify the 100% satisfaction response given.

    Although facilities understood the need for counseling services to the resident, a sizable deficiency in performance existed, and less than half of the facilities were satisfied with current counseling services being provided. Higher performance in facilities with social service staff was significant (.05). No facilities without social service staff performed at a high level, even though they did show a high understanding of the service and were motivated to improve.

Understanding of predischarge assessment of the resident was very high, and approximately half of the facilities also scored high in performance. Satisfaction was considerably higher than performance. There was no significant difference in facilities with social service staff, although performance tended to be higher in those facilities.

Understanding and performance of postdischarge contact with a resident was considerably lower than other social services to the resident. Understanding of this service was significantly higher (.01) in facilities with social service staff, and they tended to be less satisfied with their performance.

Recommendation: There is a need for educational programs to increase the understanding and performance levels of social service delivery to the individual resident. Counseling services, preadmission assessment, discharge planning, and follow-up services should be increased through support programs from community mental health centers, county welfare departments, public health nursing, and senior citizen centers.

SOCIAL SERVICES TO THE FAMILY

Facilities scored very high in understanding level and performance of preadmission contact with the family. Satisfaction also seemed appropriate when compared to service delivery level. Understanding of this service was significantly higher (.05) in facilities with social service staff. There was high understanding of the need to provide counseling services to the family, with low performance and an indication of motivation to improve service. The higher understanding and performance level of this service in facilities with social service staff was significant (.01). The need for an orientation program for the family was less clearly understood than some other services to the family. Performance was low but was significantly higher in facilities with social service staff (.01). Facilities scored high in predischarge contact with the family, but since the number of discharges was small, data did not represent a well-utilized discharge planning program. There was no significant difference in facilities with social service staff.

Recommendation: Counseling services and educational programs for the family should be developed utilizing the expertise and experience of community colleges, universities, and community mental health centers. Educational programs to increase staff understanding of family needs should be expanded. Public information programs to change the image of nursing homes would facilitate family use of social services.

SOCIAL SERVICES TO THE STAFF

There was a lack of clarity about the appropriate facility role in the staff assessment of and planning for resident discharge. Current social service was very low, and facilities show little motivation to improve delivery at this time. Performance was significantly higher (.05) in facilities with social service staff, as was satisfaction (.01).

Although staff in-service regarding social and emotional needs of residents was well understood, current delivery was not as high as might be desirable, and facilities indicate a need for stronger programs in staff training in this area. Performance was significantly higher in facilities with social service staff (.05).

Staff in-service regarding resident rights was less clearly understood than the area of social and emotional needs of residents. Facilities scored highest in social services to staff as related to the development of staff conferences and team meetings. Performance and satisfaction were significantly higher (.01) in facilities with social service staff.

Recommendation: Facilities need to consider the discharge potential of residents. Programs to increase effective discharge planning and assessment are needed. In-service programs for staff development must have a direct relationship to the changing needs of the resident, and enhance staff ability to set objectives to meet those needs.

SOCIAL SERVICES IN POLICY DEVELOPMENT

Understanding of the need for an advocate for the resident in the policy development of the facility was low, and there were many facilities without this service approach. However, satisfaction with current service delivery was high. Higher performance and higher satisfaction in facilities with social service staff were significant (.01 and .05, respectively). No facilities without social service staff performed on a high level.

Less than half of the facilities scored high in the understanding of the need to educate residents in their rights, and performance was low. Motivation to improve was also low. There was no significant difference in facilities with social service staff.

The need for some plan or structure for addressing resident grievances was somewhat better understood than other social services in the area of policy development, but performance and motivation to improve were both low. Higher performance in facilities with social service staff was significant (.05).

Only one-third of the facilities understood the need for referral of residents' grievances outside the facility at appropriate times. Current performance was critically low, and there was little motivation to improve. There was no significant difference in facilities with social service staff.

Recommendation: There is a critical need for extensive programs to educate staff on patient rights. External regulations to assist residents in assuring the implementation of their rights must be promulgated. Improved public understanding of the rights of residents in long-term care facilities is needed to increase interest and action from the community. In addition, professionals delivering social services need to develop an assertive posture in the role of advocate for the residents.

SOCIAL SERVICES WITH THE COMMUNITY

The need for ongoing relationships with community resources was well understood, and yet performance was low. A willingness to improve services was indicated. Higher performance in facilities with social service staff was significant (.01).

Although there was an understanding of the need for facility social services to give information to the public for the development of additional community resources, few facilities performed high in this service. Performance was significantly higher (.05) in facilities with social service staff.

Recommendation: Community resources must take initiative in extending their services to residents of long-term care facilities. In addition, professional social workers within long-term care settings should identify services that could be developed or adopted to serve the needs of residents.

In addition to measuring understanding, performance, and satisfaction in each social service, the five areas of social service were compared. Table 12.3 summarizes the levels found in each area of service. Table 12.4 indicates whether the social worker's presence was significant in each area of service.

For summary purposes, a collation of the 21 social services measured is shown in Figure 12.2. Part A summarizes the overall level of understanding, performance, and satisfaction. Part B compares facilities without social workers to those with social workers for significant difference. These findings confirm that the presence of social service staff generally increased the amount of service being delivered.

CONCLUSIONS

Any approach to improving social services in facilities will have to include changes in professional knowledge and society's attitudes as well as in delivery structures and personnel hours. Programs to increase understanding of the services should be directed at facilities with and without social work staff since there were only a few services where the presence of the social worker showed

TABLE 12.3

Frequency Distribution in Five Areas of Social Services (presented in percentages)

Social Service Area	Understanding			Performance			Satisfaction		
	Low	Med	High	Low	Med	High	Low	Med	High
Resident	4	35	61	69	21	10	18	37	45
Family	10	21	69	55	29	16	22	29	49
Staff	14	25	61	59	25	16	26	31	43
Policy	43	29	28	80	14	6	16	21	63
Community	16	15	69	64	10	26	51	14	35

TABLE 12.4

Cross-Tabulation of Staffing: Understanding, Performance,
Satisfaction in the Areas of Social Service

Social Service Area	Understanding	Performance	Satisfaction
Resident	No significant difference	No significant difference	No significant difference
Family	Significant difference at .05 level. Higher understanding in facilities with social service staff.	Significant difference at .01 level. Higher performance in facilities with social service staff.	No significant difference
Staff	No significant difference	Significant difference at .01 level. Higher performance in facilities with social service staff.	Significant difference at .01 level. Higher satisfaction in facilities with social service staff.
Policy	No significant difference	Significant difference at .01 level. Higher performance in facilities with social service staff.	No significant difference
Community	Significant difference at .05 level. Higher understanding in facilities with social service staff.	Significant difference at .01 level. Higher performance in facilities with social service staff.	No significant difference

a statistically significant difference in services delivered. Increases in social service staff to improve performance levels will not eliminate the need for supplementary social service programs from public and private agencies in the community. These should include at least the following: (a) increased funding to reimburse for social services in skilled nursing facilities, or more effective social service delivery through individual case management of county welfare departments; (b) legislation to require social service staffing in these facilities for certification and licensing; (c) research to clarify how social services relate to other care components; (d) more support and developmental programs from regulating agencies; and (e) public information and outreach programs to change attitudes toward long-term care facilities in particular and the aging in general.

The authors suggest the following as areas for the attention of others interested in research on social services in long-term care: (a) behavioral criteria for measuring social service outcome on individual residents; (b) interrelatedness of social service to other care components; (c) external environmental factors affecting quality of care; (d) constraints operating on social workers in facilities; (e) educational programs to raise understanding of social services; (f)

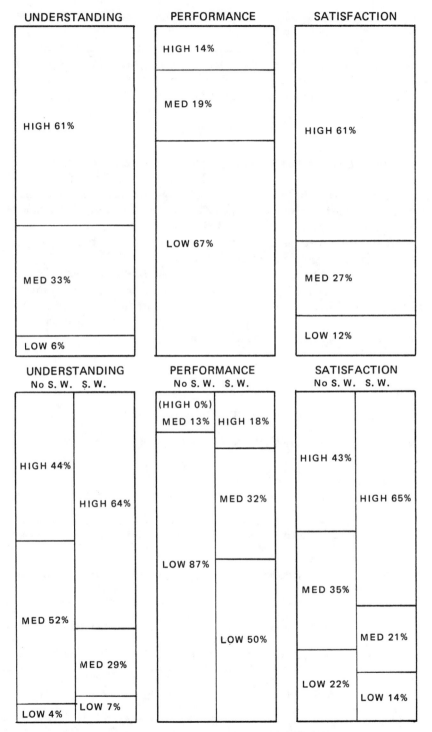

FIG. 12.2 Part A: Overall level of understanding, performance, satisfaction. Part B: Comparison of facilities without social workers (No S.W.) and those with social workers (S.W.).

comparison of full-time versus consultant social service delivery; (g) efficient and effective means of sharing social services among facilities; (h) social services that could be provided from public and private community agencies; and (i) repeat of this study for comparative data.

DISCUSSION

This study reflects the lack of value society places on older people and calls for affirmative action in professional education and public information to improve their image. In the specific area of long-term care, some immediate action is indicated in response to the deficiencies documented by the study. Until changes in state and federal regulations and reimbursement mechanisms support social services, public and private agencies have the responsibility to develop affirmative programs to provide them.

However, increasing social services will have limited effectiveness unless our thinking on older persons shifts from the traditional "medical model" toward the "balanced model." Older people in long-term care facilities deserve a total program including educational opportunities, transportation, legal assistance, general enrichment, and normalized activities of daily living.

NOTES

1. Elaine M. Brody, "Aging," in *Social Work Encyclopedia* (New York: National Association of Social Workers, 1971).
2. Eleanor Clark, "Nursing Homes," in *Social Work Encyclopedia* (New York: National Association of Social Workers, 1971).
3. *Guidelines for a Day Care Program for the Aged,* Minnesota Health Planning Office, Draft 3, January 8, 1973.
4. Jordan L. Kosberg, "The Nursing Home: A Social Work Paradox," *Social Work,* March 1973, p. 107.
5. William Barratt, Marion A. Keller, and Celia Mittleman, "Statement and Recommendations on Social Services in Health Care Related to the Proposed 1971 Amendments to the Social Security Act," National Association of Social Workers and California Society for Clinical Social Work, July 22, 1971.
6. John Wax, "Developing Social Work Power in a Medical Organization," *Social Work,* October 1968, p. 65.
7. Katherine M. Olsen and Marvin E. Olsen, "Role Expectations and Perceptions for Social Workers in Medical Settings," *Social Work,* July 1967, p. 71.
8. Warren G. Bennis, Kenneth D. Benne, and Robert Chin, eds., *The Planning of Change* (New York: Holt, Rinehart & Winston, 1969).
9. Jane Lockwood Barney, "Community Presence as a Key to Quality Life in Nursing Homes," *American Journal of Public Health,* March 1974, pp. 265–68.
10. Ruth Bennett, "Living Conditions and Everyday Needs of the Elderly with Particular References to Social Isolation," *International Journal of Aging and Human Development* 4 (1973):179–98.
11. Elaine M. Brody, ed., *A Social Work Guide for Long Term Care Facilities* (Washington, D.C.: National Institute of Mental Health, 1974).

12. Helen Gassett, *A Curriculum for Social Work Personnel in Long Term Health Care Facilities* (Washington, D.C.: Department of Health, Education and Welfare, 1974).

13. Eva Kahana, "The Humane Treatment of Old People in Institutions," *The Gerontologist* 13 (1973):282–89.

14. Dulcy B. Miller, Ada Jacobs, and Shirley Woodruff, "Life Course of Patients Discharged from Two Nursing Homes," *The Gerontologist* 14 (1974):408–13.

15. Sidney R. Saul and Shura Saul, "Group Psychotherapy in a Proprietary Nursing Home," *The Gerontologist,* October 1974, pp. 446–50.

SUGGESTED ADDITIONAL READINGS

Jorgenson, Lou Ann, and Robert L. Kane, "Social Work in the Nursing Home: A Need and an Opportunity," *Social Work in Health Care* 1, no. 4 (Summer 1976):471–82.

Austin, Michael, and Jordan Kosberg, "Nursing Home Decision Makers and the Social Service Needs of Residents," *Social Work in Health Care* 1, no. 4 (Summer 1976):447–56.

Horn, Linda, and Elma Griesel. *Nursing Homes: A Citizens' Action Guide.* Boston: Beacon Press, 1977.

Part VII

SOCIAL WORK IN PRIMARY HEALTH CARE AND PREVENTION PROGRAMS

13/APPLICATION OF KNOWLEDGE
ABOUT PREVENTION TO
HEALTH AND MENTAL HEALTH
PRACTICE*

MILTON WITTMAN

This chapter presents a brief overview of the status of preventive social work in the United States and discusses the means by which knowledge about prevention is applied in social work education and practice. During the interval between 1959, when the National Association of Social Workers published a landmark document on *Prevention and Treatment,*[1] and 1974, when the same organization published a reprint series of twelve papers on preventive intervention in social work,[2] significant progress was made toward the introduction of preventive content into social work education and practice. As it happens, 1959 was the year of publication of a national curriculum study by the Council on Social Work Education. This study took its direction from a definition of social work that introduced three core concepts: social restoration, social provision, and prevention.[3] Concurrent developments in mental health and public health occurred during the same time span. These developments have been summarized in *Mental Health: The Public Health Challenge.*[4] There is a larger context that must be considered, and this is the way in which prevention has been appearing in major national policy statements in recent years.

It is significant that for the third year in a row the *Forward Plan for Health*[5] has proposed a program theme entitled "Prevention" as a major sector for action during the next five-year period. Selected for special emphasis are the areas of health education, nutrition, child health, and environmental health. Other sections deal with drug and alcohol abuse and mental health. All of these aim in one way or another toward enhancing the preservation of life, furthering the reduction and elimination of health hazards, and helping the total population achieve the best of life chances.

*Based on a paper presented at a meeting of the Mental Health Section, American Public Health Association Annual Meeting, Miami, Florida, October 20, 1976. Content reflects the opinion of the writer and does not represent policy of the U.S. Department of Health, Education and Welfare.

While preventive medicine and preventive psychiatry are now reasonably well established and have status in the literature and in active practice, preventive social work is newer on the scene. It is a concept that has some basis in social work history. The stream of social thought that underlies social welfare stems directly from Deuteronomy XXVI: 12, which contains the injunction to tithe for the widow, the orphan, the stranger. In the eleventh century Maimonides proposed eight stages of charity, of which the highest and most beneficial was the stage that helps a person become self-supporting. Mary Richmond postulated that "legislation and propaganda, between them, will render social work with and for individuals unnecessary." She saw prevention as "one of the end results of a series of processes which include research, individual treatment, public education, legislation and then (by retraced steps) back to the administrative adaptations which make the intent of the legislation real again in the individual case."[6] This mode of thinking was reflected in the curriculum study definition advanced by Werner Boehm in 1958. The rationale for interrelated elements of social restoration, social provision, and prevention that now appear in the master's-degree curriculum can be traced to the seminal thought of this period, which antedated the introduction of a new curriculum policy statement in 1962. The macro aspects are developed in social welfare policy and services; the micro elements appear in the social work methods and the human behavior and social environment sectors. The special place of field instruction has meant that social work education has included preventive functions in field experience for students placed in mental health, public health, and school systems. These provide the facilities where the practice of prevention is most frequently found.[7, 8, 9]

There are three main sources of the knowledge base for the teaching and practice of prevention: public health, mental health, and social work. These three domains are beginning to be seen as subsumed under a single, not-well-defined rubric: "human services." All three will be discussed in detail.

THE PUBLIC HEALTH BASE FOR PREVENTION

The best single source for documentation of the relationship of public health to social work and social work education is the report of the Princeton seminar entitled *Public Health Concepts in Social Work Education.*[10] This was a landmark endeavor involving conjoint exploration of mutual concerns by the public health and social work professions. Sponsored by the Council on Social Work Education, it represented a rare instance in which several separate units of the Public Health Service were able to collaborate on a single educational enterprise. The collection of papers and the report of work group discussions pinpoint the central issues and the critical problems. Witte for social work and Porterfield for public health identify the historical roots of both fields, which extend back to the last century and illustrate the general concerns of both groups for the well-being of the individual and the community. Cassel for public health and Hamovich for social work discuss the place of epidemiology in knowledge development in these two fields. Ryder for public health, Kiesler for mental health, and Kahn for social work speak to the issues around prevention; Morris for social work and Price for public health speak of the macro issues in the large contexts for the application of knowledge about public health and social work as a means of improving the quality of life.

It is significant to note, perhaps, that this conference took place in the second year of a new national administration dedicated to social change. The Public Health Service had just undertaken a self-study of its mission and goals; a special work group was beginning to look at what might be needed to project an innovative approach to mental health service delivery; and it was this ferment that led to the passage in 1963 of the Community Mental Health and Mental Retardation Centers Act, which sparked the restructuring of the mental health service delivery system in the United States. This was a period during which joint programs in public health and social work were being developed at the Universities of Pittsburgh and Minnesota; it was also a time when notable contributions were being made by social workers in schools of public health at Harvard University and the University of California at Berkeley and Los Angeles. Throughout this period the adaptation of content from public health took into account the part of public health that relates to prevention. Witte, in his introduction to the Princeton seminar, cites Joseph W. Mountin: "Health problems cannot be isolated from the environment—both physical and social—in which they exist."[11]

The public health base for prevention derives from the wide range of continuing concerns for morbidity and disability and the means for prolonging and improving life. The preoccupation over the past few decades has been with the vulnerable sectors of the national population—the people at risk—and with means of identifying, treating, and educating them. Examples are maternal and child health, geriatrics and gerontology, multiphasic screening, mass immunization, emergency medical and health services, continuity of care, long-term care, health hazards, life cycle crises, timely intervention and treatment, health education, diet and weight control, health policy, and the structure and coordination of health service. These are among the many matters confronting the public health practitioner in the health department at the local, regional, or state level. These are what the public health planner must consider if the mission of public health is to be accomplished.

The impetus of new legislation (federal and state) is a perennial spur to action. It seems that the stage of implementation of any new legislation begets new knowledge that suggests the need for change even before the regulations are written and published. Health planning and quality assurance are examples here. The *Forward Plan* contains the general prediction that national health insurance is coming in the near future and that the whole apparatus of service structure, health professions education, and health research may soon have to come to grips with the notion of universal coverage for medical and health care (including preventive services). It is certain that the fragments of such a program that now exist (e.g., Medicare, Medicaid, the end-stage renal disease program) cannot be seen as meeting the total health needs of the nation. They simply make the gaps more obvious.

In summary, it can be said that the health base for prevention has dimensions that extend from direct application (immunization and health education) to indirect inputs (health policy and planning). Models for curriculum content emerge from the experience of joint social work and public health programs (in too few places); from the introduction of social work faculty in schools of public health (in too few places); and in the introject provided by public health-trained and medical social work faculty in graduate schools of social work (in too few places).

THE MENTAL HEALTH BASE FOR PREVENTION

This area is somewhat easier to cover because of the rich literature that has emerged in the past fifteen years. The works of Caplan in preventive psychiatry,[12] Bower[13] and Cowen[14] in psychology and prevention, Hollister[15] in public health–mental health, and Rapoport[16] and Parad[17] on social work in prevention have all drawn essentially on mental health knowledge. This knowledge is drawn from the science of human behavior, from the psychology and sociology of human relationships, and from various schools of psychoanalytic thought. Erich Lindemann, Kurt Lewin, Abram Kardiner, and Gerald Caplan have all made contributions to mental health practice because they have forced individual practitioners to look at the social context of the case. Deviant behavior, whether exemplified in schizophrenia, psychoneuroses, character disorders, situational reactions, crisis responses, delinquency, or serious crime, tends still to remain generally unpredictable. Causation is still unknown, and the rationale for successful treatment is not always understood or accepted.

It is interesting (and perplexing) to note the impressive array of distinguished mental health professionals who can be found to have assumed a derogatory stance on prevention. Sanford[18] is perhaps typical of those who feel that prevention, and especially primary prevention, has the negative effect of siphoning off professional energies that might be better devoted to using known methods in meeting the problems of mental illness and mental health. His attitudes are shared by Kolb,[19] Cumming,[20] and Garmezy.[21] In short, the question is, Should we not be working on the causation and determination of vulnerability rather than on the dissemination of information or the use of procedures (such as consultation and education) when the impact and outcome are still seen by many as dubious? This reasoning would seem warranted, especially at a time when fiscal and manpower resources are in such short supply. The argument on the other side is equally persuasive. There are many examples from the field of health demonstrating without question that intervention not only is possible but can be successful and that interventive measures can be taken to reduce illness whether or not the cause is known. The dramatic reduction of poliomyelitis through use of the Salk vaccine is one example. The relationship of water supply to the transmission of cholera is another example that comes to mind. Transpositions to the mental health field may be difficult, but they are not impossible. The variables of unemployment, poverty, and racism and their relationship to mental health and mental illness have yet to be fully analyzed and studied. Yet these are problems that must be considered for their indirect influence on human behavior and family life.

The most controversial of recent innovations in mental health is the comprehensive community mental health center. A rich literature on this subject is now available, including some informative journals. Both prevention and promotion of positive mental health are undertaken by many mental health centers. Most resource volumes on community mental health touch on the theory and practice of prevention.[22, 23] There is also an exposition of consultation and education as these bear upon prevention. Of the mental health professionals working in the area of consultation and education, social workers will be found to be making a considerable contribution. Rapoport[24] and Parad[25] are two who, from the early years of community mental health, have made contributions to practice and theory in consultation and prevention. Because the mental health center is so heavily used for field instruction by schools of social work, students have a prime opportunity for participation in treatment and preventive functions. With the advent of the learning and teaching center (a predetermined complex of agencies, institutions, and organizations linked together to provide a variety of field instruction experiences for social work students), mental health facilities have become even more intimately involved in social work education. The mental health base for prevention offers an interesting mix of behavioral science and community organization approaches. The range of interventions include such modes as parent effectiveness and teacher training, widow-to-widow programs, suicide prevention, rape counseling, geriatric mental health planning and consultation, and self-help initiatives.

THE SOCIAL WORK BASE FOR PREVENTION

As might be expected, the social work approach to prevention is related to the modalities and methods that emerged during the first several decades of this century. Beginning with social reform and charity organization and with an initial stake in the public social services, the profession has moved through a period of preoccupation with social casework and direct services (high proportions of social work students still elect the direct-treatment concentration) to a broader conception of generic social work practice and education. The notion of preventive casework emerged in 1961 (Parad[26]), and a definition of preventive social work was proposed in 1962.[27] This definition postulates preventive social work as "an organized and systematic effort to apply knowledge about social health and pathology in such manner as to enhance and preserve the social and mental health of the community." This definition suggests both micro and macro areas of social work intervention.

Rapoport reviews the definitional issues emerging from the NASW document on *Prevention and Treatment*.[28] She decries the suggestion that social work is involved only after a problem has developed. She elaborates on two phases of primary prevention to include parallels to health promotion (strengthening family life) and specific protection (maternal–child health approaches); in addition, she introduces three aspects of social work intervention that fit well into the structure of social services delivery: (1) timely intervention in family problems, (2) coordinated services (human services integration), and (3) legislative and regulation reforms aimed at preserving personal and family integrity rather than promoting partial programs. Hers is an amazing grasp of the core issues of prevention.

THE IMPLEMENTATION OF PREVENTION IN EDUCATION

The publication of *Public Health Concepts in Social Work Education* provided some stimulus to the integration of content on prevention into the social work curriculum. At least two social work texts contain sections dealing with prevention in social work.[29, 30] A continuing series of exploratory studies on prevention have been conducted at the Rutgers University School of Social Work.[31, 32] At Portland State University Collins and Pancoast have developed teaching content covering "natural helping systems" that are aimed at primary and secondary prevention.[33] Pancoast's volume contains details on the way in which natural neighbors can be brought into the picture to help not only in crises but also in relation to continuing needs such as day care for children. Levine has introduced content on social epidemiology and crisis intervention at the University of Georgia School of Social Work.[34, 35]

It is in the field work segment of the curriculum that the opportunity for direct practice experience in prevention occurs. At the Great Lakes Conference on Primary Prevention at Clymer, New York in May 1976, a number of examples of programs involving practice in primary prevention were presented. Gary Theilen of the West Virginia University School of Social Work presented the results of a student field work project in rural mental health. This took place in Preston County, West Virginia, which has a population of about 30,000. The student unit assisted the agricultural and community development agency in the county in working out the establishment of a local health council. In addition to working on water supply and improved roads in the county, this student unit helped the county obtain two physicians under the National Emergency Health Service Corps. A social work graduate from this program now serves as the health clinic coordinator. The county now has primary health care services where none existed before. The clinic has several subunits to serve more isolated Appalachian communities. County court personnel and the administrative network now have a greatly improved notion of what can be accomplished through the use of social work techniques for community organization. The high level of citizen involvement continues through the use of a local advisory committee to the health unit.[36]

PREVENTION AND SOCIAL WORK PRACTICE

The notion of crisis intervention preceded the establishment of this role in community mental health centers. Social workers now are deeply involved in special programs in suicide prevention, alcohol and drug abuse prevention, and disaster assistance. They have also taken the initiative in connection with self-help groups.[37] In a number of states parents of handicapped children have banded together to promote better protective and treatment services and improved legislation and funding. The outreach work of the War on Poverty programs has not entirely disappeared. Many of the multiservice centers and neighborhood storefronts have continued useful primary and secondary prevention functions in troubled communities. As in the case of the rural mental health example, ghetto areas in urban and suburban communities can benefit if the citizens of those communities can be helped to organize themselves in an effective manner.

There is increasing interest in finding means of using professional skills in other than treatment functions. One example is the Family Life Education program of the Family Service Association of America. Parent training, teacher education, and "family survival" projects are seen as positive mental health activities that do not involve work with ill or disturbed patients. These activities offer opportunities for "anticipatory guidance," so that the recipient of the educational program can have some notion as to how to meet perplexing individual and family problems at some future point.[38] Maternal and child health programs have the same goal.[39] A number of prenatal and postnatal clinics now employ social workers as a means of expanding service capabilities. A recent report of a National Workshop on Delivery of Hospital Social Work Services in Obstetrics/Gynecology and Services to the Newborn contains a number of illustrations of work in this important area of primary care. Breslin describes the preventive intervention conducted in a newborn special-care unit at Yale-New Haven Hospital. This unit has found that in three out of five families making use of the unit some type of direct social work intervention is needed.[40] Earlier work by Cyr and Wattenberg is also worthy of note.[41]

There has been a considerable growth of special programs in which prevention has become the main theme. Abortion and rape counseling are examples of areas in which secondary prevention becomes vastly important. Much of this experience has yet to be carefully studied for its implications as to societal policy issues. Such study may lead to better efforts at family planning, sex and marital counseling, and work with health, welfare, and correctional personnel.

NEW DIRECTIONS IN PREVENTION

It is apparent that a great deal of interest in prevention has emerged in recent years. Social work, public health, and mental health are all involved in this movement. The Public Law 94–63 amendments to the CMHS Act encourage further development of preventive functions, especially as these relate to deinstitutionalization (tertiary prevention) and the prevention of institutionalization (primary and secondary prevention). The Title XX Amendments authorize expanded social services intended to prevent inappropriate institutionalization. They also authorize the funding of day care, counseling, and chore services where these will help achieve the purposes of the Social Security Act, as amended. It should also be noted that the passage and signing of Public Law 94–484, the Health Professions Educational Assistance Act, holds open the promise of long-needed funding of health care and health administration training programs in schools of social work. Project funds and stipends will be available for this purpose. It can be expected that projects dealing with social work in primary care and in prevention will be able to compete for these funds. In keeping with this initiative, the NIMH has established a high priority for mental health training of primary health care givers, including social workers.

The small cadre of workers in primary prevention can be expected to grow as more knowledge is gained about how such programs can be made effective.[42, 43] The century-old concerns of social workers for individual and family well-being, and for policies that will bring about a better infrastructure for service delivery in health, mental health, and social welfare, clearly point to the need for more attention to prevention and to the improvement of practice in this area. As practice in prevention matures, it will become possible to extend education and training in this important part of the human services spectrum.

N O T E S

1. Bertram Beck, *Prevention and Treatment,* based on work of National Association of Social Workers, National Commission of Social Work Practice, Subcommittee on Trends, Issues and Priorities (New York: National Association of Social Workers, January 1959), 2804 s., mimeographed, 31 pp.
2. Carol H. Meyer, "Introduction/Prevention Intervention: A Goal in Search of a Method," in Carol H. Meyer, ed., *Preventive Intervention in Social Work* (Washington, D.C.: National Association of Social Workers, 1974), pp. 1–9.
3. Werner W. Boehm, "The Nature of Social Work," *Social Work* 3, no. 2 (April 1958): 16–17.
4. E. James Lieberman, ed., *Mental Health: The Public Health Challenge* (Washington, D.C.: American Public Health Association, 1975).

5. U.S. Department of Health, Education and Welfare, Public Health Service, *Forward Plan for Health FY 1978–82*, "Prevention" (Washington, D.C., 1976), pp. 69–83.
6. Mary Richmond, in Joanna C. Colcord, ed., *The Long View* (New York: Russell Sage Foundation, 1930), p. 587.
7. Rex A. Skidmore and Milton G. Thackeray, *Introduction to Social Work* (Englewood Cliffs, N.J.: Prentice-Hall, 1964), pp. 340–58.
8. Howard J. Parad, *Crisis Intervention: Selected Readings* (New York: Family Service Association of America, 1965).
9. Emory L. Cowen, Mary Anne Trost, et al., *New Ways in School Mental Health* (New York: Human Sciences Press, 1975).
10. *Public Health Concepts in Social Work Education* (New York: Council on Social Work Education, 1962).
11. Ibid., p. 8.
12. Gerald Caplan, ed., *Prevention of Mental Disorders in Chidren* (New York: Basic Books, 1961).
13. Eli M. Bower, "Primary Prevention of Mental and Emotional Disorders: A Conceptual Framework and Action Possibilities," *American Journal of Orthopsychiatry* 32, (1963): 832–48.
14. Ibid.
15. William Hollister et al., *Experiences in Rural Mental Health* (Chapel Hill, N.C.: Community Psychiatry, University of North Carolina School of Medicine, 1973–1974).
16. Lydia Rapoport, "The Concept of Prevention," *Social Work* 6 (January 1961):3–12.
17. Ibid.
18. Nevitt Sanford, "Is the Concept of Prevention Necessary or Useful?" in Stuart E. Golann and Carl Eidsorfer, eds., *Handbook of Community Mental Health,* (New York: Appleton-Century-Crofts, 1972), pp. 461–71.
19. Lawrence C. Kolb, "Against the Radical Position in Mental Health," in Harry Gottesfield, ed., *The Critical Issues of Community Mental Health* (New York: Behavioral Publications, 1972), pp. 51–70.
20. Elaine Cumming, "Primary Prevention—More Cost than Benefit," in Harry Gottesfield, ed., *The Critical Issues of Community Mental Health* (New York: Behavioral Publications, 1972), pp. 161–78.
21. Norman Garmezy, "Vulnerability Research and the Issue of Primary Prevention," *American Journal of Orthopsychiatry* 41, no. 1 (January 1971):101–16.
22. A. J. Bindman and A. D. Speigel eds., *Perspectives in Community Mental Health* (Chicago: Aldine, 1969).
23. S. E. Golann and C. Eisdorfer eds., *Handbook of Community Mental Health* (New York: Appleton-Century-Crofts, 1972).
24. Ibid.
25. Ibid.
26. Ibid.
27. Milton Wittman, "The Social Worker in Preventive Services," in *The Social Welfare Forum,* Official Proceedings National Conference on Social Welfare (New York: Columbia University Press, 1962), pp. 136–47. See also "Discussion," by Katherine A. Kendall, pp. 147–57.
28. Ibid.
29. Skidmore and Thackery, op. cit.
30. Max Siporin, *Introduction to Social Work Practice* (New York: Macmillan, 1975), pp. 15–16.
31. Ludwig W. Geismar, *Preventive Intervention in Social Work* (Metuchen, N.J.: Scarecrow Press, 1969).
32. Ludwig W. Geismar, B. Lagay, et al., *Early Supports for Family Life: A Social Work Experiment* (Metuchen, N.J.: Scarecrow Press, 1972).
33. Collins, Alice, and Pancoast, Diane, *Natural Helping Networks: A Strategy for Prevention.* Washington D.C.: National Association of Social Workers, 1976.

210   MILTON WITTMAN

34. David L. Levine, "Methodology in Developing an Epidemiology for Social Welfare," Paper presented at 89th Annual Forum, National Conference on Social Welfare, New York, May 31, 1962, mimeographed, 32 pp.
35. ———, "Crisis Intervention: Implications for Casework Practice." Address to Southern Regional Institute Medical Social Work Section, National Association of Social Workers, New York, June 11, 1962, mimeographed, 20 pp.
36. *News from West Va. University,* Release dated February 25, 1976, mimeographed, 4 pp.
37. Alfred H. Katz, "Self-Help Organizations and Volunteer Participation in Social Welfare," *Social Work* 15, no. 1 (January 1970):51–60.
38. Lois N. Glasser, "Family Services: Family Life and Sex Education," in Robert Morris et al., eds., *Encyclopedia of Social Work* (New York: National Association of Social Workers, 1971), pp. 386–93.
39. Virginia Insley, "Health Services: Maternal and Child Health," in Robert Morris et al., eds., *Encyclopedia of Social Work* (New York: National Association of Social Workers, 1971), pp. 552–60.
40. Ruth L. Breslin, "Delivery of Social Work Service in Newborn Special Care Unit," in *The First National Workshop on the Delivery of Hospital Social Work Services in Obstetrics/Gynecology and Services to the Newborn* (New Haven, Conn.: Yale-New Haven Medical Center, 1974), pp. 77–88.
41. Florence E. Cyr and Shirley H. Wattenberg, "Social Work in a Preventive Program of Maternal and Child Health," *Social Work* 2, no. 3 (July 1957):32–39.
42. Stephen E. Goldston, Ralph H. Ojemann, and Ronald H. Nelson, "Primary Prevention and Health Promotion," in E. James Lieberman, ed., *Mental Health: The Public Health Challenge* (Washington, D.C.: American Public Health Association, 1975), pp. 51–57.
43. Alfred J. Kahn, "Therapy, Prevention and Developmental Provision: A Social Work Strategy," in *Public Health Concepts in Social Work Education* (New York: Council on Social Work Education, 1962), pp. 132–148.

SUGGESTED ADDITIONAL READINGS

Bauxbaum, Carl, "Second Thoughts on Community Mental Health," *Social Work,* May 1973, pp. 24–28.
Chase, Helen, ed., "A Study of Risks, Medical Care, and Infant Mortality," *American Journal of Public Health* 63, Supp. (September 1973):1–56.
Cohen, Nathan, ed. *Social Work and Social Problems.* 1964. New York: NASW.
Hannon, Virginia, M.S.W., Sc.D. *Bibliography: Epidemiology of Mental Disorders, 1969–90,* Department of Health, Education and Welfare Publication no. (HSM) 73–9043. Washington, D.C. 1973.
Haselkorn, Florence, ed. *Mothers-at-Risk: The Role of Social Work in Prevention of Morbidity in Infants of Social Disadvantaged Mothers,* Institute sponsored by Adelphi University School of Social Work, March 1976.
Health is a Community Affair, Report of the National Commission on Community Health Services. Cambridge, Mass.: Harvard University Press, 1966.
Kelly, James. "The Quest for Valid Preventive Interventions." In *Current Topics in Clinical and Community Psychology,* vol. 2. New York: Academic Press, 1970.
Klein, Donald, "The Meaning of Community in a Preventive Mental Health Program," *American Journal of Public Health* 59, no. 11 (November 1969):2005–12.
Meyer, Henry, Edgar Borgatta, and Wyatt Jones. *Girls at Vocational High: An Experiment in Social Work Intervention.* New York: Russell Sage Foundation, 1965.
Renn, Leone. "Concepts of Prevention and Family Dynamics," Unpublished paper presented at Southern Regional Institute, Louisville, Ky., 1961.

14/ SOCIAL WORK IN PRIMARY
HEALTH CARE SETTINGS*

What is social work in primary health care? In approaching this question let us begin with a clinical illustration:

Dr. Byron is a busy gynecologist working in a fee-for-service group practice clinic in the suburbs of a large eastern city. He is meeting with a patient, Mrs. Painter, for a routine antenatal examination. As she is preparing to leave, Mrs. Painter, who is eight months pregnant, mentions that she is worried about how she will cope with her baby. She tells him that her first child, now two years old, was a very difficult baby who drove her nearly to her wits' end through exhaustion and frustration. Dr. Byron glances regretfully at his watch, remarks that he has another patient waiting, but mentions that his clinic does have a staff social worker who is available to discuss such worries. Mrs. Painter nods, somewhat diffidently, and leaves the office. She does not go to see the social worker, and Dr. Byron does not inform the social worker of his suggestion.

Two months later the social worker postpones another appointment to fit in Mrs. Painter for an urgent visit at her own request. She pours out a mixture of problems— physical exhaustion, ambivalent feelings toward her new baby, marital tension, depression, and eventually guilt over having beaten and badly bruised her two-year-old when he showed his jealousy by twisting the baby's arm.

The social worker discusses how she would like to try to help Mrs. Painter, outlining a plan involving several weekly interviews and concurrent involvement of volunteer assistants. She describes the clinic's sliding-scale fee policy for social work services, and she and Mrs. Painter agree on an appropriate weekly fee.

During the ensuing weeks events proceed according to the plan. At the final interview Mrs. Painter is quietly confident of her coping abilities. Nevertheless the mental scars of her abusive behavior still remain. The social worker wishes that Mrs. Painter had acted on Dr. Byron's original referral suggestion.

*The research drawn upon in this chapter was supported in part by the Bi-State Regional Medical Program, St. Louis, and by the Memphis Regional Medical Program (USPHS Grant No. 5 G03 RM-0051-06). However, the contents of this chapter are solely the responsibility of the author and are in no way the responsibility of the Regional Medical Programs Service, the Public Health Service, or the Department of Health, Education and Welfare.

The research was facilitated especially by Alex Cooper, William Gordon, Glenn Kelley, Sally Maki, Jean Pressburg, Ralph Pumphrey, and Emma Walker. Susan Bekenstein helped with the collation of source materials for this chapter. To all of these people I express my sincere gratitude.

The preceding sequence of events is illustrative rather than ideal or typical. Its purpose is simply to provide an example of several key facets of social work in primary health care. The *program* is located in a fee-for-service group practice *setting* in a suburban eastern area. Initially Dr. Byron attempts to provide *access* to social work service by *referring* Mrs. Painter on account of her child management concerns. This referral is not consummated at that time. We may speculate that this is due to an ambivalent *attitude* toward social workers on the part of Mrs. Painter and perhaps also on the part of Dr. Byron. Two months later Mrs. Painter does come to see the social worker after her *problems* have become more acute. A treatment *strategy* is set up and carried through, with appropriate *economic* arrangements. The following sections discuss the issues that have been introduced by the italics in this commentary.

PROGRAMS AND SETTINGS: AN OVERVIEW OF NATIONWIDE PRACTICE

There have been instances of the development of social work programs in virtually every type of primary health care setting—in prepaid group practices and health maintenance organizations;[1, 2] in fee-for-service practices and clinics, both solo[3] and group;[4] and in neighborhood and community health centers with outside funding.[5] Some programs have provided social work practicum experiences.[6] Many programs have enhanced physicians' residency experiences, especially in family medicine settings.[7, 8]

Most social workers in primary health care settings are salaried. However, an increasing minority are entering into private practice arrangements with physicians, who normally charge the social workers a certain percentage of their fees as an overhead assessment.[9] In primary health care the typical qualification level is the master's degree. There is a great diversity of job titles, with the title of "counselor" gaining increasing popularity. Social work programs are fairly well distributed throughout all geographic areas of the country, and there are instances of programs in inner-city, suburban, and rural areas. Programs in the latter category—in rural America—are relatively scarce, and yet arguably this is where they are most sorely needed.[10]

In recent years the exodus of physicians from rural areas has caused widespread concern. Remedial efforts by public and private bodies have had limited success. There are many reasons why physicians leave rural areas, but two are of particular relevance here: work overload and professional isolation. In small towns—as in the country as a whole—physicians' patients frequently present psychosocial problems. When, as often happens, there are few or no other health or social service professionals in a small town, it is hard for the town's sole physician to reduce his/her work overload by being unreceptive to patients' psychosocial problems (however disinclined, unqualified, or hard pressed he/she may feel).

Interjecting a social worker—perhaps part time—into such a situation can make a dramatic difference. The social worker might work part time with each of two or three or more solo physicians in neighboring small towns, taking over much of the physicians' psychosocial workload and at the same time providing the stimulation of interprofessional collaboration and dialog.[11]

At present social work is very far from being a normal component of primary health care nationwide. In fact even considering only clinics or centers with three or more physicians, probably no more than 3 percent currently have social worker participation. This estimate is based on extrapolation of 1974 and 1975 data compiled by the author in preparation for a 1975 nationwide mail survey of social workers in primary health care settings.[12] In this survey responses were received from social workers in 96 programs (a 60% response rate). Some of the findings are summarized in Tables 14.1 and 14.2. These tables provide an approximate quantitative profile of the field and cover several of the issues discussed in this overview.

FROM PROBLEMS TO RESPONSES: ACCESS, REFERRALS, AND ATTITUDES

In primary health care social workers are concerned with a broad range of patients' problems. These include both resource access problems—for example, difficulties in locating or applying for various benefits, services, and resources—and emotional problems (or problems with emotional bases)—for example, depression, marital tension, psychogenic sexual dysfunction, parent-child conflict, drug or alcohol or food addiction, adaptation to traumatic events or to chronic illness of self or relatives, stresses resulting in psychosomatic symptoms, anomie (especially among the elderly), and so forth.

For patients with such problems access to social work service may require passage along a pathway linking together several enabling events.[13] Major responsibility for enablement of each event may rest with one of several different system participants. However, patients and physicians are particularly important as enablers.

One of the several possible pathways to service may be conceptualized as involving the following five steps:

1. A patient recognizes the existence of his or her problem.
2. The patient presents the problem to a physician.
3. The physician says that the problem is significant.
4. The physician refers the patient to the social worker.
5. The patient presents the problem to the social worker.

Along this pathway three steps are enabled by the patient and two by the physician. Other patients' progress along this pathway might well be stymied at any particular point because of their own or their physician's lack of insight, lack of knowledge, or inhibiting attitudes. For instance, a patient may fail to present a serious marital problem to his/her physician either because he/she is unaware that the clinic has a relevant service (a social work program) or because of shame of telling anyone else about it. Even if the patient does present the problem, perhaps somewhat guardedly, his/her physician may lack

TABLE 14.1

Characteristics of Social Work Programs in Primary Health Care
Settings: Frequency Distributions (USA, May 1975, N = 96)

Characteristics	Percentages
Programs hosted by:	
Prepaid group practices	25
Residency group clinics (fee-for-service)	28
Other fee-for-service groups	47
Number of social workers in program:	
One social worker	40
Two or more social workers	60
Size of group (number of full-time-equivalent physicians):	
2 or less	14
3-5	12
6-10	13
10-19	12
20-29	10
30-40	10
50-99	14
100+	15
Region of program:	
Northeast (PHS Regions 1, 2, 3)	23
South (PHS Regions 4, 6)	15
Midwest/Mountains (PHS Regions 5, 7, 8)	36
West (PHS Regions 9, 10)	26
Population of city in which program is located (1970 census):	
Up to 9,999	15
10,000-49,999	8
50,000-99,999	20
100,000-249,999	18
250,000+	39
Social worker's remuneration system:	
Salaried (fixed wage)	89
Private practice (fee-based)	11
Social worker's qualification:	
B.A./B.S.W.	17
M.S.W. or equivalent	81
Ph.D./D.S.W.	2
Social worker with own office in group facility:	
Yes	83
No	17

TABLE 14.2

Characteristics of Social Work Programs in Primary Health Care Settings:
Mean and Median Data (USA, May 1975, N = 96)

Characteristics	Means	Medians
Social worker's working week (hours)	34	40
Social worker/patient visits (total hours per week)	17	18
Social worker/patient visits (duration in minutes)	43	45
Portion of social worker's patients referred by group's physicians	75%	81%
Social worker/patient visits per referral	5.1	4.0
Social worker/patient visit fees; fixed fee policy[a]	$24	$25
Social worker/patient visit fees; midpoint of sliding fee scales[b]	$14	$13
Private practice social worker's overhead assessments[c]	31%	29%
Years since start of social work program	7	4

[a]N = 22 (i.e., 31% of the 72 fee-for-service groups).
[b]N = 28 (i.e., 39% of the 72 fee-for-service groups). (The remaining 30% of the fee-for-service groups charge no fees for social work services.)
[c]N = 11 (the 11 groups in which the social worker's remuneration is fee-based).

insight and shrug it off as trivial or inappropriate for further attention in the context of the clinic.

A patient may be stymied somewhere along the preceding pathway but nevertheless gain access to service by taking an alternative route. For instance, to continue the preceding example, the patient may receive no encouragement from his/her physician but nevertheless—albeit atypically—may somehow find out about the social work program and on his/her own initiative make contact with the social worker. On the other hand, another patient may have a physician who is very attuned to psychosocial distress symptoms and shortens the pathway to service by suggesting referral to the social worker without the patient ever explicitly presenting an identified psychosocial problem.

Whatever the pathway under consideration, *how* a particular enabling event occurs will have much bearing on whether or not the next step will take place. For instance, in our opening clinical illustration the physician referred the patient to the social worker in a rather "take it or leave it" fashion, and unfortunately the referral was not consummated at that time. We may speculate that an opposite outcome might have resulted from more actively facilitative physician referral behavior, for example, emphasizing the social worker's professional qualifications, making a specific appointment, physically introducing the social worker or the like.

In primary health care, social work utilization rates are particularly sensitive to attitudinal factors such as anti-"welfare" prejudice, distaste for "shrinks," or physicians' ambivalence about the contributions of social workers. Many physicians will readily refer to social workers patients with problems related to resource access, but fewer consider it appropriate to refer to them patients with emotional problems. This contention is based on significant differences found during the author's two attitude surveys of primary-care physicians in a rural area[14] and in a suburban area[15] (both in the Midwest). Furthermore, over the entire range of types of patients' presenting problems, and for both surveys, on average only about half of the physicians accepted the appropriateness of referral to the social worker. In the suburban (group practice) setting the physicians' patients were also surveyed, and across a similar range of problems on an average only about half of the patients indicated that they would be willing to discuss such problems with the group's social worker.[16] These findings suggest the need for better education of both primary-care physicians and their patients regarding social workers' training and competencies.

METHODS, ROLES, AND STRATEGIES

Often an exciting aspect of social work in primary health care is the opportunity to develop one's own work style (within the limits of what is feasible). This is a young specialty. The typical program is only about four years old, and many new programs are being launched.

In most programs a considerable amount of time is devoted to individual counseling or casework, with appropriate attention being paid to backup activities, especially interprofessional liaison (for instance, at team meetings). Group work is also carried out in many programs, with the groups usually being composed of patients sharing particular types of problems, for instance, parent-child conflicts, obesity, bereavement, and the like.[17] The activities just mentioned may be considered examples of tertiary prevention—of the treating of relatively acute and overt problems in a primary setting to help prevent the necessity for later institutionalization. Many primary health care social workers are also involved in primary and secondary prevention. As part of their primary-prevention efforts, they may use community organization methods to help promote a healthier community environment—for instance, by organizing and supervising voluntary self-help projects.[18] As part of their secondary-prevention efforts, they may be involved in screening programs to facilitate the early detection of physical and/or psychosocial problems.[19] Screening programs are more commonly associated with the prepaid sector, but they may also be instituted in fee-for-service settings.[20]

Social workers in many fields are faced with the agonies of deciding how to allocate scarce time between various levels of preventive activities. What makes these decisions particularly difficult in primary health care is the situation of dual accountability—to one's professional priorities and to one's physician colleagues. In primary health care many social work programs are created and continued largely on the basis of their projected or actual contributions to the fiscal health of the clinic or center—or, to put it more bluntly, to the income of the physicians. From this standpoint the physicians welcome terti- ary- and most secondary-prevention activities. But often primary-prevention —community organization—activities generate no direct fiscal benefits for the clinic. Spending considerable time on such activities in the face of physician disapproval (covert or overt) could result in the physicians' deciding to discon- tinue the whole program. Many social workers in this field become adept strategists with a fine sense of balance—able to achieve considerable impact in the primary-prevention arena while just avoiding having their program cut from under them. As the years go by, some social workers are able to effect subtle changes in the value systems of their physician colleagues and are able to sustain work styles that are increasingly congruent with their professional priorities.

ECONOMIC ASPECTS

In this section we shall consider in more detail an issue that was touched on during the discussion of strategies, namely, the economic aspects of social work in primary health care.

As in any field, social workers in primary health care strive to make program benefits exceed costs. Thus far the literature in this field contains examinations of program cost-benefit from the standpoints of individual patients[21] and of society in general (the taxpayers).[22] Favorable program assessments from these standpoints certainly represent desirable achievements. But it is the author's conviction that such achievements must be viewed as ends that will be widely attainable only after prior focus on a more controversial means, namely, the demonstration of program cost-benefit attractiveness form the standpoint of primary-care physicians.

In primary health care social workers may or may not be employees of their physician colleagues, but virtually always the latter must be regarded as gate- keepers who make decisions regarding the initiation and continuation of social work programs within their clinics. Thus it makes sense to pay particular attention to the physicians' entrepreneurial perspective on the cost-benefit aspects of such programs.[23]

From this perspective the fiscally quantifiable component of the overall cost-benefit assessment may be viewed as the sum of two positive (benefit) terms, two negative (cost) terms, and two terms, that may be either positive or negative.

One benefit term concerns fee income. This is often substantial in fee-for- service clinics, where patients usually pay fees for social work services.[24] These fees may be fixed or individually assessed on a sliding scale. The annual total of such fees will tend to be higher in areas in which social workers have been granted vendor status by health insurance companies.

A second benefit term concerns grant income. Some programs are started with a federal or foundation grant, especially in rural and inner-city areas. However, such grants are normally phased out after one to three years.

The main cost of most programs stems from actually employing the social worker. Included in this cost term are the social worker's salary and fringe benefits and the expenses of support services—secretarial labor, telephone costs, and so forth.

A second cost term concerns space acquisition and operating costs. These will be minimal if the social worker occupies previously unused space in the clinic building. Space costs may be considerable if employing the social worker involves renting extra space or building a new office.

One of the two remaining terms may be labeled the "time effect." It is defined as the change in clinic income resulting directly from the disparities between the physicians' time allocation patterns during collaboration with the social worker and the time allocation patterns that have—or would have—occurred in the absence of such collaboration. The net time effect is often—though not necessarily—positive. Initiation of a social work program may result in a clinic's physicians being able to increase their weekly patient visit rate as a result of being able to refer to the social worker patients with time-consuming psychosocial problems. The net time effect—positive in this example—would be equal to the net clinic income resulting from the increase in the patient visit rate. In a fee-for-service clinic, extra visits would result in extra fees. In a prepaid group, extra income may come (after a time lag) from the dues of additional newly enrolled members for whom the physicians now have time to provide services.

The final term may be labeled the "drug effect." It is analogous to the time effect, but it relates to disparities in drug prescription patterns rather than time allocation patterns. From the physicians' entrepreneurial perspective the drug effect has fiscal significance only if the group pays for prescribed drugs—as sometimes occurs in prepaid group practices. A controlled study in Israel suggests that in such situations a sizable positive net drug effect could result.[25]

Individual treatment decisions may contribute positively or negatively to the overall drug effect. For instance, a positive contribution occurs if a long-term prescription of a mood-modifying drug is rendered unnecessary (or becomes needed in lesser dosage) because of the initiation of social work counseling.[26] More rarely, a negative contribution to the drug effect occurs if it becomes necessary to initiate prescription of a drug (e.g., an antidepressant) in order to stimulate verbal communication between social worker and patient.

Summing the estimated (or projected) values of the terms just discussed will generate program cost-benefit assessments based on fiscally quantifiable (objective) considerations. Such assessments are useful, but their limitations must be realized. A particular physician or group of physicians may well make a program continuation or initiation decision contrary to that indicated by the assessment because opposing subjective considerations (favorable or otherwise) have an overriding impact. For example, the physicians' philanthropic feelings *may* result in their voting to continue a program that is showing a moderate net loss from a strictly objective entrepreneurial viewpoint.

The following equation provides a summary of the preceding discussion:

Overall cost-benefit assessment of a primary health care social work program from the physicians' perspective

= fee income + grant income

− labor and support costs − space costs

± net time effect ± net drug effect

± sum of subjective considerations.

It is important to recognize that social workers' willingness to carry out program assessments within the framework just described may favorably influence the subjective components of the assessments. Such willingness may modify the attitudes of the many physicians who tend to stereotype social workers as idealists unwilling to countenance an entrepreneurial approach to primary health care.

FUTURE PROSPECTS

Throughout the primary health care field there is increasing acceptance of the need for a holistic approach to the delivery of care—for a broadening of clinic services in an attempt to relate to the totality of patients' needs, not just their somatic complaints.

The initiation of a social work program in a primary health care clinic usually markedly improves the extent to which the clinic can provide services focusing on the psychosocial needs of its patients. However, social workers have no monopoly on such services. Other types of professionals (e.g., nurse practitioners, clinical psychologists, patient educators) have varying amounts of relevant training. Each of these professional groups also has its own special area of expertise, one that is not shared by most social workers. Furthermore, the contributions of nurse practitioners, clinical psychologists, and patient educators are often better understood by physicians than those of social workers. Thus it is hardly surprising that these other professionals are fast increasing the scale of their involvement in primary health care, and indeed sometimes displacing social workers.

Social work practitioners and educators need to intensify their efforts to conceptualize their special contributions to primary health care in language that is readily understood by physicians and in ways that reflect a keen and current appreciation of the developing primary health care scene. We must not only clarify our messages but be more creative in communicating them. We need to make special efforts to communicate our messages in medical periodicals of all kinds, in books written for physician audiences, at medical conferences, and in face-to-face discussions in physicians' offices. An authoritative sociological study has indicated that the latter type of approach is a particularly effective way of promoting health care innovations.[27] It is also a feasible approach in the present context. The author's own experiences in several states indicate that many primary-care physicians *are* willing to spend a few minutes discussing the initiation or progress of a social work program. It is within the capacities of many professional groups—for example, state NASW chapters —to sponsor at least part-time advocacy of this kind.[28] The training of such advocates represents a challenge to social work educators.[29]

There is considerable growth potential for social work involvement in primary health care settings in the United States. At present there are probably at most about 1,000 social workers working full time in this field in about 300 primary health care clinics, centers, and groups—only about 3 percent of the approximately 10,000 such facilities that could plausibly be hosts for full-time social workers. (The latter figure does not include solo or two-physician practices. While there are many opportunities for part-time work in conjunction with such practices, full-time involvement normally requires collaboration with at least three physicians—and the less committed the physicians to such collaboration, the larger the number of physicians required to support full-time social worker involvement.)

In considering the import of the preceding estimates, it is necessary to bear in mind the fact that many clinics lack programs not because of lack of information, advocacy, or opportunity but because of deeply rooted contrary attitudes on the part of many physicians. Nevertheless it is the author's belief that there is potential for at least a fivefold overall expansion of the present scale of social worker involvement in primary health care.

Thus far this discussion has addressed the prospects for changes in the scale of involvement within the existing primary health care system. Certain current developments, particularly in Europe, suggest the possibility of a radical restructuring of the entire primary-care delivery system. For instance, some localities in Sweden and the Netherlands have conducted promising experiments with full physical integration of health and welfare primary-care systems—experiments in which all of a town's social workers and primary-care physicians share office space in the same building and have frequent colleagual interaction.[30, 31, 32]

The Dutch have also experimented for some years with another aspect of the integration theme—the inclusion of pastoral counseling within the primary-care concept. Especially in rural areas, frequent meetings take place between teams of pastors, physicians, social workers, and nurses.[33] They each work out of separate offices but share a common clientele and a belief in the interrelatedness of somatic, psychosocial, and spiritual problems.

There are indications that the types of integration just described may soon gain a foothold in the United States. These prospects are challenging educators and practioners to expand and develop their conceptualizations of issues such as human services integration, program administration, and interprofessional relationships.

Broad-based research efforts are needed to inform, mold, and stimulate the developments outlined in this final section. We need to carry out detailed studies of the determinants of patients' and physicians' attitudes and behaviors at the various stages along patients' pathways to social work service in primary care. For instance, we need to investigate the ways in which various fee-charging policies influence such attitudes and behaviors, and the ways these attitudes and behaviors change over time as programs mature.

We need to compile a wide range of clinical case histories illustrating patients', physicians', and social workers' perspectives. We need further study of the economic aspects of social work programs, and we especially need to attempt to document the operation of the time and drug effects. We need studies to develop guidelines regarding appropriate social worker:population and social worker:physician staffing ratios in various types of settings.[34]

We need to continue to locate relevant existing knowledge about innovation diffusion and information dissemination and to apply it to the specific context of social work program advocacy in the primary health care field. We need cross-national studies that inform us about relevant developments in other countries and analyze their implications for the domestic scene. All of these research efforts will enhance the social work profession's contributions toward the development of more humane primary health care systems.

NOTES

1. George A. Silver and C. Stiber, "The Social Worker and the Physician," *Journal of Medical Education* 32 (1957):324–30.
2. Cynthia Bell and Laurel M. Gorman, "The HMOs: New Models for Practice," *Social Work in Health Care* 1, no. 3 (Spring 1976):325–35.
3. Leonard P. Caccamo, "Using a Social Worker in the Office to Handle Family Problems," *Patient Care,* October 31, 1969, pp. 62–68.
4. Janet Winn Korpela, "Social Work Assistance in a Private Pediatric Practice," *Social Casework* 54 (1973):537–44.
5. Elizabeth J. Anderson, Leda R. Judd, Jude Thomas May, and Peter K. New, *The Neighborhood Health Center Program* (Washington, D.C.: National Association of Neighborhood Health Centers, 1976).
6. Ruth L. Goldberg, "The Social Worker and the Family Physician," *Social Casework* 54 (October 1973):489–95.
7. John A. Lincoln, Reva K. Twersky, and Dorothy O'Neil-Sale, "Social Work in the Family Medical Center," *Journal of Family Practice* 1 (November-December 1974):34–37.

8. Ann S. Frangos and Donna Chase, "Potential Partners: Attitudes of Family Practice Residents Towards Collaboration with Social Workers in Their Future Practices," *Social Work in Health Care* 2, no. 1 (Fall 1976):65–76.
9. Theresa N. Barkan, "Private Casework Practice in a Medical Clinic," *Social Work* 18 (July 1973):5–9.
10. Peter Hookey, *Social Work in a Rural Foundation Health Maintenance Organization: The Bootheel Project,* Paper presented at the American Public Health Association Meeting, Chicago, November 1975.
11. Peter Hookey, "The Establishment of Social Worker Participation in Rural Primary Health Care," *Social Work in Health Care* 3, no. 1 (Fall 1977).
12. Peter Hookey, *Social Work in Primary and Ambulatory Health Care: Access, Utilization, Attitudinal and Economic Aspects of an Emergent Field of Practice,* Doctoral Dissertation, Washington University, May 1976 (Ann Arbor, Mich.: University Microfilms International, 1976, no. 76–23,076), pp. 103–10.
13. Ibid., pp. 7–14, 76–98.
14. Hookey, *Social work in a . . . Health Maintenance Organization;* see also ibid., 28–32.
15. Peter Hookey, *A Social Worker as a Counselor in a Group Medical Practice: A New Program at the Medical Center of Florissant, Missouri,* Paper presented at the American Public Health Association Meeting, Chicago, November 1975; see also ibid., 42–49.
16. Ibid.; see also Hookey, *Social Work in Primary . . . Health Care,* pp. 49–55.
17. Korpela, op. cit.
18. Hookey, *Social Work in a . . . Health Maintenance Organization.*
19. Ibid.
20. Alastair MacLeod and Phyllis Poland, "The Well-Being Clinic," *Social Work* 6 (January 1961):13–18.
21. Frances Nason, and Thomas L. Delbanco, "Soft Services: A Major Cost-Effective Component of Primary Medical Care," *Social Work in Health Care* 1, no. 3 (Spring 1976):297–308.
22. Jane Collins, "A Cost-Effectiveness Model," in William T. Hall and Gerald C. St. Denis, Eds., *Quality Assurance in Social Services in Health Programs for Mothers and Children: Proceedings of an Institute* (Pittsburgh: University of Pittsburgh Graduate School of Public Health, 1975), pp. 103–09.
23. Hookey, *Social Work in Primary . . . Health Care,* pp. 111–38, 171–89.
24. Reva K. Twersky and William M. Cole, "Social Work Fees in Medical Care: A Review of the Literature and a Report of a Survey," *Social Work in Health Care* 2, no. 1 (Fall 1976):77–84.
25. R. Confino, "Medico-Social Teamwork in the Clinic," *Journal of the Royal College of General Practitioners* (United Kingdom) 21 (1971):230–40.
26. Colin Brewer, "Social Casework and Happy Pills," *New Psychiatry* (United Kingdom) 2 (February 13, 1975):10.
27. James S. Coleman, Elihu Katz, and Herbert Menzel, *Medical Innovation: A Diffusion Study* (New York: Bobbs-Merrill, 1966).
28. Hookey, *Social Work in Primary . . . Health Care,* pp. 152–67.
29. Peter Hookey, "Education for Social Work in Health Care Organizations," *Social Work in Health Care* 1, no. 3 (Spring 1976):337–45.
30. Claes-Göran Westrin, "Cooperation Between Medical and Social Services," *Scandinavian Journal of Social Medicine* (Sweden) 1 (1973):115–23.
31. Victor DuBois, "De wankele stabiliteit van het team van een gezondheidscentrum (door de wijziging van de samenstelling)," *Huisarts en Wetenschap* (Netherlands) 19 (1976):178–80.
32. Peter Hookey, "Social Work in Group Medical Practice: An Introduction to Developments in Ten Countries," *International Social Work* (India) 20, no. 1 (1977, in press).
33. F. J. A. Huygen, "Het home team," *Huisarts en Wetenschap* (Netherlands) 5 (1962):119–23.
34. Hookey, *Social Work in Primary . . . Health Care,* pp. 136–37.

SUGGESTED ADDITIONAL READINGS

Brunetto, Eleanor, and Peter Birk, "The Primary Care Nurse—The Generalist in a Structured Health Care Team," *The American Journal of Public Health* 62, no. 6 (June 1972):785–94.

Cohn, Helen, and William M. Schmidt, "The Practice of Family Health Care: A Descriptive Study," *The American Journal of Public Health,* 65, no. 4 (April 1975):375–82.

Forman, L. H., "The Physician and The Social Worker," *American Family Physician* 13, no. 1 (January 1976):90–93.

Gilchrist, I. G., et al., "Social Workers and Family Doctors," *The Lancet* 2, 7941 (November 8, 1875):928. (letter to the editor)

Gould, S. J., "The General Practice and Social Work: Report on a Trial," *Medical Journal of Australia* 1 (1976):669–71.

McLean, P. D., and J. E. Miles, "Training Family Physicians in Psychosocial Care: An Analysis of a Program Failure," *Journal of Medical Education* 50, no. 9 (September 1975):900–02.

"Psychiatrists, Social Workers, and Family Doctors," *The Lancet* 2, no. 7939 (October 1975): 805–06.

Part VIII

INTERPROFESSIONAL CONSULTATION AND TEACHING

15/SOCIAL WORK CONSULTATION AND TEACHING IN HEALTH AGENCIES AND MEDICAL SCHOOLS

NEIL F. BRACHT

Two aspects of social work's interprofessional contribution to health care deserve special discussion and recognition. These are (1) the expertise of social workers as consultants and (2) their role as teachers of students in other health professions. Social workers have been involved in the teaching of medical students since the 1940s and their number continues to expand. A rich body of literature documenting social work's contribution to medical, nursing, dental, and pharmacy education is summarized in this chapter. Consultation skills for social workers developed rapidly following the maternal and child health amendments to the Social Security Act in the 1930s and was given a major impetus through the enactment of the Community Mental Health Centers Act, which called for preventive intervention through consultation techniques. More recently, social work consultation is expanding to nursing homes and urban and rural outreach health demonstrations.

In this chapter we review the development of social work skills in both teaching and consultation, define the expertise required, and provide case examples illustrating social work's contribution utilizing these two methodologies. Extensive citations are provided for further study and investigation by social workers interested in improving their skills in teaching and consultation assignments. The chapter begins with a review and summary of social work teaching in medical education, followed by an elaboration of the consultation process.

SOCIAL WORK TEACHING IN MEDICAL EDUCATION

Beginning in the 1940s and continuing through the next two decades, medical educators stepped up their efforts to introduce the social-preventive and comprehensive-care aspects of medicine into medical schools.[1,2] Social workers in medical schools and teaching hospitals made contributions to these efforts, as

227

indicated in the early writings of Bartlett,[5] Cockerill,[6] and Rice,[7] which outline the problems and progress in introducing the social aspects of illness into medical education. In 1954 the National Association of Social Workers published *Medical Social Workers Participate in Medical Education, A Case Book of Illustrative Materials,* and this was followed in 1957 by a report entitled *The Psychiatric Social Worker Teaches Medical Students.* In 1959 Ullman described the functions of the social worker in teaching fourth-year medical students in a comprehensive-care and teaching program at the New York Cornell Medical Center.[8]

By 1961 two-thirds of American medical schools had social workers teaching on their faculties. The first survey of social workers participating in medical education was conducted by the National Association of Social Workers.[9]

In more recent demonstrations Edelson writes about his teaching focus with medical residents in a hospital neurological service and provides a summary. He says:

Social workers in teaching hospitals have a responsibility beyond that of instructing resident physicians in the function of a social service department in an agency setting. Since most residents go into private practice where the services of a specialist in social problems are not available to them or their patients, an important facet of their medical education is to learn to understand the patient in his environment and to utilize community resources as indicated. Social workers are uniquely qualified to impart this understanding and knowledge.[10]

Ellis, in a study of "The Social Worker as a Clinical Instructor of Medical Students," found resistance and negative attitudes on the part of medical students toward social work teaching. The difficulty of integrating the social aspects of illness has long been a problem confronting social and behavioral sciences in medical school curriculums (see Reader article in the suggested additional readings at the end of the chapter.) Ellis did find in her study, however, that patient-centered interviews followed by small-group discussion influenced in a positive direction medical students' attitudes toward the skills of social workers. She concluded that patient-centered "instructional technique is probably the most effective means of integrating the social worker's teaching into clinical instruction."[11] In 1966, the development of social work teaching in new departments of community medicine occurred. Family-centered clinical studies and community health surveys were utilized in an attempt to help medical students better understand the interrelationship between psychological and physiological aspects of health and to expose them to a larger perspective of the individual in his environment. Characteristics of teaching in community medicine are described by Bracht as follows:

The primary ingredient in any teaching effort with medical students is the essentiality of the social work consultant being firmly rooted as a contributing member of the medical school faculty. At the present time this means first the ability to collaborate on departmental research projects such as community health screening programs, epidemiologic studies and various social surveys. In one community project the social work consultant was called upon to organize a rural health referral center and utilize the findings from this experience to document health planning needs in the county. Second, the social worker must remain clinically based to provide direct social casework or consultation services when called upon. Third, the social worker must be active in planning and evaluating the community clerkship program itself. These three areas of activity are the "root ends" of the social worker's influence and visibility with both faculty and students. Additional assets that contribute to effective teaching in the community medicine program include: training in public health and medical care organization, epidemiological research methods, experience in and liking for community organization methods . . .[12]

Tanner has demonstrated the value of social work involvement in the training program of a family medicine department.[13] Soble initiated the use of social work in dental-school programs,[14] and Kilwein, Hall, and St. Denis have described the development of social work-related course content in a school of pharmacy.[15]

INTERPROFESSIONAL HEALTH TRAINING PROGRAMS

With the rise of activist student health organizations in the 1960s, a number of interprofessional student health projects were initiated that included social work participation.[16,17] Tanner and Soulary designed a program for effective interdisciplinary teamwork between students of nursing, medicine, and social work.[18] Fieldwork collaboration between medical and social work students in a rural area is reported by Bracht.[19] More recently, Quartaro and Hutchinson have described the development of a joint course in nursing and social work.[20] Williams, Williams, and Bracht have found little formal collaboration between currently practicing nurses and social workers while they were in their own individualized formal training programs.[21] This is shown in Table 15.1.

SOCIAL WORKERS ON MEDICAL SCHOOL FACULTY

In a recent study of social workers teaching in medical schools (having primary faculty appointments), it was found that among the 116 medical schools in the country nearly 600 social workers (representing 1.5 percent of all faculty) were employed members of the faculty. The range of health courses taught by social workers in medical schools is summarized by Grinnell as follows:

These courses include psychosocial implications of hospitalization; psychosocial aspects of illness and rehabilitation; death and dying; man and his environment; human behavior; human growth and development; sexuality; marriage (marital enrichment, marital dysfunction); family dynamics; interviewing; social studies; family therapy; group psychotherapy; social problems; alcoholism; drug abuse; child abuse; gerontology; family health maintenance; health care of minority groups; issues in health care organizations; plan-

TABLE 15.1

Interprofessional Contact Between Social Workers and Nurses[a]

Time Period	Mean	df	t value
Before entering school:			
Social workers	2.28	292	7.71[b]
Nurses	1.38		
During school:			
Social workers	2.51	291	4.87[b]
Nurses	1.89		
During employment:			
Social workers	3.78	291	4.80[b]
Nurses	3.23		

[a] N = 237 nurses and 60 social workers.
[b] $p < 0.001$.
Source: Cindy Williams, Reggie Williams, and Neil Bracht, "Interprofessional Experiences Between Social Workers and Nurses in Hospitals," Article accepted for publication, *Social Work in Health Care*, Vol. III (3) Summer 1978.

ning of manpower policy; fundamentals of the health care system; mobilization and utilization of community resources; function of the social worker; medical social work; urban and rural studies; rural medicine; clinical medicine; and medical ecology. The diversity of content areas being covered suggests that social workers are no longer concentrating primarily on the individual patient and his family but incorporating subject matter related to broader health care issues and concerns.[22]

METHODS OF TEACHING

A variety of methods are utilized by social workers in teaching members of other health professions. These include (1) planning and developing curriculum in medical schools; (2) offering formal courses; (3) participating in interdisciplinary team teaching, (4) clinical conferences, including going on rounds; (5) patient care coordinating demonstrations; (6) individual clinical case demonstrations through interviewing and the like; (7) consultation; (8) home visiting; (9) community field teaching; and (10) participation in epidemiologic research.

ILLUSTRATION OF SOCIAL WORK TEACHING

The following depicts the role of a social work faculty member (the author) teaching in a medical school demonstration that included *both* medical and social work students. The students lived in a rural community for six weeks and worked jointly on community and family health studies. The social worker saw the students weekly in teaching seminars conducted in the community.

The following case illustration is excerpted from a report of the total teaching demonstration.[19]

ORIENTATION SEMINAR-LAB

During the initial day of orientation for students about to depart for their specific community assignments, an orientation seminar on community survey methods is conducted jointly by the social worker and the medical anthropologist in the department. This seminar takes the form of a laboratory exercise and seeks to acquaint students with the wide range of resource data available for community assessment. This includes such items as census material, agency records, university studies, state department bulletins and geological and economic surveys. Local citizens and community leaders are also brought to the student's attention as sources of information.

CONSULTING ON COMMUNITY STUDIES

In conducting a community inventory and health assessment, it was expected that social welfare content would be emphasized in the social worker's report and health needs in the medical student's. Exchange of ideas and information was accomplished through joint visits to health and welfare institutions by the students, where both would ask questions and gather pertinent community data. Each was exposed to the way of thinking and approach of the other. Close collaboration took place when the students had to pool their information and combine their data into one community survey report. During the time in the field, the social work faculty member visited regularly with the students and provided consultation both on their community study as well as their clinical work.

PRESENTING FINDINGS

The students' presentation of their community findings to the faculty was both insightful and creative in its approach. The students decided to use specific cases of rheumatic heart disease in children as a way of assessing the variety of services, personnel, and programs in the rural community under study. This was accomplished by the two students tracing the course of the disease and relating major community services to particular patient needs and resources. For example, the medical student first described how through early detection the disease was diagnosed by the family physician. Using this introduction, the student then discussed the quality of hospital and physician services in the community. Picking up on the theme, the social work student described the effects of the disease on the child's educational progress which then led to a broader discussion of the total community's educational system and services provided for the educationally and physically handicapped. In discussing the general question of control and prevention of diseases, the students presented findings from their evaluation of the health department's chronic disease control program. The medical student discussed the "poor" record of local physician referral to the public health department for such services. The social work student found the health department's patient follow-up registry grossly inadequate and made suggestions for its improvement that were adopted while he was still in the community.

MAKING A "COMMUNITY DIAGNOSIS"

The social work student's final report also included: (a) demographic analysis; (b) history of the community; (c) assessment of political systems; (d) general social and economic factors; (e) evaluation of private and public welfare services; and (f) information on the financing and organization of health and educational services. Both students agreed in their final report that the nonaccredited status of the local hospital and its financial difficulty were serious problems confronting the community. The social work student stated in his report: "The hospital administrator, concerned about the budget deficit, is making an effort to admit only those patients who can pay either through individual resources or through limited medical care financing provided by the state. There are no licensed nursing homes in the county which will accept patients who must rely on public assistance grants. There are no services in the county for the emotionally ill." The medical student summarized the problem this way: "There is a lack of health leadership in attempting to deal with some of the very real health and social problems which exist in the community. Of the 23 reasons given for nonaccreditation of the local hospital, 21 were directly related to physician actions or omissions."

FACILITATING COORDINATED PATIENT CARE

With students living in the community, consultation and follow-up on discharged hospital patients can be undertaken. In one case, the social work student was encouraged to continue counseling with a psychiatric patient he had known at the medical center. Observing directly the patient's environment significantly increased the student's knowledge of the problems and his understanding of the inadequacy of past discharge plans. The student worked directly with the patient's local physician assisting in a plan of regular counseling follow-up visits between the patient and her local physician. The physician involved in this case was also the medical student's sponsor in the community, so there was three-way consultation on this case between the physician, the social work student, and the medical student. Casework treatment was enhanced as a result, and the interdisciplinary learning and cooperation that took place could be transferred to future practice situations.

In this teaching demonstration with students the social worker combined broad community health experience with relevant clinical case assignments. In the community the students are confronted directly with gaps in medical as well as social services. They see the effects of health manpower shortages as well as the problems of uneven distribution of such personnel. The relationship of poverty to disease is studied in bleak shacks and on barren land. Water and air pollution is recognizable where students eat and sleep. As one student summarized his experience,

The clerkship has been outstanding in my mind in that here for the first time I have been able to see the total ecology of the patient. I can see the effects of too few doctors, the impact of disease on the family and the spread of illness within a family, and the bearing of economic and social factors on the health status of the patient.

Because they were focusing on the total community as the "patient," the students were generally in unfamiliar "territory." In many respects this situation made them rely on each other's skills and knowledge to complete comprehensive community surveys and work with difficult-to-reach families. Living in the midst of deplorable health and social conditions, the students were forced to recognize the professional's responsibility as a change agent. The students did not always see eye to eye on the methods for achieving change, but because they lived together in the same town they found numerous informal opportunities to discuss traditional professional views and stereotypes. These discussions gave rise to new insights and questions, which surfaced when the faculty social work consultant visited the students in the field. The kinds of interactions reported by the students seemed, to faculty involved in the project, to be typical of future professional relationships, and perhaps these early patterns of communication would serve as some basis for continuing interdisciplinary work.

FUTURE DEVELOPMENTS

The accumulated experience of social work teaching in medical schools spans a period of some thirty years. Much can be learned from this experience that will be useful in the continuing expansion of the use of social workers in medical education. Thousands of social workers in social service departments across the country, especially in hospitals, have provided and will continue to provide *informal* teaching to students in the health professions. Among social workers with faculty appointments (formal) in medical schools, the picture remains optimistic. As Grinnell points out, 30.7 percent of social work teachers received their current medical school appointments during the years from 1966 to 1969, but 48 percent received them during the years from 1970 to the present. Grinnell also found in a survey of medical school deans that they would like to see an increase in the number of social workers teaching in medical schools.[22]

SOCIAL WORK CONSULTATION IN HEALTH PROGRAMS

Social workers have had considerable experience in using the consultative process, especially in maternal/child health programs, crippled children services, public health departments, and mental health agencies. Consultation, Bartlett comments, "is used by many professions as a way of enlarging the practitioner's knowledge and skill . . . Consultation is essentially a process of shared thinking that brings to the consultee enlarged insight, increased ability to deal with the problem, but leaves with him the responsibility for decision and action."[23] In a review of the literature on consultation, Mannino and Shore identified several types of consultation.[24] They are
1. Consultee-centered case conference consultation
2. Client-centered consultation

3. Agency-centered staff development consultation

4. Agency-centered program development and administrative consultation

5. Community-centered mental health consultation

Increasingly, interdisciplinary team consultation in health and mental health settings is gaining recognition.[25] Social work consultation to nursing homes is a more recent development. Social work consultants frequently serve as trainers in health programs and conduct inservice training programs.[26]

WHAT IS CONSULTATION?

Rapoport states that the purpose of consultation is "to introduce change in some facet of the consultee system. Thus the consultant role may be viewed as that of change agent."[27] Insley, in relating consultation to public health practice, defines consultation as

A helping process which involves the use of professional knowledge and professional relationships between one or more professional people. It takes place within the framework of an administrative arrangement officially recognized by the agency . . . Consultation is given in response to a request for help by the individual or group of individuals. The consultee is responsible for carrying out any action to be taken . . . He is free to accept or reject the suggestions made by the consultant.[28]

Social workers are most frequently involved in two major aspects of consultation: (1) case consultation and (2) program consultation. Occasionally the two can be combined. *Case consultation* is directed at individual clients and helps the consultee better identify sociomedical aspects or resources for help in treating a particular patient, group of patients, or family. *Program consultation* is directed at agency or community needs and involves help on such issues as staff motivation/development, new-program options, awareness of funding resources, and administrative efficiency. Consultation is not the same as supervision. The consultant ordinarily does not have administrative or evaluative authority over the consultee. Consultation can also be used as an effective outreach or community change strategy.[29]

Effective consultation skills develop through experience and specialized continuing-education seminars. Some research[30] focused on identifying the most important personal characteristic of successful consultants pointed to the following variables: The consultant (1) works on the *consultee's* problem, (2) has the ability to *gain the confidence* of the client, (3) has an *analytical* mind, (4) has the ability to *generate enthusiasm* for new ideas, and (5) has *patience* and *confidence* in his/her own work. Mutuality in the consultation-learning process is a must.

THE PROGRAM CONSULTATION PROCESS

Watkins,[31] in a research project to improve the effectiveness of program consultation, lists eight steps in the process:

1. *Determination of the need for consultation*
2. *Initiating the request for consultation*
3. *Organizational assessment and problem formulation*
4. *Negotiation of the contract*
5. *Setting of the consultation objectives*
6. *Determining strategies of action*
7. *Implementing the plan of action*
8. *Reporting assessment of outcome of consultation*

Watkins also highlights three major characteristics that are significant in conducting program consultations:

1. The problem formulation stage requires the consultant and consultee to use the systems approach to analyzing the organization of the health care program. They must look at the interrelationships and forces which deter achievement of the program's objectives. This approach may offer a different perspective to consultants and consultees who are clinically oriented and accustomed to analyzing a problem on the basis of accumulated experiences of patient population.

2. The objectives of the consultation process are related to advancing the objectives of the health program. The consultant and consultee are required to distinguish between the service objectives of the program and the impact objectives, that is, the desired changes in health status of the target population. This requirement of determining how the consultation will help achieve the impact objectives of the health program prevents the consultant and consultee from becoming confined to the parochialism of their own profession.

3. The assessment of outcome takes into consideration positive and negative factors which enhance or impede the achievement of the objectives of the consultation process. This not only provides a less subjective, more rational accounting for the consultation process but it also provides baseline data for future approaches in program consultation.

A typical case situation confronting a program consultant is described by Watts. The medical school consultant is working as part of an interdisciplinary team providing consultation to a county public health department.

The D County Health Department has been operating an evaluation and diagnostic clinic for mentally retarded children for some time. Its Director, Doctor P, is concerned because he does not think that his team is functioning efficiently. They are not seeing enough patients, and it takes so long for the diagnostic process that staffing conferences for diagnosis and the interpretation to parents is delayed three or four months. The problem seems to be a hold-up in pediatric evaluation and in nursing and social services studies. He writes to the maternal and child health director of the state health department and asks that a team composed of a pediatric consultant, a nursing consultant, and a medical social consultant meet with him and his staff to discuss what could be done to solve this problem.[32]

In the situation just described the state health department team discovered that much of the delay was related to inappropriate use of professional time for administrative work. A joint assessment was made and appropriate strategies of action suggested. Follow-up suggested that the outcome goals had been achieved.

ILLUSTRATIONS OF CASE CONSULTATION

In the following vignettes the use of client-centered case consultations within a rural community is illustrated by Bracht with other professionals.[33]

One aim of the social work consultant is to help familiarize the (future) doctor with the kinds of community social services he can call upon in the practice of comprehensive medicine.

CASE 1

Faced with the necessity of discharging a two-month-old baby from a community hospital, a senior medical student was presented with a dilemma. A previous child from the family had died in the hospital (malnutrition) and the present baby was about to be discharged after recovering from a similar admitting diagnosis. Perplexed by the possibility of sending the child back to a family of inadequate means and ability to care for the child, the student asked what could be done. In talking with the student, the social worker realized that the student knew very little about the family and virtually nothing about the temporary placement services of child welfare. It was suggested that a visit be made to the local Child Welfare Department. Not only was the child welfare worker well acquainted with the family, but she had previously removed children from this home and was immediately prepared to deal with a temporary placement. She spent time with the medical student explaining certain cultural and social factors that pertained directly to the parents' inability to provide for their children. The day following the consultation on this case, the child welfare worker and the medical student made a joint home visit with this family to prepare them for the necessity of temporary placement outside the home.

CASE 2

One medical student, located in a rural community with few social service resources, used the social work consultant to discuss the best approach in dealing with a sexually acting out teenager. The social worker was able to illuminate family aspects and offer tangible suggestions for the medical student's subsequent interviews with the girl. The family physician participated in the discussions and planning for this case.

CASE 3

In another consultation situation, the social worker observed a medical student's ability to secure pertinent medical as well as social information during a family interview in the home of a widowed coal miner. The widow's health concern related to the need for surgery for her young daughter. The social work consultant made suggestions as to available financial resources to pay for the girl's hospitalization and this, in turn, led to further discussions regarding the broader question of the adequacy of health insurance coverage not only of the United Mine Workers' plan but also of other health insurance plans. The medical student also wanted to discuss the opportunities for improvement in the family's situation, taking into consideration the general social and economic problems of this once prosperous coal area.

In some situations the consultant, when requested, may actually demonstrate the skill or approach being recommended. In the following example the consultant conducted an interview for demonstration purposes. The case consultation was centered on both the consultee and the client.

CASE 4

Going on "rounds" with a medical student in a community hospital offered the opportunity to address clinical aspects of a particular case and also to discuss hospital organization and issues such as accreditation and quality of services. The case situation involved an elderly hospitalized patient in which the social work consultant's requested interview with a family member revealed the harmful ingestion of a drug by the patient. Until this interview demonstration took place, medical treatment had been stymied. This case provided for the medical student a specific illustration of the use of allied health personnel.

COMBINING CASE AND PROGRAM CONSULTATION

Peterson, in an interesting description of consultation to nursing homes, discusses a process in which *program* and *case consultation* are successfully combined.[34]

CASE 5

During the period of program consultations (development of a therapeutic community) I continued the task of discussing methods for assisting individual patients to set goals for themselves... I began to meet weekly with the administrator and three staff persons: the day manager, the night manager, and the cook. The first case was presented by the administrator. It involved a resident who had posed a management problem for all staff. He was referred by the medical center and refused to assume any responsibility in the house. He failed to care for his own personal needs and kept wandering away. The administrator confessed his authoritarian stance: "Make him bathe"; "Let's increase his medications." I presented the situation from the patient's point of view, emphasizing the ultimate goal of adjustment to a community setting. The patient consistently talked about getting a job and ignored confrontations about his personal hygiene, stating that it didn't make any difference how he looked if he wasn't working—something his hospital doctor had encouraged.

I encouraged the administrator to get more information from the patient and to contact the hospital staff about their recommendations. The administrator followed through, and within a few days arrangements were made for the patient to attend a sheltered workshop nearby. The administrator had utilized this workshop before but only minimally. Now he recognized the potential of this community resource and developed a relationship with its staff.

SUMMARY

This chapter has described the work of social workers both as teachers of members of other health professions and as consultants in interprofessional health programs. Consultation is an effective approach to expanding a profession's knowledge and service to the community. The skills and characteristics of consultants have been briefly summarized, and the application of skills within selected case illustrations has been described. The reader will benefit from pursuing the references and suggested additional readings. One final note on consultation is in order. Particular problems that consultants may experience are summarized by Rapoport as follows:

Within one's own discipline it may be harder to establish and have accepted the role as expert. With other disciplines there may be problems arising from relationships with either high or low status professionals and from the need to dispel the usual interdisciplinary stereotypes and concomitant mistrust . . . [A consultant operates] in a setting in which he is only temporarily or tangentially affiliated. There is little structure in which to operate except what he creates and there is not the usual supporting framework to which he is accustomed.[35]

NOTES

(TEACHING)

1. *Preventive Medicine in Medical Schools,* Report of Colorado Springs Conference, November 1952 (Chicago: Association of American Medical Colleges, 1953).
2. P. Snoke and E. R. Weinerman, "Comprehensive Care Programs in University Medical Centers," *Journal of Medical Education* (July 1965):625–57.
3. J. Curran and E. Cockerill, *Widening Horizons in Medical Education* (New York: Commonwealth Fund, 1948).
4. Ralph Eichenberger and Robert Gloor, "A Team Approach to Learning Community Health," *Journal of Medical Education* 44 (August 1969):660
5. H. Bartlett and W. Beckman, "Teaching of Social and Environmental Factors in Medicine: Some Unsolved Problems," in D. Goldstine, ed., *Expanding Horizons in Medical Social Work* (Chicago: University of Chicago Press, 1955), p. 238.
6. E. Cockerill, "The Preparation of the Medical Student in the Recognition of the Social Component of Disease," in Goldstine, op. cit., p. 209.
7. E. Rice, "Teaching of Social Aspects in Schools of Public Health," *Medical Social Work* 2 (October 1953):148–58.
8. A. Ullman, "The Role of the Social Worker in Teaching Fourth Year Medical Students," *Journal of Medical Education* 34 (March 1959):239–46.
9. According to a 1961 study by the National Association of Social Workers, over two-thirds of the medical schools in this country had social workers participating in their teaching programs. See *Participation of Social Workers in Medical Education* (New York: National Association of Social Workers, 1961).
10. E. Edelson, "The Changing Role of the Social Worker in Medical Education," *Social Work* 10 (January 1965):81–86.
11. June Ellis, "The Social Worker as a Clinical Instructor of Medical Students," *Journal of Medical Education* 43 (April 1968):508–10.

12. Neil F. Bracht, "Contribution of Public Health Social Work in Academic Departments of Community Medicine," *Milbank Memorial Fund Quarterly* 47, no. 1, Pt. 1 (January 1969).
13. Libby Tanner and Lynn Carmichael, "The Role of the Social Worker in a Family Medicine Training Program," *Journal of Medical Education* 45, (November 1971):859–65.
14. Rosalynde Sobel and Harris Chaiklin, "Social Work and Preventive Dentistry," *Social Work,* March 1975, pp. 142–43.
15. John H. Kilwein, William T. Hall and Gerald St. Denis, "Social Science, Social Work and Pharmacy," *Social Work in Health Care* 2, no. 1 (Fall 1976):95–100.
16. Lois J. Gordon, ed., *Chicago Student Health Project, Summer 1967* (Chicago: Chicago Student Health Project, 1968).
17. *Report on the Second Assembly of Student Health Organization, "Curriculum Reform"* (New York: Albert Einstein College of Medicine, 1967).
18. Libby Tanner and Ethel Soulary, "Interprofessional Student Health Teams," *Nursing Outlook* 20 (February 1972):111–15.
19. Neil F. Bracht and Inge Anderson, "Fieldwork Collaboration Between Medical and Social Work Students," *Social Work in Health Care* 1, no. 1 (Fall 1975):7–18.
20. Emma Quartaro and Ruth Hutchinson, "Interdisciplinary Education for Community Health: The Case for Nursing and Social Work Collaboration," *Social Work in Health Care* 1, no. 3 (Spring 1976):347–56.
21. Cyndi Williams, Reggie Williams, and Neil Bracht, "Interprofessional Experiences between Social Workers and Nurses in Hospitals," *Social Work in Health Care* 3, no. 3 (Summer 1978):in press.
22. Richard Grinnell, Nancy Kyte, Ski Hunter and Thomas Larson, "The Status of Graduate-Level Social Workers Teaching in Medical Schools," *Social Work in Health Care* 1, no. 3 (Spring 1976):317–24.

(CONSULTATION)

23. Harriett Bartlett, *Social Work Practice in the Health Field* (New York: National Association of Social Workers, 1961), pp. 243–47.
24. Fortune V. Mannino and Milton Shore, *Consultation, Research in Mental Health Related Fields, A Critical Review of the Literature,* Public Health Monograph no. 79, Dept. of HEW (Washington, D.C., 1971), p. 5.
25. Constance Gross and Richard Umansky, "Problems in Promoting the Growth of Multidisciplinary Diagnostic and Counseling Clinics for Mentally Retarded Children in Rural Areas," *American Journal of Public Health* 61, no. 4 (April 1971):698–710. See also Lee E. Townsel, John Irving and Hans H. Stroo, "Mobile Consultation: An Integrative Approach to Mental Health Service to Children, *Social Work in Health Care* 1, no. 1 (Fall 1975):81–92.
26. *Social Workers as Trainers in Health Programs,* Proceedings 1971 Annual Institute for Public Health Social Workers, Berkeley, California, 1972.
27. Lydia Rapoport, ed., *Consultation in Social Work Practice* (New York: National Association of Social Workers, 1963), p. 18.
28. Virginia Insley, "Program Consultation," in Gerald Caplan, *Concepts of Mental Health and Consultation, Their Application in Public Health and Social Work,* Department of Health, Education and Welfare, Children's Bureau, Publication no. 373 (Washington, D.C., 1959), p. 235.
29. Eunice Miller, "The Social Work Component in Community-Based Action on Behalf of Victims of Huntington's Disease," *Social Work in Health Care* 2, no. 1 (Fall 1976):25–32.
30. Mannino, op. cit.
31. Elizabeth L. Watkins, "Accountability in the Practice of Program Consultation in Health Services," in *Quality Assurance in Social Services in Health Programs for Mothers and*

240   NEIL F. BRACHT

Children, Proceedings of Institute, Public Health Social Work Program, University of Pittsburgh, March 31-April 4, 1975.
32. Mary Watts, "The Process of Consultation in Public Health," unpublished paper, no date.
33. Bracht, op. cit.
34. Carolyn Peterson, "Consultation with Community Care Facilities," *Social Work in Health Care* 2, no. 2 (Winter 1976–1977):181–92.
35. Rapoport, op. cit., p. 15.

SUGGESTED ADDITIONAL READINGS

(TEACHING)

"Creative Adult Learning-Teaching: Who's the Engineer of This Train?" *Journal of Education for Social Work* 12, no. 3 (Fall 1976).
Hunt, A. D., Jr., and Neil F. Bracht, "Medical Education and the Community," *Michigan Medicine* 65 (December 1966):1061–66.
Lewis, Charles E., and Barbara A. Resnik, "Relative Orientations of Students of Medicine and Nursing to Ambulatory Patient Care," *Journal of Medical Education* 41–42 (1966):162–66.
McGavran, E. G., "Scientific Diagnosis and Treatment of the Community as a Patient," *Journal of the American Medical Association* 152 (October 1956):723–27.
Reader, George, and Rosemary Soave, "Comprehensive Care Revisited," *Health and Society,* Milbank Memorial Fund Quarterly, Fall 1976, pp. 391–414.
Tapp, J. W., Jr., and K. Deuschle, "Medical Care Teaching in the Community," *Medical Care Journal* 2 (December 1964):214–17.
Turk, H., and T. Ingles. *Clinic Nursing: Exploration in Role Innovation.* Philadelphia: F. A. Davis, 1963.

(CONSULTATION)

Mannino, Fortune. *Consultation in Mental Health and Related Fields: A Reference Guide,* National Institute of Mental Health—Department of Health, Education and Welfare, Public Health Service Publication no. 1920. Washington, D.C., 1969.
Mayer, Shirley, "Group Day Care for Children Under Three: Experience with a Program Under the Auspices of Local Health and Welfare Agencies," *American Journal Of Public Health,* January 1972, pp. 43–46.
Plog, Stanley, and Paul Ahmed, eds. *Principles and Techniques of Mental Health Consultation.* New York: Plenum, 1977.
Robbins, Paul R., Esther C. Spencer and Daniel A. Frank, "Some Factors Influencing the Outcome of Consultation," *American Journal of Public Health* 60, no. 3 (March 1970):524–34.
Signell, Karen, "Mental Health Consultation in the Field of Illegitimacy," *Social Work,* April 1969, pp. 67–74.
Signell, K. A., and P. A. Scott, "Mental Health Consultation: An Interaction Model," *Community Mental Health Journal* 7, no. 4 (December 1971):288–302.
Smyth, Wilma, "Preventive Aspects of Medical Social Work Consultation in a Rural State," *Social Work,* July 1960, pp. 91–96.
Stephenson, P. S., "Judging the Effectiveness of a Consultation Program to a Community Agency," *Community Mental Health Journal* 9, no. 3 (Fall 1973), pp. 253–59.
Warren, Roland L. *Social Research Consultation.* New York: Russell Sage Foundation, 1963.
Watkins, Elizabeth, et al., "Improving the Effectiveness of Program Consultation," *Social Work in Health Care* 2, no. 1 (Fall 1976):43–54.
Williams, Martha, "The Problem Profile Technique in Consultation," *Social Work* 16, no. 3 (July 1971):52–59.

Part IX

ORGANIZING AND PLANNING COMMUNITY HEALTH SERVICES

16/PUBLIC HEALTH SOCIAL WORK:
A COMMUNITY FOCUS
NEIL F. BRACHT

HISTORICAL DEVELOPMENT

Social workers have been employed in public health department programs since the 1920s. Initially social work in public health was simply a transplantation of medical social work as practiced in the hospital to the confines of the local public health center. Social casework services were effectively used in work with recalcitrant or hard-to-reach clients of the public health department. In its development at the local level social work was heavily identified with TB control programs in helping individuals and families deal with the traumatic impact of extended hospital stay. Case finding was also seen as a function of the social worker. While the social work focus on the individual was both supplementary and complementary to early public health practice, the development of consultation, outreach, and wider-community health action began to emerge in the 1930s and 1940s. Employment in Public Health Service hospitals, Indian health clinics, and state health department programs also emerged during this time.

In an unpublished paper by Edenka Buben entitled "Medical Social Service in a County Health Department" (written in California in 1939), a differentiation between hospital and public health practice is made: "If we were asked where there is an appreciable difference between practice in public health and the services of a hospital, we would be inclined to say that perhaps the principal difference is that in a public health setup the worker has as much opportunity for social action, and for bettering social conditions of the medically needy as she has for individual case work services." Another paper by Beatrice Hall entitled "The Role of Medical Social Service in Public Health Programs" (*The Child*, a Social Security-Children's Bureau Bulletin, February 1945) says:

The medical social worker brings to the public health program an emphasis upon the social aspects of health and medical care aspects that are of concern to all members of the medical team. In her liaison capacity she brings to welfare and social agencies a continuing explanation of health department and increased understanding of what services are available through these agencies and how their services may be utilized most effectively in the promotion of positive health for the community.

With the advent of social security and the accompanying programs for crippled children under Title V, the opportunity for public health social work services was significantly expanded. Appropriations of funds to support various Children's Bureau programs emphasized the social needs of individuals and families. A central office of medical social work in the Children's Bureau became increasingly involved in consultation to state programs regarding social service needs in child health programs. Area consultants were established in all of the regional offices of the Department of Health, Education and Welfare. It was in the meeting of these new program needs that social workers clearly moved away from the "one-to-one" approach and used their knowledge and experience to specify social and environmental considerations in both program and case planning. Rice cogently summarized this approach as follows:

In public health, the social worker is not considered to be carrying his full responsibility unless he is looking at, pointing up, analyzing and evaluating the results of his experiences, not only for his own practice but also for the values to others. Public health is not primarily interested in what happens to the individual, but is concerned with what happens to an individual as it reflects the needs of other individuals and the necessity for further community planning around these needs. In other words, the social worker in public health must get at the core of the difficulty in order to point up what is further needed to understand, solve, and prevent the problem.[1]

By the 1960s the "core of the difficulty" that Rice alluded to had become, for many, the underlying social conditions of poverty and racial discrimination. The focus of attack was on the community and organizational change. The progression to community and organizational change strategies is reflected in the writings of two other authors. Isabelle Stamm, speaking before a workshop on "Social Work in the Field of Health" in Boston (sponsored by the Council on Social Work Education, 1963), stated that "what we need are techniques and methods enabling far more people to be reached per professional person. During the next decade, one avenue of attack on the general problem of ill health and restoration will clearly involve extensive *structural* and *organizational* change." Spencer, in her chapter "Public Health Social Work," says: "In local health departments the role of the public health social worker has substantially shifted to that of consultant and *community planner*. The rapid pace at which public health is moving into new areas of concern requires a social work analysis of the *effectiveness of patterns of organization and function in meeting goals.*"[2]

Palmiere suggested that social workers should take on expanded responsibilities in the development of policy and programs in health and social services delivery:

It will not be enough, however, for social work to raise questions about the emotional and social implications of this or that biologically-oriented activity. It will not be enough to review and react to program policies and plans developed by other professions. Social work must also be willing to take on a major role in defining in human terms the objectives of public agency programs. It must be willing to accept responsibility for guidance of the use of the administrative and financial power of public agencies in the same way that it has accepted the responsibility in its traditional field of social welfare.[3]

CHANGING PROGRAMS IN PUBLIC HEALTH

Traditional public health programs are undergoing significant changes. As more primary and curative health services embody preventive and health maintenance elements, the traditional roles of public health physicians, nurses, and social workers are changing. Historically the major functions of local health departments have included the following programs:

1. environmental sanitation surveillance
2. school health and immunization programs
3. maternal and child health care
4. *limited* care for indigent patients
5. disease screening and control programs such as TB, VD

Some large-city health agencies also operate major hospitals, neighborhood health centers, and long-term care facilities. While official public health agencies still exercise control over infectious-disease control and continue to inspect for environmental and sanitary hazards, their role in environmental protection is eroding. New agencies are being created (e.g., the Environmental Protection Agency). Rearrangement of the Public Health Service at the national level has caused further blurring of the "public health" role. At the academic level, new programs in community medicine and family medicine incorporate much of the traditional content formerly "delivered" by departments of preventive medicine. While the blurring of public health roles and program efforts is a fact of life, there still exist distinct state and local health department programs. Approximately 1000 social workers are employed in these offices. A 1970 survey indicated that each year thirty M.S.W. social workers receive advanced M.P.H. degrees.

In 1962 the educational qualifications for social work practice in public health were developed.[4] A current revision is in progress under the leadership of faculty at the Berkeley Public Health Social Work Program and Professor Reichert at San Diego State University. The revised initial draft reflects significant changes in both the definition of public health and the roles of social workers. Randor has examined the expanding role of social work in case finding, consultation, and program policy planning.[5] Reichert and Morris have both written about social work roles in community health planning.[6, 7] Bracht has summarized public-policy issues for social work practice in both health maintenance organizations and neighborhood health centers.[8] These articles reflect a wide range of practice modalities for social workers in public health settings. In one sense the social worker in public health is a generalist, flexibly responding to program and population needs that cover a wide spectrum of services.

THE RANGE OF SOCIAL WORK FUNCTIONS

The services of social workers in public health are directed toward the identification and modification of social, psychological, and environmental factors that contribute to health problems or influence the use of health services, particularly at the community level. The social worker in the health agency usually discharges his/her responsibilities as a member of an interprofessional group whose close collaboration has been a traditional characteristic of public health work. Emphases in social work practice depend on the scope and organization of the total public health agency program.

Some specific functions of the social worker in public health are listed in the following pages (bibliographical references follow each function):

1. A social worker participates with other team members in case finding and planning outreach services to patients in such programs as maternal and child health, family planning, early screening, alcholism, and mental health.

Burns, Joan. "A Social Worker's Role in the Identification and Counseling of Families at Risk for Genetic Disorders." In *Family Health Care: Health Promotion and Illness Care,* edited by Robert C. Jackson and Jean Morton. Berkeley: University of California, Public Health Social Work Program, 1976, pp. 81–98.

Grass, Constance, and Richard Umansky, "Problems in Promoting the Growth of Multidisciplinary Diagnostic and Counseling Clinics for Mentally Retarded Children in Rural Areas," *American Journal of Public Health* 61, no. 4 (April 1971):698–710.

Guiliozet, Noel, "Community Mental Health—New Approaches for Rural Areas Using Psychiatric Social Workers," *Medical Care* 13, no. 1 (January 1975,) 59–67.

Haselkom, Florence, ed. *Mothers at Risk: The Role of Social Work in Prevention of Morbidity in Infants of Socially Disadvantaged Mothers,* Institute sponsored by Adelphi University School of Social Work and cosponsored by United Cerebral Palsy Association, Inc. Garden City, New York: Adelphi University School of Social Work, 1966, 160 pp.

2. A social worker provides direct preventive casework services to patients and families served by the agency, including home health care community support services when appropriate.

Cowin, Ruth, "Social Factors in Treating Burned Children," *Children* 2, no. 6 (November-December 1964):229–33.

Haggerty, Robert. "The Conceptual and Empirical Bases of Family Health Care." In *Family Health Care,* op. cit., pp. 17–26.

"San Mateo's Family-Centered Approach to Community Ill Health," *Public Health Reports* 77, no. 4 (April 1962).

Thomas, Duane. "Assessment of Family Functioning: The Transactional Analysis Model." In *Family Health Care,* op. cit., pp. 39–58.

3. Social workers function as discussion leaders or organizers of client or patient groups in promoting health education activities.

Shaw, Judith, and Robert Shaw. "Aiding Expectant and New Parents to Accomplish the Developmental Task of Parenthood." In *Family Health Care,* op. cit., pp. 59–68.
Vavra, Katharine, Lucy N. Urbain, and Annamarie Shaw, "Meeting the Challenge of Educational Care and Heart Disease," *American Journal of Public Health* 56, no. 9 (September 1966): 1507–51.

4. A social worker functions in a planning or advocacy role with other providers or consumers in comprehensive community health projects.

Barney, Jane Lockwood, "Community Presence as a Key to Quality of Life in Nursing Homes," *American Journal of Public Health* 64, no. 3 (March 1974):265–68.
Kumabe, Kazuye, "A Pre-Natal Clinic in a Rural Area," *Children* 2, no. 6 (November-December 1964):214–18.

5. A social worker provides case or program consultation (individually or as part of a team) to other staff members regarding psychosocial and community factors affecting patients and their utilization of health services.

Ardell, Donald, and Maryann Holohean, "The Effective Use of Consultant Services in Public Health Planning," *Public Health Reports* 88, no. 10 (1973):903–07.
Hayes, Charlene, "Attitudes of Public Health Nurses and Social Workers Toward Public Health Nursing and Social Work Practitioners," *Nursing Research* 19, no. 5 (September-October 1970):453–56.
"Team Problem Solving: Members of a Public Health Team Discuss the Operationalization of a Temporary Farm Labor Camp." In *Multidisciplinary Practice in Public Health,* Based on Proceedings of the 1965 Annual Institute for Public Health Social Workers, edited by Joanna Gorman and Alice M. Varela. Berkeley: University of California, School of Public Health and School of Social Work, October 1966, pp. 89–126.

6. A social worker participates with other staff in establishing policies and procedures for implementation of innovative service delivery projects.

Cowin, Ruth, Elizabeth Rice, and William Schmidt, "Social Work in a Child Health Station—Report of a Demonstration," *American Journal of Public Health* 55, no. 6 (June 1965):821.

7. A social worker works with community and consumer groups in assessing social and health needs.

Jacinta, Muriel De Garcia, "Yambele: An Experience in Community Organization in a Public Health Setting," *Social Work,* April 1961, pp. 87–93.
Planning and Implementing Social Work Programs in Community Health Services for Mothers and Children, Proceedings, Tri-Regional Workshop, Public Health-Social Work Program, edited by William T. Hall and Howard B. Monahan. Pittsburgh: University of Pittsburgh, Graduate School of Public Health, 1968.
Roberts, Pearl, "Human Warehouses: A Boarding Home Study," *American Journal of Public Health* 64, no. 3 (March 1974):270.

8. A social worker participates in research and evaluation studies.

Evaluation of Social Work Services in Community Health and Medical Care Programs, Proceedings based on 1973 Annual Institute for Public Health Social Workers, edited by Robert C.

Jackson and Jean Morton. Berkeley: University of California, Program in Public Health Social Work, 1973.

McCoy, Tommie, et al., "Clients' Reactions to an Outreach Program," *Social Work,* November 1975, pp. 442–44.

9. A social worker participates in training and staff development of paraprofessional personnel.

Bertino, Laura, and Robert Jackson, eds. *Social Workers as Trainers in Health Programs,* Proceedings of 1971 Annual Institute for Public Health Social Workers. Berkeley: University of California, School of Public Health, Program in Public Health Social Work, 1972, 83 pp.

Housman, H. Burton, "Community Organization for Treatment and Prevention of Drug Abuse." In *Social and Health Needs in Childhood and Adolescence,* Proceedings of 1970 Annual Institute for Public Health Social Workers, edited by Joanna Gorman. Berkeley: University of California, Public Health Social Work Porgram, 1970.

Richter, Ralph et al., "The Community Health Worker: A Resource for Improved Health Care Delivery," *American Journal of Public Health* 64, no. 11 (November 1974):1056–61.

KEY ASPECTS OF SOCIAL WORK PRACTICE IN PUBLIC HEALTH

A social worker new to programs in a public health agency needs to be familiar with key concepts and principles underlying public health or "community health" practice in order to integrate these "tools" with social work practice skills. These concepts and principles include such terms as "population at risk," "levels of prevention," "prevalence and incidence rates of illness," and "epidemiology." Two helpful references for the social worker in this regard are *Public Health Concepts in Social Work Education,* published by the Council on Social Work Education and Michael Murphy's article, "The Development of a Community Health Orientation Scale," in *American Journal of Public Health.* [9]* What follows is a review of three major components of social work

---

*Murphy's descriptive statements of common community health concepts are as follows:

Primary prevention: The concept of lowering the rate of new cases of illness or disease in a population by counteracting harmful forces before they have a chance to produce illness.

Population focus: The concept that the health professional should be responsible for an entire population of both identified and unidentified potentially ill members of his community as well as individual patients with whom he has contracted for treatment.

Continuity of care: The concept that there shall be a continuity of responsibility as the patient moves from one program service or organization to another in an integrated network of care-giving vehicles.

Multidisciplinary involvement: The concept that the health specialist recognizes the wide range of health disciplines and expertise in a community and that he can practice more effectively by working with and respecting these varying disciplines.

Comprehensive care: The concepts of directing care at physical and sociopsychological health needs, and of environmental health activity.

Consumer involvement: The concept that the consumer of health services should have a role in the decision-making process of service determination.

Prepayment mechanisms: The concept that various forms of prepaid medical care services should be available to population groups.

practice strategies in public health: (1) *preventive intervention utilizing the epidemologic approach,* (2) *community health assessment,* and (3) *health planning.*

UTILIZING THE EPIDEMIOLOGIC APPROACH

Epidemiology is *the study of the distribution and determinants of disease prevalence among large populations.* To put it another way, epidemiology is one of the sciences concerned with the study of the processes that determine or influence the physical, mental, and social health of people. This method has made distinct contributions to social work practice and research. Thus some familiarity with the epidemiologic approach is desirable in public health settings.

Public health professionals have used the epidemiologic method to (1) describe, (2) analyze, and (3) control major health problems among large groups of people. Some examples are yellow fever, smallpox, and tuberculosis. The substantive success achieved in controlling these problems reflects treatment based on sound knowledge of the causative agent(s). In social epidemiology the focus moves away from infectious disease to social group problems such as mental illness, alcoholism, and the like.

The epidemiologic method begins with (1) *observation and description* of the incidence and prevalence of a given disease (or social problem), the characteristics of people with the problem, and environmental factors influencing the problem; then moves on to (2) *comparison and analysis* of these data with a control group; and then (3) derives causal associations through hypothesis testing. The well-known levels of prevention frequently used in public health are shown in Figure 16.1.

In the past few years there has been growing interest within the social work profession as to how public health concepts of prevention could be applied to the study and control of major social problems. (See Chapter 13.) While social work is concerned with providing treatment services on a one-to-one basis, it needs to give equal recognition to the value of epidemiologic studies that analyze social problems and their effects on large groups. One early example of social work research done along epidemiologic lines was Bradley Buell's work in the St. Paul Study.[10] Buell provided a descriptive classification system for families and found that 6 percent of the families used 50 percent of the welfare funds. These data provided a target base for proposed intervention. A more recent study of mental subnormality in a Scottish community found that certain social characteristics found in lower socioeconomic classes were associated with a higher prevalence of subnormality. For example, family size, crowding, and mother's occupation were all linked to frequency rates 1½ to 2½ times greater than in comparison groups. More startling was a sixfold increase in prevalence rates for minimal subnormality when size of family and residence are combined, as shown in Table 16.1.

250 · NEIL F. BRACHT

Health Promotion	Specific Protection	Early Diagnosis and Prompt Treatment	Disability Limitation	Rehabilitation
Health education Good nutrition Marriage counseling and sex education Attention to personality development Provision of adequate housing, recreation, working conditions	Immunization Attention to personal hygiene Use of environmental sanitation Protection against occupational hazards Protection from accidents Use of specific nutrients	Mass and individual case-finding measures Screening surveys Objectives: To cure and prevent disease To prevent the spread of communicable diseases To prevent complications and sequelae To shorten period of disability	Adequate treatment to arrest the disease process and to further prevent complications and sequelae Provision of facilities to limit disability and to prevent death	Provision of hospital and community facilities for retraining and education for maximum use of remaining capacities Education of the public and industry to utilize the rehabilitated As full employment as possible Selective placement Work therapy in hospitals Use of sheltered colony

Primary Prevention	Secondary Prevention	Tertiary Prevention

FIG. 16.1. Levels of application of preventive measures.

Source: Hugh Leavell and E. Gurney Clark, *Preventive Medicine for the Doctor in His Community* (New York: McGraw-Hill, 1958), p. 22. Used with permission of McGraw-Hill Book Company.

The authors describe how such analysis can lead to greater precision in identifying high-risk groups:

Table [16.1] shows that each of the family characteristics results in doubling of the rate over the general prevalence for Social Class V. When both characteristics are used jointly to identify families, a six-fold increase is obtained in the prevalence rate for minimal subnormality in Social Class V compared with the overall prevalence of Social Class V. Thus, the analysis of these two family characteristics in combination within Social Class V enables us to identify with greater precision one set of families in which minimal subnormality is more likely to occur.[11]

Population studies such as those just mentioned illustrate that the real value of epidemiologic knowledge is in its illumination of the "population at high

TABLE 16.1

Prevalence of Minimal Subnormality in Social Class V
by Family Size and Area of Residence[a]

Family Characteristics	No. of Children Minimally Subnormal	No. of Children in Population at Risk	Prevalence per 1000
5 children	13	336	38.7
Residence in interwar tenement	10	234	42.7
5 children and residence in interwar tenement	9	88	102.3

[a]In Social Class V there are 18 cases of minimal subnormality, 1044 children in the population at risk, and a prevalence rate of 17.2 per 1000.

Source: Birch, Richardson, Baird, Horobin, and Illsley, *Mental Subnormality and the Community* (Baltimore: Williams & Wilkins, 1970), p. 80. Reprinted with permission of The Williams & Wilkins Co.

risk" and its potential application to preventive measures. When social workers study the influence of human factors in a group of cases and compare them to a control group, they are using the epidemiologic method. Unfortunately social work studies aimed at preventive intervention have produced few positive results.*

Social epidemiology has been underutilized by social work. Perhaps, as Kurt Reichert comments, "Social work's inability to move vigorously to develop its own variety of epidemiologic approach is due primarily to our historical, professional and institutional failure to accept that community social problems remain our collective business."[12]

Population Target Groups. Rice, in commenting on areas for preventive intervention by social workers, lists several opportunities, especially with young families:[13]

1. Experience of families in crises, such as the birth of a congenitally handicapped child, acquired handicapping conditions due to trauma or disease, the birth of a premature baby, a patient newly diagnosed as having tuberculosis or cancer, a death, or a miscarriage. These all are crises in families to which individuals will react intensely. Knowing this and working with them at the time of crisis, or preferably in advance of an anticipated crisis, will help to lessen the impact on the individual and family.

2. Early years of marriage and pregnancies at an early age.

3. Separation of the child from the family or separation of the parent from the child. In a recent study we found that the hospitalization of a parent often resulted in unfortunate experiences for the child.

*For a review of prevention studies see William Berleman et al., "The Delinquency Prevention Experiment of the Seattle Atlantic Street Center: A Final Evaluation," *Social Service Review* 46, no. 3 (September 1972):323–46.

4. Assumption of a new responsibility, such as the role of becoming a spouse, a parent, or meeting the difficulties of widowhood.

5. Pressures on both mothers and children because mothers are working.

6. Siblings of sick, disabled, or handicapped children.

7. Supportive services to adolescents who are trying to make their adjustments to adult life.

8. Children who leave school early, to become often unemployed in the labor market, or marry young, or who frequently are added to the group of our juvenile delinquents in a community.

Bracht gives several other examples of high-risk groups in which preventive interventions could be tested:

Seventy-seven thousand miners currently receive disability benefits for black-lung disease. Follow-up and continuity of care for this group are largely neglected. Although nearly 3.5 million disabled workers and their dependents receive social security disability benefits, no systematic monitoring of this population provides for tertiary prevention. In a study of the workmen's compensation program, Brinker and Murdock found that severely injured workers suffered a substantial drop in income forcing them to move to poorer housing. Their children were also adversely affected; they had a lower rate of college attendance and held poorer jobs than children in the control group.[14]

COMMUNITY HEALTH ASSESSMENT: SOCIAL WORK ROLES

Target or population groups must frequently be studied in the context of a total-community health study or assessment. Social workers can make important contributions to community health surveys.

Effecting improvements in the provision of health care for a population group requires information and objective data on both social and health care systems that exist in a community. Health care surveys are frequently used. Five types of information are critical for studying and evaluating health service programs:

1. There must be knowledge of the geographic, spatial, and environmental components of an area.

2. Knowledge of the demographic characteristics of the population, with special emphasis on data related to health-illness concerns, is needed.

3. Knowledge of the people, their social customs, their beliefs, and their political structure is necessary.

4. The socioeconomic base of a community or region must be understood.

5. Accurate information on the health care system and services available to the population should be obtained. By the health care system we simply mean the constellation of facilities (public clinics, private hospitals, etc.) and personnel (doctors, dentists, nurses, etc.) that, together with social support services, constitute the system involved in the delivery of medical care to this specific group. Economic characteristics of this system in the particular geographic area are of increasing interest to the health planner. Just as sociodemo-

graphic properties (age range, sex ratio, income, education levels, etc.) of a city's geographic subdivisions can be specified by means of census data collected by various other local government agencies, so also the properties of the health care system can be related to these geographic subdivisions.

Ideally these areas of information should be available on a continuous basis if programs are to be correlated with people's needs in a systematic fashion over time. In Figure 16.2 an outline for a community study survey is shown, with the special focus and concerns of social work highlighted. Social workers can assist in the design and implementation of survey studies or in the training of personnel to conduct household interviews.

A related issue of some importance is that of clarifying the existing *utilization patterns* of health care services. It is desirable to know, in other words, how the population currently uses existing medical facilities. Two main sources can be used to gain this information. Data can come (1) from carefully conducted household surveys and (2) from medical facilities. An enumeration of the frequency and pattern of use of relevant medical facilities, together with the underlying reasons, tells the planner how a group is currently receiving its medical care: Where do they go? With what complaints? How frequently? Are facilities near the individual's neighborhood used, or does the individual travel out of his/her immediate area? When and for what kinds of problems are private as opposed to public facilities used? The development of these data bases is an important first step in the planning process.

COMMUNITY HEALTH PLANNING

Schwebbel and his associates describe a community organization approach to the implementation of comprehensive health planning. Their model is shown in Figure 16.3. Strong emphasis, consistent with social work values, is placed on consumer participation and local citizen control. In summarizing the use of their model of planning, the authors state that

this model describes a method by which citizens, through organization techniques, can improve the quality of life in their community. As citizens form groups to begin identifying health problems, setting priorities and allocating resources, they begin developing their own health policies based on locally obtained information. Perhaps they, with some technical assistance, are the most appropriate people to develop such policy: They are closest to the problems, most affected by them, and most interested in seeing them through to solution. As the citizen groups begin to tackle local health problems, with aid from technical and other resources, they shape the course of their community's development.[15]

Levels and Types of Health Planning.   Planning means setting goals, making choices as to which needs are most urgent, deciding on and following through with appropriate strategies of intervention.

Community Study Areas	Social Work Focus and Purpose
1. *Geographic area:* Size, communications, principal towns and villages, general housing conditions, utilities, climate, flora and fauna, roads.	Importance of transportation, environment, and communications in the delivery of social and health services.
2. *Demography:* Census analysis—vital statistics, including birthrate, fertility rate, infant mortality, causes of death, divorces, accidents, etc.	Knowledge of dependency ratio, family size, percent of population increase, disease differentials is required in estimating and planning for health and welfare services. Using census material to pinpoint at-risk populations.
3. *People:* Historical-anthropological background, political affiliation, local leaders, and customs. Educational levels, social structure, associations, and interactions. Governmental and political jurisdictions. Social networks for mutual support. Religious groups, schools, arts, recreation.	Accurate knowledge of people, their heritage, and their beliefs is essential to the provision and use of health and welfare services. Knowledge of key leaders and political structure is a necessary part of community organization work.
4. *Socioeconomic:* Industrial-agricultural aspects, income levels, public assistance, social-security payments, agencies and services, community philanthropic organizations, voluntary health groups.	Causes of economic dependency that result in community social problems. Role of government in economic improvement and evaluation of current social programs.
5. *Health and social services:* Distribution of voluntary, public, local, and state agencies. Social services, mental health and official public health services, including school health, public health nursing, sanitarian, institutional facilities, nursing homes, hospitals, mental institutions, TB hospitals, and rehabilitation services. Day care voluntary agencies.	Familiarity with health programs and services and their interrelatedness to population groups served by social work agencies. Understanding of public health approach to community problems. Consumer involvement in health and social service programing.
6. *Health personnel:* Doctor:patient ratios, allied health, etc. Indigenous workers, self-help groups, volunteers.	Distribution of health professionals and attitudes of local health personnel toward social problem areas. Study of manpower shortages and estimation of future needs.
7. *Financing:* Health and welfare services, third-party reimbursement patterns, impact of Medicare and Medicaid payments, hospital commission, free clinics, union contracts and benefits, health department budget, community mental health board.	Understanding of the resources for health-welfare consumption. Analysis of problems in medical care financing and utilization. Effect of new legislation on community personnel and facilities.

FIG. 16.2. Social work outline for community health survey and assessment.

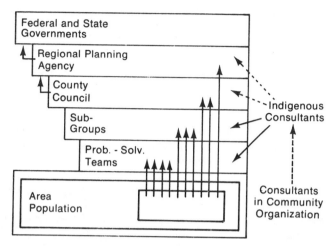

Stage 5: In the effectively organized community, health planning and decision making responsibilities rest with the area population, which is linked, through the problem-solving teams, to the county council and regional planning agency. Consultants serve as resources to the indigenous consultants.

FIG. 16.3 Stage 5: the Organized Community.

Source: Andrew Schwebbel et al., "A Community Organization Approach to Implementation of Comprehensive Planning," *American Journal of Public Health* 68, no. 8 (August 1973):679. Reprinted with permission of the American Public Health Association, Inc.

Consumer and provider participation in planning takes knowledge, involves people, holds the potential for conflict situations because of the choices to be made, and a whole host of other factors. It is a process involving many people. It takes place at many levels of community (local, state, nation), in different ways (rational, social, governmental, voluntary), in different fields of endeavor (health, rehabilitation, welfare), and with differing patterns of participation (face-to-face decision-making, representation of organizations).[16]

Palmiere, a social worker, has described three types of health planning: *dispersed, focused,* and *central.*

Dispersed planning expresses the individualistic values of our culture and continues to be the dominant approach to health planning at the present time. Focused planning reflects that segment of our value system which emphasizes voluntary cooperation. Its rapid expansion in recent years may be attributed both to its basic acceptability and its compatibility with the individualism of dispersed planning. Central planning expresses the concern of our culture for rationality and efficiency in the organization and use of resources. However, the use of power, particularly that based on governmental authority, is perceived as directly antithetical to the individualistic values of the culture. Thus, central planning has had limited expression in the health care system.[17]

Principles of Health Planning. In a report prepared for the Interagency Liaison Branch, National Institute of Mental Health in July 1971, Richard Scobie sets forth six principles to guide the planner:

1. Identify your goals, distinguishing between the basic "preamble" goals, policy, and planning goals; weighing the feasibility of each in relation to the influence you command and the resistance you anticipate.

2. Systematically analyze the setting in which you plan, including the social, organizational, political, cultural, and ideological forces at work there; assess the interrelationships between persons, formal and informal organizations determining, in the process, the loci of power and influence as they relate to relevant issues.

3. Develop your planning organization in such a way as to insure maximum information exchange, early identification and resolution of conflict, staffed with persons selected for their versatility, breadth of social outlook, and ability to relate positively in a variety of settings, especially in the target area. Avoid "tall" bureaucratic structures.

4. Develop an action system and a constituency which includes the authentic participation of those most directly affected by the programs being planned, being careful in so doing to avoid severely coopting your "lay" participants, or being coopted by established agencies with which you must deal. Accept the political nature of the planning process.

5. Analyze alternative courses of action in terms of their possible consequences, the probability and value of success, the costs in resources and influence expended, and the risks involved in each; only then should one course be selected for implementation. If unforeseen resistance occurs, repeat the analysis.

6. Provide mechanisms for information feedback, collection and analysis during the planning and implementation phases, insuring greater responsiveness to the consumers and other constituent groups, an early warning system when problems develop, and data which will be important in subsequent evaluations.

Increasingly, social workers are being employed in large numbers in community-wide health systems agencies. Among staff planners in these agencies, Finney[18] found that social work was the largest discipline represented.

Program Planning—Case Study. Not all social workers are involved in large-scale, community-wide planning activities. Particular program-planning efforts are equally important and are frequently encountered. Selig provides a case study of program planning for alcoholism:

Case Study

The purpose of this data gathering was to begin the process of problem identification in the area of alcoholism for one geographic mental health area in Massachusetts.

The setting was an inpatient ward for alcoholics located in a state mental hospital. This ward is the only inpatient service for alcoholics in its catchment area.

Two sets of data were obtained. All consecutive admissions to the ward during a 6-month period, January 1 to July 1, 1970, made up one sample; data were gathered from statistical records maintained by the hospital. The second sample consisted of all admissions to the ward during one month, August, 1971. Each respondent was interviewed, and data were recorded on a semi-structured questionnaire. The information gathered in the first sample consisted of selected demographic variables, while the second interview sample gathered information on both demographic and social variables.

Of the three communities served, one community accounts for most of the admissions, both absolutely and as a percentage of the population. Over all three communities, the divorced, widowed, and separated are overrepresented in the patient group compared to the population. Middle-aged persons (35 to 54) have higher rates of admission than other groups, and more males than females are hospitalized, the ratio being about 4:1.

Problem Identification

The case study gathered data on selected social and demographic factors of treated patients. This information fulfills only part of the problem identification function. These data do reveal something about who is presently utilizing existing services. They do not reveal the actual number of persons and families in the community who need help. They do not tell us how the problems are defined and perceived by other consumers, such as families, hospitals, social agencies, welfare departments, community organizations, etc.

The reasons that a person is admitted to the alcoholism ward are multiple. Although the attitudes influencing the decisions and pathways into the hospital were not the immediate concern in the case study, they must be dealt with in the planning of any program.

Goal Setting

Since the case study needs expansion to more validly define the problem, any further planning is limited, since it would be based on limited information. Nevertheless some examples of goals, based on the data, can be mentioned.

A significant trend in the case study is that persons separated, widowed, and divorced were overrepresented in the hospitalized group. The divorced, especially, appear to be at the highest risk of being hospitalized for alcoholism. Although which comes first, the drinking or the divorce, is unclear, a recent study suggests that divorce and separation seem to be crises that precede psychiatric difficulties. Preventing and decreasing the possible negative consequences of divorce and separation, such as depression, anxiety, and confusion, which may lead to eventual problems with alcohol, is an example of an intermediate range goal. A long range goal might be that of early identification through places of employment, unions, or children having problems in school (stemming from family problems related to alcohol), and appropriate interventions in the family system, prior to the necessity of divorce or separation.[19]

SUMMARY

In public health social work the focus of professional practice is on populations at risk, in the context of their community environment. This chapter has described the multiple roles and functions of social workers, including preventive case services, multidisciplinary consultation, epidemiologic studies, community health assessment, and the health-planning process. While more and more social workers are incorporating public health approaches in their clinical and hospital-based practice, it has been the public health social worker who has consistently maintained a community focus in addressing health and illness conditions and associated social factors. Public health social work retains a distinctive practice context, and efforts to support increased training of public health social workers should be strengthened. This is especially true in light of the significant increase in employment of social workers in health planning agencies.

NOTES

1. Elizabeth Rice, "Social Work in Public Health," *Social Work* 4, no. 1 (January 1959):82–88.
2. Esther Spencer, "Public Health Social Work," in A. Katz and J. Felton, eds., *Health and the Community* (New York: Free Press, 1965), pp. 451–65.
3. Darwin Palmiere, "The Responsibilities of Social Work in Policy and Program Development," Paper presented at the Regional Training Institute for Public Health Social Workers, "The Changing Patterns of Social Work Services in the New Health Programs," East Lansing, Michigan, August 11–14, 1966. See also Darwin Palmiere, "The Expanding Role of Social Work in Medical Care Settings," Paper presented at the National Association of Social Workers Tenth Anniversary Symposium on Social Work Practice and Knowledge, Atlanta, Georgia, May 21–23, 1965.
4. "Educational Qualifications of Social Workers in Public Health Programs," *American Journal of Public Health* 52, no. 2 (February 1962).
5. MaryAnn Randor, "Expanding Roles of Social Workers in the Health Field," *American Journal of Public Health* 62, no. 8 (August 1972):1102–04.
6. Kurt Reichert and Elizabeth Reichert, "Social Work in Health Planning: The How and What Dilemma," Paper presented at the 1968 Annual Meeting of Medical-Social Consultants in Public Health and Health Care, San Francisco, May 23. See also Kurt Reichert, "Social Work's Responsibility in Community Health," Paper presented at the 1965 Southern Regional Institute, National Association of Social Workers, Nashville, Tennessee, June 13–18.
7. Robert Morris, "The City of the Future in Planning for Health," *American Journal of Public Health* 58, no. 1 (January 1968):13.
8. Neil Bracht, "Health Maintenance Organizations: Legislative and Training Implications," *Journal of Education for Social Work* 2, no. 1 (Winter 1975):36–44, and "Medical School Sponsorship of OEO Neighborhood Comprehensive Health Centers: Issues and Implications for Social Work," in Willard C. Richan, ed., *Human Services and Social Work Responsibility* (New York: National Association of Social Workers, 1969).
9. *Public Health Concepts in Social Work Education* published by the Council on Social Work Education, 1962, and Michael Murphy, "The Development of a Community Health Organization Scale" in *American Journal of Public Health* 65, no. 12 (December 1975), pp. 1293–97.
10. Bradley Buell, "Implications for Social Work Education and the Concept of Prevention," in *Proceedings of the Annual Program Meeting,* Council on Social Work Education, 1960, pp. 139–49.
11. Herbert Birch et al., *Mental-Sub-normality in the Community* (Baltimore: Williams and Wilkins, 1970). See also Kurt Reichert, "Application of Public Health Concepts and Methods to the Field of Social Work," in *Education for Social Work,* Annual Proceedings, Council on Social Work Education, 1963, pp. 102–04.

12. Reichert, op. cit.

13. Elizabeth Rice, "Concepts of Prevention as Applied to the Practice of Social Work," *American Journal of Public Health* 52, no. 2 (February 1962):266–74.

14. Neil Bracht, "Health Care: The Largest Human Service System," *Journal of Social Work* 19, no. 5 (September 1974):532–42. See also Neil Bracht, "The Contribution of Public Health Social Work in Academic Departments of Community Medicine," *Milbank Memorial Fund Quarterly* 47, no. 1, pt. 1 (January 1969):73–89.

15. Andrew Schwebbel et al., "A Community Organization Approach to Implementation of Comprehensive Planning," *American Journal of Public Health* 68, no. 8 (August 1973):679.

16. Florence Ray Stier, "A Social Worker's View of Leadership in Program Planning Within the Community," Paper presented at the 1966 Mid-Continent Regional Institute, National Association of Social Workers, Denver, Colorado, April 18–22, 1966.

17. Darwin Palmiere, "Types of Planning in the Health Care System," *American Journal of Public Health* 62, no. 8 (August 1972):1112–15. See also Darwin Palmiere, "Lessons Learned from the Experience of Health Facilities Planning Councils," *American Journal of Public Health* 62, no. 9 (September 1972):1235–38.

18. Robert Finney et al., "Prospects for Social Workers in Health Planning," *Health and Social Work* 1, no. 3, (August 1976):7.

19. Andrew L. Selig, "Program Planning, Evaluation, and the Problem of Alcoholism," *American Journal of Public Health* 65, no. 1 (January 1975):3–75.

SUGGESTED   ADDITIONAL   READINGS

GENERAL PUBLIC HEALTH

Action for Mental Health, Final Report of the Joint Commission of Mental Illness and Health. New York: Basic Books, 1961.

Chilman, Katharine, and Paul Geasser. *Social Work Roles and Functions in Family and Population Planning,* 4 vols. Ann Arbor: University of Michigan, School of Social Work, Social Work Education and Population Planning Project, 1974.

Gentry, John, et al., "Promoting the Adoption of Social Work Services by Hospitals and Health Departments," *American Journal of Public Health* 63, no. 2 (February 1973):117.

Goldston, Steven, ed. *Mental Health Considerations in Public Health: A Guide for Training and Practice,* Department of Health, Education and Welfare, Public Health Service, Publication no. 1898. Washington, D.C., May 1969.

Kane, Robert, ed. *The Challenge of Community Medicine.* New York: Springer, 1974.

Morales, Armando. "The Impact of Class Discriminations and White Racism on the Mental Health of Mexican Americans." In *Chicanos: Social-Psychological Perspectives,* edited by Nathaniel Wagner and M. Haug. St. Louis: C. V. Mosby, 1971, p. 257.

Public Health Concepts in Social Work Education, Proceedings of Princeton Seminar. New York: Council on Social Work Education, 1962.

Rice, Elizabeth, "Concepts of Prevention as Applied to the Practice of Social Work," *American Journal of Public Health* 52, no. 2 (February 1962):266ff.

Wallace, Helen, "A Study of Services and Needs of Teenage Pregnant Girls in the Large Cities of the United States," *American Journal of Public Health* 63, no. 1 (January 1973):5–10.

COMMUNITY HEALTH ORGANIZATION AND PLANNING

Austin, Charles, "Selected Social Indicators in the Health Field," *American Journal of Public Health* 61, no. 8 (August 1971):1507–16.

Black, Bertram. "Social Work in the Planning and Delivery of Health and Mental Health Services." In *Human Services and Social Work Responsibility*, edited by Willard C. Richan. New York: National Association of Social Workers, 1969.

Bladeck, Bruce, "Interest Group Representation and the Health Systems Agencies: Health Planning and Political Theory," *American Journal of Public Health* 67, no. 1 (January 1977).

Blum, Henrik. *Planning for Health: Development and Application of Social Change Theory*. New York: Human Services Press, Behavioral Publications, 1974.

Chatterjee, Pranab, and Raymond Koleski, "The Concepts of Community and Community Organization: A Review," *Social Work*, July 1970, pp. 82–87.

Dolfman, Michael, "Health Planning—A Method for Generating Program Objectives," *American Journal of Public Health* 63, no. 3 (March 1973):238–42.

Fogelson, Franklin, "Statewide Planning in Mental Health: An Early Report," *Social Work*, October 1964, pp. 26–33.

Gonzales, Roberto, et al., "Symbiosis in Planning and Operation of a Comprehensive Health Center and Community Mental Health Program in Philadelphia," *American Journal of Public Health*, August 1972, pp. 1105–10.

Handbook for Community Fact Finders. Philadelphia: American Friends Service Committee.

Kramer, Ralph M., and Harry Specht, eds. *Readings in Community Organization Practice*, 2d ed. Englewood Cliffs, N.J.: Prentice-Hall, 1975, 386 pp.

Levy, Clifford. *A Primer for Community Research*. San Francisco: Far West Research, 1972.

Morris, Robert, "Basic Factors in Planning for the Coordination of Health Services," *American Journal of Public Health*, March 1963, pp. 32–42.

Schwartz, Edward, "Macro Social Work: A Practice in Search of Some Theory," *Social Service Review* 5, no. 2 (June 1977):207–27.

Wachtel, Dawn Day, "Structures of Community and Strategies for Organization," *Social Work* 13, no. 1 (January 1968):85–91.

Whitaker, Laighton, "Social Reform and the Comprehensive Community Mental Health Center —The Model Cities Experiment: Part II," *American Jouranl of Public Health*, February 1972, pp. 216–22.

17/ORGANIZING NONSEXIST
HEALTH CARE FOR WOMEN ELAINE SCHROEDER

American women may live longer than American men, but this does not mean that they are healthier. In fact women's illness rates are significantly higher than men's.[1] Women utilize a disproportionately large share of American medical services, averaging 25 percent more physician visits per year, consuming 50 percent more prescription drugs, and having more frequent hospital admissions than males.[2] It is not known whether this difference in illness patterns between males and females is due to health socialization, to differences by gender in life style, or to demographic factors such as the greater number of older women in the population. But it is becoming increasingly clear that the traditional health services available to women greatly need improvement.

Even though our health care system is one of the world's most costly, our infant mortality rate places us sixteenth among industrialized nations, and our maternal death rate is twelfth highest in the world.[3] Not only does the American health care system fail to provide women with quality obstetrical care, but even routine gynecological services are inadequate. For example, simple routine screening for breast and cervical cancer has not been provided for most American women (estimated at less than 20 percent a year), even though the mortality rates for these types of cancers fall steeply when identification is made early.[4]

A medical practice that is potentially hazardous to all women is the large amount of unnecessary gynecological surgery performed in the United States. Twenty-five percent of all women age 50 or over have had a hysterectomy. Currently it is estimated that over one-third of all hysterectomies are being performed unnecessarily.[5] Twice as many hysterectomies per capita are performed in the United States as in Great Britain, with the same survival rate.[6] Why is there such a high incidence of this major pelvic surgery in the United States? At least part of the answer may lie in physicians' attitudes toward women and their reproductive organs. Excessive pelvic surgery is nothing new. In the nineteenth and early twentieth centuries female castration (öophorectomies) was practiced to cure women of such problems as masturbation as well as for eugenic purposes.[7]

Breast cancer is also treated differently in the United States than in other countries with high medical standards. The most common American surgical procedure for breast cancer is a radical mastectomy, which involves removing the entire breast plus all the axillary nodes and the pectoral muscles. There are other surgical alternatives, including simple mastectomy and radiation. Dr. George Crile, a specialist in breast cancer surgery, asserts that in many cases less extensive surgery is indicated.[8] The result is fewer complications and less discomfort and disfigurement.

Women have often unknowingly been subjects for drug experiments, especially those involving IUDs and hormonal preparations. In one notorious study sponsored by a large pharmaceutical company, women—mainly Chicanas—participated in a double-blind study of the side effects of birth control pills.[9] Unfortunately one side effect for the placebo group was pregnancy. In the 1940s and 1950s diethylstilbesterol (DES) was given to women with threatened miscarriages. It is now known that DES is hazardous to female offspring. Even after DES was linked to vaginal cancer in those offspring, the drug was still sometimes prescribed to prevent miscarriage.

The hazards of oral contraception have until recently been downplayed in the United States, even though early British studies have established associated risks of blood clotting and heart disease. Much of the available information on the effectiveness and safety of oral contraceptives is published by the drug companies that sell the product. One certainly wonders about the accuracy of these contraceptive reports when drug companies, like any business, are concerned with profits. Pharmaceutical companies are also our major source of information on IUD safety and effectiveness. The abrupt removal of one type of IUD, the Dalkon shield, from distribution (owing to associated deaths) and the numerous reports linking all types of IUDs with increased risk of pelvic inflammatory disease[10] point to the need for improved research before a contraceptive is widely distributed. Even when the dangers of birth control methods are known by physicians, this information is too seldom communicated to the patient.[11]

SEXISM AND MEDICINE

There are other women's-health issues, like the ones just discussed, that call for improved standards of treatment: obstetrical care, sterilization, mood-altering drugs, abortion, menstruation, and more. Perhaps it is more important here to examine briefly the origins of sexist practices and attitudes among health care providers and within the medical system in general. Social workers need to be sensitive to the sexual prejudices that pervade the health care institutions in which they work. Some alternatives to traditional medical care for women will be examined later in the chapter.

Although women have historically had a major role in providing health care, either as lay healers or as learned physicians, today's situation does not reflect that legacy. With the advent of organized Christianity in Europe* and the formal exclusion of women from centers of learning, women's role in the provision of health services has diminished. Their numbers are still great—in fact 70 percent of all health workers are women—but women's influence and power are small. Only 9 percent of American physicians are women, and less than 4 percent of obstetrician-gynecologists are female. Within the health care professions the doctor is on top in prestige, power, and income. Women, whether nurses, social workers, or aides, are at the lower end of the health care hierarchy. They traditionally have little power in the decision-making process; their role is to follow "doctor's orders."

Physicians' attitudes toward the treatment of women can be seen to originate in a sexist society and, more specifically, in physicians' medical training. Two medical sociologists have examined the contents of gynecology texts used in medical schools and have found that women are "consistently described as anatomically destined to reproduce, nurture and keep their husbands happy."[13] Texts published as late as 1970 describe women as narcissistic, masochistic, and passive. A 1971 gynecology text[14] is astoundingly ignorant of female sexuality and describes the female sex drive as less than the male's* (and as dependent on marital love!), despite the well-known Masters and Johnson findings that disprove this antiquated misogynist view.

Women patients are too often viewed as neurotic and psychosomatically ill. One medical-journal article concludes that a fairly common vaginal infection, trichomonas vaginitis, is due primarily to the "effects of disturbed emotions; depression . . . emotionally unstable patients with known moral laxity who had a reactive anxiety to fornication."[15] It is sad to imagine what this physician's attitude would be toward a single female requesting contraception. Two physicians writing in the *New England Journal of Medicine* conclude that supposed psychosomatic disorders in women, such as dysmenorrhea, nausea of pregnancy, and painful labor, are possible manifestations of prejudice against women.[16]

American medicine, especially around the turn of the century, treated women as inherently sickly—prone to emotional upsets and frail in constitution. Pregnant women were "indisposed"; menstruation was seen as a chronic disorder; menopause was treated as a disease; childbirth was treated like surgery.[17] Today we are left with the legacy of these discriminatory medical practices and attitudes toward women as patients.

---

*During the fourteenth to seventeenth centuries women healers and midwives were often accused of witchcraft. Vast witch hunts executed millions of women, many of whom were accused only of healing.[12]

*This text states that "though the instinctive sexual drive of the male . . . is greater than hers, it is nevertheless of fundamental importance for the woman . . . to make herself available for the fulfillment of this drive . . . Herein lies her power and purpose—to preserve the family unit . . ."

THE WOMEN'S-HEALTH MOVEMENT AND FEMINIST CLINICS

Today, owing to many factors, primarily the women's movement, women are beginning to complain openly about sexist medical practices. Women's magazines now include articles about how to find a nonchauvinist gynecologist or a critical appraisal of breast cancer treatment. An important component of the feminist movement is the attention given to women's bodies in both their reproductive and their sexual capacities. The current resurgence of the women's movement owes much of its direction to early suffragists who were concerned with women's control over reproduction—only then they termed it "voluntary motherhood." Linda Gordon, a social historian of birth control in America, concludes that "birth control represents the single most important factor in the material basis of women's emancipation in the course of the last century."[18] Gordon sees women's increased control over their reproduction as a reflection of other changes in women's social role. Fertility control is a matter not merely of improved contraceptive technology but of women's *access* to that technology. Lack of access to either contraception or abortion acts as a restraint on sexual activity that punishes the woman with special severity.

The women's-health movement does not focus solely on matters of reproduction. The general health needs of women of all ages are increasingly a concern of feminist clinics. Much of traditional medicine, which emphasizes treatment of symptoms, fails to consider the whole woman, her mind and her social environment as well as her body. Social workers, among all health professionals, should find a holistic health care philosophy particularly compatible with their professional goals.

Feminist clinics emphasize preventive care and health education. The patient is seen as a participant in her own health care. Such clinics are either free or very low cost, further distancing themselves from the traditional American health care system with its fee-for-service requirements. The funding of feminist health clinics is often unstable, relying on donations and government grants that may not be renewed. This sparse or uncertain funding can affect the stability of the staff and the continuity of care.

Rather than compromise on quality, most feminist clinics limit patient enrollment. These clinics may take considerable time with each patient, sometimes up to an hour or more, in order to teach and to involve the woman in her care. This unhurried pace is in stark contrast to many private physicians' allowance of fifteen minutes for each appointment. It requires at least half an hour to perform a routine pelvic exam and properly fit and instruct a woman in the use of a diaphragm. Many private-practice physicians do not take the time to instruct; the result is possible misunderstandings that lead to ineffective contraceptive use.

One primary goal that unites the different elements of the women's-health movement is to make health care more responsive to women's needs. Helen Marieskind[19] has identified three broad areas of focus for women's-health activists: changing consciousness, working for change in existing health institutions, and providing alternative services.

The first priority, changing consciousness, involves both patients and health care providers. The self-help component of the movement encourages women to examine their own and each other's bodies and to be prepared to engage actively in the care of their bodies. In self-help clinics the patient does not lie passively on the examining table but instead is shown how to examine her cervix and breasts. The practitioner is more like a teacher or facilitator of the health care process. Knowledge that was formerly esoteric or monopolized by males is now demystified and shared. In this self-help process women are provided the knowledge to gain control over their bodies. The solidarity women experience when working and learning together promotes a change in consciousness about their right and power to exercise that control.

An interesting example of changing consciousness about contraceptive responsibility is the recent establishment of a male birth control clinic in San Francisco. The usual female focus of birth control services has promoted the stereotype that it is the woman's responsibility to avoid pregnancy. But if there is no place for the man to comfortably go for information or contraceptives, his sharing in this responsibility is hindered. "Reproductive counseling" is an additional service birth control clinics could offer that would greatly change consciousness about the inevitability of childbearing. In reproductive counseling couples or individuals are assisted in weighing the pros and cons of childbearing so as to make a decision consonant with their values and life situation.[20]

The second focus involves going beyond the supportive confines of the movement and confronting established and traditional medical institutions that treat women. Feminists demand an end to sexism in the health care system. Evidence of the effect of these confrontations has begun to appear in public health settings such as the separate women's clinics in university student health services and in large hospitals. We can also see signs of feminist influence in improved emergency room procedures for the treatment of rape victims, in the utilization of nurse practitioners who spend more time in educational activities as well as with direct care, and in the provision of abortion services that include adequate counseling and follow-up.

All of these changes may be accomplished from within as well as from outside the system. Change from within the medical system may be illustrated by an experience I had while I was employed at a university women's clinic. Over several years it became apparent that many patients desired counseling regarding sexuality as well as contraception. In fact sexual concerns were seen by some patients as more acute than their routine gynecologic needs. Because the clinic was medically rather than psychologically oriented, patients with sexual concerns originally were not accorded the same priority of care as women requesting birth control services. Sexuality counseling was seen as a luxury the clinic could not easily afford. Eventually a solution was reached that pleased both patients and clinic administrators: group treatment for sexual problems.* These sexuality groups were time and cost efficient (one social worker could treat up to eight women in one hour) and highly effective in treating orgasmic dysfunction and providing general sex education.

Social workers employed by a health agency or institution are in a uniquely effective position for improving health services for women, as they are often the link between the patient's social/emotional and physical needs and care. Women's consciousness is changing, and more women are vocalizing their demands for nonsexist treatment. The social worker's task is, then, to promote the institutional changes necessary for the provision of nonsexist services.

ORGANIZING ALTERNATIVE SERVICES

The final component of the women's-health movement is to organize alternative services for women. All over the United States, and in European countries too, there has developed a network of autonomous women's-health-related services ranging from rape crisis centers to abortion referral groups. Most numerous among these feminist services are women's-health clinics—at least one feminist clinic now exists in every major United States city, and more are being organized in small cities and towns.

In 1971 I, along with several other women, organized a free women's clinic in the Pacific Northwest. The idea for the clinic developed out of individual women's dissatisfaction with the sexist medical care they were receiving and with the health care system in general. Most of the organizers had already been involved in some feminist project. Unlike many feminist clinics, which operate solely on patients' donations, the organizers chose to seek government funding —and were successful in obtaining support from the Department of Health, Education, and Welfare for 1000 patients per year. Additional patients were served through contributions. The interior of an older building was remodeled by a woman architect and numerous women volunteers who learned the carpentry skills necessary to transform a large, empty storage space into a colorful women's clinic with a laboratory. Examining rooms were designed to accommodate several people (the patient, her partner, a paramedic, and perhaps a doctor or nurse), with attractive graphic designs decorating the walls.

Patients were served without cost, although the prices for similar services through private physicians were posted on the wall to educate patients about the high cost of care outside this free clinic. Many patients spontaneously made donations to support the care of women not covered by the HEW grant. Drugs

---

*For a description of preorgasmic group treatment, see Lonnie Barbach, *For Yourself: The Fulfillment of Female Sexuality* (Garden City, N.Y.: Doubleday, 1975).

The clinic is described in the past tense only because some clinic procedures have evolved and changed over the past few years. The clinic continues to operate even though it now has no government funding.

and medications were available for prices much below pharmacy charges. The clinic offered complete gynecologic care (except for abortions), including
• contraception
• routine pelvic exams and Pap smears
• detection and treatment of urinary-tract infections, vaginitis, and VD
• breast exam/self-exam instruction
• information and counseling about menstruation, menopause, sexuality, and lesbianism

The clinic was staffed entirely by women—physicians, nurses, and paramedics.

The training of paramedics was one of the first tasks of the clinic's organizers. Women volunteers with or without health care experience were provided with comprehensive women's health care knowledge and supervised practice. Several local physicians and other health professionals volunteered to teach sections of the paramedic training program. The paramedic was seen as more than a physician's helper. Paramedics could do routine pelvic exams, fit diaphragms, and take tests for cervical cancer, vaginitis, and venereal diseases. The paramedic was trained to explain the process to the patient as she proceeded with the exam. A female physician was available for consultation. Paramedics and other clinic staff were sought from the community that provided the clinic's clientele, including minorities and women of all ages.

The clinic's staff was organized collectively. All staff members were paid equal salaries, and all had an equal vote in decision making. A clinic board, called the Coven, was composed of patients and unpaid staff. The Coven determined basic clinic policy. Physicians at this feminist clinic had no greater force in determining clinic policy than did a paramedic. The expertise of certain individuals and professions was utilized, but this knowledge was not equivalent to hierarchical power. In essence, then, the traditional medical professional hierarchy was eliminated.

The fact that all clinic staff were women created a special atmosphere that was attractive to many patients who were uncomfortable with a male examiner. The all-women character of the clinic was also instructive. Women could —and did—take control over their health care and their bodies. Out of an awareness of the existing inadequacies in women's health care, the organizers and staff created an alternative service and a new concept in health care: one that is nonsexist, focused on prevention and education, and freely available.

NEW DIRECTIONS

Out of this clinic and the women's center that housed it developed additional alternative services for women. For social workers who are institutionally employed, these examples of extensions of the women's-health movement may provide useful alternatives to traditional and ineffective treatment for women. Four specialized projects will be discussed: sexuality groups, abortion referral service, rape crisis intervention, and a menopause study group. All these projects were sponsored by the feminist clinic described here or by the women's center in which it was located.

Among the services offered by the clinic was one-on-one counseling. But so many women had numerous questions about their sexuality that a lecture series/rap group on the topic of sexuality was organized. By this time some clinic staff members had developed their own specialties in the area of female sexuality. A weekly series of lectures for about thirty participants was developed that included the anatomy and physiology of sexual response, myths about female sexuality, sexual dysfunction, and body image work. At one lecture the participants were offered the opportunity to watch a complete pelvic examination. Following each lecture the participants gathered into small groups that met for one hour and provided the setting in which to confidentially discuss personal concerns about their bodies and sexuality. Each group was led by a facilitator from the clinic. In the past year groups for preorgasmic women have been organized.

The clinic provided abortion referrals for its own patients, but many more women from all over the city needed a centralized, reliable source for abortion referrals. Learning a lesson from New York State, where abortion was legalized earlier and where expensive, profit-making referral agencies developed, the Northwest feminists organized a free telephone and walk-in abortion referral service. In addition to facilitating women's access to the abortion services of private physicians, the referral service monitored the quality of these physicians' services, thereby acting as a true client advocate. In addition, it kept the cost of abortion down. Since this service was the major source of abortion referrals in the city, and since overpriced physicians were usually excluded from the referral list, the women-controlled service effectively regulated the cost of abortions locally.

A third extension of this nucleus for feminist services was a rape crisis center that eventually grew into an autonomous agency with government funding and paid staff. The original organizers, including the author, envisioned a service that provided trained advocates to assist the rape victim through the maze of medical and legal procedures, as well as to provide ongoing counseling. A telephone "hot line" was established with advocates on call during the peak hours when most rapes occurred and when women needed immediate assistance. The organizers also confronted the established institutions that come into contact with rape victims—the police and hospital emergency rooms. Eventually rape crisis center workers were involved in the training of police cadets and were influential in changing the police department's response to charges of rape. Rape crisis center workers contacted hospital and emergency room administrators and promoted in-service staff training for the treatment of rape victims.

One final and unusual example of feminist health-related services is the organization of a menopause study group. This group is based on the recognition that the meaning of menopause and middle age for women needs to be redefined. The plight of middle-aged women in American society has been investigated by sociologist Pauline Bart, who writes about the "empty-nest syndrome" or the loss of the mothering role and, therefore, societal recognition at the time of menopause.[21] From an examination of cross-cultural data Bart concludes that it is societal attitudes in addition to hormonal changes that determine how a woman experiences menopause. In this society menopause is associated with physical discomfort, irritability, and depression. Middle-aged women account for a disproportionate share of psychiatric care and tranquilizer use.[22] There is currently a controversy over the long-term risks and benefits of estrogen replacement therapy. The menopause study group was organized by middle-aged women who sought to examine the psychosocial and physiological aspects of menopause in order to establish a nonsexist knowledge base from which health and social services for middle-aged women might develop. The study group sponsors rap groups for "women in midstream" so that through mutual support they may discover strengths and directions traditionally unavailable to older women.

SUMMARY

Women's special health concerns and the origin of sexist medical practices have been examined in this chapter. The emergence of the women's-health movement has radically changed concepts of medical care for women by focusing on three areas: changing consciousness, working for change within the health care system, and providing alternative services. Examples of interventions in these three areas, particularly the description of one feminist clinic and its offshoot services, provide social workers with models for change.

Not only are women increasingly defining their health needs and demanding improved, nonsexist medical services, but health care providers, including social workers, are becoming sensitized to issues of sexism.* Women have long sought to exercise control over their bodies, especially their reproductive capacities. Patriarchal medical institutions deny women access to that control. The revolution in women's health care is due in great part to the organization by women of alternative services—services that they control as providers and patients.

NOTES

1. Lois M. Verbrugge, "Females and Illness: Recent Trends in Sex Differences in the United States," *Journal of Social and Health Behavior* 17 (1976):387–403.

*In the 1930s the birth control movement led by Margaret Sanger had to convince reluctant social workers that their clients needed contraceptive services.

2. Boston Women's Health Book Collective, *Our Bodies, Our Selves* (New York: Simon and Schuster, 1976), p. 337.
3. Ibid., p. 338.
4. Ibid., p. 339.
5. Ibid., p. 148.
6. John Bunker, "Surgical Manpower," *New England Journal of Medicine* 282, no. 3 (Jan. 15, 1970):135–43.
7. Helen Marieskind, "Gynecological Services: Their Historical Relationship to the Women's Movement with Recent Experiences of Self-Help Clinics and Other Delivery Methods," unpublished dissertation, University of California, Los Angeles, 1976.
8. George Crile, Jr., *What Women Should Know About the Breast Cancer Controversy* (New York: Macmillan, 1973).
9. *Medical World News,* April 1971, p. 19.
10. Lars Westrom et al., "The Risk of Pelvic Inflammatory Disease in Women Using Intrauterine Contraceptive Devices Compared to Non-users," *The Lancet,* July 31, 1976.
11. Helen Marieskind, "Restructuring Ob-Gyn," *Social Policy,* September-October 1975.
12. Barbara Ehrenreich and Deirdre English, *Witches, Midwives and Nurses: A History of Women Healers* (Oyster Bay, N.Y.: Glass Mountain Pamphlets, n.d.).
13. Diane Scully and Pauline Bart, "A Funny Thing Happened on the Way to the Oriface: Women in Gynecology Textbooks," *American Journal of Sociology* 78, no. 4 (January 1973).
14. Thomas Green, *Gynecology: Essentials of Clinical Practice* (Boston: Little, Brown, 1971).
15. S. F. Moore and J. W. Simpson, "The Emotional Component in Trichomonas Vaginitis," *American Journal of Obstetrics and Gynecology* 68 (October 1954):984.
16. K. Jean Lennane and R. John Lennane, "Alleged Psychogenic Disorders in Women—A Possible Manifestation of Sexual Prejudice," *New England Journal of Medicine* 288, no. 6 (February 1973).
17. Barbara Ehrenreich and Deirdre English, *Complaints and Disorders, The Sexual Politics of Sickness* (Old Westbury, N.Y.: Feminist Press, 1973).
18. Linda Gordon, *Woman's Body, Women's Right* (New York: Grossman, 1976), p. xiii.
19. Helen Marieskind, "Gynecological Services: Their Historical Relationship to the Women's Movement with Recent Experiences of Self-help Clinics and Other Delivery Methods," unpublished dissertation, University of California, Los Angeles, 1976.
20. Lee Roy Beach, B. Townes, F. Campbell, and G. Keating, "Developing and Testing a Decision Aid for Birth Planning Decisions," *Organizational Behavior and Human Performance* 15 (February 1976):99–116.
21. Pauline Bart, "Depression in Middle-aged Women," in V. Gornick and B. Moran, eds., *Women in Sexist Society* (New York: New American Library, 1971).
22. Ellen Frankfort, *Vaginal Politics* (New York: Quadrangle Books, 1972), p. 108.

SUGGESTED ADDITIONAL READINGS

Boston Women's Health Book Collective. *Our Bodies, Our Selves.* New York: Simon and Schuster, 1976.
Ehrenreich, Barbara, and Deirdre English. *Complaints and Disorders, The Sexual Politics of Sickness.* Old Westbury, N.Y.: Feminist Press, 1973.
Social Work 21, no. 6 (November 1976), special issue on women.
The Source Collective. *Organizing for Health Care.* Boston: Beacon Press, 1975.
Veninga, Robert, "The Management of Organizational Change in Health Agencies," *Public Health Reports* 90, no. 2 (March-April 1975):149–154.

Part X

STRATEGIES FOR
RESEARCH

18/SEVEN STEPS IN APPLIED

HOSPITAL SOCIAL WORK

RESEARCH*

BARBARA BERKMAN

HELEN REHR

~~~~~~

Prior to the 1970s there was limited social work research in hospital settings. This deficiency was often attributed to lack of funds to support such research. What is happening currently is that the public accountability of hospitals is being extended to their social service programs, with the expectation that professional standards review systems will be implemented. These demands, influenced by government mandate as established in the Professional Standards Review Organization (PSRO) legislation, come from program directors who must account for the value of their services, from funding agencies, professional groups, clientele, and a more sophisticated general public, as well as from our own profession. Systematic applied research studies are a form of audit in that they devise methods to clarify concepts of performance and delineate the role of the social worker. Research, in this role, can be indispensable in meeting the accountability demands of public and private funding agencies, hospital administrators, and consumers.

Traditionally medical social work has been housed in institutions in which "financial" accountability has been a primary concern. Statistics have often been gathered by hospital administrators for cost analyses but not to assess and evaluate performance. In addition to the issue of "financial" accountability, the question of "performance" accountability must now be answered.[1] Is social work reaching the needs of the people it serves by the treatment provided? Are the services provided comprehensive enough?

During the past ten years the Social Work Services Department of the Mount Sinai Hospital in New York City has completed numerous studies that were similar in approach and in attempt but varied in terms of the division of social work involved and the populations studied. Many research questions

*An earlier version of this paper appeared in *Social Work in Health Care* 2, no. 3 (Spring 1977).

were pursued. Based on these experiences in doing intradepartmental research, an approach to conducting necessary application studies has been developed and is being used effectively with minimal cost expenditure, frequently without benefit of outside funding.

This chapter discusses the steps involved in implementing intradepartmental applied studies that can document the contribution that social workers make to the management of the social component of illness. The approach discussed involves the study of what psychosocial needs or problems social workers say they deal with (their objectives) in a particular case; the social workers' judgment of "outcome" for each need they identify; and the study of clients' perceptions of their needs and their perceptions of the role of social workers in meeting those needs. The specific delineation of clients social needs and the outcome of intervention as directly related to client needs are essential components of this audit system. The assumption being made in this approach is that consumer evaluation is one of the primary sources of validation of the social worker's role with clients, and that some indication of their support and satisfaction should be secured. These types of classification of information make review and assessment feasible by making social-need identification and treatment plans, as well as outcome, reviewable. The basic steps involved in conducting such applied research will be discussed in the following pages.

STEP 1: DETERMINING THE RESEARCH QUESTIONS

The first step in the design of a study is to determine the question or questions to be answered. Some common interrelated issues that can be studied to meet accountability demands are the following: (1) Who was served (e.g., in sociodemographic terms)? (2) How did the client get into the care system (who referred him/her)? (3) What did the referrer request? (4) What services were given and over what period? (5) What was the outcome of the intervention as perceived by the social worker? (6) What were the social needs as perceived by the referrer and the social worker? (7) Was the patient and/or family satisfied? (8) Did the recipient and the referrer understand the benefit from the service? In addition, more complex questions can be asked, such as: Do social workers' perceptions of outcome vary according to the types of social needs involved? Do social workers and clients agree on outcome? Do social needs and outcome vary according to whether the patient is an inpatient or an outpatient? Are there certain normative ranges of intervention patterns related to particular problems?

In designing inexpensive studies a principle to keep in mind is not to expect to answer all possible questions in one study but, rather, to focus on answering a small percentage of those questions. Then in the next study add pieces onto the original one. Studies should be planned so that they build on one another.

STEP 2: ADMINISTRATIVE ISSUES[2]

The first administrative issue involves the need for close collaboration between the people conducting the study and the department's social work service personnel. The explication of concepts and the development of the study design should be done with the cooperation of staff members. This is necessary if the study is to be viable within the department. The people heading the research should have a plan (design) of how to do it and a good grasp of the variables for study, but then the staff should be engaged in the research process in order to ensure their continued cooperation in its implementation and in the collection of data.

Another administrative issue is the clarification of any ethical problems related to research involving human subjects. This is of particular concern if consumer follow-up is planned. The hospital's research administration committee (or whatever the responsible administrative body is called) must be asked for guidelines as to its prerequisites for patient interviewing. Many hospitals have a standard form that patients must sign before they can be involved in research. For example, in the Adolescent Unwed Mother Clinic and in the Pregnancy Interruption Clinic at Mount Sinai studies have been done over the past few years using a research questionnaire that the social workers follow in the first and last interviews with their clients. Aside from this questionnaire, the information collected consisted of data that the social worker normally obtained during the course of his/her interviews with patients and their families. Such studies must guarantee the interviewee confidentiality and anonymity with respect to data collection and reporting, while securing truly informed content. This means the patient and/or family must not feel that they will be in jeopardy if they are unwilling to participate, and that they must have a clear understanding of their involvement.

The third administrative issue involves avoiding overuse of a subject for research purposes. This probably happens more often in psychiatric settings, where there are many different professions doing the same types of research and asking for the same types of data, than in medical settings, in which the social service department might be the only one collecting psychosocial data.

STEP 3: DETERMINING THE VARIABLES

One of the major problems encountered in implementing studies is that of specifying the concepts that are involved and determining and specifying the independent and dependent variables. Independent variables can be explained as those that are thought to be independent of social work services intervention and do not vary over the time of the study. Examples of independent variables are the sex of the patient, the patient's age at the time of the study, and the patient's marital status. There are a number of such client social indicators that can be considered independent variables. The dependent variables, on the other hand, are those that may vary according to different conditions (e.g., psychosocial needs). For example, do the elderly (independent variable) have different psychosocial needs (dependent variable) than a younger age population? Psychosocial needs are conceived of as varying in relation to the age of the patient. There can be complex independent variables. For example, does an elderly black man living alone (complex independent variable) have different psychosocial needs than an elderly white man living alone?

The independent variables are usually not very difficult to understand or explicate. Measuring the dependent variables, the concepts that are to be studied, is more difficult. For example, without an acceptable, valid classification system of "psychosocial needs" as the dependent variable, it is impossible to collect the necessary data to answer questions such as: What are the psychosocial needs of patients referred to social work services? or What were the psychosocial needs as perceived by social workers? or What are the needs as perceived by clients?

Thus the major task of the type of study suggested here is to utilize a classification system that clearly delineates the psychosocial needs social workers deal with. Much work has been done in this area, and the use of available valid classification systems is not only acceptable but probably the most advantageous approach to take. For example, a social-need classification system, first published in 1972,[3] has been replicated and validated for different patient groups, and in fact was recently piloted in thirty-five hospital social work services departments across the state of Massachusetts with 237 social service cases.[4] This system has been proved applicable to most adult medical and surgical social service cases in the general acute-care hospital, and is currently being revised for pediatric and psychiatric services. This, of course, does not mean that an existing classification system cannot be modified to fit a particular social work services clientele more perfectly if indicated.

STEP 4: SAMPLE SELECTION

A major research issue, after the question for study has been determined and the variables specified, is the definition of a "case." What should be considered a case? Is a situation involving one interview a case? What about two or more interviews? What is a social service "consultation?" Often these concepts are not well defined, and the result is a set of cases selected for study, some with client interviews and some without interviews. Who is the primary client of social work intervention? Is it the patient, or is it the patient and his/her family? This question is particularly relevant for a study that involves follow-up interviews, and the answer must be determined prior to data collection. If follow-up interviews are planned, it would not be valid to interview a patient who had seen the social worker only once if it was the patient's husband who had been the primary focus of the intervention.

Closely related here is the problem of deciding whether or not to conduct follow-up interviews with relatives of deceased patients if the relative was the primary client. A great deal of resistance may be encountered from social workers in doing any follow-up interviewing of grieving relatives or even of other clients. If the social worker believes a primary client should not be interviewed, give him/her the opportunity to explain why the client should not be contacted, but determine in advance what types of decisions will be acceptable in omitting someone from a follow-up.

Another sample selection problem involved in interviewing clients is that of simply getting accurate names and addresses necessary to find them. Hospital and social service records are frequently incomplete, or may be lost or outdated in terms of addresses and telephone numbers. Thus if retrospective data (closed-case records) are used, there is usually a real problem in finding the current addresses or telephone numbers needed for a follow-up study. A prospective study alleviates this problem, although one must always anticipate not being able to locate some of the clients who move away or die after the period of hospitalization.

STEP 5: ACCOUNTING FOR SAMPLE ATTRITION

Taking these steps in stride, let us assume that a sample has been selected and a prospective study of 100 social service clients is to be conducted by gathering data from social workers through precoded questionnaires, to be followed by telephone interviews of a random sample of these clients. There is always going to be a percentage of clients who cannot be reached, who have either died, moved away, or just will not answer questions. This problem is to be expected and is called "sample attrition." It must be remembered that there are always some data available on clients that one cannot reach, and these data can be analyzed. In the study model suggested, patient social-indicator data and social worker judgments of social needs and outcome are available. It is necessary to determine whether clients not interviewed are significantly different from those interviewed. For example, in one study at Mount Sinai we found that we were able to interview significantly fewer family members of patients who had died during the hospitalization period than family members of other patients. This definitely put a different light on the meaning of our data. The findings had to be interpreted in view of the fact that certain data were missing and that the findings could not be generalized to family members of the patients who had died.

STEP 6: DATA COLLECTION

In determining the methodological design for data collection, the actual operation of the hospital and the department's system of practice must be considered. Each hospital has certain unique aspects to its system that must be taken into consideration when designing a research study. For example, in determining the viability of content analysis of previously recorded information, hospital records must be examined to make sure that they contain the necessary information. If retrospective data from case records are to be used, the issue of missing data must be considered.

Thus the method of data collection requires a research decision as to the use of closed or open cases from which to obtain data. There are many problems in retrospective closed-case data. Closed cases have been recorded for purposes other than the current research and may not be able to provide the kinds of information that is sought. Lately at Mount Sinai we have been doing prospective studies, which means that the audit is conducted on cases, for example, that are open during a one-month period and closed over the following two to three months.

However, there are also problems in prospective data collection. If one is going to conduct a prospective study that has social workers completing a special questionnaire, the question of the reliability and validity of their answers must be considered. While there may be no absolute way to alleviate this problem, there are research methods to account for most problems of this sort. For example, the use of several questions to get the answers to one issue is one way of ascertaining the validity or "truth" of the findings.

A prospective study method utilizing telephone interviews with clients assumes that client judgment has some validity and will reflect certain problems in the program. One methodological argument that has been raised against consumer evaluation is that the clients do not have the necessary qualifications to evaluate professional services and the findings will be biased or superficial. This type of evaluative approach using client judgments is methodologically valid, especially in looking at basic accountability issues such as the clients' views of accessibility of service, acceptability of service, and continuity and comprehensiveness of care. Around these issues the consumer can and does make an assessment of the services received, decide whether to return, and decide whether to recommend the services to others. And within this frame of reference the client is probably the only valid source or criterion of whether service is achieving its goals.

But what of the client who is going to continue to come to the hospital because of his/her outpatient status, for instance? Will such clients commit errors of omission or commission because they are fearful of saying what they really feel? We must consider this as a possible validity problem and analyze our data with the possible implications in mind.

Another issue is whether to use questionnaires that respondents fill out themselves or whether to use a more expensive interview approach. What about telephone versus direct interviews? What about questions in which the full answer given to us by the client is written out versus questions that have "closed" answers (in other words, open-ended questions versus precoded answers that have been determined to cover all possible answers, with perhaps a category for "other")? Exploratory interviews with clients that allow for open-ended responses to in-depth questions may be more cogent and valid than other approaches using quantitative measurements. Through direct questioning of clients we are able to explore areas that at this time in our research practice sophistication would be limited and invalid if we used standard codifiable measurements. These types of research issues can be answered on the basis of the system in which one is operating, and there are many standard research texts that give the various pros and cons of each approach.[5] What must be kept in mind is that there is never one superior, "only" method of doing a study but, rather, that the research design must be developed within the context and limitations of the setting in which the study is being conducted.

STEP 7: ANALYSIS

In the analysis and interpretation of findings the data should be treated as exploratory and one must be aware of the many variables that have not been available so that in explaining the findings one does not get fooled by one's own design weaknesses. The meaning of the data should be discussed with the staff in order to get the full breadth of the analysis. In each step of the audit analysis one must be aware of the pros and cons of the study design chosen. There may have been only one way to design the study that was feasible or economical at a certain point in time. The researcher should be aware of this, and in the writeup the limitations of the methodology as they may have affected the data obtained should be clearly stated.

At Mount Sinai we have done a number of studies literally on a shoestring because we have had the encouragement of the administration and workers in the department who are willing to examine their caseload and to follow certain structured, often precoded questionaires that may be a little time-consuming. The studies can be done in a minimum amount of time. Data can be collected for one month and the analysis done in staff meetings where the implications of the findings can be openly discussed. There is no longer the time to ask the question: Should we do applied studies? The demands for accountability require that we systematically examine our practice and account for our contributions to the care of patients and their families.

To be accountable as a profession we need to answer the question: What is unique about social work?[6] This question can be answered through the use of an appropriate social-need data system. We can indeed show what it is that we work on that other health professionals do not. It is our premise at Mount Sinai that through some such social-need/outcome approach we will eventually be able to answer consistently the questions of relevance, efficiency, and effectiveness posed to us by consumers, other health professionals, and reimbursing agencies, as well as by the profession of social work itself.

NOTES

1. Eveline Burns, "Health Insurance: Not When but What Kind?" *American Journal of Public Health,* Univ. of Pittsburgh 16, no. 11 (November 1971):2164–73.

2. The authors are indebted to Molly Grob's excellent paper "Teaching Graduate Students Accountability to the Agency Through Evaluative Studies," presented at the Annual Program Meeting, Council on Social Work Education, Chicago, March 3, 1975.
3. Barbara Berkman and Helen Rehr, "Social Needs of the Hospitalized Elderly: A Classification," *Social Work* 17, no. 4 (July 1972):80–88.
4. Barbara Berkman, "Are Social Service Audit Systems Feasible? Experiences with a Hospital-Based and Regional Approach," Paper presented to Society for Hospital Social Work Directors PSRO-UR and Social Work Workings Conference, Fort Worth, Texas, January 18–21, 1976.
5. Two excellent research texts are Clair Selltiz et al., *Research Methods in Social Relations* (New York: Holt, Rinehart and Winston, March 1962), and William Goode and Paul Holt, *Methods in Social Research* (New York: McGraw-Hill, 1952).
6. William Hall and Gerald St. Denis, "Accountability: A Critical Issue in Social Services," Report of meeting, Webster Hall Hotel, Pittsburgh, June 19–22, 1972.

SUGGESTED ADDITIONAL READINGS

Evaluation of Social Work Services in Community Health and Medical Care Programs, Proceedings, 1973 Annual Institute for Public Health Social Workers, University of California, School of Public Health, Program in Public Health Social Work, Berkeley, 1973.

Ferguson, Kris, et al., "Initiation of a Quality Assurance Program for Social Work Practice in a Teaching Hospital," *Social Work in Health Care* 2, no. 2 (Winter 1976):205–17.

Fischer, Joel, "Is Casework Effective?" *Social Work* 18, no. 1 (January 1973):5–20.

Gurman, Allen, "The Efficacy of Therapeutic Interventions in Social Work: A Critical Reevaluation," *Journal of Health and Social Behavior* 15, no. 2 (June 1974):136–41.

Haggerty, Robert J. "Family Diagnosis: Research Methods and Their Reliability for Studies of the Medical-Social Unit, the Family," *American Journal of Public Health* 55, no. 10 (October 1965):1521–44.

Linn, Margaret W., and Bernard S. Linn, "Narrowing the Gap Between Medical and Mental Health Evaluation," *Medical Care* 13, no. 7 (July 1975):607–14.

McCollum, Audrey T., "A Clinical Caseworker in Interdisciplinary Research," *Social Work*, January 1956.

Meredith, Jack, "Program Evaluation Techniques in the Health Services," *American Journal of Public Health* 66, no. 11 (November 1976):1069–80.

Neser, William B., Stanley L. Silberg, and Henry M. Parrish, "The Host-Agent Model in Social Work Research," *Social Work* 13, (April 1968):96–100.

Ogren, Evelyn H., "Sample Bias in Patient Evaluation of Hospital Social Services," *Social Work in Health Care* 1, no. 1 (Fall 1975):55–63.

Quality Assurance in Social Services in Health Programs for Mothers and Children, Proceedings, Institute sponsored by University of Pittsburgh, School of Public Health, Public Health Social Work Program, Pittsburgh, March 31–April 4, 1975.

Rosenberg, Marvin L., and Ralph Brody, "The Threat or Challenge of Accountability," *Social Work* 19, no. 3 (May 1974):344–50.

Seaberg, James R., "Systematized Recording: A Follow-up," *Social Work* 15, no. 4 (October 1970):32–41.

Starr, Philip, "Use of Research in Social Work Practice," *Social Work in Health Care* 2, no. 3 (Spring 1977).

Struening, Elmer L., and Marcia Guttentag. *Handbook of Evaluation Research*. Beverly Hills, Calif.: Sage Publications, 1975.

Wechsler, Henry, et al. *Social Work Research in the Human Services*. New York: Human Sciences Press, 1976.

Weiss, Carol H., "Alternative Models of Program Evaluation," *Social Work*, November 1974.

19/FACILITATING PATIENT COMPLIANCE WITH MEDICAL PROGRAMS: AN AREA FOR SOCIAL WORK RESEARCH AND INTERVENTION

RONA LEVY

THE PROBLEM

Medical care typically involves the active participation of the patient. Patients are asked to eat certain things, take medications at specified times, exercise, monitor and report the presence—or absence—of physiological signs, return for follow-up visits, stop doing some things and start doing others. Patient compliance with these requests is usually as essential, if not more so, for the satisfactory completion of the medical program as what goes on in a physician's office. Compliance is defined here as occurring when the patient follows instructions given to him or her in a treatment setting.

Noncompliance seriously affects the delivery and cost of medical services. The sheer size of the medical literature on compliance or noncompliance is an indication of the recognition of its importance. Literally hundreds of compliance-related studies appear each year (cf. *The Medline Bibliographic Citation List*). Most of the concern is around issues of patient care. For example, Eney and Goldstein studied asthmatic children to determine whether their oral medication was being taken in prescribed amounts. Only 11 percent of these children were found to have taken the appropriate medication dosage, and 23 percent had no measurable medication in their systems! The remaining group was found to have taken less than therapeutic amounts.[1] Similarly, in Seattle's Harborview Medical Center Pediatrics Unit adults are bringing in their children only 40 percent of the time for appointments that have been previously scheduled. This situation makes it extremely difficult to schedule clinic visits efficiently (McCann).[2]

Compliance problems have also been cited in the treatment areas of hypertension control (Silverberg;[3] Briggs, Lowenthal, Cirksena, Price, Gibson,

281

and Flamenbaum[4]), diabetes diets (Williams, Martin, Hogan, Watkins, and Ellis),[5] ophthalmic treatment (Bigger),[6] prescription (Waters, Gould, and Lunn),[7] and taking medication (Kellaway and McCrae),[8] to name a few.

While reported compliance rates do differ, they are almost uniformly low enough to indicate that a serious problem exists. In one study Stewart and Cluff reported that 20 to 82 percent of all patients did not take their medications as prescribed.[9] However, there have been some measures of medication adherence that go as low as 8 percent (Bergman and Warner).[10] Sackett and Haynes cite studies that report appointment-keeping rates of from 37 to 87 percent.[11]

In addition to patient care problems, a less discussed but important concern is that of medical researchers who find that tests on experimental treatments are often invalidated by "compliance bias" (Feinstein).[12] A compliance bias problem can occur when, for example, a new medication is tested for its effect in reducing hypertension. Let us say that the medication must be taken three times a day and that many patients often forget to take it once or twice each day. When many patients do not improve, researchers do not know whether this failure is due to ineffectiveness on the part of the medication or to the fact that it was not taken as prescribed.

THE ROLE OF SOCIAL WORK

Social workers, as members of the health care team, are in an excellent position to do something about the problem of noncompliance. The social worker's role in the health care setting includes the recognition of human behavioral and social factors that contribute to a positive state of health. Medical social workers, for example, often try to alter a patient's living patterns and/or housing arrangements when designing discharge plans to optimize recovery from an illness. One way that these patterns influence health is by supporting or not supporting the following of medical regimens. Therefore the application of social work expertise to the problem of noncompliance is a logical component of our services.

The compliance literature is introduced here to facilitate the involvement of social workers in this critical area of medical treatment. Social workers have two main responsibilities in this field. First, they should be familiar with the findings reported in the literature. By being aware of the variables associated with noncompliance, social workers can take part in case finding in the area of potential compliance problems. (The major variables that have been investigated for their association with compliance will be discussed later.) By knowing the methods that have been tested to enhance compliance, they can offer solutions when noncompliance occurs or is anticipated. (Some specific techniques that have been shown to positively affect compliance, such as providing the patient with a reminder cue, are also given later.) Second, social workers should contribute to the development of a compliance enhancement technology in a medical setting. This would require that they participate in research studies that experimentally test potential enhancement techniques. Some of the author's efforts in that direction are discussed, among others, in the following review.

An additional issue should be recognized here, although an extended discussion is beyond the scope of this chapter. This issue addresses, if you will, the "other side" of compliance and questions whether compliance, and the "medical model" system that this term implies, are actually desirable. The interested reader is referred to a recent article by Stimson on this issue.[13] For the purposes of this chapter we will consider only the enhancement of compliance, with the assumption that compliance is indeed appropriate.

VARIABLES ASSOCIATED WITH COMPLIANCE

Finding cases of potential noncompliance can be enhanced by knowledge of factors that have been found to be associated with noncompliance. Unfortunately, contradictory findings have been reported for many associations. The relationship between compliance and such patient characteristics as age, sex, education, socioeconomic status, and race, as well as certain beliefs, has not been consistently demonstrated by investigators. While many studies do report a positive association between each of these variables and compliance, an even larger number have found no such association (Silverberg;[3] Sackett and Haynes[11]). The only exceptions to this are the data that report the consistent underutilization of health care facilities by the poor and by members of minority groups. However, while the issue of utilization is an important one, it will not be addressed here or considered to be a component of compliance as defined earlier. We will be concerned only with the situation in which patients do or do not follow instructions after initial utilization or contact with the health facility has been established. Investigators also have not yet been able to find an association between compliance and various features of the disease, such as diagnosis, severity, and duration. Thus case finding based on the available literature must go beyond patient characteristics and disease features.

Other groups of variables have been studied for their association with compliance and have produced more useful information. For example, some features of the therapeutic regimen have been tested for their association with compliance. There does seem to be an inverse relationship between compliance and the complexity of the regimen, the length of time over which it is to occur, and the change from normal life patterns that it requires. For example, a powdered medication that must be dissolved in water and taken four times a day could require quite a disruption in living patterns to patients whose daily activities do not conveniently place them near a glass and a water source. An ointment that must be applied on one's feet twice during the day is equally problematic to most life styles. A request that a patient take baths when there is no bathtub in the home also has a low probability of compliance. The social worker who is sensitive to the issues in the patient's life, as well as the therapeutic regimen, can strive to either make compliance easier to carry out or alter the regimen's requirements by communicating potential problems to other health professionals.

A number of variables concerning the way the health professional and the patient interact have also been shown to be related to compliance. Davis,[14] Francis, Korsch, and Morris,[15] and Korsch and Negrete[16] report a positive relationship between compliance and such physician behaviors as friendliness, attention, laughter, joking, and positive affect. These findings are not surprising and certainly are consistent with the work in social psychology that states that "source attractiveness" is related to the source's degree of influence (McGuire).[17] Here again, social workers should be aware that the presence of these positive interaction qualities is highly associated with compliance.

EXPERIMENTAL RESEARCH

The studies discussed so far are correlational—the presence of one variable (regimen type or interaction behaviors) has been shown to be related to the presence of another—in this case, compliance. Correlational studies can provide valuable information. However, to truly say that a relationship is causal —that, for example, physician friendliness causes greater compliance—an experimental study must be conducted. In a basic experimental design paradigm to test a compliance enhancer, the independent variable of interest (the compliance enhancer) is systematically introduced to a group of patients whose compliance rates (the dependent variable) are compared to those of patients who did not receive the independent variable. The value of an experimental study as a contribution to the development of compliance enhancement in medical practice can be gauged by the extent to which it meets the following three criteria:

1. It should test "the efficacy of interventions that appear realistic and feasible in light of the circumstances surrounding current provision of health and medical care services."[18]

2. It should be methodologically respectable. In addition to design concerns, this criterion includes clear operational definitions of the independent variable(s) and reliable and valid dependent variable(s).

3. It should go beyond the study of simple variables. Many levels of a factor or the interaction of two or more factors must be considered if results are to be meaningfully interpreted and utilized. The effect of an intervention, for example, could vary as utilized by different therapists or under different circumstances. Sackett states that "we need to learn much more about the compliance distributions of different treatments, for different diseases, among different patients, and at different points in time and space."[19]

Enhancers that have been tested can be generally conceptualized as falling into two broad categories. Methods that increase the probability that a patient will remember an assignment at the correct (performance) time involve the use of some form of cue. Another group of methods addresses the issue of actually doing an assignment that has already been remembered. The experimental studies in both these areas will be discussed in the following pages, with particular attention being paid to examples of studies that are strong or weak in relation to the preceding criteria.

ALTERING THE PROBABILITY OF DOING AN ASSIGNMENT

Experimental studies that have tried to alter the probability of doing an assignment often have not adequately met one or more of the criteria listed here. Relocating the health facilities to the patient's employment site, for example (Sackett, et al.), has only limited utility (and also happened to prove ineffective in this study).[20]

Patient education methods often try to alter patients' knowledge about the disease or the regimen in a direction that would facilitate compliance. Unfortunately most of these studies do not specify the components of the educational package and/or do not assess the effect of each component individually (Fletcher, Appel, and Bourgeois;[21] Katkin, Zimmerman, Rosenthal, and Ginsberg;[22] Dickey, Mattar, and Chudzik;[23] Anderson, Rowe, Dean, and Arbessar;[24] Hecht[25]).

Another packaged technique, employing attention, praise, self-monitoring, and monetary reimbursement, has been shown to reduce hypertension levels.[26] Further research should investigate whether this technique is particularly feasible with all patients as well as whether the entire package is needed to show an effect.

Another serious problem in compliance research is the choice of dependent variables. Gordis provides a summary of the difficulties in evaluating the dependent variables used in compliance research.[27] Measures such as studying urinary secretion are often time limited. That is, often only medications taken within the last 24 hours are present. Counting the number of pills a patient has after a given period and comparing this number to how many should be missing also is far from problem free. Whether the pills were taken by the patient with the correct between-dosage intervals, or by other family members, is not detectable using this method. Physician opinion and patient report are both inaccurate and subject to bias.

Levy and Carter present to casework practitioners a list of recommendations for the enhancement of compliance.[28] These recommendations are based on studies that have received support from good empirical research, and therefore address some of the problems discussed earlier. Most of their practice propositions have been studied in the medical situation. The use of *positive reinforcement* (e.g., the presentation of some praise or reward for assignment completion), for example, has been recommended and tested in the treatment of obesity (Williams, Martin, and Foreyt)[5] and with dental care (Levy, Weinstein, and Milgram;[29] Stachnik and Talsma[30]). The lack of *specificity* (e.g., detail relevant to carrying out the assignment) on medical prescriptions is believed to be a big source of patient nonadherence to medication regimens (Mazzullo, Lasagna, and Griner).[31]

The *overt commitment* is one enhancer that is feasible to use in clinical practice, has been clearly defined, and has been tested using a reliable and valid dependent measure. Levy[32] gave parents in a treatment project the assignment to call the agency at a specified time. They were then either asked to make a verbal commitment or a verbal plus a signed commitment to do so. A control group was given only the instructions; no commitment was requested. For all subjects there was a significant relationship between commitment condition and compliance rates. However, only the verbal and signed commitment group differed significantly from the no-commitment group. One explanation for the success of the verbal-and-signed condition might be its resemblance to a treatment contract procedure. As Zifferblatt and Dunbar point out,

The contract technique would ... serve as a medium by which self-management of the drug regimen could be taught, and maximize the probability of reinforcement for adherence from the health worker or others. Additionally, it minimizes ambiguity in instructions and elicits a formal commitment to adhere.[33]

While the numbers were too small to merit separate analyses, the pattern for black subjects appears to be somewhat different from that for white subjects. For example, all of the noncompliers in the verbal-and-written condition were black. Since all the therapists were white, it is suggested that a possible factor might be the interracial therapist-patient pairing (Grantham;[34] Ledvinka[35]). Further studies are needed with larger numbers that also pair black interviewers with white clients and black interviewers with black clients.

The verbal commitment alone has been tested in one medical setting.[36] Patients receiving flu inoculations were given postcards on which they were to indicate any symptoms that followed the shot within forty-eight hours. Patients asked to give a verbal commitment when they were told to return the cards returned significantly more cards, and did so significantly sooner, than patients in a control condition.

ALTERING THE PROBABILITY OF RECALL

One area of research that has been fairly rigorous methodologically and has produced useful information is the investigation of cues that increase the likelihood that a patient will remember something. Shepard and Moseley[37] and Gates and Colborn[38] compare compliance rates for patients who received mailed or phone reminders about their appointments to the rates for control (no-reminder) groups. Both types of reminders significantly improved compliance rates for these subjects over rates for subjects in the control condition. These studies do meet the first two criteria mentioned earlier, using sound methodology to test realistic techniques. However, further research is needed in order to meet the third criterion, measuring the effects of enhancers under varying conditions. We should have finer discriminations on the type of cue and its effect over time. Nazarian, Mechaber, Charney, and Coulter compared the effects of two types of reminder cards on appointment keeping.[39] Both cards indicated the date and time of the appointment, and one also noted the physician or nurse and the reason for the appointment. No difference was found between the effects of one type of card and those of the other type.* However, both groups receiving cards had a significantly higher appointment-keeping rate than the control group. Also interesting was the indication that the reminder seemed to have a greater effect as the interval between appointments increased. The smallest appointment interval was twelve days.

Levy and Claravall studied the use of a reminder call on appointment keeping for patients with between-interval appointments that went as low as three days.[40] Thus many of the immediate-return patients who had been excluded in the study by Nazarian and his associates could be included here. In this study patients were randomly assigned to a call or a no-call condition. Patients in the call condition received a phone reminder from a social worker informing them of the date and time of their appointment. Those in the no-call condition received no reminder. The reminder call had a significant effect on patients whose appointments were more than two weeks apart, but no significant effect on patients whose appointments were scheduled within a two-week period. These findings would seem to indicate that with limited resources a first priority would be to use a reminder cue with patients who have long intervals between their appointments. Future research into this type of cue and other enhancers should continue to discriminate the differential effects of enhancers under many varying conditions.

CONCLUSION

Noncompliance is a serious problem in medical treatment affecting both the quality and the cost of services. The growing body of literature on compliance or noncompliance recognizes this fact. The source of the problem(s) can lie in the selection of an appropriate regimen, the manner in which the regimen is communicated to the patient, or the ability of the patient to recall the regimen at the appropriate time. Some of the preliminary findings on factors related to and affecting compliance have been presented. An exhaustive review has not been attempted. The field of compliance research and intervention is rapidly expanding, and new ideas are constantly being tested. This chapter has attempted to provide an incentive for social work interest in this field. Social workers need to be alert to the problem of noncompliance and knowledgeable

---

*This finding should not be interpreted as a failure to confirm previous studies on specificity, since knowledge of the health worker and the reason for the appointment was not necessary to the completion of the assignment. The patient, for example, who arrived as scheduled was considered as a complier whether or not she/he went to or asked for the correct worker.

288   RONA LEVY

regarding new compliance studies; indeed, they should participate in such
studies. Social workers will then be in an excellent position to make a major
contribution to this important area of health care.

NOTES

1. R. D. Eney and E. O. Golstein, "Compliance of Chronic Asthmatics with Oral Administration of Theophylline as Measured by Serum and Salivary Levels," *Pediatrics* 57 (April 1976):513–17.
2. John McCann, M.D., Harborview Medical Center, Seattle (personal communication, 1976).
3. D. S. Silverberg, "Long-term Follow-up of a Hypertension Screening Program," *Canadian Medical Association Journal* 114 (March 1976):425–28.
4. W. A. Briggs, D. T. Lowenthal, W. J. Cirksena, W. E. Price, T. P. Gibson, and W. Flamenbaum, "Propranolol in Hypertensive Drug Dialysis Patients: Efficacy and Compliance," *Clinical Pharmacology and Therapeutics* 18 (November 1975):606–12.
5. F. Williams, D. Martin, M. Hogan, J. Watkins, and E. Ellis, "The Clinical Picture of Diabetic Control, Studies in Four Settings," *American Journal of Public Health* 57 (March 1967): 441–51.
6. J. F. Bigger, "A Comparison of Patient Compliance in Treated vs. Untreated Ocular Hypertension," *Transactions of the American Academy of Ophthalmology and Otolaryngology* 81 (March–April 1976):277–85.
7. W. H. Waters, N. V. Gould, and J. Lunn, "Undispensed Prescriptions in a General Mining Practice," *British Medical Journal* 1 (May 1976):1062–63.
8. G. S. Kellaway and G. McCrae, "Non-compliance and Errors of Drug Administration in Patients Discharged from Acute Wards," *New Zealand Medical Journal* 81 (June 1975): 508–12.
9. R. B. Stewart and L. E. Cluff, "A Review of Medication Errors and Compliance in Ambulant Patients," *Clinical Pharmacology and Therapeutics* 13 (July–August 1972):463–68.
10. A. B. Bergman and R. J. Werner, "Failure of Children to Receive Penicillin by Mouth," *New England Journal of Medicine* 268 (June 1963):334–38.
11. D. L. Sackett, "Priorities and Methods for Future Research," in D. L. Sackett and R. B. Haynes, eds., *Compliance with Therapeutic Regimens,* pp. 169–89.
12. A. R. Feinstein, "Biostatistical Problems in 'Compliance Bias,'" *Clinical Pharmacology and Therapeutics* 16 (5) (November 1974):846–57.
13. G. V. Stimson, "Obeying Doctors' Orders: A View from the Other Side," *Social Science and Medicine* 8 (February 1974):97–104.
14. M. S. Davis, "Variations in Patients' Compliance with Doctors' Advice: An Empirical Analysis of Patterns of Communication," *American Journal of Public Health* 58 (February 1968):274–88.
15. F. Francis, B. M. Korsch, and M. J. Morris, "Gaps in Doctor-Patient Communication: Patients' Response to Medical Advice," *New England Journal of Medicine* 280 (March 1969):535–40.
16. B. M. Korsch and V. F. Negrete, "Doctor-Patient Communication," *Scientific American* 227 (August 1972):66–74.
17. W. J. McGuire, "The Nature of Attitudes and Attitude Change," in G. Linzey and E. Aronson, eds., *The Handbook of Social Psychology,* 2d ed., vol. 3 (Reading, Mass.: Addison-Wesley, 1969).
18. M. H. Becker, "Sociobehavioral Determinants of Compliance," in D. L. Sackett and R. B. Haynes, eds., *Compliance with Therapeutic Regimens* (Baltimore: Johns Hopkins, 1976), p. 50.
19. Sackett, op. cit., p. 172.

20. D. L. Sackett, R. B. Haynes, E. S. Gibson, B. C. Hackett, D. W. Taylor, R. S. Roberts, and A. L. Johnson, "Randomized Clinical Trial of Strategies for Improving Medication Compliance in Primary Hypertension," *Lancet,* May 1975, pp. 1205–07.

21. S. W. Fletcher, F. A. Appel, and M. A. Bourgeois, "Management of Hypertension. Effect of Improving Patient Compliance for Follow-up Care," *Journal of the American Medical Association* 233 (June 1975):242–44.

22. S. Katkin, V. Zimmerman, J. Rosenthal, and M. Ginsberg, "Using Volunteer Therapists to Reduce Hospital Readmissions," *Hospital and Community Psychiatry* 26 (March 1975): 151–53.

23. F. F. Dickey, M. E. Mattar, and G. M. Chudzik, "Pharmacist Counseling Increases Drug Regimen Compliance," *Hospitals* 49 (May 1975):85–88.

24. F. P. Anderson, D. S. Rowe, V. C. Dean, and A. Arbessar, "An Approach to the Problem of Non-compliance in a Pediatric Outpatient Clinic," *American Journal of Diseases of Children* 122 (August 1971):142–43.

25. A. B. Hecht, "Improving Medication Compliance by Teaching Outpatients," *Nursing Forum* 13 (2) (1974):112–29.

26. R. B. Haynes, D. L. Sackett, E. S. Gibson, D. W. Taylor, B. C. Sackett, R. B. Roberts, and A. L. Johnson, "Improvement of Medication Compliance in Uncontrolled Hypertension," *Lancet,* June 1976, pp. 1265–68.

27. L. Gordis, "Methodologic Issues in the Measurement of Patient Compliance," in Sackett and Haynes, op. cit., pp. 51–66.

28. R. L. Levy and R. D. Carter, "Compliance with Practitioner Instigations," *Social Work* 21 (May 1976):188–93.

29. R. L. Levy, P. Weinstein, and P. Milgram, "Behavioral Guidelines for Plaque Control Programs," *Dental Hygiene* 51 (January 1976):13–18.

30. T. Stachnik and E. Talsma, "Oral Health Practices in Children: A Behavioral Analysis of Why Brushing and Flossing Is Not Their Idea of a Good Time," *Journal of the Michigan Dental Association* 55 (February 1973):38–41.

31. J. Mazzullo, L. Lasagna, and P. Griner, "Variations in Interpretation of Prescription Instructions," *Journal of the American Medical Association* 227 (February 1974):929–31.

32. R. L. Levy, "Relationship of an Overt Commitment to Task Compliance in Behavior Therapy," *Journal of Behavior Therapy and Experimental Psychiatry* 8 (January 1977): 25–29.

33. S. M. Zifferblatt and J. Dunbar, "Increasing Adherence to Medication Through the Use of Behavior Modification Strategies," unpublished manuscript, Stanford University, p. 9.

34. R. Grantham, "Effects of Counselor Sex, Race, and Language Style on Black Students in Initial Interview," *Journal of Counseling Psych.* 20 (November 1973):553–59.

35. J. Ledvinka, "Race of Employment Interviewer and Reasons Given by Black Job Seekers for Leaving Their Jobs," *Journal of Applied Psychology* 58 (December 1973):362–64.

36. R. L. Levy, D. Yamashita, and G. Pow, "A Verbal Commitment as a Compliance Enhancer with Symptom Reporting," in preparation.

37. D. S. Shepard and T. A. Moseley, "Mailed vs. Telephoned Appointment Reminders to Reduce Broken Appointments in a Hospital Outpatient Department," *Medical Care* 14 (March 1976):268–73.

38. S. J. Gates and C. K. Colburn, "Lowering Appointment Failures in a Neighborhood Health Center," *Medical Care* 14 (March 1976):263–67.

39. L. F. Nazarian, J. Mechaber, E. Charney, and M. D. Coulter, "Effect of a Mailed Appointment Reminder on Appointment Keeping," *Pediatrics* 53 (March 1974):349–51.

40. R. L. Levy and V. Claravall, "Differential Effects of a Phone Reminder on Appointment Keeping for Patients with Long and Short Between-Visit Intervals," *Medical Care* 15 (May 1977):435–38.

PART XI

ADMINISTRATION AND ACCOUNTABILITY IN SOCIAL SERVICE PROGRAMING

20/PARTICIPATORY GOVERNANCE: A MODEL FOR SHARED DECISION MAKING*

SIDNEY HIRSCH

LAWRENCE C. SHULMAN

The model for staff participation in administrative decision making for social work departments in health and hospital settings presented here is consonant with the emerging view of professional accountability. Medical and other health professions recognize that they must take the initiative in the developing of professional standards and criteria for organizational structure, program development, and service delivery; professions must also develop methods for monitoring, auditing, and assuring quality of services. To the degree that the professional response to these external and internal pressures is responsible, realistic and rapid, results for the health care institutions and the people they serve will be positive.

An assumption underlining these changes in the health field is that the delivery of service is not only an institutional or departmental responsibility but the responsibility and concern of the various professionals delivering services within the health care setting. Professionals are being held accountable for their practice, both by their peers and the organizational structure within which they work. Accountability has shifted from the administrative levels, the director and supervisory personnel, to the practitioners. The growth of utilization review committees, hospital audit committees, peer review committees, and quality assurance programs has involved all levels of professionals in the setting up of standards, criteria, programs, and the monitoring of services.

What implications do these developments have for administrative processes within a hospital department of social work? The organizational model that has until now prevailed in hospital departments of social work has been predominantly authoritative in structure. In its traditional and rigid form this

*Reprinted with permission of the authors from *Social Work in Health Care* 1, no. 4 (Summer 1976).

is no longer a viable model. New forms of governance must evolve and be tested.

The proposed model of governance is characterized by a more mature partnership between the social work administrator and staff. The means for implementing such a model of staff participation in department decision making and minimizing the risks involved will be considered.

DEFINITION OF GOVERNANCE

Social work administration encompasses the spectrum of operations enabling all levels of staff to carry out their professional duties and responsibilities effectively.

The governance component of administration is that parameter limited to the decision-making processes that determine or affect policies, procedures, and the direction in which goals, programs, and services will evolve.

Another way of looking at governance is as a process of keeping the institution's and the department's goals in viable balance: the operational needs and imperatives such as ward coverage, patient discharge, community services, teaching and research. Decision making is the fulcrum on which these forces are balanced and kept in a homeostasis that enables the department to be productive and effective.

The literature of administrative decision making in social work and in other professions reflects a basic concept of the role of the administrator as the one in whom the decision-making authority and responsibility is lodged,[1] but who, if he is to be effective, must utilize, whether formally or informally, the competence and expertise of various levels of personnel within his staff in the decision-making process.[2]

In contrast to Max Weber's[3] traditional model of the "pure" type of bureaucratic organization, and its modes of decision making through defined hierarchical roles and relationships, a further examination of the more recent literature of decision making indicates the value of participation in this process.[1,4] Obviously, unanimity of those affected by the decision cannot always be achieved. While some staff may disagree, for a decision to be effective a basic consensus must be obtained.

A corollary rationale for participation in governance evident in the literature is that participation can improve morale, productivity, and the quality of output.[5]

Implementing staff participation in governance, particularly within the complex organization of a hospital, is an awesome task. It is easier to ride the authoritative tide of formally mandated rather than participatory governance. The implementing of staff participation must grow out of conviction of its value.

PROPOSED MODEL OF GOVERNANCE

In participatory-collateral governance there is an assignment of flexible roles. Decision making is not by fiat or mandate from above, but rather by explicitly delineated collateral participation of departmental staff at all levels. Necessary accountability, authority, and responsibility on the part of the director of the social service department is simultaneously retained.

Discussion is restricted by parameters that encompass the intradepartmental factors, dynamics, and processes of a social service department within a hospital. The rationale for participatory-collateral governance is rooted in the ethical values and practice principles of the social work profession and in the sociopolitical philosophy of our democratic society.

If we expect openness and honesty in practice in order to help patients, and in supervision in order to promote workers' professional growth and development, must we not therefore also expect it in administrative practice to promote departmental growth and the accomplishment of its mission?

Can most directors of hospital social work departments meet this value test in their administrative practice? Unless they can, administrative problem solving and decision making will not be optimal for the effective accomplishment of the department's mission.[6] In the long run, the collective judgment and wisdom of those affected and involved in government and decision making is sounder than that of any one person. This belief in a democratic rather than an elitist philosophy underlies the premise of participatory governance.

PREREQUISITES

In order to achieve maximum effective participatory governance, certain conditions are prerequisites:

1. The basic core of accountability, within a professionally staffed department, rests with the individual staff member. The social worker must be a self-governing, responsible person whose professional objectives and activities are aligned and consonant with the goals of the department as well as the overall goals of the institution.

2. The professionally knowledgeable, administratively experienced or talented director must be secure enough to risk self in order to reach for higher levels of departmental effectiveness. Openness and honesty are essential. The respect and confidence of his hospital executive body as well as that of his staff and his other professional colleagues are also prerequisite.

3. The director and his staff must be confident in their shared capabilities to deliver a quality level of social work services.

4. Ideally, the time to initiate participatory governance is when there is a relatively stable staff, relative freedom from "anger" in staff relationships, and relative freedom from active conflict between staff and director. Antagonistic forces are rarely willing to risk themselves in ways that participatory gover-

nance requires. However, a crisis that confronts the department may impel the finding of a common base to engage in a shared governance venture.

5. The director must work closely and sensitively with supervisors on all levels. A great deal is being asked of this group. The remodeling of their roles is matched only by the remodeling required of the director himself. Their concerns and anxieties must be elicited if they are to be able to risk authority, prerogative, and traditional roles, because they see the higher value potential of participatory governance in program development and service delivery.

The director is caught in a squeeze play similar to that of the supervisors. In attempting a collateral governance approach, he "gives up" some authority and control to staff while still himself subjected to the controls of the hierarchical governance system of the institution. He remains accountable for the decisions and actions of his department even though he no longer has the total "command power." Control now flows from different sources, for different reasons, with different effects.

Ideally one should not attempt to mandate participatory governance. It should evolve and develop over a period of time out of needs and experiences of a department that call forth a structuring or restructuring of: committees with specific tasks; group supervision methods; creative use of staff meetings for shared work; experiences with staff around operational problems. The ultimate goal is to develop a group crossing all levels and programs that is concerned with overall policies and operations of the department.

The evolutionary flow offers staff, supervisors, and the director opportunities to share responsibilities and professional developmental experiences on peer collateral levels as well as in joint endeavors across hierarchical lines. If such experiences and episodes have proved constructive and valuable, a fertile, mature base has been established to take the next "natural" step toward participatory governance.

In the event that the life space of the department has not fostered such an evolutionary process, opportunities may arise out of crises. Crisis calls forth opportunities for staff to face, with the administrator, challenges that may commit the department to serious modification of program and mission. Staff participation in decision making may grow explicitly at such a time.

For the director of a small social work department, there is a trap that must be understood. Such a director may say, "Since we are such a small department, and see each other daily, I speak with my staff continually, and we really have a shared process of decision making in the department." However, on closer examination the director may find that he is describing close interpersonal relationships and contacts, while actual direction and governance follows a hierarchical and largely director-centered pattern. Unless a director consciously absorbs the concept of collateral governance, and translates this into a structure that involves staff in its development, it will not come to pass. Merely intensified interpersonal relationships are not participatory governance.

The director of a large social service department faces a different trap, with a net effect of maintaining a hierarchical, vertical governance system. His pseudo-participatory governance may take the following shape: The director uses a number of supervisors or program chiefs with whom he meets regularly as an advisory cabinet. The director of such a department may pride himself on the fact that he has direct linkages and input from the front lines of staff, but this is not so. Since the supervisory group tends to have the same perspective of authority as he does, the director is not under the same pressure to accept or utilize their advice, nor do the supervisors react as staff would if their advice is not heeded. They have incorporated and emotionally accepted the hierarchical model of governance of which they, themselves, are a significant part. The director is, in effect, isolated from the rank and file staff and really is talking with other "selves" who are extensions of himself.

STAFF DYNAMICS

The creative use of peer responsibility promotes the model in that the peers can with more credibility come to their fellow staff members with their suggestions, recommendations, and queries: "Do we have your trust and mandate to go ahead?" On an unconscious level, the transferential situation of the nuclear family is recreated by virtue of the power attributed to the directorial (dictatorial) position. This transferential power exists regardless of age or sex of the director or the size of the staff whether it is visible or submerged. Thoughtful input is more readily elicited by peers; in contrast, expectation of conformity by the director; hence the value of this model in tapping creative resources, talents, and full staff investment in the operations, goals, and growth of the department.

ORGANIZATIONAL DYNAMICS

Can there be truly shared responsibility in governance of social work departments within social institutions that are vertical monoliths? Hospitals tend to be organized in a feudal (or baronial) model with a king (administrator, director, executive vice-president, or medical director) who oversees and mediates among strong barons and governs through a bargaining-negotiating process. His role is to maintain the viability and existence of the organization. Decisions are made, sometimes for the good of the total institution, sometimes for the people it serves, but often in deference to the muscle power of particular barons (services or departments), singly or in concert. The least powerful barons exist because of their essentiality to the institution and to the functioning of the most powerful departments.

In a general hospital more complex and powerful forces are at work than in any other social care institution. The key differentiating factor is the duality of systems: the "cure system" and the "care system." The "cure system" is that set of services and people mobilized to save and sustain life in the biological-physical-medical sense. When this system determines that it has priority in a situation, it commands all resources on an immediate basis. The physician is in command of the cure system. He makes the decisions, and all systems' resources must respond promptly and appropriately. This is in the traditional mission of the hospital, the "repair station" function, mandated by society.

The "care system" is composed of all nonemergency, non-life-and-death services and personnel. It is geared to a slower, sustaining pace with the occurrence of life-and-death crises being the exception. In those crises, the care system serves, and is subserved by, the cure system. It waits upon the cure system and for the cure system. The social worker is part of the care system. Not only is the physician in command of the cure system, but he also has an unparalleled mobility (and, therefore, power) between both systems.

The director of social work must be clear about the actual power structure in his institution because his decisions have to be made with a realistic understanding of the impact of these decisions on the administrator and the departmental chairman. An understanding of the tensions among them is essential for the social work department because any decision has not only an impact on but a potential for redistributing or altering the relative power and status of the departments.

The challenge for the social work director is to represent the department's decisions to this "field system" and to enable his staff to understand the realities of the forces at work within the organization. If staff are, indeed, going to be part of a participatory departmental governance, they must understand the effects of decisions in order to share in making them competently.

Social workers may be confused as they experience participatory decision making with the department and, at the same time, are confronted by an authoritarian model on the ward or service program. This system, with the physician as captain of the "team," rewards those members of the team who unquestioningly accept the authority and decisions of the leader. For social work staff to influence decisions significantly within the cure system, even though many of these may actually fall within other than medical competence, involves tremendous effort in developing working relationship strategies. The mature staff member uses his executive ego capacities to deal with conflicts that arise in moving from one system to another and responding appropriately just as he does within societal subsystems. To live with the differences in decision making that exist between these subsystems is a learned survival technique.

The differences between an intradepartmental mode of participatory governance and the type of governance in the rest of the institution are stressful for the director as well as for staff. The director is called upon by administration, by other departmental chairmen, or by the situation itself to make on-the-spot decisions. The director cannot become a captive of the participatory governance mode existing within the department. To delay an expected answer, or to say he must consult with staff, would obviously project an image of weakness in critical situations requiring strength, credibility, and decisiveness.

In the sharing of relevant information the director is sometimes placed in an existential bind. He is privy to confidential, restricted information given to him with the understanding that it is not to be "publicly" shared. Yet this kind of information about budgets, planning decisions, personnel changes, contemplated policy changes that involve delivery of services, construction of new facilities, sensitive community negotiations, and critical union negotiations that may involve social work staff may be precisely what staff must have if they are to participate in valid and sound governance. Since a basic prerequisite for sound decision making is the availability of all known pertinent and relevant information, then how can the director engage in other than a game of participatory governance when he is bound to withhold significant information from his staff?

This issue has to be resolved within the constraints of individual institutions. However, a useful principle is the director's sharing all he is able to and defining broadly what at the time cannot be shared. The director has responsibility not to "cop out" behind this contractual shield.

APPROPRIATE ISSUES FOR COLLATERAL DECISION MAKING

In developing an effective collateral governance process it is necessary to be clear about what are appropriate and inappropriate areas for the collateral decision-making process.

There are certain responsibilities that cannot be delegated to staff without undermining the role of the director and the viability of the department:

1. Hiring of personnel. It is possible, however, for staff to have input in evaluating potential staff members.

2. Taking action to separate or fire a staff member.

3. Promotion and/or deciding to increase professional responsibilities, such as student supervision or major program assignment. However, in the climate of open communication the administration's evaluation of staff members often coincides with the staff's assessments. Staff members evaluate each other as peers, the director evaluates on behalf of the organization.

4. Budget negotiations with hospital management. The development of program ideas and goals is appropriate to the collateral decision-making process and can be utilized by the director in his budget negotiations.

5. Certain interagency relations cannot be shared appropriately with staff. Negotiations between the director and a community agency initially may require confidentiality because of sensitive political and professional considerations. However, when this is not the case, or at a later point in time, appropriate sharing with staff is possible and necessary.

6. Responsibility for determining the timing and nature of negotiations between elements of the hierarchical hospital organization, such as other

department heads, clinical chiefs, and the social work staff. For example: the decision regarding the input of social work into a new clinical program, or, conversely, when social work will have a new input into an existing clinical program.

Matters of mutual concern can readily be categorized into negotiable (soft) and nonnegotiable (hard) issues. If the director seeks every opportunity for engaging the staff in collateral governance around negotiable items, a foundation is built that enables staff to accept with confidence the director's assessment that a specific matter is not negotiable. If this process is unsuccessful and the director increasingly finds it necessary to invoke his authoritative role, credibility is lacking or, at least, failing. The relationship between the director and his staff has to be reexamined and reworked.

The selective use of collateral and unilateral decision making relates to a clear understanding of the differentiated accountability requirements laid on the director and on staff. The director is responsible to the hospital organization for the social work department no matter how the decision or viewpoint he is representing is developed within the social work department. He is responsible to his staff for creating a climate and structure in which the professional functions productively.

In a hierarchical system, there is continual contraction of the parameters within which staff can participate in decision making that affects their professional roles, responsibilities, and duties. Their input to the basic core of staff programs and innovation is restricted. If growth and development of individuals and organizations are seen by the director as related to the release of creative potentials, then approaches and structures that will promote participatory effort will be found.

STRUCTURE: SOME MODELS OF COLLATERAL GOVERNANCE

There are numerous ways of approaching participatory governance. One important consideration is the size of the staff. In a small staff comprised of a director and perhaps one or two staff people, problems of organization and structure are minimal. What is significant is the way in which this staff, which can function as a committee of the whole, is perceived by the director. If the director adopts and accepts a philosophy of participatory governance, then all his dealings and relationships with staff will reflect a seeking of appropriate input and participation by that staff. As the size of a social service department increases, there is reached a certain point where this "town meeting" approach to collateral governance is no longer viable. Five or six people are the maximal optimal number for a committee of the whole approach. Anything larger than that results in a time-consuming and unmanageable process in which too many people are tied up in too many meetings resulting in too little being accomplished.

In larger social service departments of six or more staff people, a small group or committee structure is most feasible. As long as the committee sizes are kept within manageable limits, the committee structure is a realistic and manage-able vehicle for the development and implementation of a collateral governance approach. Committees are traditional and noncontroversial structures within all organizations and therefore are readily accepted by all parties involved as a means for communication. Committees have always been used as part of the process of problem or task solving. Regardless of whether the committee structure is implemented through mandate or through an evolutionary process, the end result must be a formal representational group that can engage with the director in collateral governance.

Governance committees can be structured along horizontal or vertical staff lines. In the horizontal structuring each professional level or discrete subgrouping forms committees out of its own ranks which then meet with the director. Examples of this are a supervisory level committee, a staff level committee, a nonprofessional staff level committee, or a group from the medical unit or the psychiatric unit. In vertical models, a committee or committees with representatives from all these levels meet together with the director.

In the early developmental stages of a participatory governance model it may be more comfortable or convenient for all parties concerned to establish a horizontal committee structure. The structure may shift from horizontal to vertical with representatives of all levels meeting in committee together.

Whether horizontal or vertical committee structures are most effective will depend on the developmental point of time within the organization, the specific goals or tasks that need to be accomplished, and the readiness of the group and the director to engage at either or both levels. There are idiosyncratic factors both within the staff and the director that need to be considered before establishing a formal committee structure. While the vertical model offers a more representational input, and thereby reduces the need for coordination and communication among levels, this is not postulated as the optimum model for all institutions.

ADVISORY COMMITTEE

An Advisory Committee can achieve staff participation in administrative decision making. In order to provide continuity as well as opportunity for new input, membership in this committee can be rotated every 2 years on a staggered basis. Thus, for a four-member committee, it would be possible to have an annual selection in which two new members are selected to replace two members who retire from committee service. In determining committee size, we suggest a minimum of three staff members and a maximum of six, depending on total size of the department.

As the advisory council to the director, this committee provides consultation derived from its own collective expertise. The fact that the committee members are selected by staff, and are also closer to the day-to-day delivery of services, lends considerable value to its point of view and counsel on matters of general staff concern.

The Advisory Committee should meet at least biweekly, for approximately 1 to 1½ hours. The agenda is determined by the director, with additions from the committee. The director serves as chairperson, in that the committee is "advisory" to him or her. A brief record of items discussed and any decisions made should be kept and distributed to all the committee members by the director.

A report by the committee should be made at monthly administrative staff meetings. Staff are thereby assured that there have been no secret or privileged communications within the structure of the advisory process, and that members have not been co-opted. It provides an opportunity for full staff airing and input on selected issues of their concern. Our experience is that staff trust their representatives and do not seek to duplicate the committee's role, except around those issues of pressing general concern. Thus, the work of the Advisory Committee helps to identify and focus these special concerns for full staff input.

Matters that are the proper concern of the Advisory Committee can be of current importance, related to crises, or can lead to substantive change or policy alterations of a lasting nature.

Members of the Advisory Committee, by virtue of its specific mandate, must be seen as advisers and not implementers of change. The normal departmental structures and processes, such as task forces and standing committees, are still required.

The responsibility of staff members on this committee is of a high level, and appropriate recognition for service should be given.

RISKS OF OLD AND NEW GOVERNANCE FORMS

Historically, the most common means for receiving staff input has been through the supervisory structure. Because the supervisory group is closely identified with administrative goals, concerns, problems, and strategies, it forms an Inner Council. This may create a sense of strain within staff, if no other means for direct exchange with the director exist. Staff do not necessarily regard the supervisor as having the type of front-line experience that they have and feel that the supervisory group cannot necessarily represent their concerns fully and feelingly (the gut feeling). A feeling of a communications barrier eventually develops among rank and file staff. Administrators, generally speaking, have a reluctance to use staff committees. To them it seems and feels easier to communicate with supervisory group members who are in a similar operational responsibility level and who indeed act for the director, on occasion, in his absence. This approach is ego-syntonic and comfortable for the director, "as if the parents were discussing the activities of the children" in privacy, without having to be bothered by the participation of the children who may be "unruly."

The supervisory group meets, decides, goes to staff to pronounce the decisions. It is at that point that one of two things happens: (a) staff outwardly and passively "accept," inwardly and covertly may resist and undermine; (b) an open clash—a staff peer group coalesces and resists as a combined pressure group. Battle may then ensue, which no one really wins. The department and its mission suffer.

Participatory decision making can become a Pandora's box. Once opened, it may be difficult or impossible to close off the forces generated. To gain an even greater dividend in program effectiveness by obtaining staff participation a director can take some risks. There are no easy solutions, but clarity on the following points can avoid some pitfalls:

1. Participatory governance is a contract, which must be drawn with certain clearly defined elements. The mutual roles and responsibilities of director and staff have to be clearly explicated and understood in the process of governance. The identification of appropriate and inappropriate agenda items for a participatory decision-making process must be integral parts of the contract.

2. To the degree that the prerequisites for achieving maximum effective participatory governance have been taken into account the risks of contractual breakdown or abrogation will be lessened.

3. Participatory governance requires an ongoing process of examination of the contractual requirements and the experiences that ensue, and a joint continual reevaluation, by all parties involved, of the mutual roles and responsibilities as well as the ways in which they have been reflected in the everyday practice of governance.

4. Effective participatory governance requires a built-in mechanism and process for immediate alert warnings and open exchanges of views and differences resulting from episodic occurrences that have potential for undermining or abrogating the governance covenant. The cumulative effect of negative or negatively perceived mutual experiences that have not been promptly and openly discussed holds the greatest danger to the success of the participatory governance model.

5. The director's anxiety about the potential Pandora's box effect may cause him to project this fantasy upon staff, and so conduct himself as to create a self-fulfilling prophecy. On staff's part, the lack of trust in the director and his intentions may cause them to set up test situations (traps) that may have the effect of conveying to the director the message of their distrust of his authoritative role. An action-reaction process may ensue that will fulfill the staff's "fantasy-prophecy."

6. Participatory governance should be viewed as a vehicle for releasing creative and constructive forces within the staff, rather than as a defense mechanism against institutional pressures and problems. While mutual support is valid, and is derived through this model, its primary purpose is not to defend the department, director, or staff.

Within every staff there may be conflicting subgroups, and there are ambivalent feelings about authority. Staff need to be controlled and also to resist control. Whatever tendencies exist among staff to separate from each other along subgroup lines or self-interests are less powerful than the thrust of healthy individuals to achieve interdependence in their personal and professional relationships. Our knowledge of personality development validates the capability of staff to adopt and develop decision-making roles. While situational forces can obscure and delay the process, maturational forces are in the direction of greater satisfaction and fulfillment in participating in the governance of their department than in fostering division within it.

CONCLUSION

Participatory governance is not easy. The director must be prepared to develop structures that enable staff to move toward maximum participation in the governance processes. Problems of differences within staff can be overcome.

Accepting the validity of appropriate sharing, collateral work between staff and director has to be lived out in day-to-day process. The process is a laboratory for testing out the needed changes in professional relationships. It can strengthen practice capability and resourcefulness and can enhance intra- and interdepartmental work. Risks exist, but in a climate of mutual trust and respect, they need not be formidable.

NOTES

1. Harleigh B. Trecker, *Social Work Administration: Principles and Practices* (New York: Association Press, 1971).
2. James D. Thompson, ed., *Comparative Studies of Administration* (Pittsburgh: University of Pittsburgh Press, 1959).
3. Max Weber, *The Theory of Social and Economic Organization,* translated by A. M. Henderson (New York: Oxford University Press, 1947).
4. Joseph I. Hungate, Jr., *A Guide for Training Local Public Welfare Administrators* (Washington, D.C.: U.S. Department of Health, Education and Welfare, Bureau of Family Services, Division of Technical Training, 1964).
5. F. J. Peirce, "Student Involvement: Participatory Democracy or Adult Socialization?" in Patricia J. Stickney, ed., *Decision-Making in Graduate Schools of Social Work and in Higher Education* (New York: Council on Social Work Education, March, 1972).
6. Winifred Bell, "Educational Bases for Student Involvement in the Administration of Social Work Schools," *Social Work Education Reporter,* December 1969, pp. 13–46.

SUGGESTED ADDITIONAL READINGS

Bohr, Ronald, et al., "Value Conflicts in a Hospital Walk Out," *Social Work,* October 1971, pp. 33–42.
Carmody, Francis, "Planning Social Work Services for an Army General Hospital," *Military Medicine,* March 1976, pp. 170–76.

Collins, Jane. "Assessment of Social Services in a Large Health Care Organization: A Social Work Administrator's Perspective." In *Evaluation of Social Work Services in Community Health and Medical Care Program,* 1973 Annual Institute for Public Health Social Workers edited by Robert C. Jackson and Jean Morton. Berkeley: University of California, Public Health Social Work Program, 1973, pp. 57–70.

Hirsch, Sidney, and Abraham Lurie, "Establishing a Hospital Social Service Department," *Social Work* 4 (April 1959):86–93.

Lurie, Abraham, "Staffing Patterns: Issues and Program Implications for Health Care Agencies," *Social Work in Health Care* 2, no. 1 (Fall 1976):85–94.

Nacman, Martin, "A Systems Approach to the Provision of Social Work Services in Health Settings—Part I and II," *Social Work in Health Care* 1, nos. 1 and 2 (Fall 1975):47–53.

Phillips, Beatrice. "Facilitating Communication: Social Work and the Problem Oriented Record System." In *Evaluation of Social Work Services in Community Health and Medical Care Program,* 1973 Annual Institute for Public Health Social Workers, edited by Robert C. Jackson and Jean Morton. Berkeley: University of California, Public Health Social Work Program, 1973, pp. 93–114.

Schoenfeld, Harvey, "Opportunities for Leadership for the Social Worker in Hospitals: An Administrator's Expectation," *Social Work in Health Care* 1, no. 1 (Fall 1975):93.

Spano, Robert, and Sander Lund, "Management by Objectives in a Hospital Social Service Unit,' *Social Work in Health Care* 1, no. 3 (Spring 1976) pp . 267–76.

Weiner, Hyman. "Workshop on Administration." In *Social Services in Pediatric Hospitals,* edited by Lang M. Lewis and sponsored by the James Whitcomb Riley Hospital for Children. Washington, D.C.: U.S. Department of Health, Education and Welfare, Public Health Service, Maternal and Child Health Service, 1972, pp. 15–28.

21/SOCIAL WORK INFORMATION AND ACCOUNTABILITY SYSTEMS IN A HOSPITAL SETTING*

PATRICIA VOLLAND

"To move forward in the coming decade, social work must make substantial progress in at least three tasks: (1) to find better ways to account for what it does, (2) to determine the effectiveness of its programs, and (3) to develop more potent means of effecting change in social problems."[1] To do what Dr. William Reid suggests, and to do it responsibly, the profession must continue to develop and perfect information and accountability systems that collect, store, and analyze a wide range of information to answer questions of program effectiveness, costs, and operating systems. It is to the credit of the profession that social work is asking these questions of itself in planning for a future where nothing will be taken for granted. All services in the health care sector are coming under critical scrutiny in an attempt to provide the highest level of care at the lowest possible cost. Health care providers are being asked to define and account for their services through cost-effective processes. Both third-party payers, including government agencies, and consumers are focusing on the escalating cost of health care and understanding the quality of the care provided.[2] Where social work is part of a health care delivery system, the profession is participating in this process.

This chapter describes the design and implementation of an information and accountability system within a university hospital. It reviews the purposes of the system and relates these to the needs of the profession in general, and social work in health care in particular.

ACCOUNTABILITY AND SOCIAL WORK INFORMATION SYSTEMS

There are forces at local and federal levels that sharpen the need for definitions of quality and quantity of work by the profession. In the state of Maryland,

---

*Reprinted with permission of the author from *Social Work in Health Care* 1, no. 3 (Spring 1976).

the Maryland Health Services Cost Review Commission has been established.[3] This commission has responsibility for investigating, reviewing, and establishing rates of reimbursement for hospital services. In establishing a rate review methodology, this commission has accepted the Revenue Center as a means for defining service. Each revenue center makes bills and establishes relative value units. Departments of social work are not considered revenue centers. Rather, social work services are charged off through the per diem established within the revenue center where the service is provided. A relative value unit has been established for each professional service; for social work this unit of measure is total number of cases. This unit of measure does not accurately define quality or quantity of services provided or their benefit to patients. In response to this, directors of social work departments, through the Maryland Chapter of the American Society for Hospital Social Work Directors, have taken responsibility for defining and ranking types of social work services.[4] One approach to relative value is time spent in delivering each service with level of professional skill necessary to provide these services.

On the federal level, passage of Professional Standards Review Organization (PSRO) regulations mandates the requirement for both concurrent and retrospective review.[2] The objectives of this legislation suggest that reduction of health care costs is compatible with increased effectiveness of service. Establishment of criteria for a standard for services for each health care professional addresses the possibility of reduced cost and increased effectiveness. One approach for the establishment of such criteria for social work is through defining service categories with minimum criteria necessary to deliver these services effectively,[4] a process that is part of an information system.

In addition to addressing accountability, a good information system has potential as the basis for research and evaluation of services. Attempts within the profession of social work to research adequately the content and effectiveness of services have tended to be anecdotal and limited to case examples at best.[5] Predictions for future studies suggest that future focus will be on effectiveness of certain techniques, established in advance, rather than total review of process retrospectively.[1] Emphasis is on defining and testing observable changes or "hard" data. One approach to developing these data is to categorize psychosocial problems that are frequently utilized to define cause and effect relationship to illness and health. These psychosocial problems, frequently used to define need for social work interventions in health care, could form the basis for a taxonomy of "hard" data.

Changes in The Johns Hopkins Hospital focused on decentralized management and implementation of "Management By Objectives" concepts. The Department of Social Work experienced a change in leadership. This resulted in overall goals being sharpened, as the new leadership was charged with defining program objectives and establishing effectiveness criteria while understanding the costs to a given revenue center. A cost system was needed to establish this clearly. These developments reflect the situation faced by many departments of social work.

ESTABLISHMENT OF SYSTEM OBJECTIVES

Having considered all of these factors, what then should the objectives of an information and accountability system in a large university hospital setting be? This author determined that a multifaceted system with the following objectives would be functional for the Department of Social Work at The Johns Hopkins Hospital:

1. To establish and define social work services.
2. To communicate these services to all other health care professionals.
3. To measure the outcome of these services.
4. To develop an information system that lays a basis for developing and executing research projects on health care problems pertinent to social work interventions.

The first approach was a review of developments in other hospital social work departments. In Maryland, one such program with potential for adaptation was developed at the Sinai Hospital of Baltimore.[6] The consultant to that program was employed by our department to review our needs and to assist in the design of a workable system. The system that has been developed at The Johns Hopkins Hospital refects and has similarities to the design developed at the Sinai Hospital of Baltimore.

The system at The Johns Hopkins Hospital has been developed within the framework of problem indentification, goal-directed services provided to alleviate the defined problem, and measurement of service outcome. In setting such a framework, services are defined into categories; each category has a set of criteria that will be utilized in the peer review process.[2,7] Further definition of services results from collection of demographic information on each patient. For example, review of patients who receive discharge planning services clearly establishes patients at risk for this service. Patients needing social work services can be defined and enter the social work system more effectively. This also leads to implementation of concurrent review[2] as has already been demonstrated at The Johns Hopkins Hospital where patients "at risk" are automatically referred to the Department of Social Work by the Quality Assurance Office. Effective implementation of concurrent review is accomplished, and outcome of such service delivery benefits the patient (effective discharge planning) and the hospital (improved utilization of beds).

Objective definition of services leads to a better understanding of social work services. Further, by comparing time spent and level of professional expertise necessary to provide said service, a relative value for each service category will be established. Service categories will then become the unit of measure for defining the cost of social work service, thus providing a more accurate cost base and a more effective means of comparing for social work departments within like hospitals. The potential of charging for social work services, based on actual services provided, should have greater appeal for third-party payers in considering separate reimbursement for social work.

Collection of data, both qualitative and quantitative, can lead to demonstration of cost-effectiveness. For example, when the commission or hospital administration questions the high cost of social work services in an outpatient clinic where service to patients in groups is focused on reducing somatic complaints while dealing with psychosocial problems of depression and social isolation, this service can be demonstrated as being less costly than utilization of physician time with patients individually. The above discussion of objective data collection also has value in working with hospital administration. Psychosocial problems that interfere with or complicate health and medical care are defined for a particular patient population. Such systematic problem identification combined with defined service categories and measurement of outcome of such services defines for hospital administration the type of program being implemented and the contribution it makes to the hospital's objective to provide quality care. Effectiveness of program planning is demonstrated by comparing services with outcomes such as length of stay in the hospital. The potential for reducing length of stay in the hospital through early entry into the social work system can be demonstrated while providing comprehensive service to the patient. Through preliminary review, the Department of Social Work has demonstrated already that time is lost in planning when the patient's refusal to cooperate is disregarded.[8] Further, both service definition and outcome measures are better understood through the reporting of obstacles to service. Internal and external obstacles such as late referral or lack of resources are known. This information can be utilized to define ways of saving health costs. Communication through objective methodologies and utilizing the concept of problem-oriented record keeping enhances understanding of social work services while leading to clarification of role responsibilities for patient care. Problems and service intent are clearly stated to enhance team responsibilities for patient care.

Finally, there is great potential for such a system to lay a basis for developing and executing research projects. Demographic patient information, problem taxonomy, service goals and outcomes, and obstacles to service delivery can be compared and studied separately in evaluative as well as descriptive research projects.

DESCRIPTION OF THE SYSTEM

The Recording and Reporting System itself contains a standardized problem list and four recording forms. The problem list has two levels:

1. *Initial problems* represent the point of entry into the social work system from the overall health care system. Classifications include: (a) difficulties with medical regime; (b) acceptance/adjustment to conditions; (c) inadequate/harmful care; (d) personal adjustment/behavior problem; (e) environmental difficulties; and (f) terminal illness.

2. *Follow-up or resultant problems* are defined following a social work assess-ment. The problems here may coexist with health-related problems, or they may be the cause or result of these health-related problems. Classifications include the following: (a) individual function related to illness; (b) family conflicts; (c) living conditions; (d) interpersonal relationship difficulties; (e) economic conditions; (f) other specific conditions; and (g) individual psychiat-ric disorders—behavioral symptomatology, thought and feeling disorders, and lifelong maladaptive behavioral patterns. Each is further broken down into specific problem areas to aid in focusing for social work services. Each problem is numbered for computerization.

RECORDING FORMS

Patient Case Record.   This form is completed by the social worker at the time of referral for assessment. It contains demographic information regarding the patient and his family, a medical diagnosis, as well as a description of the referring agent and the referring problem. This form never appears in the Medical Record, as all information contained on it should already be there. One copy of this form goes to data processing; the social worker keeps the other for his own records.

Service Plan.   Following initial assessment where the social worker decides to open a case, this form is completed and a copy is placed in the Medical Record within 48 hours. The Service Plan Form contains specific problems identified for social work services. Service goals are defined, and activities to be per-formed are described. These are coded for computer analysis.

Service Completion Form.   At the completion of a service episode this form is completed. A copy is placed in the Medical Record. Problems worked, service goals and activities, and outcome achieved for each are recorded de-scriptively and coded. Obstacles that may have interfered with the social work services are described and coded. The worker then has the option of closing the case or redefining problems and new services to be provided.

Service Plan Change.   When, in the process of providing service, the worker determines a need to redefine problems and/or services, the Service Plan Change Form is completed. A copy is placed in the Medical Record. This represents either a shift in problem focus or in goal focus. The Service Plan Change is similar to the Service Plan. It is primarily an indicator of the shift. With the decision to computerize this system, it becomes possible to store information indefinitely and to expand the number of variables to be com-pared. In devising and implementing this system, it was determined that a system was needed that served both recording and reporting purposes. Each suggested design was analyzed for its potential usefulness in collecting the necessary information and then was tested on limited staff. Attention was focused on creating a problem list that contained mutually exclusive items. The current problem list is close to this goal. A sample system was devised and implemented on a trial basis in April of 1975 and was utilized through August of 1975. Feedback was gathered from each of the staff members with suggestions for improving the system. The formal system was implemented in September 1975.

IMPLEMENTATION AND POTENTIAL VALUE

No formal system of recording existed previously. Therefore, worker response to this system was very ambivalent: There was excitement in developing and participating in a new system; however, the ultimate expectation that each worker would be required to utilize it created concern. Time considerations in learning to use and maintain such a system are still being discussed. Social workers tend to view this process of record keeping as unneccessary paperwork. Time spent away from direct contact with patients and/or family is frequently seen as time wasted. Administrative staff spent much time attempting to resolve such concerns.

The value of this system in planning and implementing comprehensive treatment services was stressed as was the responsibility for maintenance of profession accountability within the hospital. Since the administration of The Johns Hopkins Hospital views any attempt at objective definition and planning of services within realistic cost as positive, necessary funds to develop and build this system were readily available. The Medical Records Department was reluctant to approve still another form for the Medical Record. However, this was a minor obstacle, and the focus on problem-oriented records further reduced resistance as Medical Records would like the hospital to adopt this format.

Building a foundation for future research projects posed a minor problem in that it was necessary to develop a system that combined a mutually exclusive problem list and collected relevant patient demographic information. Outcome measures, while somewhat objective, will need continued review.

The value of this system can be stated in terms of how it benefits and relates to: (a) outside regulatory agencies such as the Maryland Health Services Cost Review Commission; (b) hospital administration; (c) the director and supervisory personnel of the social work department; (d) the social work profession, particularly as it has impact on PSRO regulations and research potential; and (e) patients and families.

As previously stated, the Department of Social Work's relationship to the Maryland Health Services Cost Review Commission is in establishing service categories as the unit of measure and of costing social work services more effectively. Future budgets will be built on this cost system, not on total number of cases or total number of staff. At any given time the director of the

Department of Social Work is prepared to say, by revenue center, exactly what social work services are provided, to what population, with what problems, at what cost (time and money), with what outcome.

Management information, for the director and supervisory staff, is gathered and disseminated in a useful form. The social work administrator utilizes this information to understand and evaluate the quality of work of each staff member. Services can be understood both as they alleviate problems for patients and their families and as they alleviate problems within the institution. Comparison of services for a given problem will aid in understanding which services for which problem are most effective within the shortest time and the least cost to the patient and the institution. The teaching of medical students and other health care professionals about patient and family psychosocial needs is more clearly focused. Subjective assessment of quality of work is reduced as is assessment of clinical social work skills. Activities can be reviewed regularly, and innumerable variable comparisons can be retrieved.

When cost reduction programs are begun, the social work administrator is prepared to define what these potential reductions will mean. Conversely, when fiscal year budgets are submitted the administrator is prepared to demonstrate need and value (outcome) for additional services. Thus by defining costs for each service the administrator can compare this with the potential cost to the institution when a service is not provided. Future program planning becomes a process of defining services necessary within a given patient population. These objective data presented to the chief of a medical division allow him to establish a value for these services, plan for quality patient care, and analyze where dollars will be most effectively spent.

For the social work professional the system's problem, service, and outcome criteria are readily adaptable for PSRO requirements. It represents a conceptual framework through which social workers in a health care setting can function effectively. This framework is not new. With the focus on objectifying problems and goal expectations it allows the social worker to anticipate service effectiveness and validate this by outcome measures. The social worker must contract with a patient and/or his family for specific service focused on clearly defined problems, which reinforces the social work principle of self-determination.

Such a system tends, as well, to reduce jargon and to clarify role responsibilities for social work within the health care team. Services provided for the psychosocial needs of patients, from a variety of health care professionals, can be compared in terms of process as well as outcome effectiveness. The profession has labored diligently to establish a role as evaluator and treater of psychosocial factors that affect health and medical care. The medical profession has struggled to understand the effect of these factors on illness and health. Objectifying problems in a systematic taxonomy can establish a basis through which we view psychosocial factors as they affect or cause illness.

A standardized problem list is a beginning step for building a system taxonomy as a scientific framework through which social work research can focus in the future on specific etiologies of medical problems. Collection of demographic information regarding population served establishes potential for reviewing and comparing populations within a given health care system. Comparisons between the population receiving social work service and the population that is not can prove invaluable for understanding the effectiveness and the future of social work programs in health care planning.

Definitions of social work services with outcome measures established are the basis of evaluation of effectiveness. The service categories are defined objectively, and standardized outcomes have been established. Evaluative research projects can be conducted easily, where population allows, emphasizing objective factors to be considered.

This chapter has described the forces that moved a department of social work toward an experimental information and recording system and has emphasized the potential in such a system. This effort is being paralleled in many other departments of social work within health care settings. It is essential that those experiences be shared with the social work community in health settings with the goal of a single system combining the most productive components of each system.

REFERENCES

1. William Reid, "Developments in the Use of Organized Data," *Social Work* 5 (1974):585–93.
2. Department of Health, Education and Welfare, PSRO *Program Manual* (Washington, D.C.: United States Government Printing Office, 1974).
3. State of Maryland, Health Services Cost Review Commission, "Position Paper on Selected Problems and Issues" (Baltimore, Maryland, May 1975).
4. American Society for Hospital Social Work Directors, Maryland Chapter, Ad Hoc Committee on Peer Review, *Final Report,* in process. Documentation available in minutes of chapter meetings from September 1975 through present. Unpublished.
5. Joel Fischer, "Is Casework Effective: A Review," *Social Work* 18 (1973):5–20.
6. Jacqueline D. Fassett, Paper presented at the 1974 Annual Meeting of the Society for Hospital Social Work Directors.
7. PSRO *Basic Information for Social Workers Action Guide* (Washington, D.C.: NASW, 1975).
8. The Johns Hopkins Hospital, Department of Social Work, "Nine Month Report from Continuity of Care Office" (Baltimore, Maryland, September 1975). Unpublished.

SUGGESTED ADDITIONAL READINGS

Ferguson, Chris, et al., "Initiation of a Quality Assurance Program for Social Work Practice in a Teaching Hospital," *Social Work in Health Care* 2, no. 2 (Winter 1976-1977):205–18.
Lurie, Abraham, and Rosalind Chernesky, "The Functional Analysis Study: A First Step in a Quality Assurance Program," *Social Work in Health Care* 1, no. 2 (Winter 1975-1976):213–24.
Miller, Roy, et al., "Psychiatric Peer Review: The Ohio System," *American Journal of Psychiatry* 131, no. 12 (December 1974):1367–70.
National Federation of Societies for Clinical Social Work. *Standards for Health Care Providers in Clinical Social Work.* San Mateo, Calif., 1975.

Proceedings, Working Conference on Minimum Review Criteria for Professional Social Work Practice, University of Pittsburgh Graduate School of Public Health, Public Health Social Work Program, edited by Florence Stein, William Hall, and Christine Young. Pittsburgh, 1976.

Quality Assurance in Social Services in Health Programs for Mothers and Children, Proceedings, Conference held at William Penn Hotel, Pittsburgh, Pennsylvania, 1975, edited by William T. Hall and Gerald C. St. Denis. Pittsburgh: University of Pittsburgh, Graduate School of Public Health, Public Health Social Work Program, 1975, 115 pp.

Rehr, Helen. *Professional Standard Review and Utilization Review: The Challenge to Social Work,* Paper delivered at Social Work Conference sponsored by NASW and Society for Hospital Social Work Directors, Dallas-Ft. Worth, Texas, January 18–21, 1976.

Report of the Task Force on Cost Finding, Society for Hospital Social Work Directors, Eleanor Klein, chairperson, October 11, 1976, mimeographed, (interim report).

Weiss, Carol, "Alternative Models of Program Evaluation," *Social Work,* November 1974, pp. 675–87.

Westerman, John, et al., "Public Accountability, Quality Assurance and Social Work," *Social Work in Health Care,* 2, no. 1 (Fall 1976):33–42.

Part XII

EDUCATION FOR HEALTH CARE PRACTICE

22/BUILDING A HEALTH CARE CONCENTRATION: CURRICULUM GUIDELINES FOR SCHOOLS OF SOCIAL WORK

NEIL F. BRACHT

In recent years there has been a modest growth of health care concentrations and/or health courses in schools of social work. Recent amendments (1976) to the Federal Health Professions Educational Assistance Act include training funds for schools of social work. With federal funds there is likely to be pressure for more standardization of health care concentrations (sometimes refered to as specializations) in schools of social work. While academic innovation and flexibility must be maintained, this chapter presents a framework for the discussion and development of guidelines for health care concentrations in schools of social work that have the interest, skills, and resources to develop such concentrations.

Large numbers of social work students are placed in health care settings and particularly in new health care delivery programs such as neighborhood health centers, HMOs, interdisciplinary team projects and the like.[1,2] Finney found that one in four social work students placed in health-planning agencies for practicum experience were hired on a full-time basis following completion of their master's degree.[3] In a related study Finney reports a significant increase in the number of social work doctoral students (104) who are concentrating in the health policy planning area, and in the number of social work faculty affiliations with community health-planning programs.[4] (Social work faculty in 11 schools serve as members of the board of directors of comprehensive health-planning agencies; in 30 other schools faculty are represented on health-planning committees or task forces and also serve as consultants.) Joint health courses and programs between schools of social work and medical centers are also on the increase.[5] Several schools have joint social work (M.S.W.)-public health (M.P.H.) degree options at both the master's and doctoral levels.[5] A growing number of social work faculty have additional training in public health.

WHAT IS A HEALTH CARE CONCENTRATION?

Students in accredited schools of social work will be prepared for careers in health care organizations and systems through the *concentration mechanism* of the curriculum. Health courses and health practicum experiences are integrated in a *planned* way (see Figure 22.1) with *core professional courses* (e.g., social policy, research, human behavior and the social environment, minority content, etc.) and *specialized practice (track) courses* (e.g., social work methods, CO practice, etc.). Students generally choose one of two major practice streams or emphases within their specialization: (1) direct service delivery (individual and group interventions at the *micro* practice level) or (2) community organization and planning (organizational, management, and policy interventions at the *macro* practice level). Health courses may be linked to one of these practice specializations (e.g., "crisis intervention in clinical settings" for the micro practice level or "health planning" for students in the macro-level specialization). Such courses may cut across specializations and serve common learning needs of students in either specialization (e.g., courses on "health care systems" or "social impact of illness and disability").

In contemporary social work practice in health care settings, rigid distinctions between these two specializations are at times difficult to maintain, and many social workers find that they need skills obtained from both micro and macro practice. Experience indicates that master's-level social workers move rapidly into supervisory and administrative positions. Students specializing in direct service delivery are often encouraged to take health courses in planning, administration, and supervision, since in a very real sense they are being prepared for future administrative positions in health care.

ARTICULATION

In light of the facts that an increasing number of doctoral programs have students who are specializing in the health policy planning area and that undergraduate programs are also making available courses in health as part of the base for social work practice, graduate schools, where applicable, *should be able to describe how their health care concentration articulates* with other school-university components, such as undergraduate programs, doctoral studies, continuing education, health science center affiliations, and so forth (see Figure 22.2). This articulation standard should be general in nature but should adequately reflect a coordinated and planned effort to relate health care concentration resources and programs to other relevant components of the school, including perhaps other specialized concentrations (e.g., aging). Where undergraduate programs are separate from graduate schools of social work, consideration should be given to the type of "base" courses in health and their relationship to advanced health courses at the graduate level.

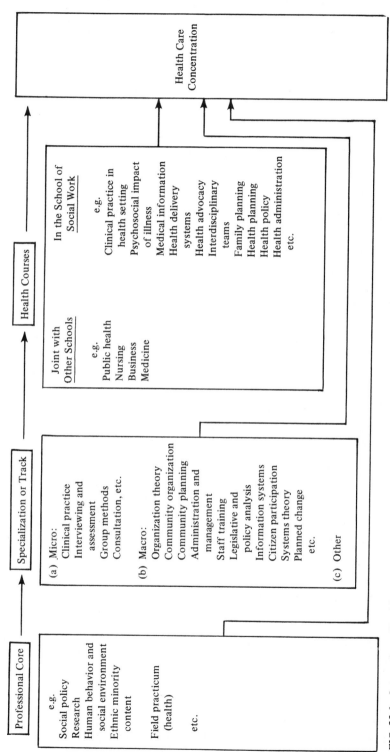

FIG. 22.1. Integration of health concentration into social work curriculum (master's program model).

Professional Core

e.g.

Social policy
Research
Human behavior and
social environment
Ethnic minority
content

Field practicum
(health)

etc.

Specialization or Track

(a) Micro:
Clinical practice
Interviewing and
assessment
Group methods
Consultation, etc.

(b) Macro:
Organization theory
Community organization
Community planning
Administration and
management
Staff training
Legislative and
policy analysis
Information systems
Citizen participation
Systems theory
Planned change
etc.

(c) Other

Health Courses

Joint with
Other Schools

e.g.
Public health
Nursing
Business
Medicine

In the School of
Social Work

e.g.
Clinical practice in
health setting
Psychosocial impact
of illness
Medical information
Health delivery
systems
Health advocacy
Interdisciplinary
teams
Family planning
Health planning
Health policy
Health administration
etc.

**Health Care
Concentration**

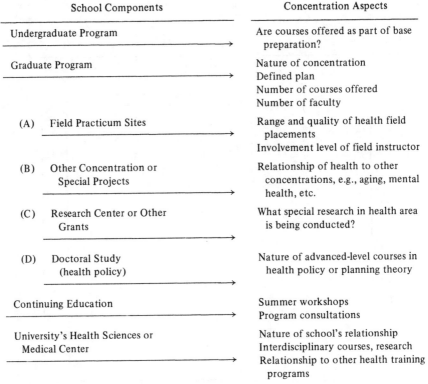

School Components	Concentration Aspects
Undergraduate Program	Are courses offered as part of base preparation?
Graduate Program	Nature of concentration Defined plan Number of courses offered Number of faculty
(A) Field Practicum Sites	Range and quality of health field placements Involvement level of field instructor
(B) Other Concentration or Special Projects	Relationship of health to other concentrations, e.g., aging, mental health, etc.
(C) Research Center or Other Grants	What special research in health area is being conducted?
(D) Doctoral Study (health policy)	Nature of advanced-level courses in health policy or planning theory
Continuing Education	Summer workshops Program consultations
University's Health Sciences or Medical Center	Nature of school's relationship Interdisciplinary courses, research Relationship to other health training programs

FIG. 22.2 Health care concentration: articulation to other school-university components (conceptual scheme).

GOAL AND OBJECTIVES OF THE HEALTH CARE CONCENTRATION

In July 1975 the Council on Social Work Education issued a memorandum summarizing a meeting on "development of manpower for the health field." In brief, the Council recommended that

1. Health care education should be directed toward training social workers to coordinate efforts with other members of the health care team, both in direct services and work with patients and families, and as contributors to health planning.

2. Social work should emphasize prevention, teach epidemiologic approaches, and program planning skills.

3. There is a need for a much stronger biological and physiological base in social work education.

4. Schools should develop linkages with systems in medical centers and schools in other health professions.

Schools must be allowed to develop unique approaches to their health concentrations. In general, a health care concentration should have as its basic goal the preparation of social workers for specialty practice in the health care field (including both direct service and planning-administration skills). In developing health care concentrations, as stated earlier, it must be recognized that the demands made of contemporary social work practitioners in the health care field require that a student's professional education cut across specializations at both the micro and macro levels of intervention. Health care concentrations should emphasize training to prepare practitioners for settings characteristically categorized as health care settings, and this includes such organizations as hospitals, public health departments, neighborhood health centers, home health agencies, public health nursing homes, health maintenance organizations, chronic-disease programs, and maternal and child health programs. Social work administrators and planners are needed in many of the newer outreach and preventive health delivery programs.

OBJECTIVES FOR STUDENTS IN HEALTH CARE

Possible outcomes or educational objectives of the health care concentration might include, but are not limited to, the following:
• Be able to identify major components of the health care system and analyze current policy issues.
• Be able to list specific research contributions of social work services to patients in health care settings.
• Be able to understand and have experienced the team process in health care settings.
• Be knowledgeable about the distribution of disability and illness in contemporary society and its changing patterns.
• Have knowlege of the distribution and contribution of social work throughout all aspects of the health care system.
• Be able to apply research methodology to practice in health care settings, including epidemiologic methods.
• Be familiar with the patient-consumer movement and issues of advocacy, including patient rights, medical experimentation and informed consent, malpractice, and right-to-die legislation.
• Be able to assess one's own continuing-education needs.
• Have developed specialized skills in administration, including consultation, staff selection training, cost analysis, budgeting, information systems, grant writing, and quality assurance methods.
• Be able to apply psychosocial assessment, treatment, and measurement skills to patient illness. Understand both normal and abnormal human functioning.
• Have developed specialized skills in planning and policy analysis, including community assessment, citizen participation, survey design, program analysis and evaluation, staffing committees, plan development and follow-through, and the role of health systems planning agencies; have knowledge of the community network of support services.

• Have completed at least one year of direct fieldwork (practicum) in health care settings.
• Provide students with basic evaluative skills in assessing effectiveness and cost-benefit of social work services in health settings.
• Provide students with skills in analyzing differences between and among illnesses and normal conditions.
• Show ability to plan and coordinate health care services with community social support services.

THE RANGE OF HEALTH COURSES OFFERED IN SCHOOLS OF SOCIAL WORK

The following list is a sampling of the diverse courses offered in health and health-related subjects at selected schools of social work:*

Health Care Systems

Health Care Delivery Issues
Public Health
Health Care Administration
Health Planning
Community Health

Social Work Practice in Health
Health Characteristics of the Poor

Research in Consumer Health
Citizen Participation–Advocacy
Organizational Theory
Future Trends in Health Care Delivery

Social Policy and Mental Health
Human Ecology

Social and Behavioral Aspects of Illness
Crisis Intervention in Health
Gerontology
Interdisciplinary Team Process
Cultivating Health
Medical Information for Social Work
Family Planning

Alcoholism
Social Work Practice in Health
Death and Dying
Social Work in a Medical Setting

Work with the Developmentally Disabled
Sexual Dysfunction and Health
Cultural Aspects of Health and Illness

As can be seen, schools of social work offer a wide range of health-related courses. These courses may reflect a particular school's philosophy, urban or rural regional health needs, or specialized interests of faculty and community field instructors.

In summary, the following categories of courses can be listed as a guide for selective use in expanding or developing a health care concentration in the

*Based on a review of seven schools' health care concentration statements (1976).

curriculum. In some instances field instructors from teaching hospitals and community health agencies can be called upon to teach in these areas.

1. *Health care systems analysis:* Analysis of the American health care system would deal with delivery problems of health care, aspects of our health care crisis, and delineation of organizational, financing, and manpower characteristics of the current system.

2. *Health and disease characteristics of population groups:* Course content in this area would provide students with a broader understanding of the epidemiology and distribution of illness in America and the shift in chronic-disease categories, with emphasis on preventive potential in certain kinds of infectious and chronic illnesses. Special topics on the health aspects of minority populations should be included.

3. *Application of the public health model to social work practice:* Students should generally be familiar with the public health practice model and the levels-of-prevention concept that frequently will be utilized in health care organizations. They should be familiar with new health-screening procedures and general public health resources in the community.

4. *Interdisciplinary collaboration:* Courses in this area would deal with new family and community medicine programs, new types of outreach centers, and the growing importance of interdisciplinary teamwork. Discussion of role diffusion among health disciplines should also be considered, especially among nursing, family medicine, and social work professionals.

5. *Health policy and legislative issues:* Depending on the particular curriculum needs of any one school, a survey course outlining the major legislative health proposals of recent years and a discussion of policy questions related to national health insurance would be germane to content in this section. Content dealing with the increasing role of social workers in health planning and the important developments in comprehensive health planning should be highlighted. The community organization faculty at the school might be interested in the development of specialized courses in community organization and planning for health care programs.

6. *Social work practice in health care settings:* In this course(s) a framework is set for social work practice in health care settings. A survey of modalities (both clinical and community organization) would be explicated. Special emphasis on psychosocial assessment of illness and crisis intervention would be given. Additional courses would deal with specialized case services related to social and health problems such as child abuse, rape, and psychological aspects of patients with kidney and heart conditions. Other courses could deal with the social work administrator or planner in health care settings.

NUMBER OF COURSES

How many health courses should there be in a concentration? If a rule of thumb is to be adopted, it would seem that, in addition to core and specialization (or track) courses, *at least five* courses clearly designated as related to health would be adequate to fulfill requirements for a health care concentration. Most schools of social work that have a health care concentration offer a range of 8–15 courses and usually require anywhere from 12 to 15 credit hours specifically in health.

FIELD PRACTICUM EXPERIENCE

In addition to field training in more traditional settings, social work students are increasingly deployed in community health outreach and referral programs, health maintenance organizations,[6] prevention and early screening programs, halfway programs in long-term care, home health, community and state health planning agencies, and interdisciplinary teams[7] in maternal and child health and developmental disabilities. They are also serving as health advocates in nursing homes and other institutions. Social work students are also assigned to ambulatory-care settings such as solo physician offices,[8] group medical practices, and special rural health projects.[9]

As regards *criteria for practicum experiences* in health, it seems reasonable to set a standard that requires that at least one year of the student's practicum experience be in a health care setting. Some schools will probably exceed this. Lurie and Pinsky make a convincing case for a two-year placement.[10]

The field component for the concentration is organized to provide the student with practice experiences in *breadth and depth*. The first-year experience could be designed to present a wide array of case situations of individuals, families, groups, dealing with problems of normal daily living or community social problems. This would include such agencies as family and children's agencies, schools, mental health centers, and United Way planning components. This field experience provides the student with knowledge of common problems faced by individuals, families, and communities, and ways of coping or dealing with these problems. The second year of fieldwork, however, would be designed to provide the student with in-depth experience in helping individuals and families deal with health and illness problems. For the student interested in macro-level practice, the experience would focus on the activities of health planning, administration, or analysis and development of health policy. This combination of field experiences should enable the student to recognize and assess the effect of health problems on normal human functioning and help him or her discern and extrapolate problems that are uniquely associated with health.

Close liaison between practice sites and the school's health concentration faculty should be encouraged. Hookey describes a systems conceptualization of *the relationship between the practice community and schools of social work.*[11] Implementation of strong ties to the practice community is critical. A community advisory group for the health care concentration is recommended.

Through their health curricula schools of social work can greatly influence the quality of social work practitioners in the health care system. While health curriculum reform in the graduate school itself is important, social work educators should not neglect the many opportunities available for interdisciplinary teaching and research with faculty of related health professional schools, e.g. medicine, nursing, dentistry (approximately one-half of all schools of social work are located in universities with medical schools or health sciences' centers). Collaboration between schools of social work and university health science centers[12] can be a productive way to both enhance health curriculum content and to influence health care delivery at the university level. If the benefits for patient and family of interdisciplinary health team practice are to remain viable, early exposure to health team functioning and research among students of all the disciplines becomes a necessary prerequisite.

NOTES

1. Edgar Perretz, "Social Work Education for the Field of Health: A Report of Findings from a Survey of Curricula," *Social Work in Health Care* 1, no. 3 (Spring 1976):357–66.
2. Neil Bracht, "Community Field Work Collaboration Between Medical and Social Work Students," *Journal of Social Work in Health Care* 1, no. 1 (Fall 1975):7–18.
3. Robert Finney et al., "Prospects for Social Workers in Health Planning," *Health and Social Work* 1, no. 3 (August 1976):7.
4. Robert Finney and Larry Matheis, "Educating Social Workers as Health Planners," Unpublished manuscript, 1977.
5. Eugene Hooyman et al., "Social Work and Public Health: An Interdisciplinary Joint Degree Program," CSWE Annual Program, Phoenix, 1977. See also note 12.
6. Neil Bracht, "Health Maintenance Organizations: Legislative and Training Implications," *Journal of Education for Social Work* 11, no. 1 (Winter 1975):36–44, and Cynthia Bell and Laurel Gorman, "HMO's, New Models for Practice," *Social Work in Health Care* 1, no. 3 (Spring 1976):325–36.
7. Libby Tanner and Ethel Soulary, "Interprofessional Student Health Teams," *Nursery Outlook* 20, no. 2 (February 1972):111–15.
8. Ruth Goldberg, "The Social Worker and the Family Physician," *Social Casework,* October 1973, pp. 489–95.
9. Neil Bracht, "Contributions of Public Health Social Work To Academic Departments of Community Medicine," *Milbank Memorial Fund Quarterly* 47, no. 1, pt. 1 (January 1969): 73–89.
10. Abraham Lurie and Sidney Pinsky, *Social Work Education for Health Care,* Paper presented at Annual CSWE Meeting, Phoenix, March 2, 1977.
11. Peter Hookey, "Education for Social Work in Health Care Organizations," *Social Work in Health Care* 1, no. 3 (Spring 1976):337–46, and Phyllis Caroff, "A Study of School Agency Collaboration in Social Work in Health Curriculum Building," *Social Work in Health Care,* 2, no. 3 (Spring 1977).
12. Neil F. Bracht and Scott Briar, "Relationship of Schools of Social Work to University Medical Centers: The University of Washington Experience," paper presented at Annual Program Meeting, Council on Social Work Education, Philadelphia, February, 1976.

SUGGESTED ADDITIONAL READINGS

Bassoff, Betty Zippin, "Interdisciplinary Education for Health Professionals: Issues and Directions," *Social Work in Health Care* 2, no. 2 (Winter 1976–1977):219–28.

Caroff, Phyllis, "A Study of Agency Collaboration in Social Work in Health Curriculum Building," *Social Work in Health Care* 2, no. 3 (Spring 1977):329–40.

Carroll, Nancy, "Areas of Concentration in the Graduate Curriculum: A Three Dimensional Model," *Journal of Education for Social Work* 11, no. 2 (Spring 1975):3–10.

Cramer, Margery Fay, "Fieldwork Preparation for Entrance into Mental Retardation Practice," *Journal of Education for Social Work* 13, no. 1 (Winter 1977):37–43.

Dalgleish, K. B., R. A. Kane, and J. J. McNamara, "Rotating Social Work Students within a Medical Center," *Health and Social Work* 1, no. 2 (May 1976).

Kane, Rosalie, "Interprofessional Education and Social Work: A Survey," *Social Work in Health Care* 2, no. 2 (Winter 1976–1977):229.

Lurie, Abraham, and Sidney Pinsky, "Queens Field Instruction Center: A Field Instruction Center for Multilevel Education in Social Work," *Journal of Education for Social Work* 9, no. 3 (Fall 1973):39–44.

"Position Statement on Preparation for Practice of Social Work in the Health Field," Statement approved by House of Delegates, Society of Hospital Social Work Directors, American Hospital Association, Chicago, February 4, 1975.

"Practice Standards for Social Work Practice in the Health Field," Ontario Association of Professional Social Workers, adopted at OAPSW Board Meeting, December 1975. Toronto.

Rusnack, Betty, "Planned Change: Interdisciplinary Education for Health Care," *Journal of Education for Social Work* 13, no. 1 (Winter 1977):104–11.

White, Grace. "Preparation of Social Workers for Interprofessional and Interagency Collaboration." In *Education for Social Work,* 1960 Proceedings. New York: Council of Social Work Education, 1960.

APPENDIX A/ABBREVIATIONS AND
SYMBOLS USED IN
CLINICAL MEDICINE

The following abbreviations are used in clinical practice, particularly in patients' charts. They are not standardized and differ with locale and according to specialty. Their use carries some risk as misunderstandings, sometimes with adverse consequences, do occur. Familiarity with these terms, however, is important for the social worker as is medical terminology as discussed in Chapter 5.

ADL	activity on daily living	CCU	coronary-care unit
ad lib	ad libitum (at pleasure)	CHF	congestive heart failure
AKA	above-knee amputation	cm.	centimeter
amt.	amount	CNS	central nervous system
ANS	autonomic nervous system	COPD	chronic obstructive
aq.	aqueous		pulmonary disease
ASA	aspirin	CO_2	carbon dioxide
ASHD	arteriosclerotic heart	C&S	culture & sensitivities
	disease	CVA	cerebral vascular accident
		CVD	cardiovascular disease
Ba	barium		
bid	bis indie (twice daily)	d.c.	discontinue
BKA	below-knee amputation	D_5W	dextrose 5% water
BM	bowel movement	DOA	dead on arrival
BP	blood pressure	DT	delirium tremens
BRP	bathroom privilege	Dx	diagnosis
BR	bedrest	D.M.	diabetes mellitus
ca	carcinoma; cancer	EKG	electrocardiogram
CAD	coronary artery disease	ENT	ear, nose, throat
Cath	catheterization	ER	emergency room
CBC	complete blood count	ETOH	ethyl alcohol
cc.	cubic centimeter	exp.	expired

fl.	fluid	N&V	nausea & vomit
F/U	follow-up	NPO	nothing by mouth
fx	fracture	NSR	normal sinus rhythm
GC	gonorrhea	O_2	oxygen
GI	gastrointestinal	OBS	organic brain syndrome
gm.	gram	OD	right eye
GSW	gunshot wound	OR	operating room
gtt.	drop	OS	left eye
GU	genitourinary	OT	occupational therapy
GYN	gynecology	OU	both eyes
		oz.	ounce
HCVD	hypertensive cardiovascular disease	PAD	peripheral artery disease
Hct.	hematocrit	PE	physical examination
H_2O	water	PID	pelvic inflammatory disease
hr.	hour		
h.s.	at bedtime	p.o.	by mouth
Hx	history	P.O.	postoperative
Htn	hypertension	POMR	problem-oriented medical record
ICU	intensive-care unit		
IPPB	intermittent positive pressure breathing	Pre-op	preoperative
		Prn	as need requires
I&O	intake & output	PT	physiotherapy
IV	intravenous	PTA	prior to admission
		PUD	peptic ulcer disease
kg.	kilogram		
L&W	living and well	q.d.	quaque die (every day)
LLE	left lower extremities	q.h.	every hour
LLL	left lower lobe	qid	four times a day
LLQ	left lower quadrant	qod	every other day
LPN	licensed practical nurse	q2h	every two hours
LUL	left upper lobe	qqh	every 4 hours
LUQ	left upper quadrant	qs	sufficient quantity
MD	medical doctor	RN	registered nurse
mgm.	milligram	R/O	ruled out
MI	myocardial infarction	ROM	range of motion
MICU	medical intensive-care unit	RUL	right upper lobe
		RUQ	right upper quadrant
ng.	negative	Rx	take, therapy
NHP	nursing home placement	RHD	rheumatic heart disease

s.c./s.q.	subcutaneous	tid	three times a day
SICU	surgical intensive-care unit	TKO	to keep open
		TPR	temperature, pulse, respiration
Sig.	signetur (let it be labeled)		
SOB	shortness of breath	TB	tuberculosis
S/P	status post	UTI	urinary-tract infection
ss	one-half	UA	urinalysis
STAT	statim (immediately)		
Staph	staphylococcus	VD	venereal disease
Strep	streptococcus	VNS	visiting nurse service
Surg.	surgery		
		WBC	white blood cells
T.	temperature; thoracic	WC	wheelchair
tab.	tablet	WNL	within normal limits
tbsp.	tablespoon		
TIA	transient ischemic attack		

X-RAYS

CX	chest	GB	gallbladder
IVP	intravenous pyelogram	IVC	intravenous cholecystogram
UGI	upper GI		
LGI	lower GI	PEG	pneumoencephalogram
BE	barium enema		

ELECTRICAL TRACINGS

ECG (EKG)	electrocardiogram	EEG	electroencephalogram
		EMG	electromyogram

MISCELLANEOUS

CC	chief complaint	VC	vital capacity
ROS	review of systems	p̄	after
Imp.	impression	ā	before
C/O	complaint of	c̄	with
Sx	symptom	s̄	without
H/O	history of		

SYMBOLS

*	Birth	♂	Male
†	Death	♀	Female

APPENDIX B
SELECTED FEDERAL HEALTH ACTS, 1935–1975*

1935	74-241	Social Security Act	Provided for the first time grants-in-aid to States for such public health activities as maternal and child care, aid to crippled children, blind persons, the aged, and other health-impaired persons.
1936	74-846	Walsh-Healy Act	Authorized Federal regulation of industrial safety in companies doing business with the government.
1937	75-244	National Cancer Institute Act	Established National Cancer Institute to coordinate research related to cancer.

*Excerpted from U.S. Department of Health, Education and Welfare, Health Resources Administration, *Health in America: 1776–1976*, Publication no. (HRA) 76-616 (Washington, D.C., in press). Reprinted in Department of Health, Education and Welfare, *Baselines for Setting Health Goals and Standards*, Publication no. HRA 76-640 (Washington, D.C., September 1976).

Year	Number	Act	Description
1938	75-540	LaFollette-Bulwinkle (VD Control) Act	Provided grants-in-aid to States and other authorities to investigate and control venereal disease.
1938	75-717	Federal Food, Drug and Cosmetic Act	Extended Federal authority to act against adulterated and mis-branded food, drug, and cosmetic products.
1941	77-146	The Nurse Training Act	Supported schools of nursing to increase their enrollments and help strengthen their facilities.
1943	78-38	Act to Provide for the Appointment of Female Physicians and Surgeons in the Army	Gave women and men equal rank, pay, allowances, and privileges in the Army Medical Corps.
1944	78-410	Public Health Service Act	Consolidated all PHS authorities into a single statute (42 USC).
1946	79-293	Medical and Surgical Act	Established a Dept. of Medicine and Surgery in VA; removed it from Civil Service control; authorized medical student residencies in VA hospitals.
1946	79-396	National School Lunch Act	Authorized a national school lunch program.
1946	79-487	National Mental Health Act	Authorized major Federal support for mental health research, diagnosis, prevention, and treatment; changed PHS Division of Mental Health to National Institute of Mental Health; established State grants-in-aid for mental health.

Appendix B

Year	P.L.	Act	Description
1946	79–725	Hospital Survey and Construction Act	The Hill-Burton Act to support surveys, plans, and new facilities.
1948	80–655	National Heart Act	Authorized aid for research, training, and other programs related to heart disease; established the National Heart Institute; acknowledged a plural NIH.
1948	80–755	National Dental Research Act	Authorized aid for research on dental diseases and conditions; established a National Institute of Dental Research at NIH.
1948	80–845	Water Pollution Control Act	Authorized PHS to help States develop water pollution control programs and to aid in the planning of sewage treatment plants.
1949	81–380	Hospital Survey and Construction Amendments	Increased Federal financial assistance to promote effective development and utilization of hospital services and facilities.
1949	81–439	Agricultural Act of 1949	Authorized donations of commodities acquired under price support programs for school lunch and for feeding the needy.
1950	81–507	Act to Establish a National Science Foundation	Set up an autonomous NSF and strengthened the concept of Federal support for university-based research in physical, medical, and social sciences.
1950	81–692	National Research Institutes Act	Expanded the National Institutes of Health to include research and training relating to arthritis, rheumatism, multiple sclerosis, cerebral palsy, epilepsy, polio, blindness, leprosy, and other diseases.

Year	Number	Act	Description
1954	83–482	Medical Facilities Survey and Construction Act	Extended aid to chronic care hospitals, rehabilitation facilities, and nursing homes.
1954	83–568	Act to Transfer Indian Health Responsibility to the Public Health Service	Placed responsibility for maintenance and operation of Indian health facilities in PHS rather than Bureau of Indian Affairs.
1955	84–159	Air Pollution Control Act	Provided aid to States, regions, and localities for research and control programs to protect air quality.
1955	84–182	Mental Health Study Act	Authorized grants to nongovernmental organizations for partial support of a national study and reevaluation of the human and economic problems of mental illness.
1955	84–377	Polio Vaccination Assistance Act	Provided assistance to State vacination programs.
1956	84–569	Dependents Medical Care Act	Set up program of primarily inpatient medical care for dependents of military personnel (CHAMPUS).
1956	84–652	National Health Survey Act	Provided for a continuing survey and special studies of sickness and disability in the U.S.
1956	84–835	Health Research Facilities Act	Aided construction of research facilities.
1956	84–911	Health Amendments	Increased mental health staff and skills.
1956	84–941	National Library of Medicine Act	Transferred responsibility for the library to the Public Health Service.

Appendix B

Year	P.L.	Act	Description
1957	85–151	Indian Health Assistance Act	Provided for construction of health facilities for Indians and others.
1958	85–340	Social Security Amendments	Provided States with minimum maternal and child health grants and extended authority to Guam.
1958	85–929	Food Additive Amendments to the FD&C Act	Required pre-marketing clearance for new food additives; established a GRAS (generally recognized as safe) category; prohibited the approval of any additive "found to induce cancer in man or animal" (the so-called "Delaney clause").
1959	86–382	Federal Employees Health Benefits Act	Authorized program of prepaid health insurance for employees of Federal Executive and Legislative Branches.
1960	86–613	Federal Hazardous Substances Labeling Act	Required prominent label warning on hazardous household or workplace chemical products.
1960	86–778	Social Security Amendments	Authorized grants to States for medical assistance for the aged.
1961	87–395	Community Health Services and Facilities Act	To improve community facilities and services for aged and others.
1962	87–692	Assistance to Migratory Workers Act	Authorized Federal aid for clinics serving migratory agricultural workers and families.

Year	Number	Act	Description
1962	87–838	National Institutes of Child Health and Human Development and General Medical Sciences Act	Established an institute to coordinate and expand research into child-hood diseases and human growth and a second institute of General Medical Sciences to coordinate inter-Institute research and handle "all other" diseases.
1963	88–129	Health Professions Educational Assistance Act	Aided training of physicians, dentists, public health personnel, and others. 1976 amendments (sections 791–792) include schools of social work.
1963	88–156	Maternal and Child Health and Mental Retardation Planning Amendments	Initiated program of comprehensive maternity and infant care and mental retardation prevention.
1963	88–164	Mental Retardation Facilities and Community Mental Health Centers Construction Act	Provided aid for the construction of these facilities and centers; became the basic law for mental health centers' staffing, programming, etc.
1964	88–352	Civil Rights Act	Title VI provided that "no person in the United States shall, on the ground of race, color or national origin, be excluded from participation in, be denied the benefits of, or be subjected to discrimination under any program or activity receiving Federal financial assistance."
1964	88–525	Food Stamp Act	Authorized food stamp program for low-income persons to buy nutritious food for balanced diet.

Appendix B

Year	Number	Act	Description
1965	89–74	Drug Abuse Control Amendments	Established enforcement procedures to control depressants, stimulants, and hallucinogens.
1965	89–92	Federal Cigarette Labeling and Advertising Act	Informed the public of health hazards of cigarette smoking.
1965	89–97	Social Security Amendments	Established health insurance for aged and grants to States for medical assistance programs (Medicare and Medicaid).
1965	89–239	Heart Disease, Cancer, and Stroke Amendments	Established Regional Medical Programs for research training and sharing of new knowledge in heart disease, cancer and stroke.
1966	89–563	National Traffic and Motor Vehicle Safety Act	Provided for a coordinated national safety program and established safety standards for motor vehicles in interstate commerce.
1966	89–614	Amendments to CHAMPUS (Military Dependents Act)	Broadened eligibility to CHAMPUS and extended benefits beyond impatient care.
1966	89–642	Child Nutrition Act	Established Federal program of research and support for child nutrition; authorized school breakfast program.
1966	89–749	Comprehensive Health Planning and Public Health Services Amendments	Promoted health planning and improved public health services; authorized broad research, demonstration, and training programs in Federal-State-local partnership.
1966	89–751	Allied Health Professions Personnel Act	Initial effort to support the training of allied health workers; also provided student loans for health professionals.

1967	90–222	Economic Opportunity Amendments	Authorized grants for Comprehensive Health Services and other health programs.
1967	90–248	Social Security Amendments	Consolidated maternal and child health authorities, extended grants for family planning and dental health.
1968	90–574	Health Services Amendment	Extended grants for RMP's and migrant health services; provided treatment facilities for alcoholics and narcotic addicts.
1969	91–173	Federal Coal Mine Health and Safety Act	Protected the health and safety of coal miners.
1969	91–190	National Environmental Policy Act	Stated the concern of Congress for preserving the environment and to "stimulate the health and welfare of man"; created the Council on Environmental Quality to advise the President; required environmental impact statements before major Federal actions.
1970	91–211	Community Mental Health Centers Amendments	Extended grants for community mental health centers and facilities for alcoholics and narcotic addicts and established programs for children's mental health.
1970	91–513	Comprehensive Drug Abuse Prevention and Control Act	Increased aid for research; strengthened prevention, treatment, rehabilitation programs.
1970	91–517	Developmental Disabilities Services and Facilities Construction Amendments	Assisted States to develop and implement plans for provision of comprehensive services to persons affected by mental retardation and other developmental disabilities.

Appendix B

Year	P.L.	Act	Description
1970	91–519	Health Training Improvement Act	Provided expanded aid to all allied health professions.
1970	91–572	Family Planning Services and Population Research Act	Expanded and coordinated services and research activities.
1970	91–596	Occupational Safety and Health Act	Provided Federal program of standard-setting and enforcement to assure safe and healthful conditions in the workplace.
1970	91–604	Clean Air Act Amendments	Strengthened and expanded air pollution control activities; placed broad regulatory responsibility in new Environmental Protection Agency, in operation as of December 2, 1970.
1970	91–616	Comprehensive Alcohol Abuse and Alcoholism Prevention, Treatment, and Rehabilitation Act	Established National Institute of Alcohol Abuse and Alcoholism; provided a comprehensive aid program to States and localities.
1970	91–623	Emergency Health Personnel Act	Provided assistance to health manpower shortage areas through a new National Health Service Corps.
1972	92–294	National Sickle Cell Anemia Control Act	Provided for control of and research into sickle cell anemia.
1972	92–500	Federal Water Pollution Control Amendments	Totally revised Federal water program; shifted efforts from the preservation of available water quality to the improvemen of quality through technology; set as a goal the elimination of pollutant discharges from all navigable waters.

Year	Number	Act	Description
1972	92–603	Social Security Amendments	Extended health insurance benefits to the disabled and to end-stage renal disease patients; established Professional Standard Review Organization program, and expanded research and demonstrations of financing mechanisms.
1972	93–154	Emergency Medical Services Systems Act	Provided aid to States and localities to establish coordinated, cost-effective, areawide EMS systems.
1973	93–222	Health Maintenance Organization Act	Assisted in the establishment and expansion of HMOs.
1974	93–247	Child Abuse Prevention and Treatment Act	Created a National Center on Child Abuse and Neglect; authorized research and demonstration grants to States and other public and private agencies.
1974	93–270	Sudden Infant Death Syndrome Act	Provided assistance for research, training, and extensive public education concerning SIDS.
1974	93–286	Research on Aging Act	Established National Institute on Aging within the NIH.
1974	93–640	National Arthritis Act	Established National Commission on Arthritis and coordinated arthritis programs in NIH.
1975	93–641	National Health Planning and Resources Development Act	Authorized major Federal reorganization of health planning programs, including Hill-Burton; set up national designation of local Health Systems Areas and governing agencies.

Year	No.	Act	Description
1975	94–63	Health Revenue Sharing and Nurse Training Act	Established National Center for Prevention and Control of Rape; revised and extended National Health Service Corps, Community Mental Health Centers, migrant health, family planning, and other programs; strengthened the nurse training program.
1975	94–103	Developmentally Disabled Assistance and Bill of Rights Act	Expanded national effort and protected rights of the developmentally disabled.

INDEX